DOMESTIC STRUCTURES AND INTERNATIONAL TRADE

STUDIES IN EUROPEAN LAW AND INTEGRATION

Titles in this Series

Rein Wesseling: *The Modernisation of EC Antitrust Law*

Candido Garcia Molyneux: *Domestic Structures and International Trade: The Unfair Trade Instruments of the United States and the European Union*

Francis Snyder (ed.): *The Europeanisation of Law: The Legal Effects of European Integration*

Domestic Structures and International Trade

The Unfair Trade Instruments of the United States and the European Union

CANDIDO TOMAS GARCIA MOLYNEUX

·HART·
PUBLISHING
OXFORD – PORTLAND OREGON
2001

Hart Publishing
Oxford and Portland, Oregon

Published in North America (US and Canada) by
Hart Publishing c/o
International Specialized Book Services
5804 NE Hassalo Street
Portland, Oregon
97213-3644
USA

Distributed in the Netherlands, Belgium and Luxembourg by
Intersentia, Churchillaan 108
B2900 Schoten
Antwerpen
Belgium

Hart Publishing Ltd is a specialist legal publisher based in Oxford, England.
To order further copies of this book or to request a list of other
publications please write to:

Hart Publishing Ltd, Salter's Boatyard, Folly Bridge,
Abingdon Road, Oxford OX1 4LB
Telephone: +44 (0)1865 245533 or Fax: +44 (0)1865 794882
e-mail: mail@hartpub.co.uk
WEBSITE: http//www.hartpub.co.uk

British Library Cataloguing in Publication Data
Data Available
ISBN 1 84113–132–6 (cloth)

Typeset by Hope Services (Abingdon) Ltd.
Printed and bound in Great Britain by
Lightning Source UK Ltd

Foreword

FRANCIS SNYDER

Globalisation is a fact of modern life. Buzzword, symbol, ideology, goal, challenge, or fear, it represents a powerful current in the contemporary world. In significant ways, it distinguishes today from the past. Sociologists, economists, political scientists and other social scientists, as well as journalists, have explored many of its facets already. Legal scholars, however, have lagged somewhat behind. Sticking too close to our last, we have frequently been loath either to engage in what might seem to be mere speculation, at best an unnecessary distraction, or alternatively to cast our net so widely as to risk losing our professional identity.

This powerfully argued book is an exception. It demonstrates that legal scholars have a good deal to say about the causes and implications of globalisation. It gives the lie to the generalisation that books about law have failed, on the whole, to come to grips theoretically with globalisation as a significant determinant of contemporary legal arrangements. Written by a lawyer, it breaks new ground in presenting a theoretically informed, yet empirically grounded comparative study of globalisation and the law. It thus has much to offer to all social scientists and others who are concerned with the interplay between globalisation and regulation, in particular by means of legal institutions, norms and processes.

This book, like many good books, is based on a deceptively simple idea. It begins from the premise that societies have different histories, and consequently different constitutional frameworks and economic arrangements. In particular, they diverge in the strength of government and the organisation of markets. From this starting point, the author of this book argues the case for the constraining power of history. In the language of institutional economics, change is path-dependent. Globalisation, despite its homogenising tendency, can therefore eliminate structural differences among countries only to a limited extent. Our age of globalisation thus is characterised by both homogeneity and diversity.

The flesh on this theoretical skeleton consists of a detailed comparative analysis of trade law and policy in the European Union and the United States. It helps us to appreciate the political, economic, social and legal reasons for the author's general conclusion. It also casts a powerful theoretical light on the formulation and implementation of trade policy measures in the EU and the USA, as well as on the role of different EU Member States, notably France and Germany, in the formation of EU economic policies toward the rest of the world. Obviously this discussion also provides us with the theoretical, conceptual tools for understanding the roles of other EU Member States also. But this book goes further. One of its special merits is to enable us to grasp some of the implications of US and EU trade policy for globalisation and the regulation of globalisation. It thus will be indispensable reading for anyone interested in the role of the World Trade Organization in the governance of international trade.

Candido Garcia Molyneux has written a stimulating and critical book. It challenges us to re-examine some received wisdom, not only about globalisation but also about europeanisation. His analysis emphasises the diversity of constitutional and market structures within the European Union, as well as the differences between the EU and the USA. This intra-EU diversity has important consequences for EU trade policy. It also, however, has profound implications for the future development of a European identity, polity and forms of governance. Of course, not all of these implications can be elaborated and analysed here. But this book provides the basis for a much more systematic rethinking of the relationship between europeanisation and globalisation, one that takes seriously and indeed values the diversity of political and economic structures within the EU but at the same time seeks to imagine new forms of EU governance. Drawing on history, this book invites legal scholars to come to grips with some of the most significant issues confronting the EU in the 21st century. It should be essential reading to all concerned with EU-US relations, the role of the EU in the world, and the challenges posed by globalisation to the construction of the EU in the future.

Francis Snyder
Berlin
September 2000

Contents

PART II: THE EUROPEAN UNION'S COMMON COMMERCIAL POLICY

Table of Cases

1. GATT/WTO ARBITRATIONS

2. EUROPEAN COURT OF JUSTICE CASES

3. EUROPEAN COMMUNITY DECISIONS

4. UNITED STATES CASES

4. UNITED STATES DECISIONS

Table of Legislation

1. GATT

2. EUROPEAN COMMUNITIES

3. UNITED STATES

4. NATIONAL LEGISLATION

Canada

Introduction

This book's point of departure is the idea that, despite globalisation, societies organise themselves differently and have diverse expectations of their governments and market actors. The book asks how these differences affect the trading partners' policies in an age where nearly everything can be considered as a matter of commerce. It explores how domestic structures affect trade policy when the external world has a strong impact on the domestic sphere.

Globalisation is a fundamental concept in this book. It is seen both as a process where states play an active role, characterised by both homogeneity and diversity, and as being biased. First, despite the importance of technological improvements and the development of multinationals, it is argued that globalisation is also the result of state action. Globalisation is seen as a struggle to impose the rules of the game. Second, while acknowledging that globalisation has an impressive impact on states' domestic spheres by constraining the behaviour of governments and domestic market actors, it is arguable that globalisation fails to change states' fundamental characteristics and expectations. Thus, as the result of globalisation, there are states which are better off, and those which are worse off. Finally, globalisation is seen as nothing other than the internationalisation of the American system.

As trading partners, this book focuses on the United States and the European Union. For domestic structures it takes the constitutional cultures of each. It focuses on both the constitutional rules and the socio-economic structures in which national markets are rooted. Constitutional rules are considered to be part of a much wider socio-economic context which defines the behaviour of states. States diverge in the historically rooted roles of their governments in the market and the organisation of their market actors.

By trade policy, this book focuses on different institutional and substantive features of the unfair trade instruments of the United States and the European Union. The countervailing, anti-dumping and market access instruments of both trading partners are seen as an attempt to deal with the external world, while taking into account the conditions and constraints posed by domestic constitutional and socio-economic structures.

Unfair trade instruments are viewed as a reflection of the constitutional systems of each trading partner from three perspectives, which the study tries to merge. First, unfair trade instruments are seen as a necessary *ad hoc* protection to compensate for domestic constraints imposed by globalisation. Second, they are seen as intertwined with the country's constitutional culture and trade policy-making process. Third, it is argued that unfair trade instruments carry, in their concept of fairness, parochial views on the market behaviour of governments and market actors.

The book is divided into six chapters and has two parts. Chapter I introduces the argument and outlines the theoretical framework. It offers insights with regard to the persistence of different domestic structures in which markets are embedded, the friction among states as a result of global diversity, the relation between the domestic and the external sphere and, finally, how unfair trade instruments are a form of *ad hoc* protectionism.

Part I, on the United States' Trade Policy, includes chapters two and three. Chapter two presents a theoretical background of the US trade policy by outlining the domestic constitutional and socio-economic structures of the United States. It first explains, in brief, the socio-economic structures of America. It describes their historical origins, the limited role of the US government in the market and the pluralistic organisation of its market actors. Thereafter, it describes the constitutional actors and process of US foreign trade policy by focusing on the plenary trade powers of Congress, the role of the Executive, the increasing delegation of powers to regulate foreign trade from the former to the latter, as well as the fast track procedure to implement international trade agreements. Chapter three takes a more practical approach and presents three case studies: the United States implementation of the Uruguay Round Research and Development Subsidies Agreement; the United States' countervailing duty methodology; and Section 301 of the 1974 Trade Act. These show how America's unfair trade instruments reflect its domestic system. It is argued that despite all the rhetoric, unfair trade instruments formed part of a dialogue between Congress and the Executive to develop a consensus policy which provided *ad hoc* protection at home and established the rules of the game abroad.

Part II, on the European Union's Common Commercial Policy, includes chapters four and five. Chapter four outlines the domestic structures of the European Union by highlighting the persistence of market differences within Europe and the influence this has upon the entire trade policy making process. The Community's trade policy reflects a shifting balance between the absence of uniform European domestic structures, on the one hand, and the need to act together to face the challenge of globalisation, on the other. Thus, Chapter five first analyses the domestic structures of France and Germany. The approach is based not on a systematic comparison but, instead, highlights their different market economies as a whole. These two Member States have been chosen for their historical importance in the project of European integration and because they symbolise the Community's divisions over trade policy, between free trade and protectionism. Chapter four thereafter analyses the Community's trade policy process, the legal framework as well as the actors, taking into account the different market economies of the Member States. Chapter five presents two cases, an analysis of the European Union' methodology used to determine the existence of dumping, and an analysis of its Trade Barriers Regulation. The two cases seek to show how the European Union's trade policy reflects its domestic constitutional system. Thus, it is argued, the persistence of market differences in Europe leads it to the implementation of second best unfair trade instruments.

Chapter VI presents some conclusions.

This book is based on the Ph.D. dissertation I defended in June 1999 at the European University Institute. Two other papers have been published on the basis of this dissertation. Volume 5 of the *European Law Journal* included "The Trade Barriers Regulation: The European Union as a Player in the Globalisation Game". A piece entitled "Establishing the Rules of the Game: Domestic Structures and International Trade" is being published in Francis Snyder & Goncalo Cabral (eds.), *Global and Regional Regulation of International Trade* (Oxford, Hart Publishing, 2000).

During the years I have been researching and writing my Ph.D. dissertation and this book, I have had the support of several institutions and many people. I would like to thank the Universidad Autonoma de Madrid, the Georgetown University Law Centre and the European University Institute, which continues to be one of the best research environments in Europe. I also wish to thank the European Commission which hosted me for some months, and in particular those officials who supported and gave me advice during my stay.

Working with Professor Francis Snyder has been a remarkable experience. I wish to thank him for his support and most of all for his trust. I have also benefited from conversations with Shirley Coffield, Don Wallace, David Trubek, John Greenwald, Jacques Bourgeois, Claus D. Elhermann, Song Ying, Stephen Clarkson, and several government officials. Professors Jacques Bourgeois, Thomas Risse, Freidl Weiss and Francis Snyder were the members of the jury of my Ph.D. dissertation. They provided useful comments that have helped me to improve my work, for which I wish to thank them. I also wish to thank Andrew and Diamond for their useful proof reading and corrections.

Working on this project would have been impossible without the friendship and love of many people. Not everybody could be there at the same time, but there has always been someone. Thus, I dedicate this book to my family, Nico, Vickie and Marta with love. This book is also dedicated to all the Cristinas, Mireias, Yadiras, Agustins, Andreus, Davides, Filips, Ignacios and Sergios of the world.

Cala Panizo, Almeria.
May, 2000.

A las bellas casualidades, las ilusiones y los cuentos.
Para que nunca perdamos de vista la realidad.

1

Theoretical Background

1.A. STATES AND GLOBALISATION

I.A.1. The Approach

GLOBALISATION IS A reality.[1] Our world is one in which events, decisions and activities in one part of the globe have significant consequences for individuals and communities in other very distant parts.[2]

The globalisation process is unique in that it is both a quantitative and qualitative phenomenon. Globalisation refers to an idea of magnitude. The number of contacts and volume of flow between the various participants in the global economy has increased extraordinarily. However, globalisation refers also to an idea of increased sensitivity. The extent to which consumption and production patterns, money and capital markets in one country are influenced by policies and developments outside its borders has drastically increased. The key element of globalisation is the blurring of the line between the domestic and the external sphere.

To a very great extent, globalisation is the result of technological improvements. The process of globalisation is possible due to important developments in communication systems, allowing the rapid flow of information, in transport systems which make possible the flow of goods, in new production processes which result in new products and services, in new financial systems which permit the accumulation and movement of capital, etc. Globalisation can also be seen as the result of the increase in foreign direct investment and the development of multinational corporations.[3]

This book, however, adheres to the perspective that globalisation is the result of state policies and international institutions which have promoted a liberal economic system.[4] It considers globalisation not as simply a mechanical process

[1] See R Went, "Globalization: Myths, Reality and Ideology: The EU in a Globalized World" (1997) 26(3) *Int'l J. Political Economy* 35–59; See also P Hirst, "The Global Economy—Myths and Realities" (1997) 73(3) *Int'l Affairs* 409–425.

[2] See The Group of Lisbon, *Limits to Competition* (Cambridge, MIT Press 1995), 34.

[3] H Milner, *Resisting Protectionism: Global Industries and the Politics of International Trade* (Princeton, Princeton University Press, 1988); see also J Grunwald and K Flamm, *The Global Factory: Foreign Assembly in International Trade* (Washington, The Brookings Institute, 1985).

[4] See J Scholte, "Global Capitalism and the State" (1997) 73(3) *Int'l Affairs* 427–452, 441; see also J Zysman, "The Myth of a Global Economy: Enduring National Foundations and Emerging New Realities" (1996) 1(2) *New Political Economy* 157–184, 164; and G Underhill, "Markets Beyond Politics? The State and the Internationalisation of Financial Markets" (1991) 19 *European J. Political Research* 197–225, 200.

but rather as the result of the interaction, negotiation and policies decided among states.[5] Globalisation is a reality but it is not inevitable. It exists because some want it to.[6] Globalisation is the result of political will and of law.

It is in this context that the developments concerning the international trading system are taking place. On 15 December 1993, more than one hundred and twenty countries concluded the Uruguay Round,[7] the eighth multilateral trade negotiations held under the auspices of the General Agreement on Tariffs and Trade.[8] The Uruguay Round resulted in the most ambitious trade agreements package ever concluded. First, by establishing the World Trade Organisation,[9] the GATT contracting parties have finally recognised the inevitable: the existence of an international trade organisation. Second, the Uruguay Round strengthened disciplines already contained in previous agreements. Third, it incorporated into GATT discipline international trade issues such as services, telecommunications and intellectual property rights.[10] Finally, and probably most importantly, the contracting parties achieved the consensus needed in order to strengthen its dispute settlement procedure.[11]

The final outcome of the Uruguay Round has been described as a step forward to trade multilateralism which, if it succeeds, will bring uniformity to the law of international trade.[12] But, in fact, the Uruguay Round trade agreements were much more than that. They added an important stone in the construction of a neo-liberal economic system and provided the legal instruments for the globalisation our world faces. The agreements legally sanctioned the end of "embedded liberalism": the balance between the domestic and the external spheres.[13] Governments are no longer free to develop their own policies in their domestic sphere.

[5] In this sense, the interests of states and multinationals do not necessarily have to be divergent. See T Bottomore and Bryen Brian, *The Capitalist Class: An International Study* (Hemel Hempstead, Harvester Wheatsheaf, 1989).

[6] S Strange, *Casino Capitalism* (Oxford, Basic Blackwell, 1986).

[7] The Uruguay Round was launched on 20 September 1986 in Punta del Este, Uruguay. See GATT BISD 33 Supp. 11 (1987). It was concluded, in Geneva, on 17 December 1993. Its Final Act was signed in Marrakesh on 15 April 1994. After ratification by most Contracting Parties it entered into force on 1 January 1995. See 33 I.L.M. 3 (1994).

[8] General Agreement of Tariffs and Trade, 29 October 1947, 61 Stat. A3, T.I.A.S. No 1700, 55 U.N.T.S. 187 (entered into force on 1 January 1948). [Hereinafter GATT]; see J H Jackson, *World Trade and the Law of the GATT* (Indianapolis, Bobbs Merrill, 1969).

[9] *Agreement Establishing the World Trade Organisation*, 33 I.L.M. 13 (1994). The web site of the WTO is available at <http://www.wto.int>.

[10] *General Agreement on Trade in Services*, 33 I.L.M. 44 (1994); See also *Agreement on Trade Related Aspects of Intellectual Property Rights*, 33 I.L.M. 81 (1994).

[11] *Understanding on Rules and Procedures Governing the Settlement of Disputes*, 33 I.L.M. 112 (1994).

[12] A Lowenfeld, "Remedies Along Rights: Institutional Reform in the New GATT" (1994) 88 *Am. J. Int'l L.* 477–488, 478; see also E U Petersmann, "The Transformation of the World Trading System Through the 1994 Agreement Establishing the World Trade Organisation" (1995) 6 *Euro. J. Int'l L.* 161–221.

[13] For the concept of embedded liberalism, see Section B of this Chapter.

To understand the globalisation process as one ruled by states, it is possible to adopt different approaches. First, one can analyse the manner in which states act collectively to establish and preserve their trade relations. Thus, we may adopt an upward looking analysis and ask what impact certain state actions have on the system as a whole, or a downward looking analysis by enquiring how the whole system affects the policies of individual states.[14]

Secondly, taking into account the important role that states play in the globalisation process, we may question what are the determinants of a state's trade policy. Several approaches may be taken to answer this question. Realist or systemic approaches tend to focus on the system as a whole, considering the state to be a rational and unitary actor. These theories consider state preferences to be constants, rather than variables. States are assumed to have stable and broadly similar domestic preferences, decision-making procedures and abilities to extract resources from society. Thus, trade policy will shift only in response to constraints and incentives that derive from the broader structure of interstate relations.[15]

Domestic level approaches, however, consider the state not as a rational unitary actor but, rather, analyse its policies as resulting from different domestic factors such as its society, culture and political institutions. Domestic groups, social ideas, the character of constitutions, economic constraints, historical social tendencies, and domestic political pressures are considered to play an important role in the selection of a trade policy.[16] The diverse domestic level approaches explain a state's trade policy in different ways. Pluralists consider the strategic interaction among all domestic actors, either inside or outside the government or in the economic culture. Cognitivist analysis addresses the social perceptions that guide policy making; analysing the cultural perceptions to which the entire policy making leadership is subject.[17] Structuralists, instead, focus on the economic structure which determines the possibilities of public and private actors and results in a certain trade policy.[18]

Probably the best way to explain the role that states play in the globalisation process would be to take into account all approaches. First, an understanding of a state's trade policy requires taking into account both domestic structures and

[14] B Cohen, "The Political Economy of International Trade" (1990) 44 *Int'l Org.* 261–281. For the impact that the international system has on individual states, see H Milner and R Keohane, *Internationalization and Domestic Politics* (Cambridge, Cambridge University Press, 1996).

[15] See A Moravcsick, "Introduction: Integrating International and Domestic Theories of International Bargaining" in P Evans, H Jacobson and R Putnam (eds.), *Doubled-Edged Diplomacy; International Bargaining and Domestic Politics* (Berkeley, University of California Press, 1993), 3–42, 5.

[16] R Rosecrance and A Stein (eds.), *The Domestic Bases of Grand Strategy* (Ithaca, Cornell University Press, 1993), 5.

[17] See P Rohrlich, "Economic Culture and Foreign Policy: The Cognitive Analysis of Economic Policy Making" (1987) 41 *Int'l Org.* 61–92.

[18] P Katzenstein, "Introduction: Domestic and International Forces and Strategies of Foreign Economic Policy", in P Katzenstein (ed.), *Between Power and Plenty: Foreign Economic Policies of Advanced Industrial States* (Madison, The University of Wisconsin Press, 1978).

international constraints.[19] Understanding the role of a state in the international trading system requires considering the effects of the system on the state. Second, though we may consider that the trade policy of states is basically determined by its domestic structures, this should not prevent us from accepting that, sometimes, states will rationally pursue defined goals. States are in fact constrained by a tension between the need to act rationally and unitarily and the reality of their domestic structures.

This study, while taking into account the relevance of the impact of globalisation on states and assuming the possibility of their acting rationally, attempts to explain a trading partner's trade policy as a result of domestic factors. The unfair trade instruments of the US and the EU are considered to be an attempt of these trading partners to deal with the external world whilst taking into account the conditions and constraints posed by their domestic constitutional and socio-economic structures.

First, this book analyses the substantive and institutional elements of unfair trade instruments resulting from a state's domestic constitutional structure. National constitutions and legal constraints are considered as fundamental in the process of formulating foreign economic policy.[20] The way in which the distribution of power between the different political units is constitutionally articulated will be considered as having an important impact upon the adoption and practice of unfair trade instruments. Thus the book looks at the distribution of power between the central-regional governments and between the executive, parliamentary and judicial branches. Unfair trade instruments are intertwined with a wider constitutional trade policy process.

However, this book also takes into account socio-economic structures as determinants of unfair trade instruments. Trade policy is also the result of domestic socio-economic structures which rule a state's economy. The approach analyses the strength or weakness of the government and the organisation or plurality of the market. It focuses first on how the market is organised. It takes into account how industry is organised in a specific country, the relationship between export-led and domestic industry, the relationship between industry and finance and the relation between business and labour. Secondly, it looks at the interaction between the state and the market. Thus, it examines the state and its ability to interfere with business. It analyses whether a given state has a "government intervention" or "hands off" tradition, whether there is a

[19] P Evans, "Building an Integrative Approach to International and Domestic Politics: Reflections and Projections", in P Evans, H Jacobson and R Putnam (eds.), *Double Edge Diplomacy: International Bargaining and Domestic Politics* (Berkeley, University of California Press, 1993), 397–430, 397; see also R Schmidt, "International Negotiations Paralyzed by Domestic Politics: Two-Level Game Theory and the Problem of the Pacific Salmon Commission" (1996) 26 *Environmental L.* 95–139; and V Mahler, "Domestic and International Sources of Trade Policy: The Case of Agriculture in the European Community and the United States" (1991) 24 *Polity* 27–47.

[20] J H Jackson, J V Louis and M Matsushita, *Implementing the Tokyo Round: National Constitutions and International Economic Rules* (Ann Arbor, The University of Michigan Press, 1984), 2; see also P Cowhey, Domestic Institutions and the Credibility of International Commitments: Japan and the United States (1993) 47 *Int'l Org.* 299–327.

strong government capable of influencing the market or not, etc. All states intervene in the market but they may do so in very different ways. States may influence, regulate, mediate, distribute, redistribute, produce and plan the market.[21] How governments intervene in the market depends both on the nature of the market and the state.[22]

1.A.2. The Structural Approach: Globalisation and Diversity

Analysing a state's foreign economic policy from a domestic structural perspective implies a critical approach to the normative idea of free trade by rejecting a-historical and structure-blind assumptions and asserting the primacy of social, economic and political structures.[23]

Free trade is an extension of the regime of free markets to the international sector. It prescribes that all countries will gain economically if each first specialises in the production of those goods and materials in which it has a comparative or absolute advantage.[24] In the absence of distorting constraints individuals will engage only in economic exchange if it brings them benefit. The market is considered to be a device through which individuals voluntarily interact in their capacities as producers and consumers to exchange goods and services. Price is the mechanism which transmits information to both consumers and producers; enabling them, through demand and supply, to determine exactly what is produced and in what quantity. Thus, without central direction, millions of individual economic decisions are co-ordinated to utilise resources in the most efficient manner possible to determine optimum production.

The idea of free trade requires the separation of economics from politics. Politics should not interfere in the market process. However, the extent to which classical economic theory is genuinely apolitical is doubtful.[25] The free market economy tries to subject everything to the rule of profit and considers labour,

[21] T Biersteker, "Reducing the Role of the State in the Economy: A Conceptual Exploration of IMF and World Bank Prescriptions" (1990) 34 *Int'l Studies Quarterly* 477–492, 480.

[22] A good example of the different ways through which a government can influence the market is the practice of administrative guidelines in Japan. Such guidelines are not considered to be law in force and are not legally binding. This practice has been examined under different GATT dispute settlement panels. In *Japan, Restrictions on Imports of Certain Agricultural Products*, L/6253, 22 March 1988, BISD 35 S/163; see also *Japan, Trade in Semi-Conductors*, L/6309, 24 March 1988, BISD 35 S/116. Other GATT cases dealing with different socio-economic structures are *EC: Anti-Duties on Audio Tapes in Cassettes Originating in Japan*, ASP/136, April 8, 1995; *United States: Imposition of Countervailing Duties on Certain Hot-Rolled Lead and Bismuth Carbon Steel Products Originating in France, Germany and the United Kingdom*, SCM/185, 15 November 1994; *Japan: Measures Affecting Consumer Photographic Film and Paper*, WTO/DS44/R, 31 March 1998.

[23] See S Hix, "The Study of the European Community: The Challenge of Comparative Politics" (1994) 17 *West European Politics* 1–30, 9.

[24] See D Ricardo, *The Principles of Political Economy and Taxation* (London, I. M. Dent & Sons, 1973), 77–93.

[25] See G Myrdal, *The Political Element in the Development of Economic Theory* (London, Routledge & Kegan Paul, 2nd ed., 1955); see also C B Macpherson, *The Political Theory of Possessive Individualism: Hobbes to Locke* (Oxford, Oxford University Press, 1964).

land and money as nothing more than commodities. What distinguishes the self-regulating market from any other economic system is that it subjects the whole of society to its own rules.[26]

Yet, markets are neither neutral nor exist in isolation. First, markets are a source of political power and thus affect political life. Political life is entangled with the workings of markets and market institutions. Second, markets are embedded in political and social institutions.[27] A global market does not result from the elimination of barriers. The systematic elimination of tariffs and non-tariff trade barriers, known as negative integration, mandated by neo-liberal ideology, does not create a unified economic space because it fails to address the importance of the political and social peculiarities in which market exchange takes place.

Capitalism may be defined by the existence of free markets and private property rights. However, economic action is shaped not just by markets and private property but also by a wide range of institutions.[28] The market is just one institutional device among others co-ordinating the governance of a society.[29] Markets and property rights are always part of, and modified by, local institutional contexts which are not economic. These social and political institutions surrounding markets and property rights are the source of differences amongst capitalist economies.[30] Thus, it is not clear that the globalisation process brings uniformity among nations.[31] Production methods, industrial relations, technology processes, taxation and economic policy styles remain very specific to each country. In fact, increased interdependence implies the growing significance of domestic structural differences.[32] The reduction of barriers in the form of tariffs or different government interventions in the market highlights the importance of the different socio-economic structures in which national markets are rooted.

[26] K Polanyi, *The Great Transformation: The Political and Economic Origins of Our Time* (Boston, Beacon Press, 1957). On the different visions of market society, see A Hirshman, "Rival Views of Market Society", in A Hirshman *Rival Views of Market Society and Other Recent Essays* (New York, Viking, 1986), 105–141.

[27] See J Zysman, *Government, Markets and Growth: Financial Systems and the Politics of Industrial Change* (Ithaca, Cornell University Press, 1983), 17.

[28] G M Hodgson, "The Evolution of Socioeconomic Order in the Move to a Market Economy", 11 *Rev. Int'l Pol'y Economy* 387 at 395.

[29] See J R Hollingsworth and R Boyer, "Coordination of Economic Actors and Social Systems of Production", in J Hollingsworth and R Boyer (eds.), *Contemporary Capitalism: The Embeddeness of Institutions* (Cambridge, Cambridge University Press, 1997), 1–48.

[30] See J R Hollingsworth, P Schmitter and W Streeck, "Capitalism, Sectors, Institutions and Performance", in J. R Hollingsworth, P Schmitter and W Streeck (eds.), *Governing Capitalist Economies: Performance & Control of Economic Sectors* (Oxford, Oxford University Press, 1994), 3–17, 5.

[31] See R Boyer and D Drache, "Introduction", in R Boyer and D Drache (eds.), *States Against Markets: The Limits of Globalization* (London, Routledge, 1996), 1–26.

[32] J G Ruggie, "Trade, Protectionism and the Future of Welfare Capitalism" (1994) 48 *J. Int'l Affairs* 1–11, 7.

Following Katzenstein, it is possible to divide countries into four types with regard to their socio-economic structures:[33]

GOVERNMENT		MARKET: ORGANIZED	MARKET: PLURAL
	STRONG	1 STRONG ORGANIZED	3 STRONG PLURAL
	WEAK	2 WEAK ORGANIZED	4 WEAK PLURAL

This model is a very abstract one. Countries cannot definitively be placed in one category. However, for the sake of clarity it is useful to classify countries into these four categories. Types 1 and 2 are countries which tend towards a corporativist system characterised by the existence of a highly organised market. These countries are likely to have strong and highly organised trade unions, strong trade and industrial associations, a very strong banking system, itself capable of financing and controlling industry, a strong tendency towards consensus within industrial relations, the reliance on technically correct solutions, a strong and fluid dialogue between government and industry, etc. Types 1 and 2 differ from each other with regard to the strength of their governments. Under model 1, the government will be strongly interventionist. It will tend to develop an industrial planning policy. An example of model 1 would be Japan.[34] A good example of model 2 could be Germany which, as the result of the Nazi tragedy, has developed a tradition of non-intervention and governmental division of power, becoming instead an enabling state.[35] Generally, examples of countries falling under models 1 and 2 are small European countries such as The Netherlands, Denmark, Sweden, Finland, Austria or Belgium.[36]

[33] P Katzenstein, "Conclusion", in P Katzenstein, *supra* n. 18, at 324. An alternative way of understanding market diversity is by focusing on the three elements which are necessary for the existence of a market economy, i.e. property rights, governance structures and rules of exchange. See N Fligstein and I Mara-Drita, "How to Make a Market: Reflections on the Attempt to Create a Single Market in the European Union", 102 (1) *Am. J. Sociology* 1; see also N Fligstein and R Freeland, "Theoretical and Comparative Perspectives on Corporate Organization", 21 *Annual Rev. Sociology* 21.

[34] See Chapter 5.A.3 of this book

[35] See Chapter 4.B.3 of this book, on the domestic structures of Germany.

[36] See P Katzenstein, *Small States in World Markets: Industrial Policy in Europe* (Ithaca, Cornell University Press, 1985).

Model 3 is characterised by the existence of a strong government, by strong government intervention in the economy, and the authoritative imposition of such, but also by a pluralist society. These countries, such as France, Spain or Italy, are those with a strong government interventionist tradition but which have a market characterised by the existence of weak trade unions, or trade unions which are not taken into account, by a weak banking system, by weak trade associations and by the incapability of industrial actors to reach solutions through consensus.[37]

Pluralist Anglo-Saxon countries such as the United Kingdom and the United States fall under model 4. These countries are characterised by the weakness of their governments and by a plural, unorganised market. Trade unions tend to be very weak, there is a consistent lack of strong trade associations, industry tends to finance itself through the stock market due to the weakness of the banking system, there are difficult relations between industry and government and, in general, industrial actors are unlikely to reach a consensus.[38]

These different socio-economic structures, of which national markets are part, result from different historical experiences. Societies' economic organisations and arrangements are path-dependent. The way in which the state and society are actually linked is historically conditioned.[39] The capacity of the state in a capitalist economy to mobilise and use resources effectively is conditioned by ideologies and institutions, and, at a deeper level, by the historical and structural factors that have shaped the development of these.[40] The way the market actors interact with each other, even without the intervention of the state, depends on their expectations. Such expectations, however, are rooted in their past experiences. Although identical technologies and market conditions make for similarities in the industrial organisation and the governance of sectors across countries, there are still significant differences due to different past experiences.[41]

It is important to distinguish between governmental policies and socio-economic structures. While it would be possible to change and control the different policies of a state from the external sphere, it would be much more difficult to change the structures of the same country which are firmly rooted historically. The structures which rule the organisation of the market and strongly condition the role of the state in the market would have to undergo a

[37] See Chapter 4.B.2, of this book, on the domestic structures of France.

[38] See Chapter 2.B of this book, on the domestic structures of the United States.

[39] H Kitschelt, P Lange, G Marks and J Stephens, "Convergence and Divergence in Advanced Capitalist Democracies" in H Kitschelt, P Lange, G Marks and J Stephens (eds.), *Continuity and Change in Advanced Capitalist Democracies* (Cambridge, Cambridge University Press, 1999), 427–460, at 440.

[40] K Dyson, *The State Tradition in Western Europe* (Oxford, Martin Robertson, 1980); see also J Zysman, "How Institutions Create Historically Rooted Trajectories of Growth" (1994) 3(1) *Industrial & Corporate Change* 243–283, 245.

[41] C Crouch, "Sharing Public Space: States and Organized Interests in Western Europe", in J. Hall (ed.), *States in History* (Oxford, Basil Blackwell, 1986), 177–210.

much slower erosion process.[42] Although it is possible that some models would be better off than others, as market institutions are path-dependent and part of an entire socio-economic context, countries would not be able to adapt themselves smoothly to different domestic structures.[43] Thus, globalisation is characterised both by homogeneity and diversity. Globalisation does not create a completely homogenous world-wide market place. Instead, while enforcing a thin Anglo-Saxon market uniformity, it puts together different market frameworks.[44] That is, globalisation makes the interaction between different systems possible.[45]

1.A.3. The Link Between Constitutional and Socio-Economic Structures: Diversity and Domestic Legitimacy

The constitutional and structural approaches to understanding a state's unfair trade instruments as a result of domestic factors are linked. Globalisation creates a paradox for all countries. The challenge for each trading partner in managing globalisation is learning to deal with global diversity while obtaining the necessary domestic legitimacy. However, legitimacy can only exist within a country's socio-economic context.

The persistence of different domestic socio-economic structures within the globalisation process results in a constant exchange of goods and services and capital between different market frameworks. As the flow of trade and investment has a great impact on the domestic life of each trading partner and yet, domestic socio-economic structures are not easily subject to change, states try to protect their domestic spheres by means of participating in bilateral and multilateral negotiations and unilateral unfair trade instruments, in order to influence the rules of the market. Globalisation becomes a cut-throat struggle in which the trading partners try to protect themselves by imposing policies, which

[42] D Soskice, "Different Production Regimes: Coordinated and Uncoordinated Market Economies in the 1980s and 1990s" in H Kitschelt, P Lange, G Marks and J Stephens (eds.), *Continuity and Change in Contemporary Capitalism* (Cambridge, Cambridge University Press, 1999), 101–134, at 123.

[43] But see M Albert, *Capitalism versus Capitalism* (New York, Four Walls Eight Windows, 1993); see also M Hodges and S Woolcock, "Atlantic Capitalism versus Rhine Capitalism in the European Community" (1993) 16 *West Euro. Pol'y* 329–344 (arguing the existence of a competition between different capitalist models from which one model will finally impose itself).

[44] See C Jones, "Capitalism, Globalization and Rule of Law: An Alternative Trajectory of Legal Change in China" (1994) 3 *Social & Legal Studies* 195–221, 202–203.

[45] See P Cerny, "Globalization and Other Stories: The Search for a New Paradigm for International Relations" (1996) *Int'l J.* 617–635, 625; see also R Boyer, "The Convergence Hypothesis Revisited: Globalization but Still the Century of Nations?", in S Berger and Ronald Dore (eds.), *National Diversity and Global Capitalism* (Ithaca, Cornell University Press, 1996), 29–59, 51. In this sense multinational corporations, considered by many authors to be the main actors in the globalisation process, continue to have their patterns of internal governance and financing determined by their background nationalities. See P Doremus, W Keller, L Pauly and S Reich, *The Myth of the Global Corporation* (Princeton, Princeton University Press, 1998), at 139.

accord with their domestic structures, on others.[46] Thus, unfair trade instruments reflect, in their conceptions of fairness, the different socio-economic frameworks in which markets are embedded.

Unfair trade instruments are rationalised on grounds of fairness. The trading system in place since the end of World War II, is not based on the idea of unilateral free trade but rather on a cosmopolitan free trade idea.[47] Free trade must be reciprocal and under certain rules. Free trade is argued not to mean free for all but rather free and fair trade.[48] Fair trade is supposed to be concerned with the equitable treatment of all participants in international trade.[49] It is related to the notion of a level playing field. Competition in international trade should be played according to a set of rules which all participants must share.

However, societies and their economic systems differ so much that what seems to be unfair for one state it may seem perfectly reasonable to another.[50] Hence, it is difficult to agree to a uniform set of market rules. This interdependence between different economic systems may cause harm and economic dislocations to some. Trade instruments can thus be seen as buffer mechanisms, as interface instruments to share the burden of the adjusting costs between different systems.[51] States will use trade instruments in order to limit the dislocation costs caused by goods and services coming from different economic systems. They will impose their own domestic socio-economic standards as their fairness benchmarks. The fair trade notion will extend to any foreign government policy or institution that is different from ones own.[52] Globalisation instead of a process of tolerance and mutual acceptance is simply one of *campanillismo*. The relationship between the state and its private industry and the relationships between its market actors will be the models used to evaluate the trade practices of other nations.[53] No country may assist its home industry or interfere with consumer market preferences to a greater extent than is done in the targeting country. Likewise, foreign market actors may not organise to a greater extent than it is done in the targeting country.

[46] De Sousa Santos considers that one of the process of globalism is globalised localism whereby a local phenomenon is successfully globalised. Globalised localism is paralleled by localised globalisation which is the restructuring and adjustment of the local sphere as a result of globalisation. See De Sousa Santos, "Globalization, Nation-States and the Legal Field: From Legal Diaspora to Legal Ecumenism?", in *Toward a New Common Sense: Law, Science and Politics in the Paradigmatic Transition*, 250–377, 263 (New York, Routledge, 1995).

[47] J Bhagwati, *The World Trading System at Risk* (New York, Harvester Wheatsheaf, 1991), at 50–51.

[48] A Tondson, "Beating Back Predatory Trade" (1994) 73 (4) *Foreign Affairs* 123.

[49] P Nicolaides, "How Fair is Fair Trade?" (1987) 21 *J. World Trade L.* 147–162.

[50] J H Jackson, *The World Trading System: Law and Policy of International Economic Relations* (Cambridge, MA, The MIT Press, 1989), at 218.

[51] R Dore, "Convergence in Whose Interest?", in S Berger and R Dore (eds.), *National Diversity and Global Capitalism* (Ithaca, Cornell University Press, 1996), 366–374, at 371.

[52] See J Bhagwati, "Fair Trade, Reciprocity and Harmonization: The New Challenge to the Theory and Policy of Free Trade", in Deardorff and Stern (eds.), *Analytical and Negotiating Issues in the Global Trading System* (Ann Arbor, The University of Michigan Press, 1994) 547–593, at 584.

[53] J Goldstein, "Ideas, Institutions and America's Trade Policy" (1988) 42 *Int'l Org.* 179, 198.

Furthermore, unfair trade instruments can also be a method of competition between different market economies. Because the elimination of tariff and non-tariff barriers does not lead *per se* to a neutral and global market economy but rather to a variety of market systems each with its own peculiarities, states will compete in the establishment of an international trade legal system which reflects their own domestic sphere. Thus, trade instruments can be understood not only as buffer mechanisms between markets with different socio-economic frameworks but also as states' means of protecting their own structures by trying to change the policies and structures of others.

In the world of globalisation all states are sensitive to interdependence. However, some states are more vulnerable than others.[54] States may have bigger export or import markets or they may be more import- or export-dependent than others. This creates an asymmetrical relationship which will imply the existence of power of one state over another. Power can be defined as the ability of one actor to get others do something they otherwise would not do.[55] Unfair trade instruments may be seen as examples of both relational and structural power. Relational power would be the power of state A to get state B to do something it would not otherwise do. Structural power is the power to shape and determine structures of the global economy within which other states, their political institutions and economic enterprises have to operate.[56]

By using unfair trade instruments a state may use its power to intervene in a foreign country's domestic structure in order to undo the latter's institutional advantages or to impose the same socio-economic framework that it itself has.[57] By simply using the power of its import market a state may impose the conditions of trade and thus alter the policies and structures of a foreign country.[58] Trade instruments are nothing more than the old strategy of "the carrot and the stick".[59] Reverse convergence—the adaptation to its own domestic structures—may be demanded as a condition for free trade when access to the market of a larger country is made conditional on the smaller country accepting foreign

[54] R Keohane and J Nye, *Power and Interdependence* (Boston, Little Brown and Co., 4th ed, 1977) 11–13.

[55] Ibid. at 11.

[56] S Strange, *States and Markets* (London, Pinter Publishers, 1988), at 24.

[57] J Hollingsworth and W Streeck, "Countries and Sectors: Concluding Remarks on Performance, Convergence and Competitiveness", in Hollingsworth, Schmitter and Streeck (eds.), *Governing Capitalist Economies: Performance & Control of Economic Sectors* (Oxford, Oxford University Press, 1994), 270–300, 282–283.

[58] J H Jackson, "Perspectives on Countervailing Duties" (1989) 21 *L. & Pol'y Int'l Bus.* 739–761.

[59] A way of understanding this is through game theory. See R Diamond, "Changes in the Game: Understanding the Relationship Between Section 301 and US Trade Strategies" (1990) 8 (2) *B. U. Int'l L. J.* 351–361; see also K W Abbot, "Modern International Relations Theory: A Prospectus for International Lawyers" (1989) 14 *Yale J. Int'l L.* 335–411, 354; see also K Oye, "Explaining Cooperation Under Anarchy" (1985) 38 *World Pol'y* 1–24; see also R Axelrod, *The Evolution of Cooperation* (New York, Basic Books, 1984); and S Coffield, "Using Section 301 of the Trade Act as a Response to Foreign Government Trade Actions: When, Why and How" (1981) 6 *N. C. J. Int'l L. & Com. Reg.* 381–405.

intervention in its domestic structures.[60] However, reverse convergence will be much more successful when addressing government policies, than when dealing with those practices affecting trade which are deeply embedded in a market's industrial organisation and wider society.[61]

Trade instruments may also be used to build up an international trade regime which is compatible with a state's own domestic structures.[62] By using trade instruments against foreign countries, states may create precedents and establish the standards of the future international regime. An international regime may be defined as a set of explicit or implicit principles, norms, rules and decision-making procedures around which actor expectations converge in a given area of international relations.[63] International trade regimes are institutions that establish the standards for the socio-economic world market framework. However, they reflect the underlying power and interests of the dominant hegemonic states. Powerful states will try to impose regimes which reflect their own market economy's framework.

One way of understanding this is to focus on subsidies. A state can impose countervailing duties to restrain the use of subsidies and influence the future agenda of negotiations on subsidies. However, despite its possible economic rationale, limiting subsidies is not neutral. Restraining the use of subsidies implies limiting a way of government intervention in the economy. Such limitation benefits most those countries which traditionally have had a weak government and thus, even if international rules allowed for subsidies, it would not be so easy for it to grant them. On the other hand, limiting subsidies will seriously handicap countries which traditionally have had a strong and interventionist government.

Distinguishing between defensive and offensive trade instruments is somewhat limited. Arguably anti-dumping and countervailing duties would protect domestic producers from the unfair trade of foreign producers, whereas market access instruments would try to open up unfair foreign markets for domestic producers. But this is only to a certain extent. In practice, defensive instruments, may also indirectly (and therefore less efficiently) be offensive. It all depends on

[60] See G Saxonhouse, "A Short Summary of the Long History of Unfair Trade Allegations against Japan", in J Bhagwati and R E Hudec (eds.), *Fair Trade and Harmonization: Prerequisites for Free Trade?* (Cambridge, The MIT Press, 1996), 472–513, 401 (analysing US Super 301 and the Structural Impediments Initiative against Japan. But the author considers that the US initiative was successful because in Japan there were some domestic calls, such as the Maekawa Commission Report, for such changes); see also N Zuberi, "Disregard for EU Laws Would Mean Ouster from World Market", *Business Recorder*, March 12 1997, at 8.

[61] See J McMillan, "Why Does Japan Resist Foreign Market-Opening Pressure?", in J N Bhagwati and R E Hudec, *supra* n. 60, 515–541.

[62] See D Leebron, "Lying Down with Procrustes: An Analysis of Harmonization Claims", in J Bhagwati and R E Hudec, *supra* n. 60, 41–117 (arguing that instruments such as Section 301 could be means of unilateral harmonisation. The author considers, however, that such efforts are only partially successful and are, for the most part, aimed at bilateral harmonisation rather than multilateral harmonisation).

[63] See J Finlayson and M Zacher, "The GATT and the Regulation of Trade Barriers: Regime Dynamics and Functions" (1981) 35 *Int'l Org.* 561.

the magnitude of the asymmetrical relationship between the different trading partners. Unfair trade laws benefit countries with large import and export markets in contrast with countries with small markets.[64]

An example of how anti-dumping and countervailing duties can be offensive in an indirect manner could be the case of the People's Republic of China.[65] The PRC is desperate to obtain foreign income in order to import new technologies and improve its economy. The main way for China to obtain income is by exporting.[66] But between 1987 and 1997, the PRC has been the country which has been most affected by anti-dumping investigations.[67] This implies that the PRC's exports have been severely punished by anti-dumping duties. The anti-dumping laws of the most frequent anti-dumping users, the United States, the European Union, Mexico and Australia have tended to use dumping methodologies which clearly discriminated against non-market economies. Systematically, the exports of the PRC receive higher duties than those of market economies. What can the PRC do? It can keep its non-market economy and thus, its export products, or it can start to change its economy, play by the rules, and improve its anti-dumping profile.

The ability to impose the rules of the game does not rely exclusively on economic power but also depends on the domestic structures which affect the taking of trade policy decisions. To influence the international regime for their benefit, states have to act rationally and as monoliths. States are required to act efficiently and with one voice as if there were no internal domestic differences. But globalisation itself creates the paradox. Due to the increasing effects of globalisation within the internal sphere, trade relations can no longer be considered to be an issue for a reduced number of experts. Rather, all different constitutional units of power within a state will want to have a voice.[68] States will need to develop constitutional procedures which will provide the necessary domestic legitimacy to act effectively in a global system characterised by diversity. Through constitutional procedures, states will try to solve the paradox by creating mechanisms for co-operation which allow a voice to the different powers while at the same time permitting the state to have a uniform voice in the external sphere.

However, political action prescribed by formal constitutions is part of a much wider socio-economic context.[69] Because countries have diverse market

[64] See J H Jackson, *Restructuring the GATT System* (London, Pinter, 1990), 69–74.

[65] I take this example from conversations with professors Song Ying and Francis Snyder, European University Institute, January 1999. The PRC is a radical example because it is a non-market economy.

[66] It could also do so by attracting foreign investment.

[67] See J Miranda, R Torres and M Ruiz, "The International use of Anti-dumping, 1987–1997" (1998) 32(5) *J. World Trade* 5–71, 11.

[68] G Winham, "Robert Strauss, the MTN, and the Control of Faction" (1980) 14 *J. World Trade L.* 377–397.

[69] T Prosser, "The State, Constitutions and Implementing Economic Policy: Privatization and the U.K., France and the USA" (1995) 4 *Social & Legal Studies* 507–516.

frameworks, they respond differently to globalisation.[70] To comprehend why constitutional political actors behave as they do it is important to consider their socio-economic context. Thus not all trading partners can solve the paradox to the same extent. While the United States till now has been able to create a trade policy which allows its constituencies to voice their concerns, grants selective protectionism and at the same time empowers the executive to strongly influence the developments of globalisation, the European Union has created a rather chaotic trade policy which reduces its role in the international trade scene to one which is certainly not in accordance with its factual trade significance. While the United States has one market embedded in one socio-economic framework, the Community has fifteen markets, or perhaps one market in fifteen different socio-economic frameworks. Because the Community's trade policy is the result of different socio-economic structures it lacks a coherent and strong uniform Common Commercial Policy. As long as Europe does not recognise the existence of different socio-economic structures in the Community we will lack a coherent trade policy. Constitutional reform will not be enough without strong positive integration.

1.B. UNFAIR TRADE INSTRUMENTS AND PROTECTIONISM

The most widely used unfair trade instruments are anti-dumping, countervailing measures and market access instruments. These are protectionist instruments used by governments as a means to aid their national industries. Furthermore, they are trade barriers that imply a threat to the international trading system by creating a bad trade relations environment within which a feeling of mutual distrust and retaliation prevails. The irony is, however, that unfair trade instruments are the result of free trade ideas. Their internal rationale implies a perfect market standard where no social or political constraints limit market actors. Second, the application of unfair trade instruments shows no more than the inability of most states to cope with a global interdependency in which states increasingly see themselves incapable of developing their own domestic policies.

1.B.1. The Basic Elements of Anti-dumping and Countervailing Measures

Anti-dumping and countervailing duties are intended to defend against the introduction of unfairly low priced imports into the domestic market. Anti-dumping measures aim at offsetting the distortive effects which dumping practices from foreign firms cause in the domestic market. Countervailing measures

[70] As to the different reactions to globalisation on the basis of different domestic structures, see Section B of this chapter.

have the purpose of offsetting the distortive effects in the domestic market resulting from unfair government subsidisation.

A country may take anti-dumping measures if it makes an affirmative determination of both dumping and injury.[71] A product is considered to be dumped if the export price of the export product is less than the comparable price, in the ordinary course of trade, for the like product when sold in the domestic market of the exporting country.[72] Where there are no sales in the ordinary course of trade in the exporting country,[73] the importing country authorities may use the price of the like product when exported to a third country, or the cost of production in the country of origin plus a reasonable amount for administrative, selling and other costs and profit. In practice, the importing country will generally determine whether the product is sold in its market below cost of production and profits.

A country may impose a countervailing duty if it makes an affirmative determination of both the existence of a countervailable subsidy and injury to its domestic industry.[74] A countervailable subsidy is one which is specific *de iure* or *de facto*[75] and is not subject to any exceptions as a non-actionable subsidy.[76] A subsidy is deemed to exist if there is a financial contribution by a government or any income or price support, within the meaning of article VI of GATT, which confers a benefit to the recipient.[77]

The imposition of both countervailing duties and anti-dumping measures requires an affirmative determination of the existence of injury to the domestic

[71] Article VI of GATT; see also Agreement on the Implementation of Article VI of GATT, O.J. 23.12.94 L 336/103 [Hereinafter Anti-dumping Code]; see also J H Jackson and E. Vermulst, *Antidumping Law and Practice: A Comparative Study* (New York, Harvester Wheatsheaf, 1990); see also F Snyder, *International Trade and Customs Law of the European Union* (London, Butterworths, 1998) 212–258. The European Community's anti-dumping law is now contained in Council Regulation No 384/96, O.J. 6.3.96 L 56/1, as amended by Council Regulation 2331/96, O.J. 6.12.96 L317/1 and Council Regulation 905/98, O.J. 30.4.98 L128/18. The United States anti-dumping law is now contained in Sections 731–739 of the Tariff Act of 1930, as amended; 19 U.S.C. 1673 (1996).

[72] Article 2 of the Anti-dumping Code. Concerning the discussion on the definition of dumping, see Chapter 5.A.

[73] As to sales of the like product in the exporting country, see Article 2(2)(1) of the Anti-dumping Code.

[74] Article 6 of GATT; see also Agreement on Subsidies and Countervailing Measures, O.J. 23.12.94 L 335/156 [Hereinafter ASCM]; see also G Horlick and P Clarke, "The 1994 WTO Subsidies Agreement", in G Lew (ed.), *The Commerce Department Speaks on International Trade and Investment* (New York, Practising Law Institute, 1994) 685–719; see also Terry Collins-W and G Salembier, "International Disciplines on Subsidies" (1996) 30 (91) *J. World Trade* 5–17; see also R Behboodi, *Industrial Subsidies in World Trade: Trade Policy or Trade Politics* (London, Routledge, 1994). The European Community's countervailing duty law is contained in Council Regulation 2026/97, O.J. 21.10.97 L 288/1. The United States countervailing duty law is contained in Section 701 of the Tariff Act of 1930, as amended; 19 U.S.C. 1671 (1996).

[75] Article 2 of the ASCM. The specificity test has basically been copied from US countervailing duty law.

[76] As to the concept of non-actionable subsidies see Article 8 of the ASCM; see also G Kleinfeld and D Kaye, "Red Light, Green Light?: The 1994 Agreement on Subsidies and Countervailing Measures, Research and Development Assistance, and US Policy" (1994) 28 (6) *J. World Trade* 43–63; see also Chapter III.A of this book.

[77] Article 1 of the ASCM.

industry.[78] This implies two determinations. First, the importing country authorities must establish the existence of injury in the sense of material injury, threat of material injury or material retardation to the domestic producers of a product which is like the one which is subsidised or dumped. Second, they must determine the existence of a causal link between the dumped or subsidised imports and the injury. It is desirable that the duty be less than the margin of dumping or subsidisation if such lesser duty would be adequate to remove the injury to the domestic industry.[79]

Both countervailing duties and anti-dumping measures are substantially and procedurally biased toward protectionism. From the perspective of the importing country they most probably reduce its aggregate economic welfare. From a free trade perspective, cheap imports are good regardless of their cause.[80] The wealth increase of consumers is higher than the reduction of wealth of producers. However, it could be argued that anti-dumping duties and countervailing measures are a way of preventing a transfer of income from producers to consumers due to abnormal cheap imports.[81] But the distortion that may be caused because of this transfer of income could be best restored by other forms of domestic intervention such as adjustment relief rather than protectionist measures.[82]

From the perspective of the importing country, anti-dumping and countervailing measures would only make economic sense as prevention against economic predation. The predatory argument assumes that the exporter will maintain its low prices until it has eliminated competition in the importing country.[83] While consumers in the short run enjoy the low prices characterised by dumping and subsidised imports, the manufacturer is more than repaid in the form of higher prices once competition has been eliminated. Yet, the real possi-

[78] Article VI of GATT. See also Article 15 of the ASCM; Article 3 of the Anti-dumping Code; and A Pangratis and E Vermulst, "Injury in Anti-Dumping Proceedings—The Need to Look Beyond the Uruguay Round Results" (1994) 28(5) *J. World Trade* 61–96.

[79] Article VI of GATT; see also Article 9 of the Anti-dumping Code; and Article 19 of the ASCM. European Community law requires the EC institutions to follow the lesser duty rule. See Articles 7(2) and 9(4) of Council Regulation No 384/96, O.J. 6.3.96 L 56/1, as amended; and Articles 12(1) and 15(1) of Council Regulation 2026/97, O.J. 21.10.97 L 288/1; see also Joined Cases 277 and 300/85, Canon Inc. *v.* Council [1988] ECR 5731; and Case 256/84, Koyo Seiko *v.* Council [1987] ECR 1899 (requiring the Community authorities to ascertain whether the amount of the duties is necessary in order to remove the injury). No such provisions exist in United States Anti-dumping and Countervailing duty law.

[80] J M Finger, "Anti-dumping and Antisubsidy Measures", in J Finger (ed.), *The Uruguay Round: A Handbook for Multilateral Trade Negotiations* (Washington, World Bank, 1988) 153–161, 157.

[81] B Hindley, "Subsidies, Politics and Economics", in D Wallace, F Loftus and V Krikorian (eds.), *Interface Three: Legal Treatment of Domestic Subsidies* (Washington, International Law Institute, 1984) at 29.

[82] K Stegemann, "The Efficiency Rationale of Anti-dumping Policy and Other Measures of Contingency Protection", in J Quinn and P Slayton (eds.), *Non-Tariff Barriers After the Tokyo Round* (Montreal, The Institute, 1982), 21–67.

[83] J Barcelo, "Antidumping Laws as Barriers to Trade—The United States and the International Antidumping Code" (1972) 57 (4) *Cornell L. Rev.* 491, 500.

bility of predation is very doubtful. The predator should be able to prevent the re-entry into the market of competitors after the prices are raised at monopoly levels. An industry which featured many product substitutes would thus hinder the predator in raising prices. Furthermore, from an international trade perspective, the predator should be able to establish a world-wide monopoly. Eliminating domestic producers from one market would not prevent competing firms from entering the market once the predator had risen its prices.

From the specific point of view of countervailing measures, the predatory intent of subsidies could be more credible. Predation could be more likely in the case of subsidies because governments, and especially those of big countries, are usually stronger than firms. Yet, predation would still be extremely difficult to prove.[84] This would particularly be so in the case of domestic subsides. Subsidisation may be the result of a country's will to achieve certain domestic goals and not related to predation. Likewise, dumping can result for reasons other than predation; such as market segmentation, fluctuations in demand, or shifts in supply or a different distribution of costs. In any case, neither anti-dumping nor countervailing laws require the determination of any predatory intent.[85] In fact, these instruments only call for the existence of injury to domestic competitors and not to competition itself. Thus, it has been argued that, from an economic point of view, the best thing an importing country can do when receiving cheap imports resulting from dumping or unfair subsidisation is to send a "Thank You" note to the exporting country.[86]

The economic rationale for anti-dumping and countervailing measures could also be argued, however, from a world-wide approach. Countervailing and anti-dumping measures would be efficiency-enhancing because they would deter the use of subsidies or the practice of dumping. The deterrence argument of countervailing duties would assume that all subsidies are distortive in one way or another.[87] The argument that subsidies distort trade is based on the idea that the market is always perfect. It unrealistically assumes full internal efficiency within every national economy. Subsidies would distort comparative advantages and lead to an inefficient allocation of global economic resources. However, there may be imperfect competition, market externalities or market rigidities. Subsidies can thus compensate for market imperfections or externalities. Similarly, it is also very doubtful whether global efficiency would suffer if dumping were permitted. Only if dumping were the result of a monopoly

[84] J H Jackson, *The World Trading System: Law and Policy of International Economic Relations* (Cambridge, The MIT Press, 1989) at 253.

[85] The exception to this is the US 1916 Anti-dumping law. See Chapter 5.B.

[86] See J Bhagwati, *Protectionism* (Cambridge, MIT Press, 1988), 43–59.

[87] This is the argument of the anti-distortion school of thought, in contrast to the injury school of thought which considers that only subsidies which really affect the industries of the importing countries should be countervailed. See G Hufbauer and S Erb, *Subsidies in International Trade* (Cambridge, MIT Press, 1984), at 19. By defining a subsidy as a distortion of the market *per se*, the United States authorities would adopt the anti-distortion approach and follow the deterrence argument. See *Carbon Steel Wire Rod from Poland*, 49 Fed. Reg. 19374 (1984).

enjoyed by the firm in the exporting country, would those consumers in such country suffer from the monopoly prices.[88]

It could also be argued that countervailing and anti-dumping measures are necessary to protect firms from an unfair advantage. Foreign firms should compete at the same level and under the same conditions as domestic firms. Domestic firms should not be allowed to compete against foreign firms that enjoy an unfair advantage due to subsidisation or market monopoly. From this perspective dumping could be considered unfair because it is not cost justified but rather based on the monopoly the firm enjoys in its domestic market. Yet, even if the foreign firm were enjoying a monopoly in its domestic market this would not necessarily allow it to dump in the importing market.[89] Furthermore, while this argument would require a substantially fair analysis, anti-dumping duties are substantially protectionist as they systematically discriminate against the foreign firm. First, they establish an asymmetry in the comparison between the normal value and the export price. They establish different treatment of the expenses for the export price and the domestic market.[90] Second, they make an unfair comparison of normal value average with individual export prices.[91] Third, most anti-dumping practice establishes the existence of dumping by determining the constructed value of the product. By requiring the foreign firm to sell above all costs (fixed and variable costs) and profit, the practice does not take into account the economic rationale of selling below fixed cost but above variable costs.[92] Furthermore, the anti-dumping laws call for an arbitrary minimum amount of selling and general administrative costs and profit.

[88] See J Barcelo, *supra* n. 83, at 513.

[89] Ibid. at 507.

[90] This has been limited only partially by the new anti-dumping code. See Article 2(4) of the Anti-dumping Code. On the practice of asymmetry in EC anti-dumping law, see Chapter 5.A; see also E Vermulst and P Waer, "The Post Uruguay Round EC Anti-Dumping Regulation: After a Pit Stop, Back in the Race" (1995) 29(2) *J. World Trade* 53–76. On the United States practice, see E McClafferty, "Identifying Level of Trade in US Antidumping Law" (1996) 36(4) *Virginia J. Int'l L.* 1021–1078.

[91] Again, the new anti-dumping code has only limited this to a certain extent. See Article 2(4)(2) of the Anti-dumping Code. On the EC practice see Article 2(11) of Council Regulation No 384/96, as amended. For previous Community practice see *Powdered Activated Carbon from the PRC*, O.J. L 192/14 (1995); see also *Certain Magnetic Disks from the United States, Mexico and Malaysia*, O.J. L 249/3 (1995); see also Case 204/84, *Toyo Bearing* v. *Council* [1987] ECR 1809; see also Case 255/84, *Nachi Fujikoshi* v. *Council* [1987] ECR 1861; and Case 256/84, *Koyo Seiko* v. *Council* [1987] ECR 1899 (upholding this practice on grounds that otherwise it would not be possible to countervail dumping practices). Again, US anti-dumping law and practice is basically the same. See D Palmeter, "The Capture of Antidumping Law" (1989) 14 *Yale J. Int'l L.* 182–198.

[92] K Matsumoto and G Filayson, "Dumping and Antidumping: Growing Problems in World Trade" (1990) 24 (4) *J. World Trade* 5–19; see also P Waer, "Constructed Values in EC Dumping Margin Calculations: Fiction or a Realistic Approach" (1993) 27(4) *J. World Trade* 5–22. The Uruguay Anti-dumping code has limited this only to a certain extent. See Article 2(2) of the Anti-dumping Code. The Community will basically continue to ignore economic rationale in applying its constructed value analysis. See Article 2(3) of Council Regulation No 384/96, as amended. On the EC practice see Chapter 5.A. US law also ignores the economic rationale of selling below fixed costs in times of slack demand.

Countervailing duties could also be justified from an entitlement approach.[93] It could be argued that it would be unfair to make domestic firms and workers compete with foreign subsidised products. The purpose of the entitlement argument would be to protect the competitive position that the domestic producers would have occupied had the foreign subsidy never existed. However, not all subsidies would have a distortive effect in foreign countries.[94] A countervailing duty would only be required if the subsidy lowers the variable costs.[95] However, the countervailing duty laws do not contain any distortion across the border test. The laws only require the government authorities to look at the difference in cash flows without taking into account whether such difference in fact enables the foreign firm to sell at a lower price. Thus, the countervailing duty is much higher than that necessary to counter the effects of the subsidy.[96]

From a procedural point of view, countervailing and anti-dumping measures are also biased.[97] The procedural rules lay down an inquisitorial rather than an adversarial system as the government authorities both investigate the allegations of unfair trade and resulting injury and impose the final duty.[98] Once the initial threshold of sufficient evidence is presented, it is basically the government authority which does all the work. This, in one way or another, will frustrate the petitioner who will always think that it itself could have found a higher subsidisation or dumping rate. This in turn puts much more pressure on the government authorities who consequently become more and more demanding towards the foreign firms. Thus, the procedural rules are full of protectionist tilts. The initiation standards are easy to meet, the duties apply in principle to future exports, the refund procedures are generally limited, there are enormous administrative burdens and costs for the foreign firms and governments, there are no penalties against frivolous complaints, etc.

1.B.2. The Basic Elements of Market Access Instruments

The market access instruments of the United States and the European Union are Section 301 of the Trade Act of 1974 and the Trade Barriers Regulation

[93] C Goetz, L Granet and W Schwartz, "The Meaning of Subsidy and Injury in the Countervailing Duty Law" (1986) 6 *Int'l Rev. L. & Econ.* 17–32.

[94] See R Diamond, "Economic Foundations of Countervailing Duty Law" (1989) 29 *VA. J. Int'l L.* 767.

[95] This is because the firm could sell cheaper as it is always rational to sell below variable costs.

[96] J Francois, "Countervailing the Effects of Subsidies: An Economic Analysis" (1992) 16 *J. World Trade*. 5–13, 8.

[97] M Rowat, "Protectionist Tilts in Antidumping Legislation of Developed Countries and the LDC Response: Is the Race to the Bottom Inevitable?" (1990) 24 (6) *J. World Trade* 5–27; See also Palmeter and Anspecher, Conceptual and Procedural Biases in the Administration of Countervailing Duty Law, in R Boltuck and R Litan (eds.), *Down in the Dumps: Administration of the Unfair Trade Laws* (Washington, The Brookings Institute, 1991), at 95.

[98] D Palmeter, "Torquemada and the Tariff Act: The Inquisitor Rides Again" (1985) 20 (2) *Int'l Law*. 641–657.

respectively.[99] Their objective is to increase or create export markets for domestic firms by challenging foreign practices that are considered to be obstacles to trade. They provide private petitioners and government authorities with a mechanism to enforce international trade agreements or to eliminate what are considered to be unfair foreign trade practices by threatening trade retaliation and engaging in international negotiations and dispute settlement procedures.

Though based on the idea of opening markets and, thereby, on a presumed free trade rationale, market access trade instruments reflect a mercantilist approach to trade and risk becoming export protectionist instruments. By means of these instruments, governments, instead of protecting domestic firms from foreign imports, support firms in exporting to foreign markets.[100] They are means for governments to interfere in the market and improve the welfare of their industry. They result from domestic pressures and the inability of states to pursue their own domestic policies. Governments will try to limit import protectionism and domestic government intervention by promoting export industries.[101] Even if their use is justified under international trade rules they still consist of government action trying to improve conditions for domestic firms.[102]

It could be argued that, from a free trade perspective, market access instruments can be welfare enhancing.[103] Through the use of threats they may eliminate trade barriers and increase trade. However it is important to distinguish between two situations. First, these instruments may be used against practices which are considered to be GATT/WTO illegal. In such a situation the use of these instruments would be trade enhancing only if used successfully. Only if the targeted country responds positively to the threat, and thus complies with the international trade standards by eliminating the trade barrier, would the use of the instrument be trade enhancing. If the targeted country refuses to comply with GATT and the targeting country decides not to stand by its threat then nothing will have changed. Furthermore, if the targeting country decides to retaliate there will be two trade distortions: the original violation of GATT and the new retaliatory measure. But, even if the targeted practices are clearly

[99] Section 301 of the United States Trade Act of 1974 is codified in 19 U.S.C. 2411 (1996). On the development of Section 301 of the 1974 Trade Act see Chapter III. C. As to the Trade Barriers Regulation, see Council Regulation (EC) No 3286/94, O.J. 31.12.96 L 349/71 (1994), as amended for technical reasons by Council Regulation (EC) No 356/95, O.J. 23.2.95 L 41/3 (1995). As to the developments of the Trade Barriers Regulation, see Chapter 5.B.

[100] M Hirsh, "Toying with Trade Wars", *Newsweek*, July 1996, at 34.

[101] J Bhagwati, "Aggressive Unilateralism: An Overview", in J Bhagwati and H Patrick (eds.), *Aggressive Unilateralism: America's 301 Trade Policy and the World Trading System* (New York, Harvester Wheatsheaf, 1991), at 14.

[102] In this sense, they may be an example of how international trade rules can justify some government intervention while prohibiting others. Domestic government intervention would be wrong but promoting firms in third markets could be justified. This is not something neutral. Whereas some countries have certain structures which favour domestic government intervention others will have domestic structures which make it easier to act in the foreign sphere through the use of these trade instruments.

[103] A Sykes, "Constructive Unilateral Threats in International Commercial Relations: The Limited Case for Section 301" (1992) 23 (2) *L. & Pol'y Int'l Bus.* 263–330, 265.

GATT illegal, there is still the risk of world-wide distortion. The use of these instruments will only be credible when the targeting country is one with a big market. Under these instruments, and even under the WTO Dispute Settlement Mechanism, the distortions most likely to be removed will in fact be those of small countries. Retaliation against a big state, even under the auspices of WTO, will very rarely make sense to a small country.[104] Furthermore, in times of economic decline or trade deficit, if the use of these trade instruments under the rules of WTO does not result in the opening of foreign markets which improve the domestic economy, protectionism will continue to put pressure on government authorities and these will try again and again to reinterpret the rules in order to further open foreign markets.[105]

Second, if the use of market access instruments is not based on international law standards, but is instead the result of a unilateral interpretation of trade fairness, there will be a stronger risk of trade distortion.[106] In particular, the instruments could be used to secure domestic firms exports to foreign countries without taking into account whether such exports displace those of a third country.[107] Moreover, using these instruments without having regard to international trade rules may increase the threat of counter-retaliation in response to what is perceived to be an unfair retaliation. Thus, unilateral interpretations of the standards of trade can create a climate of unfairness which may, in turn, limit the willingness of governments to keep their markets open.

Like anti-dumping and countervailing duty investigations, market access instrument procedures are also often biased. In the investigation phase of the procedure there seems to be a feeling of us against them. The administration in charge of these instruments and policies would feel pressure to achieve results. There is a need to prove that it is possible to open third markets and improve the domestic economy through these instruments. Thus, sometimes the procedure is more focused on proving the illegality of the foreign countries practices' than on objectively determining whether the facts alleged by the claiming party are true. This is particularly true if investigations can only be initiated as a result of a complaint rather than *ex officio*.[108]

[104] J Bello and A Holmer, "US Trade Law Policy Series No 24: Dispute Resolution in the New World Trade Organization: Concerns and Net Benefits" (1994) 28 (4) *Int'l Law* 1095–1104.

[105] "Now, It's About Beef: America Retargets EU", *International Herald Tribune*, Tuesday, 23 March 1999, at 1.

[106] J Jackson, "US Threat to the New World Trade Order", *Financial Times*, 23 May 1995, at 17.

[107] See *Japan, Trade in Semi-Conductors*, L/6309, 24 March 1988, BISD 35 S/116 (where the panel analysed the negative trade effects which the agreement between Japan and the US ending US Section 301 threats had for third countries).

[108] Interview at the Commission, Brussels, May 1997.

1.B.3. The Background of Unfair Trade Instruments: The Relation between the Domestic and the External Sphere

Anti-dumping and countervailing duties, together with market access instruments, are ways by which domestic governments attempt to improve their national economies. Unfair trade instruments result from the inability of governments to develop their policy goals within their domestic sphere. This in turn is due to the effects of globalisation on most states.

To understand the relation between globalisation, its effects on the domestic structures of most states, and the use of trade instruments as protectionist devices, it may be useful to analyse states according to the relation between their domestic and external policies. Following Keohane, states may be classified with regard to the relation between the domestic and the external in the following way:[109]

	DOMESTIC	
	A	C
	EXT OPEN DOM LAISSEZ FAIRE	EXT OPEN DOMESTIC EMBEDDED
EXTERNAL		
	EXT CLOSED DOM LAISSEZ FAIRE	EXT CLOSED DOM EMBEDDED
	B	D

The development of anti-dumping and countervailing duty laws are the result of a misconception. They are an example of how ideas, by being solidified in institutions, may have an impact even after they are no longer considered satisfactory.[110] Trade instruments were basically a creation of the nineteenth century economic system; a period in which countries of models (A) and (B) tended to prevail. Liberal countries falling into category (A) are those characterised by an external openness, a basic commitment towards the free trade system, and a domestic *laissez faire* system in which government intervention in the market is limited. These domestic and foreign economic policies reflect a domestic system characterised by a weak government and a plural and unorganised market that will favour a hands off policy, in which the government will refuse to intervene in the economy and generally refuse to grant protection. However, in practice,

[109] R Keohane, "The World Political Economy and the Crisis of Embedded Liberalism", in J Goldthorpe (ed.), *Order and Conflict in Contemporary Capitalism: Studies in the Political Economy of Western European nations* (Oxford, Clarendon Press, 1984), 15–38.

[110] J Goldstein, *Ideas, Interests and American Trade Policy* (Ithaca, Cornell University Press, 1993).

countries such as these have rarely existed.[111] Only under conditions of economic hegemony, have some states like the United Kingdom in the second half of the nineteenth century and the United States after the Second World War, allowed themselves to come close to this category. One of the main characteristics of liberal countries which are not hegemonic is a tendency towards trade conflict through the externalisation of domestic problems.[112] In times of economic crisis, the governments of such countries would grant *ad hoc* protectionism. One way of doing so is by means of unfair trade instruments.

Closely related to the liberal model are the self-help countries characterised by a closure towards the trading system, protectionism, and a domestic system where a free market economy and low government intervention is pursued. As with liberal countries, model (B) countries result from the existence of a plural society and a weak government. The inability of the state to pursue domestic policies and the incapacity of its market to organise itself results in strong calls for protectionism. Trade instruments would flourish within this system.

Although there had already been early claims against allegedly unfair foreign trading practices, the United States was the first country to develop strong countervailing and anti-dumping laws.[113] Such developments were to take place in a system of domestic *laissez faire* and strong protectionism towards the external sphere which characterised the United States during the nineteenth century.[114] The new America, characterised by the absence of a state tradition and a plural society based on the principle of extreme individualism, would embrace Locke's liberalism in domestic politics but not Adam Smith's nor David Ricardo's external free trade. It would pursue a liberal internal market sheltered by a strong protectionist foreign economic policy.

Despite the popular myth to the contrary, the US would follow Hamilton's suggestion of protectionism and economic isolation to allow American industry to flourish. One of Hamilton's justifications for protectionism was the unfair trading practices of foreign countries.[115] In the medium run the United States would embrace such policy. American society realised that the creation of an identity and of a national liberal market required the establishment of a strong protectionist foreign economic policy.[116]

[111] J Hagelstam, "Mercantilism Still Influences Practical Trade Policy at the End of the Twentieth Century" (1991) 25 (1) *J. World Trade*, 95–105, 99.

[112] A good example of this could be the United States during the steel crisis in the 1980s. See J Berkey, *International Trade: Countervailing Duties and the European Steel Imports* (1989) 23 (2) *Harvard. Int'l L. J.* 443.

[113] J Viner, *Dumping: A Problem in International Trade* (New York, Augustus M. Kelly Publishers, 1966), at 374.

[114] A Eckes, *Opening America's Market* (Chapel Hill, The University of North California Press, 1995), 28–59.

[115] A Hamilton, "Report on Manufactures: Communicated to the House of Representatives on December 5, 1791", in H Lodge (ed.), *The Works of Alexander Hamilton* (New York, Haskell House Publishers Ltd., 1971), Volume IV, 70–164, 106.

[116] On the relation between the creation of a national identity and a liberal domestic market and protectionism, see M Wolf, "Cooperation or Conflict? The European Union in a Liberal Global Economy" (1995) 71 *International Affairs* 325–337.

The first trade instrument to be adopted as a protectionist device was the countervailing duty legislation against subsidised foreign products. The United States enacted the first countervailing duty provisions in the Tariff Act of 1890 as part of a reinforcement of its tariff laws.[117] The countervailing provision applied only to sugar imports from countries which paid, directly or indirectly, a bounty upon exportation.[118] The law was intended to retaliate against Russian subsidies on exported sugar. The countervailing duty provisions, however, did not contain any requirement of injury to the domestic industry. This was due to the fact that the provision's intention was not to protect the US undistorted market but to protect its tariffs.[119] Russian export subsidies were considered to be wrong because they limited the effects of US tariffs on sugar that were intended to protect the US sugar industry.

The law was further developed by the Tariff Act of 1897[120] which introduced the first countervailing duty law against all export subsidies and by the Tariff Act of 1921[121] which required the imposition of a countervailing duty against both export and domestic subsidies. As the original countervailing duty provisions, their intent was to safeguard the United States' protectionist policy. Thus, not only did they follow the absence of an injury requirement in the original provision, but furthermore, such provisions did not apply to duty-free imports. In fact, because the law was intended to protect US protectionist foreign economic policy and not the unknown idea of an undistorted market, the courts interpreted the definition of a subsidy as broadly as possible, without taking into account any economic considerations.[122] These basic principles of countervailing duty law which were part of a protectionist policy would thereafter remain in the US trade laws. Other countries would follow the United States in enacting countervailing duty laws.[123] However, unlike the US provisions, their application was not mandatory and, in practice, most countries only threatened their use. Only India and British South Africa ever applied their anti-subsidy laws.

Canada, another Anglo-Saxon and liberal country, would be the first to enact an anti-dumping law in 1904.[124] But it was not until after the First World War that anti-dumping laws spread around the world as result of the protectionist sentiments and the fears of ruinous German dumping. Again, the United States

[117] Tariff Act of 1890, ch. 1244, Sect. 237, 26 Stat. 584, as cited in G Bryan, *Taxing Unfair International Trade Practices* (Lexington, Lexington Books, 1980), at 250.

[118] See J Viner, *supra* n. 113, at 168.

[119] R Mundheim and P Ehrenhaft, "What is a Subsidy? A Discussion Paper", in D Wallace, F Loftus and V Krikorian (eds.), *Interface Three: Legal Treatment of Domestic Subsidies* (Washington, International Law Institute, 1984) at 95.

[120] Tariff Act of 1897, ch. 11 Sect. 5, 30 Stat. 205.

[121] Tariff Act of 1922, ch. 356 Section 303, 42 Stat. 935.

[122] See *Downs* v. *US*, 187 US 496 (1903); see also *Nicholas & Corp. v. US*, 249 U.S. 34 (1919).

[123] Belgium in 1892, India in 1899, British South Africa in 1903, Switzerland in 1902, Serbia in 1904, Spain in 1906, France and Japan in 1910, Portugal in 1921. See Jacob Viner at 169.

[124] An Act to Amend the Customs Tariff of 1897, 4 Edw. 7, c. 11, S 19 (1904) as cited in J Barcelo, "Antidumping Laws as Barriers to Trade—The United States and the International Antidumping Code", *supra* n. 83, at 517.

would be the main user of such laws. Its first anti-dumping provisions were adopted in the Revenue Act of 1916.[125] The act was the result of domestic outrage against German steel producers who were accused of by-passing US tariffs through dumping practices. Some years later, the US would further develop and strengthen such provisions with the Tariff Act of 1922 as part of a new wave of protectionism.

Thus, the rise of countervailing and anti-dumping laws was part of a protectionist policy which arose from a system characterised by a domestic liberal tradition. Such rise was stronger in countries, such as the United States, with a weak government tradition and a plural market strongly based on individualist principles. The weakness of government and the lack of social organisation between market actors called for a domestic hands off government approach linked to strong protectionism in the external sphere. While the unfair trade instruments were intended to allow or protect the protectionism granted to the domestic industry, they were based on the liberal rationale of the states which developed them.

Unfair trade instruments were institutionalised during the peak years of protectionism but continued to exist even after the establishment of an open trading regime. They would quietly survive the establishment of the multilateral trading system forged as part of the post-Second World War deal. However, when this deal was broken, when the balance between the domestic and the external sphere was lost, trade instruments would rise again.

In the aftermath of the Second World War, the economic gap between the United States and the rest of the world was so wide that it allowed the US to become an economic hegemon; opening itself to world trade. The United States and its Allies considered that the war and the disastrous effects resulting therefrom had been, to an important extent, the result of the economic isolation and protectionism which characterised the inter-war period.[126] This political and economic environment had reflected in turn the domestic liberal policies which many countries had pursued during the nineteenth century.[127] The economic system of the nineteenth century caused social and economic tensions which resulted in many countries becoming nationalist or totalitarian countries as those of model (D). These countries such as Franco's Spain, Hitler's Germany or Italy under Fascism were characterised by a protectionist approach towards the trading system and very strong government intervention.

Thus, the United States executive would pursue the establishment of a worldwide economic liberal order, within a multilateral trading system, with the purpose of avoiding past economic failures. This new foreign economic policy in fact internationalised the substitution of the discussion on the redistribution of resources with that of a common goal of productivity and efficiency that took

[125] Revenue Act of 1916, ch. 463, SS 800–01, 39 Stat. 798, 15 U.S.C. SS 71–72 (1970).

[126] See R Gardner, *Sterling-Dollar Diplomacy in Current Perspective* (New York, Columbia University Press, 1980).

[127] See Polanyi, *supra* n. 26.

place at the American domestic level.[128] However, due to both the reaction of foreign countries and its own domestic constraints, the United States would have to settle for a much more balanced compromise. The international economic order established by the Bretton Woods system would follow the embedded liberalism of model (C).[129] The essence of such an order was to devise a form of multilateralism compatible with the requirements of domestic stability. Governments would seek to encourage an international division of labour which, while multilateral in form and reflecting some notion of comparative advantage, also promised to minimise socially disruptive domestic adjustment costs as well as any national economic and political vulnerabilities that might accrue from international functional differentiation. Embedded liberalism was a compromise based on a balance between the external sphere, which would be open, and the domestic arena which would be protected. The international economic order would be multilateral in character but unlike the *laissez faire* system of the nineteenth century, its multilateralism would be predicated upon domestic intervention.[130]

The embedded liberalism of the multilateral trading system was part of a wider socio-economic context. It made sense in a system where most countries had adopted Keynesian macroeconomic policies and a system of production characterised by Fordism. Its basic feature was that it allowed all states to choose their domestic policy, no matter what their domestic structures were. Whether states had weak or strong government, or a plural or organised market, did not affect their ability to implement their own domestic policies as long as they remained, to a certain extent, open to international trade.

The international trading system was not based on free trade but rather on a compromise of multilateral openness based on reciprocity. The GATT did not necessarily intend to push countries towards more market-like principles. Instead, the reduction of tariffs was considered to be a means to give states reciprocal benefits under the agreements. A good example of this was the nullification and impairment clause in the dispute settlement provisions.[131] The basic

[128] C Maier, "The Politics of Productivity: Foundations of American International Economic Policy after World War II", in P Katzenstein (ed.), *Between Power and Plenty: Foreign Economic Policies of Advanced Industrial States* (Madison, The University of Wisconsin Press, 1978), 23–29.

[129] J G Ruggie, "International Regimes, Transactions, and Change: Embedded Liberalism in the Postwar Economic Order" (1982) 36(2) *Int'l Org.* 379–415.

[130] J G Ruggie, "Trade, Protectionism and the Future of Welfare Capitalism" (1994) 48 *J. Int'l Affairs* 1–11, 3.

[131] Paragraph 1 of Article XXIII reads:

> "If any contracting party should consider that any benefit accruing to it directly or indirectly under this Agreement is being nullified or impaired or that the attainment of any objective of the Agreement is being impeded as the result of
>
> (a) the failure of another contracting party to carry out its obligations under this Agreement, or
>
> (b) the application by another contracting party of any measure, whether or not it conflicts with the provisions of this Agreement, or
>
> (c) the existence of any other situation, the contracting party may, with a view to the satisfactory adjustment of the matter, make written representations or proposals to the other contracting party or parties which it considers to be concerned. Any contracting party thus approached shall give sympathetic consideration to the representations or proposals made to it."

requirement for a dispute settlement claim was the existence of nullification or impairment. This had two legal consequences. First, a GATT violation *per se* without a nullifying or impairing effect on a country, could not give rise to an act of retaliation.[132] Furthermore, an action was possible without a GATT violation as long as a country had suffered nullification or impairment.[133] The party claiming nullification and impairment in non-violation complaints, however, should explain in detail the benefits accruing to it under the tariff concessions or trade negotiations which had been nullified or impaired.[134] Yet, in non-violation cases where the Panel had found nullification or impairment to exist, the contracting powers could not require another contracting party to remove the nullifying or impairing measure, but only allow the claiming party to take compensatory measures.[135] The Agreement's intent, was thus to maintain the reciprocity achieved during the tariff negotiations. Countries could take measures to protect their reciprocal benefits. The benefits could be the establishment of tariffs at a certain level but also, as we shall see, the protection of their domestic sphere, such as their own domestic market system.[136]

The cornerstone of the international trading legal system was the Most Favoured Nation treatment clause contained in Article I of GATT.[137] It required the contracting parties to grant unconditionally all benefits listed in

[132] See *Uruguayan Recourse to Article XXIII*, L/1923, 16 November 1962, BISD 11 Supp. p.95, paragraph 13; see also *Japan, Trade in Semi-Conductors*, L 6309, 24 March 1988, BIUSD 35 Supp. p. 116, paragraph 130.

[133] See *Italian Discrimination Against Imported Agricultural Machinery*, L/833, 23 October 1958, BISD 7 Supp. p. 68, paragraph 18; see also *Panel on Vitamins*, L/53331, 18 June 1982, BISD 29 Supp. p. 110, paragraph 22 (g); see also *Treatment by Germany of Imports of Sardines*, G/26, 31 October 1952, BISD 1 Supp. p. 53; see also *German Import Duties on Starch and Potato Flour*, BISD 3 Supp. p. 78 (1955); and *Australian Subsidy on Ammonium Sulphate*, 6 November 1950, BISD 7 Supp. p. 68.

[134] *Uruguayan Recourse to Article XXIII*, L/1923, 16 November 1962, BISD 11 Supp. p. 95, paragraph 14; see also *United States—Restrictions on the Importation of Sugar and Sugar-Containing Products Applied under the 1955 Waiver and under the Headnote to the Schedule of Tariff Concessions*, L/6631, 22 June 1990, paragraph 5.21; and *Japan, Trade in Semi-Conductors*, L 6309, 24 March 1988, BISD 35 Supp. p. 116, paragraph 131. However, the claiming party is not obliged to provide statistical evidence showing the nullification or impairment. The benefits impaired could encompass future trading opportunities. See *European Economic Community, Production Aids Granted on Canned Peaches, Canned Pears, Canned Fruit Cocktail and Dried Grapes*, L/5778, 20 November 1985, paragraph 77.

[135] See *Australian Subsidy on Ammonium Sulphate*, 6 November 1950, BISD 7 Supp. p. 68, paragraph 16. The case law of the GATT Dispute Settlement regarding non-violation cases of nullification or impairment was introduced in article 26 of the Understanding on Rules and Procedures Governing the Settlement of Disputes annexed to the WTO Agreement; see also P Pescatore, "Drafting and Analyzing Decisions on Dispute Settlement", in Pescatore, Davey and Lowenfeld (eds.), *Handbook of WTO/GATT Dispute Settlement* (New York, Transnational Juris Publication Inc., 5th ed., 1995), Volume I.

[136] R E Hudec, "Regulation of Domestic Subsidies Under the MTN Subsidies Code", in D Wallace, F Loftus and V Krikorian (eds.), *Interface Three: Legal Treatment of Domestic Subsidies* (Washington, International Law Institute, 1984) 1–18; see also J P Robe, *Countervailing Duties, State Protectionism and the Challenge of the Uruguay Round* (Florence, European University Institute Working Paper No 372, 1989).

[137] J H Jackson, *World Trade and the Law of GATT* (Indianapolis, The Bobbs-Merrill Company, 1969), 249–278.

Article I granted to any other country, whether or not a member of GATT. Together with the national treatment requirement of Article III, Article I would establish a new multilateral system based on unconditional reciprocity. However, the GATT drafters were careful enough to introduce the necessary safeguards to allow for the promised system of embedded liberalism. The Agreement contained exceptions allowing states to deviate from the multilateral trading system in times of either economic crisis or political constraint such as restrictions to safeguard the balance of payments,[138] general security exceptions,[139] health and public moral exceptions,[140] emergency action on imports of particular products,[141] customs unions and free trade areas,[142] etc. Furthermore, the General Agreement would only enter into force by virtue of the Protocol of Provisional Application.[143] Such protocol made parts I and III of GATT provisionally applicable.[144] Part II would be only provisionally applicable to the fullest extent not inconsistent with existing domestic legislation. Thus, all those rules which were incompatible with Part II of GATT could be maintained if they could not be removed by a simple administrative act but instead required legislative action. The reason for this exception was that while US officials would not accept any trade agreement without such part, most contracting parties, especially the United States, did not have the power to enter into international agreements which dealt with non-tariff barriers such as those contained in Part II of GATT.[145]

Article VI of GATT, regulating anti-dumping and countervailing duty laws, was one of the exceptions to Article I of GATT.[146] Thus there was no paral-

[138] Article XII of GATT.

[139] Article XXI of GATT.

[140] Article XX of GATT.

[141] Article XIX of GATT.

[142] Article XXIV of GATT.

[143] J H Jackson, *supra* n. 137, at 88–118.

[144] Part I refers to Articles I and II. Part III refers to Articles XXIV to XXXV.

[145] G Ikenberry, "Creating Yesterday's New World Order: Keynesian 'New Thinking' and the Anglo-American Postwar Settlement", in J Goldstein and R Keohane (eds.), *Ideas and Foreign Policy: Beliefs, Institutions and Political Change* (Ithaca, Cornell University Press, 1993), 57–86, 59; see also J H Jackson, "The General Agreement on Tariffs and Trade in United States Law" (1967) 66 *Mich. L. Rev.* 250; see also Reciprocal Trade Agreements Act of 1934, Pub. L. No 73–316, 48 Stat. 943.

[146] See J H Jackson, *supra* n. 137, at 410; see also S Alessandrini, "Subsidies, Strategic Trade Policies and the GATT", in J Bourgeois (ed.), *Subsidies and International Trade: A European Lawyer's Perspective* (Deventer, Kluwer Law and Taxation, 1991), 5–16, at 5; see also E Vermulst and N Komuro, "Anti-Dumping Disputes in the GATT/WTO: Navigating Dire Straits" (1997) 31 (1) *J. World Trade* 5–43. There has been a very important controversy with regard to whether article VI of GATT is an exception to the Most Favoured Nation clause or instead it is a provision on its own right. This controversy is extremely important because it affects the interpretation of such Article. If Article VI is an exception, the right of imposing anti-dumping or countervailing duties unilaterally must be interpreted in a narrow way. Conversely, if Article VI is interpreted not as an exception but rather as a provision offering rights of its own then there is no reason to apply a narrow interpretation and thus the possibilities of applying unilateral measures are broader. The GATT Dispute Settlement has explicitly considered, in two countervailing duty panels, that, unlike the case in anti-dumping disputes, Article VI is an exception. See *United States, Countervailing Duties on Fresh, Chilled and Frozen Pork from Canada*, DS7/R* 18 September 1990, adopted on

lelism between either the regulation of subsidies and countervailing duties or between anti-dumping and the regulation of competition. Until the Agreement on Subsidies and Countervailing Measures, resulting from the Uruguay Round, there was never any correlation between the regulation of subsidies and the right to impose unilaterally countervailing duties.[147] Likewise, the contracting parties have never been able to reach an agreement on competition rules but instead have simply allowed the parties to apply unilaterally anti-dumping measures. Unfair trade instruments were part of the embedded liberalism deal included in GATT. To the same extent that some governments would remain free to intervene in their market, others would be able to keep unfair trade instruments in their economic toolkits as protectionist devices or to protect their markets from the alleged distortions caused by either foreign anti-competitive practices or subsidisation. Furthermore, the anti-dumping laws of the United States would benefit from the grandfather clause which affected Part II of GATT and would not need to include the injury test required by GATT.

For many years the unfair trade laws would be like sleeping giants in the statute books. The deal of embedded liberalism allowed for both economic growth and a government freedom to intervene in the domestic economy. Trade instruments, as part of the deal, would be used from time to time in order to overcome transitional periods of crisis without causing mayor problems to the trading system.[148] The United States, the main user of trade instruments, continued to be an economic hegemon which could overlook foreign trading

11 July 1991 BISD 38 Supp. p. 30, paragraph 4.4; *United States, Definition of Industry Concerning Wine and Grape Products*, SCM/71 (24 March 1986) adopted by the Committee on Subsidies and Countervailing Measures on 28 April 1992 BISD 39 Supp. p. 436, paragraph 4.5. Some contracting parties have argued that considering Article VI as an exception implies that the right to impose duties under such Article should be interpreted narrowly and thus the party invoking the exception has the burden of demonstrating that it has met all the requirements of the provision in question. See Arguments of Norway in *United States, Imposition of Countervailing Duties on Imports of French and Chilled Atlantic Salmon from Norway*, adopted by the Committee on Subsidies and Countervailing Measures on 28 April 1994, (GATT Doc. SCM/153, 4 Dec. 1992). An extreme interpretation of the exceptional character of Article VI would be to consider that any method or concept that is not expressly allowed in Article VI or in the Codes developing it should be prohibited. See Arguments of Japan in EC, *Anti-Dumping Duties on Audio Tapes in Cassettes Originating n Japan*, ADP/136, 28 April 1995, paragraph 54.

[147] Horlick, R Quick and E Vermulst, "Government Actions Against Domestic Subsidies, an Analysis of the International Rules and an Introduction to US Practice" (1986) 1 *L.I.E.I.* 1–56; see also R Rivers and J Greenwald, "The Negotiation of a Code on Subsidies and Countervailing Measures: Bridging Fundamental Policy Differences" (1979) 11 *L. Pol'y Int'l Bus.* 1447–1495; see also Holmer, Haggerty and Hunter, "Identifying and Measuring Subsidies under the Countervailing Duty Law: An attempt at Synthesis", in *The Commerce Department Speaks on Import and Export* (New York, Practising Law Institute, 1984), 301; but see F Benyon and J Bourgeois, "The EC–US Steel Arrangement" (1984) 21 *C.M.L. Rev.* 305–354.

[148] F Davis, "The Regulation and Control of Foreign Trade" (1966) 66 *Columbia L. Rev.* 1428; see also I V Bael and J F Bellis, *International Trade Law and Practice of the European Community: EEC Anti-Dumping and other Trade Protectionist Laws* (Bicester, CCH Editions, 1985), 12 (arguing that from the establishment of the Common Commercial Policy until 1977, only 26 anti-dumping cases were initiated).

practices. Thus, for example, until 1974 the United States had imposed less than fifty eight countervailing duty cases.

However, the very success of embedded liberalism led to the disruption of the balance between the domestic and the external sphere. The rise of interdependence proved that in the long run the system was biased.[149] The reduction of trade barriers, through the successive GATT rounds, implied the emergence and development of phenomena such as interdependence and globalisation. This was first the case with the movement of goods, but within time, the movement of capital would follow. The emergence of a liberal international trade order, where trade barriers had significantly diminished, strengthened the power of capital against governments and labour. Capital was mobile and could choose to invest in those countries where labour and government provided for the best conditions; labour and government were not. In the long run, the openness towards trade undercut the ability of governments to intervene domestically.

Under the new conditions of economic interdependence, the maintenance of an embedded liberalism system for most states was no longer guaranteed. States started to experience the widening of a power gap between political authority and the forces of the market.[150] Only states with strong corporativist structures, such as Germany, The Netherlands, Denmark, Sweden etc, where the market actors were able to organise themselves and reach decisions by consensus, would be able to remain open to the trade system while keeping their ability to develop their own domestic policies.[151] The flexibility provided by the strong organisation and collaboration between industry, labour and government allowed these countries to remain faithful to the system of embedded liberalism. However, strong states but with plural and unorganised societies would, as a result of the economic crisis and globalisation, tend to slip down into policies similar to those of category (D) countries. Countries like France or Italy, were originally able to remain open to the trading system under the embedded liberalism deal. In the long run, however, they reinforced the role of the state in providing industrial adjustment assistance and were inclined to grant import relief measures in the way of quotas, safeguards, voluntary restraint agreements and anti-dumping measures. These different reactions to the effect of globalisation are the cause of enormous distress to the Community's Common Commercial Policy.

Similarly, countries such as the United States, with weak states and plural markets, would favour a hands off policy in which the government would refuse to intervene in the economy and generally refuse to grant protection. However, in times of economic crisis such countries would adopt certain features of model (B) countries and take *ad hoc* protectionist measures by the way of trade instru-

[149] S Hymer, "The Internationalisation of Capital" (1972) 6 *J. Economic Issues* 91–11 (1972).

[150] S Strange, "The Power Gap: Member States and the World Economy", in Brouwer, Lintner and Newman (eds.), *Economic Policy Making and the European Union* (London, The Federal Trust, 1994), 19–26.

[151] See R Keohane, *supra* n. 109, at 35.

ments. The 1980s in the United States characterised by Reaganomix policy was a good example of this.[152] The Reagan administration pursued a radical government hands off policy but was compelled, to adopt *ad hoc* measures in order to grant protection to its declining domestic industry. Again, as in Hamilton's nineteenth century America, protection was granted on the basis of fair trade. Trade instruments were used as *ad hoc* measures to protect declining American industry. Trade aggressiveness was linked to domestic neo-liberal policies.

The neo-liberal wave of the Uruguay Round and the Single Market Initiative, at a regional level, further destroyed the system of embedded liberalism, thus resulting in an increased use of trade instruments. The trade agreements were basically biased. One of their main achievements has been the reduction of the role of the government in the market place. Such a policy, however, has only benefited countries with both weak governments and small government intervention traditions. For states with strong governments but weakly organised markets the major means to achieve society's goals—government intervention—has been seriously jeopardised. Because in the short-medium term it is very difficult to adopt the domestic structures of corporativist countries, such states have been constrained to adopt policies similar to those of liberal countries, that is, a hands off approach in the domestic and external spheres.

Yet, since in the long run societies tend to protect themselves from the harsh rule of the market, countries unable to do this through the organisation of their market actors will have recourse to *ad hoc* protectionism in the form of unfair trade instruments. Thus, the economic liberalism of our world's globalisation tends to reinforce the role of the state as a protector.[153] As the globalisation process has taken away their sovereignty in the domestic sphere, states are increasingly acting in the external sphere. One way to increase their role is through the use of trade instruments that theoretically cost nothing and may be justified on grounds of fairness.

Good examples of this have been the external trade policies of both the European Union and the United States. The two trading partners have entered into a race of trade instruments. Between 1980 and 1999, the United States initiated 315 countervailing duty procedures[154] and 784 anti-dumping investigations.[155] Its trade protectionist policy was further strengthened by the use of Section 301 as an export protectionist instrument. The Community would also follow the same policy. The economic liberalisation resulting from both European and world-wide developments would cause the Community increasingly to adopt trade instruments as protectionist measures. From 1980 to 1999 the Commission initiated more than seven hundred and fifteen anti-dumping

[152] See J Bhagwati, *Protectionism* (Cambridge, MIT Press, 1988).

[153] W Streck, "Public Power Beyond the Nation State: The Case of the European Community", in R Boyer and D Drache (eds.), *States Against Markets: The Limits of Globalization* (London, Routledge, 1996), 299–315.

[154] See <http://www.ita.doc.gov/import_admin/records/stats>.

[155] Id.

and countervailing duty cases.[156] Although such protectionism only affected a small part of the total imports to the Community, they have been concentrated on certain strategic countries and industrial sectors.[157] Thus, trade policy would reflect domestic policy. The increasing use of trade instruments as protectionist devices would be part of the bargain between the domestic and the external spheres: a bargain by which an aggressive foreign trade policy would allow for domestic economic liberalisation.[158]

[156] This figure results from my calculations after going through the annual European Commission's Communications to the European Parliament on the Community's anti-dumping and anti-subsidy activities. As to the latest communication, see Commission of the European Communities, *Seventeenth Annual Report from the Commission to the European Parliament on the Community's Anti-Dumping and Anti-Subsidy Activities (1998)*, COM (1999) 411 final (Luxembourg, Office for Official Publications of the EC).

[157] During the last years, anti-dumping and countervailing measures have been concentrated against Eastern European counties, Japan, Korea, Turkey, China and Taiwan. They have also targeted especially high technology and high added value products such as those of the electronics sector. See Commission of the European Communities, *Fourteenth Annual Report from the Commission to the European Parliament on the Community's Anti-dumping and Anti Subsidy Activities (1995)*, 2 COM (96) 146 final (Luxembourg, Office for Official Publications of the EC).

[158] J Miranda, R Torres and M Ruiz, "The International Use of Antidumping: 1987–1997" (1998) 32(5) J. World Trade 5–71.

Part I

United States Trade Policy

2

The Domestic Structures of United States Trade Policy

2.A. INTRODUCTION

IN JANUARY 1998, in his State of the Union Speech, President Bill Clinton asked for the renewal of a fast track procedure to negotiate and implement trade agreements with foreign countries.[1] The President's call took place within the context of a dramatic standstill in United States trade policy.[2] It followed the failure, of both the Administration and Congress, to implement the procedure during the previous autumn when a humiliated Clinton requested the House Speaker to postpone indefinitely the vote on such a bill due to the lack of the votes necessary to ensure its passage.[3] Opposition to the re-enactment of fast track could be found within the ranks of both parties. Yet, whereas the Republican leaders had been able to get together around one hundred and seventy affirmative votes, only forty Democratic representatives, that is only one out of five, would support the re-enactment of fast track.[4] As Democratic leader Gephardt made clear, the overwhelming majority of Democratic representatives would not vote for any trade negotiation powers unless these incorporated the

[1] "Trade Policy: Clinton Signals Intent to Pursue Fast Track in State of the Union Speech", 15(4) *BNA Int'l Trade Reporter* 140 (28 January 1998).

[2] As of March 2000, the US Congress has not yet adopted fast track. The renewal of fast track is in fact unlikely in the year 2000 as Presidential primaries and elections must take place. See R Dale, "Thinking Ahead/Commentary: New Trade Round? Not Under Clinton", *Int'l Herald Tribune* 22 February 2000. 9. There have been, however, some attempts in Congress to redraft a new fast track bill. See "Finance Committee Mark Up Omnibus Trade Bill", Press Release # 105–387, 31 July 1998, available at <http://www.senate.gov/finance>.

[3] R Brevetti, M Felsenthal and Cheryl Bolen, "Trade Policy: Clinton Conceded Defeat on Fast Track; Pledges to Pass Legislation Next Year", 14 (45) *BNA Int'l Trade Reporter* 1944 (12 November 1997). The legislation proposal was named "The Export Expansion and Reciprocal Trade Agreements Act of 1997". The full text of the bill is available at <http://www.whitehouse.gov>.

[4] Of the 228 Republican House Representatives in the 105th Congress, around 58 opposed the bill. For a profile of the members of the 105th Congress, see *CRS Report for Congress: Membership of the 105th Congress: A Profile*, 97–37 GOV, available at <http://www.senate.gov/rules>. In the Senate, the re-enactment of fast track would have been guaranteed as it had been voted for 69 to 31, on a closure petition allowing consideration of the legislation to move forward. See R Brevetti and C Bolen, "Trade Policy: Fast Track Bill Clears First Senate Vote After Administration Makes Commitments", 14 (44) *BNA Int'l Trade Reporter* 1923 (5 November 1997).

goal of establishing adequate international labour and environmental standards and tackled the democratic deficits of fast track.[5]

United States trade policy seems to be on the edge of a U-turn. For the last 60 years, US foreign economy policy has been the story of a success: being able to allow the input of domestic constituencies while making sure that the country would speak uniformly and strongly in the international trading system. Most of the literature has argued that the key feature of United States' success has been the device of adequate co-operation procedures between its Presidency and Congress.[6] Despite the tensions and strong divisions between the different constitutional powers, the plurality of the American system and its democratic and legalistic manners, the establishment of balanced procedures, which while delegating the necessary powers and credibility to the President allowed Congress to keep tight control of the process and make sure that the claims of its constituencies were taken into account, has permitted the United States Executive to maintain world leadership and to pursue successfully American interests in the international trading system.[7] This was first achieved by means of the Trade Reciprocal Agreements program under which Congress delegated powers to the President to negotiate with foreign countries, and proclaim, in the form of Congressional-Executive Agreements, the reduction of tariffs on the basis of reciprocity.[8] Thereafter, as the international trading system started to focus on non-tariff barriers and the domestic impact of interdependence increased, Congress and the Presidency devised the fast track procedure as a rule of the House of Representatives and the Senate which would facilitate the approval of legislation to implement trade agreements by allowing Congress, by way of a Congressional-Executive agreement, to ratify the trade agreements negotiated by the President by passing implementing legislation, but without being able to subject such legislation to any amendments.

[5] See "Trade Policy: Gephardt Outlines Trade views, Develops New Fast-Track Proposal", 14(49) *BNA Int'l Trade Reporter* 2116 (10 December 1997). Opposition to the re-enactment of fast track also came from Republican members; during previous years they opposed any legislation which would make reference to international labour or environmental standards. See L Santos, "Trade Politics of the American Congress" (1995) 29 (6) *J. World Trade* 74–78; see also "Trade Policy: Kober Says GOP May Accept Fast Track if Labor-Environment Provision Restricted", 14 (18) *BNA Int'l Trade Reporter* 772 (30 April 1997).

[6] S O'Halloran, *Politics, Process and American Trade Policy* (Ann Arbor, The University of Michigan Press, 4th ed., 1997); see also R Pastor, *Congress and the Politics of US Foreign Economic Policy 1929–1976* (Berkeley, University of California Press, 1980); and I Destler, *American Trade Politics*, 2nd ed. (Washington, *Institute for International Economics*, 1992).

[7] On the plurality, institutional division of powers and democratic and legalistic manners characteristic of the US trade policy process in general see J H Jackson, "Perspectives on the Jurisprudence of International Trade: Costs and Benefits of Legal Procedures in the United States" (1984) 82 *Mich. L. Rev.* 1570–1587; see also J Garten, American Trade Law in a Changing World Economy (1995) 29(1) *Int'l Law.* 15–41.

[8] On the 1934 Reciprocal Trade Agreements Act and its renewals See M Bailey, J Goldstein and B Weingast, "The Institutional Roots of American Trade Policy" (1997) 49 *World Politics* 309–338; see also D Tarullo, "Law and Politics in Twentieth Century Tariff History" (1986) 34 *UCLA L. Rev.* 285–370.

Yet, just as the United States appears to be succeeding in modelling a world that is a reflection of its own, it seems to take a U-turn and retreat from the international trade *fora*. Not renewing the fast track procedure implies the absence of serious discussions for a WTO Millennium Round, no incorporation of Chile into the NAFTA, no Free Trade Agreement of the Americas (FTAA) nor any credible negotiations within Asia Pacific Economic Cooperation (APEC). As the failure of the OECD Shipbuilding Subsidies Agreement has proved all too well, it is worthless to negotiate with a US Executive that lacks fast track.[9] United States trading partners know that without fast track any legislation implementing the agreements will become hopelessly bogged down in Congress.[10] Much less problematic than negotiating international agreements with a US Executive lacking fast track would be the impossible task of negotiating them with the entire Congress. Thus, without fast track, the United States has lost diplomatic strength and leadership in the international trading system. US trade officials have approached trade *fora* by focusing on negotiations which did not require changes in US domestic legislation and which could be based on the residual powers of the Uruguay Round Agreements Act,[11] and by putting great emphasis on dispute settlement under Section 301 of the 1974 Trade Act.

The United States' domestic response to this situation has been divided.[12] On the one hand, some have advocated the urgent renewal of fast track to maintain both United States world leadership and free trade.[13] They have argued that fast track is an adequate vehicle for power sharing between Congress and the Presidency which is essential for continuing US leadership in world trade and guaranteeing the continuance of free trade, both world-wide and at home, thus maintaining United States' world market shares.

[9] After the OECD Shipbuilding Subsidies Agreement was signed by the OECD contracting parties, the US Executive presented it, together with its implementing legislation, to the House of Representatives. Because there was no fast track commitment, the House amended the agreement and the proposed implementing legislation in such a way that it would have required its renegotiation. Thus, the implementation bill was dropped, without even being presented to the Senate and the agreement remains in suspension.

[10] P J Kuypjer, "The EC's Common Commercial Policy: Which Way the Swing of the Pendulum?", in *The Future of the President's Authority to Negotiate International Trade Agreements after NAFTA and the Uruguay Round: What Should Congress Delegate?, Proceedings of the 88th Annual Meeting of the American Society of International Law*, Washington DC, 6–9 April 1994.

[11] Uruguay Round Agreements Act, P.L. 103–465; 108 Stat. 4809 (1994). Examples of these agreements have been the GATS agreements on financial services, telecommunications, or the agreements on information technology or technical standards.

[12] The National Economic Council, *Future Visions for US Trade Policy* (Washington, The Council of Foreign Economic Relations, 1998).

[13] American Bar Association, Section of International Law and Practice Report to the House of Delegates, "Fast Track Negotiating Authority" (1997) 31(3) *Int'l Law*. 955–959; see also J Schott, "Wither Fast Track?", in J Schott (ed.), *Restarting Fast Track* (Washington, Institute for International Economics, 1998) at 29–40; see also C. F Bergsten, "Trade Policy and Trade Legislation" in 1998, Jeffrey Schott (ed.), *supra* at 3–8; see also I Destler, *Renewing Fast Track Legislation* (Washington, Institute for International Economics, 1997); and <http://www.fast track.org>.

On the other hand, an increasing number of scholars have argued against fast track on grounds of its democratic deficit and its lack of sensitivity towards labour and environmental problems. First, they have criticised the lack of democratic accountability both at the international level, where negotiations are usually secretive and obscure, and at the US domestic level, due to the implementation process required by fast track where no amendments are possible and public participation is limited.[14] Second, they have supported the Democrats' request for international labour and environmental standards in order to protect the US domestic system.[15] According to this approach, while the US as a whole is one of the countries which has benefited most from globalisation, domestically the latter has created much distress by accentuating the economic and political asymmetry of social groups and increasing the feeling of social insecurity.[16] Many have claimed that domestic programmes for worker adjustment are simply not enough and that the protection of US standards and citizens requires the establishing of fair international trade rules.

Whereas some have focused on the teleological argument of the need for fast track in order to achieve US international trade goals, others have put into question the substance of such objectives. But the fact is that, for 50 years, the success of United States trade policy was not due simply to its co-operation procedures between the different constitutional institutions but also to the fact that it was based on a broad national consensus. Despite the constitutional struggles for power between Congress and the Presidency, their politics of blame avoidance, the calls and cries for protectionism and its unilateral aggressive trade policies based on retaliation, the United States has been committed to a long-standing and widely agreed policy which clearly reflected and fitted its domestic structures.[17] Starting in the 1930s, and in a U-turn from its previous

[14] P Goldman, "The Democratization of the Development of United States Trade Policy" (1994) 27 *Cornell Int'l L. J.* 631–697; see also R Housman, "Democratizing International Trade Decision-Making" (1994) 27 *Cornell Int'l L. J.* 699; M Ritchie, "Democratizing the Trade Policy-Making Process: The Lessons of NAFTA and Their Implications for the GATT" (1994) 27 *Cornell Int'l L. J.* 749–754; C O'Neal Taylor, "Fast Track, Trade Policy, and Free Trade Agreements: Why the NAFTA Turned into a Battle" (1994) 28 *Geo. Wash. J. Int'l L. & Eco* 1–132; and <http://www.tradewatch.org>. Against these arguments, see R Hudec, "Circumventing Democracy: The Political Morality of Trade Negotiations" (1992) 25 *N.Y. U. J. Int'l L. & Pol'y* 311–322.

[15] S Charnovitz, "Labor and Environmental Issues", in Jeffrey Schott (ed.), *supra* n. 13, at 55–88; see also R Howse and M Trebilock, "The Fair Trade-Free Trade Debate: Trade, Labor and the Environment" (1996) 16 *Int'l Rev. L. & Economics* 61–79, 62.

[16] D Rodrik, *Has Globalization Gone Too Far?* (Washington, Institute for International Economics, 1997); see also G Burtless, R Lawrence, R Litan and R Shapiro, *Globaphobia: Confronting Fears About Open Trade* (Washington, The Brookings Institution, The Progressive Policy Institute and The Twentieth Century Found, 1998).

[17] On the politics of blame avoidance between Congress and the Executive, see P Nivola, "Trade Policy: Refereeing the Playing Field", in T Mann (ed.), *A Question of Balance: The President, the Congress and Foreign Policy* (Washington, The Brookings Institution, 1990) at 201–253; see also P Low, *Trading Free: The GATT and the US Trade Policy* (Washington, Twentieth Century Fund Inc., 1993). On the cries and calls for protectionism, see R Pastor, "The Cry and Sigh Syndrome: Congress and Trade Policy" in A Schick (ed.), *Making Economic Policy in Congress* (Washington: American Enterprise Institute for Public Policy, 1983), at 159–195.

nineteenth century policy characterised by high tariffs and strong domestic division, the US would agree to develop a policy which, while not seriously questioning redistributional issues and the share of wealth of each social group, would attempt and succeed in increasing the pie so that everybody could benefit from it.[18] To this end, the US would start and maintain over five decades, a policy of free and reciprocal trade complemented by *ad hoc* protectionism and fair trade that would assure its world trade dominance, increase its standards of living and, most of all, fit its domestic system.[19] Unlike Europe, the United States has known who it is, what it wanted from the international trading system and how to get it. Congressional delegations of powers to the President and the fast track procedure were merely designed to grease the wheels for a policy that had broad support and only minor opposition.[20]

Unfair trade instruments have been a fundamental pillar of this widely agreed trade policy. Anti-dumping, countervailing duties and Section 301 are trade instruments inherent to the US domestic system. In the late 1970s, after forty years of silence, unfair trade instruments re-emerged in a two-way dialogue between Congress and the Executive to deal with international trade. They were part of a policy aimed at reaching a balance between providing *ad hoc* protectionism as an exception to the general rule of free trade and establishing the rules abroad; a balance between the protectionist worries of Congress and the export enhancing policy of the Executive.[21] Such trade instruments were *ad hoc* protectionist measures inherent to the American domestic system because while providing protection on the politically appealing grounds of fairness they were not attempting to plan or interfere within the domestic industry. They provided protectionism without industrial policy.[22] Furthermore, by doing so they served the US government's goal of trying to create a system of international rules which built upon the American domestic experience.[23] Regardless of the economic and efficiency arguments that are supposed to be their underlying rationale, unfair trade instruments in practice establish only standards embedding

[18] On US nineteenth century tariff policy, see A Eckes, *Opening America's Market: US Foreign Trade Policy Since 1776* (Chapel Hill, The University of North Caroline Press, 1995); J Goldstein, *Ideas, Interests and American Trade Policy* (Ithaca, Cornell University Press, 1993); and J Dobson, *Two Centuries of Tariffs: The Background and Emergence of the US International Trade Commission* (Washington, United States International Trade Commission, 1976).

[19] See D Yoffie, "American Trade Policy: An Obsolete Bargain", in J Chubb and P Peterson (eds.), *Can the Government Govern?* (Washington, The Brookings Institution, 1989) at 100–138; see also S Schwab, "Politics, Economics and US Trade Policy" (1987) 23 *Stanford J. Int'l L.* 155–176.

[20] See S Charnovitz, "The Future of Fast Track in US Trade Policy", 14(15) *BNA Int'l Trade Reporter* 655 (9 April 1997).

[21] See A Puckett and W Reynolds, "Rules, Sanctions and Enforcement under Section 301: At Odds with the WTO?" (1996) 90 *American J. Int'l L.* 675–689, 687.

[22] J Greenwald, "Protectionism and US Economic Policy" (1987) 23 *Stanford J. Int'l L.* 233–261.

[23] On the argument of the US government creating a system which is a reflection of the US, see A Wolf, "The Failure of American Trade Policy", in Howell, Wolf and Gadbow (eds.), *Conflict Among Nations: Trade Policies in the 1990s* (Boulder, Westview Press, 1992), 469–526, 524.

implicit parochial views on the behaviour of political institutions and market actors.[24]

The United States' long standing consensus on trade policy may have fallen apart during the last few years.[25] The very same domestic structures which led the US to succeed may now push it into retreat. The dramatic increase of globalisation and its resulting impact on, and disembeddedness of, the domestic sphere has created two effects.[26] It has enhanced the interest of American constituencies in trade policy and, thus, the calls for the democratisation of the trade policy process. Secondly, and most importantly, globalisation has broken the American deal by both increasing inequality and impoverishing certain groups of society. The United States lacks the necessary domestic structures to implement any credible domestic adjustment and the redistribution programs necessary to cope with globalisation. Thus, the US need to externalise the problem and call for international labour and environmental standards.[27] The discussion on international labour and environmental standards consists only in advancing one step further the case for countervailing, anti-dumping duties and Section 301. Instead of business dumping it is now eco-dumping or labour dumping. The same domestic structures which have made impossible any domestic economic planning or economic concertation, and thus resulted in unfair trade instruments as *ad hoc* protectionist measures, are now requiring international standards on labour and the environment to provide *ad hoc* solutions to US domestic problems in coping with globalisation. The resulting hint may be that unless the US moves to establish such international standards there will be no fast track.

Hence, to understand US trade policy, and the role played within it by fast track and unfair trade instruments, it is important to analyse the domestic structures of the country. The development of the 1934 reciprocal trade agreements program, fast track, unfair trade instruments and the current impasse are all a clear reflection of the American domestic system.

[24] D Tarullo, "Beyond Normalcy in the Regulation of International Trade" (1987) 100 *Harvard L. Rev.* 547–628.

[25] Some have argued that the turning point was the implementation process of NAFTA. See J Bello and A Holmer, "US Trade Law and Policy Series No 23: Reflections on the NAFTA as a Turning Point in American Foreign Policy" (1994) 28(2) *Int'l Law.* 425–432. The increasing divisions in Congress concerning trade policy can be seen by examining the records of previous Congressional votes in passing the different trade agreements. In 1979, the Tokyo Round agreements were approved by a vote of 336–40 in the House and 83–9 in the Senate. In 1985, the Israel FTA was passed by 422–0 in the House and a voice vote in the Senate. In 1988, the Canada FTA was approved by 395–7 in the House and 61–38 in the Senate. But, NAFTA was passed in 1993 by 234–200 in the House and 76–24 in the Senate. Finally the Uruguay Round, was also passed with a strong division, by 288–146 in the House and 76–24 in the Senate.

[26] On the disembeddedness of the domestic sphere as a result of globalisation and its inherent dangers to the international system, see J Ruggie, *Winning the Peace: American and World Order in the New Era* (New York, Columbia University Press, 1996).

[27] On the US tendency to exteriorise its domestic economic problems by means of trade policy See P Katzenstein, "Conclusion: Domestic Structures and Strategies of Foreign Economic Policy", in Peter J. Katzenstein (ed.), *Between Power and Plenty: Foreign Economic Policies of Advanced Industrial States* (Madison, The University of Wisconsin Press, 1978), at 295–336.

2.B. THE DOMESTIC SOCIO-ECONOMIC STRUCTURES OF THE UNITED STATES

2.B.1. The Origins

Unlike most countries in the world, America's national identity is not defined so much by a common history and a tradition as by an ideology. The American creed can be described as liberty, democracy, egalitarianism, defined as equality of opportunity and respect, individualism, populism, meritocracy and *laissez faire*.[28] What distinguishes most the US from all other countries is its radical liberalism. America's exceptionalism derives from the unique development of a capitalism and democracy which neither confronted nor benefited from the existence of medieval institutions or the idea of class, and which took place in a blessed land.

The point of departure of US liberalism was a *tabula rasa*. There was no feudal system against which to fight. "Men were born equal instead of becoming equal".[29] Whereas Locke's liberal thought implied two steps, the idea of a state and thereafter the idea of limiting the powers of such state, since in the US there was no state to start with, America would focus only on one side of Locke's theory and put much emphasis on the limitation of powers. The absence of a feudal system and a hierarchical church implied, on the one hand, the lack of any commitment towards social and collective values and, on the other hand, disregarding the state as there was no need of its power to displace a previous system.

Furthermore, America was the "blessed land". The United States was born and grew in a territory of unlimited wealth where it was possible to increase the standards of living of everybody without any need to question the distribution of wealth nor to challenge the dominance of any group. Whereas in Europe, there would be a class struggle and thus, the different social groups would develop class consciousness as well as links of solidarity among them, in the United States, both the wealthy and the poor would not accept the idea of a rigid hereditary class and instead would be much more disposed to think they lived in a meritocracy where individual hard work, education and ambition were the key to success.[30]

American capitalism developed freely in a blessed land without constraints. While most other states in capitalist societies increased their role and power as industrialisation proceeded, the authority and size of the American state remained relatively small. The US government nurtured its infant industry by

[28] S Lipset, *American Exceptionalism: A Double-Edge Sword* (New York, W.W. Norton & Company, 1996), at 19.

[29] L Hartz, *The Liberal Tradition in America* (New York, Harcourt, Brace & World, 1955); see also J Young, *Reconsidering American Liberalism: The Troubled Odyssey of the Liberal Idea* (Boulder, Westview Press, 1996).

[30] J Fallows, *More Like Us: Making America Great Again* (Boston, Houghton Mifflin Company, 1989).

simply protecting it from foreign competition; and letting it take full advantage of the huge American market. Whereas the government did help its industry in the form of protection, construction of infrastructure and banishing away the Indian tribes, it did not attempt to interfere with nor plan its industry. As the basis of economic growth moved from trade and agricultural exports to industry, the emerging industrial elite began to outgrow the need for any governmental domestic participation in the economy. With the defeat of the South and its economic interests, the American bourgeoisie's triumph in civil society was virtually complete. It had neither aristocracy nor church to overthrow, no foreign armies to mobilise against and basically no foreign products to compete against. American capitalism was left to grow on its own and without any need to organise nor create any links of solidarity within itself. The benefit of large foreign investment would enable firms to raise long-term debt and risk capital on terms developed in capital markets without the need to depend on banks and financial institutions nor on large public funds.[31]

As a result of these developments, state societal arrangements in the US are characterised by both decentralisation and pluralism. America is a capitalist system which combines a fragmented government with a strong yet disorganised business sector and extremely weak labour.[32] It is a system where democracy is identified with *laissez faire* and where the idea of the proper role of the government is limited to acting as an impartial arbiter of fairness between competing individuals, groups and enterprises rather than as a promoter of any particular interest which may result in particular rights and obligations.[33]

2.B.2. The Weakness of the US Government

In the Constitution, the basic plan is the diffusion and fragmentation of power.[34] Hence the creation of a federal system and strong separation of powers within the federal government.

Federalism implies a division of powers between the federal government and the states as well as a system of competition between all entities at federal, state and local levels.[35] At the level of federal government, decentralisation means division and competition as between and within different constitutional branches. The system of checks and balances between the Presidency, Congress

[31] T Rybcynski, "Industrial Finance System in Europe, US and Japan" (1984) 5 *J. Economic Behaviour & Org.* 275–285, 280.

[32] J Hart, *Rival Capitalists: International Competitiveness in the United States, Japan and Western Europe* (Ithaca, Cornell University Press, 1992), at 224.

[33] A Wolf, "The Failure of American Trade Policy" in Howell, Wolf, Bartlet and Gadbow (eds.), *Conflict Among Nations: Trade Policies in the 1990s* (Boulder, Westview Press, 1992) 469–525, 480; see also A King, "Ideas, Institutions and the Policies of Government: A Comparative Analysis, Part III" (1973) 3 *British J. Pol'y Science* 409–423, 419.

[34] R Denenberg, *Understanding American Politics* (London, Fontana Press, 4th ed, 1996), at 22.

[35] T Dye, *American Federalism: Competition Among Governments* (Lexington, Lexington Books, 1990).

and the Judiciary implies not mere independence but interdependence. The American Constitution does not grant each branch a different and clearly defined set of powers but instead requires common action between these competing branches before any governmental policy can take place. However, to preclude the possibility of collusion and guarantee that the different branches will be predisposed to compete, each branch is tied to different constituencies of base of support. The party which controls Congress need not necessarily be that which supports the President. Indeed, from 1973 to 2000 (or from the 93rd Congress to the 106th Congress) the political system has been characterised by one of divided government. The only exceptions have been the 95th and 96th Congress when President Carter ruled with a Democratic majority in both houses, and the 103rd Congress when President Clinton ruled with a Democratic Congress. All other Presidents during the last 25 years have had to face a Congress under the control of the opposing party.[36] The idea is to render government incapable of action unless the various branches, representing diverse constituencies and chosen at different times, are in agreement.[37] Moreover, within each branch there are also divisions. Both Congress and the Executive are characterised by decentralisation and competing interests, making impossible any action unless there is a broad consensus.

2.B.2.a. The Decentralisation of Congress

Congress is popularly described as a sleeping giant. It has organised itself in a decentralised way that impedes the building of consistent majorities able to pass coherent legislation on difficult issues. It is divided into a House and a Senate. The House, under federal law, is composed of 435 constituencies of more or less 750,000 people from the same state. The Senate is composed, under the Constitution, by one hundred seats: two for each of the states of the Union.[38] Furthermore, whilst all the Representatives in the House are elected every two years, the Senate is renewed only partially every two years with Senators enjoying a term of six years. These different terms imply that the majority party may not be the same in both houses as well as that the political behaviour of Senators will be different from that of House Representatives who are much more concerned with the local politics of their electoral districts.

In Congress, legislators struggle to maintain a balance between being ambassadors who congregate in Washington DC to pursue the interests of the individual states and electoral districts, and becoming a single deliberative assembly addressing national issues and reaching accords that may serve the broad collective interests of the nation as a whole.[39] Many times Congressmen cannot

[36] S Smith, *The American Congress* (Boston, Houghton Mifflin Company, 1995), at 176.
[37] See Denenberg, *supra* n. 34, at 23.
[38] Article I, Section 1 US Constitution; see also Article I, Section 3 ibid.
[39] B Loomis, *The Contemporary Congress* (New York, St. Martin Press, 1996), at 6.

represent the national interest but only the parochial interests of their constituencies.

The atomism of the members of Congress results from America's pluralism and its electoral system.[40] In the US, political parties have been proven much weaker and less capable of producing the strong centripetal effect within the legislature that parties in most other democracies have. The need to gain wide support to elect one national president implies that although most members of Congress share emotional attachments to their party, and regard it as one means to exercise power, the labels of the Democrat and Republican party are, in fact, a catch all for a broad spectrum of political tendencies. They mask a pluralism of geographic, social, ideological and organisational sources of identification, support and loyalty. Furthermore, the fragmentation of the electoral base in different districts implies the local nature of Congressional elections, especially for House Representatives whose districts remain relatively homogenous.

For the most part, American legislators are on their own as they seek election and re-election. Congressmen are in practice political entrepreneurs; independent from their national parties. They develop their own campaign organisations, raise their own money and set their own political strategies; rarely with any support from their label parties. As a result, both the House and the Senate lack any centralised leadership. Congress members, knowing they are on their own when it comes to re-election, have little reason to be deferential to party leaders who, in turn, have relatively few resources that can influence their electoral prospects.[41]

Both the House and the Senate have created standing committees which collect information through hearings and investigations, draft and report legislation and oversee Executive branch activities.[42] Committees are divided in subcommittees but although most of the House committee's work is done in subcommittees, in the Senate, with much fewer members, most issues are in fact dealt with at the committee level.

Standing committees have a positive and a negative legislative power. Positive power implies their ability to gain approval for legislation opposed by others by persuading members of Congress on the basis of superior argument and information, threatening unfavourable action on Congress members' bills if they do not co-operate, and by strategically employing the legislative process, such as the conference negotiations between the two houses, to gain the endorsement by the chamber for the policy provisions favoured by the committee. Negative

[40] B Loomis, *The Contemporary Congress* (New York, St. Martin Press, 1996), at 50.

[41] See S Smith, *supra* n. 36.

[42] Standing committees have been created by Congress under the powers granted by Article 1 Section 5 of the Constitution which reads "each House may determine the rules of its proceedings". See C Deering and S Smith, *Committees in Congress* (Washington, Congressional Quarterly Press, 3rd ed, 1997); see also C Campbell and R Davidson, "US Congressional Committees: Changing Legislative Workshops" (1998) 4(1) *Legislative Studies* 124–142. Whereas the House has 22 standing committees, the Senate has 16. See <http://www.senate.gov/committees>; see also <http://www.house.gov/committees>.

power refers to the fact that committees act as gatekeepers of legislation. Bypassing the committee stage and bringing legislation to the chambers' floor without the committees' approval is nearly impossible. Committees are free to act as they consider appropriate on most legislation that is referred to them. They may simply refuse to act, may hold hearings but take no legislative action, may amend the legislation in any way or accept the legislation without changes, and report to the floor the legislation with a recommendation that it pass, with no recommendation or with one that it be rejected.[43]

Standing committees were created to relieve the workload of their chambers and speed up the legislative process. Yet, they do not limit the decentralisation of Congress instead tending to divide their parent chambers into different rival factions. Members of Congress will sit in different committees depending on their interests, their personal prestige and their support in the chambers. Seats in the committees are usually allocated in proportion to the size of the parties in each house. The majority party will assign the chairman of the committee while the party in minority will assign the minority-ranking leader. Usually assignment to the most prestigious and powerful committees is done on the basis of seniority. Yet Congressmen will attempt to sit on those committees which are of most interest to their constituencies and which may attract most political and economic support. Thus, committees are not necessarily representative of the houses as a whole but may in fact represent the interests of those constituencies which support the electoral expectations of their members. The latter, therefore, must, in fact, balance the opposing interests of their parent chamber, their party and their constituents. Furthermore, often different committees will compete for the legislative competence on a specific issue.

During the last decades one of the most important developments in Congress has been the enormous expansion of staff and access to information. To keep pace with the Executive's policies both Congressmen and standing committees have made increased recourse to the hiring of expert staff and research services. However congressional staff are not civil servants but can be hired and dismissed at will. Committee staff reflect the same interests and influences that determine the policy preferences of the Committee members. They are influenced by the same interest groups that support the members of their committees.[44]

Thus, Congress is stacked against action, particularly as against quick action. The best way to describe the legislative process is as an obstacle course in which majorities must be created at several stages among different groups of legislators. Getting a major bill passed involves attracting majority support in successive stages of the standard process: in committees and their subcommittees, on the floor, in conference between the two houses if there are differences between

[43] See S Smith, *supra* n. 36, at 213.

[44] M Shapiro, "The Politics of Information: US Congress and European Parliament", in Craig and Harlow (eds.), *Law Making in the European Union* ((The Hague, Kluwer Law, 1998), 187–208, at 189.

them, and on the floor again for the conference report. Even if Congress can produce a piece of legislation, it may still face the presidential veto.[45] After being passed by Congress, the bill is sent to the President who may sign the bill or veto it by doing nothing. If the President vetoes the bill, Congress may overrule such veto only with a two thirds majority in each of its houses.[46] This implies that enacting any legislation requires reaching a broad consensus between the three different constituencies which are represented in the Senate, the House and the Presidency. As Dahl and Lindblom put it:

> "In the United States the structure of government prescribed by the Constitution, court decisions, and traditions vastly increases the amount of bargaining that must take place before policies can be made . . . The necessity for constant bargaining is . . . built into the very structure of American government."[47]

Thus, very rarely, indeed only after historic realigning elections which produce a large shift of loyalties from one party to another, will a party be able to push any legislation on its own without arranging some sort of compromise with members of the other. As a result, few bills pass and those that do tend to be either very specific ones on behalf of narrow interests or extremely broad ones that distribute benefits widely and, usually, without discrimination or programmatic rationality.[48]

Congress carries more weight in economic policy than does the legislative branch of any other large capitalist country. It controls economic policy because it is responsible for all legislation and it has the power of the purse, it must amend and authorise the national budget proposed by the President.[49] Congress also has explicit, and in principle exclusive, powers to tax, regulate interstate commerce and trade with foreign nations.[50] Congressional power over economic policy implies on the one hand that such policy will reflect the institution's decentralisation and be predisposed to be slow, ambiguous and distributional rather than redistributional. On the other hand, as divided government is the most common political state in Washington DC, and Congressmen are not necessarily loyal to their parties, economic policy is subject to a constant struggle between the President and Congress and, hence, is limited.

[45] See Article I, Section 7(2) US Constitution.

[46] On the importance of divided powers, bicameralism and presidential veto in the legislative process, see *Immigration and Naturalization Service* v. *Chadha et al.*, 462 U.S. 919, 958; 103 S. Ct. 2764; 1983 U.S. LEXIS 80 (1983); see also *Youngstown Sheet & Tube Co. et al.* v. *Sawyer*, 343 U.S. 579; 72 S. Ct. 863; 1952 U.S. LEXIS 2625 (1952). However, the US Constitution does provide some restricted exceptions to such division of powers, see *Chadha*, *supra* n. 46, at 955.

[47] R Dahl and C Lindblom, *Politics, Economics, and Welfare* (New York, Harper and Brothers, 1953), at 335, as quoted by C Jones, *The Presidency in a Separated System* (Washington, The Brookings Institution, 1994), 10.

[48] See E Krauss and J Pierre, "Targeting Resources for Industrial Change" in R Weaver and B Rockman (eds.), *Do Institutions Matter: Government Capabilities in the United States and Abroad* (Washington, The Brookings Institution, 1993), 151–186, 177.

[49] Article I, Section 7(1) US Constitution.

[50] Article I, Section 8 (2) US Constitution; see also Article I, Section 8(3) ibid.

2.B.2.b. The US Executive

The decentralisation of Congress, together with the congressional-presidential struggle for power and the phenomenon of divided government has shaped the administrative structure of the Executive.[51] Congress accepted only the development of the bureaucracy as long as power within the Executive branch remained functionally decentralised along the same lines as the legislature. Thus, the Executive is not modelled in a rational way according to a plan but rather has grown by accretion; different units having been created as *ad hoc* responses to problems that were acute at some point in US history. This implies that the policies of the different units are not necessarily co-ordinated and may even conflict as between themselves. Furthermore, Congress has tended to keep a very tight control over the bureaucracy by passing very detailed legislation, keeping control over funding for the most specific purposes through its power to ratify the budget, and monitoring thoroughly the work of the Executive through its committees and subcommittees.[52] The bureaucracy has been designed not to be effective but to be capable of being under control and being representative.

Within the Executive it is important to distinguish between the departments, the agencies or commissions and the Executive Office of the President. The departments most relevant to economic and industrial policy are the Department of Treasury, the Department of Commerce, the Antitrust division of the Department of Justice and especially the Department of Defence which in recent years has increasingly become more involved in matters of economic policy and has shown a serious concern on industrial policy. Indeed, Defence is the most important of all the departments in the development of industry specific policies. It is one of the few departments which has created tutelar relations with its contractors and with other firms in order to build industrial strength in areas that are deemed important for national security purposes.[53]

The different Departments may reflect competing interests with regard to economic policy. Whereas Commerce and Defence may tend to show a concern for nurturing American domestic industry, the Treasury, followed by Justice and the State Department, will advocate for more *laissez faire* oriented policies. These divisions are not simply among bureaucracy officials but also take place at the political level. Although the Secretaries of the Departments sit as cabinet members, their authority is exercised not collectively on a council presided by the President but severally as the overseers of their departments.[54] As a result there is not necessarily a common commitment to one economic policy.

[51] J Chubb and P Peterson, "American Political Institutions and the Problem of Governance" in J Chubb and P Peterson (eds.), *supra* n. 19, at 1–43, 36.

[52] Krauss and Pierre, *supra* n. 48, at 180.

[53] Hart, *supra* n. 32, at 228.

[54] Denenberg, *supra* n. 34, at 144.

Next to the departments there is a *de facto* headless fourth branch of government: a collection of regulatory commissions and agencies that operate semi-autonomously of the President and thereby increase the Executive's decentralisation and its lack of co-ordination.[55] Commissions are Congress' *ad hoc* solution to meet the different demands put upon the federal government while limiting the delegation of standard-setting power to the Presidency. They are agencies with administrative power but which are subject to a greater control by Congress than by the Presidency. On the one hand, presidents appoint the members of the different agencies, but these must be confirmed by the Senate. Furthermore, because the lengthy terms of office which commissioners may serve may exceed that of the President, the latter will be able to name only a fraction of any commission. Moreover usually there is a requirement that no commission may house more than a certain number of commissioners representing the views of either of the two major parties. On the other hand, commissions are subject to the strict control of Congress by means of budget constraints, annual reports and Congressional hearings.

The main function of the President, as the head of the Executive, is to attempt to co-ordinate the policies of the bureaucracy and make proposals for legislative action. To do so it is aided by the Executive Office of the President (EOP) which includes the President's closest staff and advisors.[56] This office has different units that vary in number and in size dependant on the interests of the President and Congress. Usually, it is composed by the Council of Economic Advisors, the National Security Council, the Office of Policy Development, the Bureau of Management and Budget, the Office of Administration, the National Economic Council, the Office of National Drug Control, the Office of the United States Representative, the Council of Environmental Quality and the Office of Science and Technology.[57] However even at EOP level the control of the President is limited as Congress may also influence the structure and composition of the office. The Presidential appointment of many of the senior members to the different units is subject to the Senate's confirmation. Congress can further influence the EOP by simply enacting legislation, through budget constraints or by holding oversight hearings. Many times the President may have to tolerate a Congressionally supported unit within his EOP which he dislikes or, conversely, he may have to fight to maintain a unit which displeases the legislature.

In their respective areas, the different units of the EOP are involved in policy advice to the President, policy making, policy implementation, political strategy as well as co-ordination of Executive branch activities. But many times such co-ordination never materialises and the units of the EOP end up doing the work that the Departments should have done in the first place. Frequently, the work of the EOP overlaps, second-guesses or conflicts with the work done in the

[55] <http://www.whitehouse.gov/WH/Independent_Agencies/html/independent_links.html>.

[56] C Jones, *supra* n. 47, at 52–112.

[57] J Hart, *The Presidential Branch: From Washington to Clinton* (Chatham, Chatham House Publishers, 2nd ed., 1995).

departments and agencies. In fact there is usually an adversarial relationship between the EOP and the different departments and agencies as they respond to different constituencies and are controlled by different personalities.

The inability of the Executive to develop a co-ordinated economic policy is due not only to its institutional decentralisation but also results from its bureaucracy. Unlike European countries, the US does not have a group of career senior administrators in charge of making and implementing policy. The US Executive branch is managed by people who are hardly in place long enough to learn their immediate responsibilities, let alone the intricacies of participating meaningfully in policy making and the politics of a separated system.[58] The majority of US administrators in the most responsible posts are amateurs with very little knowledge of how their administration works. Every time there is a change in the Presidency or in Congress, there is a cut-throat struggle between different constituencies and interests to allocate the thousands of senior posts changing hands. Public service is not seen as a long life commitment but rather as a way of gaining experience, networking or trying to benefit the interests of specified constituencies. These temporary public servants may not necessarily be committed to the program of their President but may be in Washington DC to have their own 'intellectual fling' and promote their own views.

2.B.2.c. The United States Government's "hands off" Policy

US government is thus characterised by decentralisation and federalism, catch-all party organisations, a highly autonomous and decentralised Congress, an institutionally constrained Presidency and an uncoordinated and porous bureaucracy. Thus, even if there were the political will to implement domestic interventionist policies in the economy it would be very unlikely that any rational and coherent policy would develop.[59] Further, it would still have to face the long-standing adversarial approach of business towards government. Indeed, America's business community is deeply biased in its belief that "government intervention is bad; the less government intervention the better; no government intervention is best". As a result of its historical development, the most characteristic and distinctive belief of corporate America is an underlying suspicion and mistrust of government.[60] Though business may welcome governmental help for specific industries in exceptional circumstances and on a temporary basis, it has historically opposed any intervention or planning that might limit its autonomy. Business will only support indirect help in the form of lower tax burden and costs of doing business, enabling consumers to buy their products

[58] C Jones, *supra* n. 47.

[59] A Shonfield, *Modern Capitalism: The Changing Balance of Public and Private Power* (Oxford, Oxford University Press, 2nd ed., 1970), 298–357.

[60] D Voguel, "Why Businessmen Distrust their State: The Political Consciousness of American Corporate Executives" (1978) 8 *British Pol'y Science* 45.

and protection from foreign products.[61] American executives want their government to do more for them by taking less from them.

As a result, the US government has no other alternative than to rely upon market forces. If one reserves the term industrial policy to signify an explicit, co-ordinated and institutionalised industrial strategy, then it can be said that America lacks an industrial policy.[62] Instead it has only a series of policies that stress the use of tax, defence procurement and technology policies and rely mainly on the large size of the US market and the enterprise of domestic firms to retain competitiveness in world markets. While the federal government is involved in many activities, intervention has been totally uncoordinated and in no way is it part of a comprehensive strategy for industrial growth and change.[63] Moreover, the radical liberal bias of American society will imply that whilst the government may provide specified benefits to its business, it will in no way try to plan or establish a government organised industrial strategy.

Furthermore, and in contrast to other countries that also tend to refrain from domestic industrial planning, the US will be handicapped by being unable to develop any domestic policies which may imply a serious redistribution of wealth.[64] The need to base all policies on a wide consensus, together with the possibility of small groups obstructing the policy making process and, most of all, the lack of any collective and social values, are insurmountable obstacles to the implementation of any serious domestic social programs necessary for a smooth domestic adjustment to the changes taking place in the international trading system. The US government lacks the necessary tools to develop any successful domestic policies to cope with the internal social effects of globalisation.

2.B.3. The Plurality of the American Market

Unlike other capitalist countries, the inability of the American state to intervene domestically so as to meet the challenge of international trade competition – either by industrial planning or social adjustment—is unfortunately paralleled

[61] A Wildavsky, "Squaring the Political Circle: Industrial Policies and the American Dream" in C Johnson (ed.), *The Industrial Policy Debate* (San Francisco, ICS Press, 1984), 27–46, 29.

[62] J Freyman, "Industrial Policy: Patterns of Convergence and Divergence" in J Waltman and D Studlar (eds.), *Political Economy: Public Policies in the United States and Britain* (Jackson, University Press of Mississippi, 1987), 44–68, 58. But see D Vogel, "Government-Industry Relations in the United States: An Overview" in S Wilks and M Wright (eds.), *Comparative Government-Industry Relations: Western Europe, the United States and Japan* (Oxford, Clarendon Press, 1987), 91–116.

[63] Krauss and Pierre, *supra* n. 48, at 176; see also R Lawrence, "Myths and Realities on America's Need for an Industrial Policy" in Steven A. Shull and J Cohen (eds.), *Economics and Politics of Industrial Policy: The United States, and Western Europe* (Boulder, West View Press, 1986), 15–26.

[64] D King and S Wood, "The Political Economy of Neoliberalism: Britain and the United States in the 1980s" in H Kitschelt, P Lange, G Marks and J Stephens (eds.), *Continuity and Change in Contemporary Capitalism* (Cambridge, Cambridge University Press, 1999), 371–397, at 379.

by its private market actors' failure to develop any concerted domestic responses to external challenges. While the US government is characterised by decentralisation, its market can be described by the absence of any concertation or corporativism.

The power and influence of business on the government and the political system has been constant throughout American political history.[65] Corporate America in general has been able to dominate on its own the economic and political debate in the United States. But despite business being able to do what it wanted it do, it has not been capable of generating rational economic outcomes. The fact that capitalism in America has traditionally been unchallenged, either by medieval institutions or by a socialist working movement, has inhibited American business from developing a sense of unity. The business community is largely a community in name only; its internal structures of authority remain remarkably decentralised and its investment decisions are made by firms or industries relatively independent from each other.[66] The absence of a class consciousness has resulted in a lack of a sense of solidarity and responsibility towards other firms. American capital is the most fragmented of all western countries.

The representation of business in the US is divided into the US Chamber of Commerce[67] and the National Association of Manufacturers,[68] which represents around 80% of the national industrial output. Whereas the Chamber of Commerce voices the interests of both small and large enterprises, the NAM tends only to represent the interests of large enterprises, thus causing conflict and competition between both associations. In fact, the US lacks an essential ingredient of a corporativist system: a limited number of peak associations.[69] Peak interest groups in the US have great difficulty in achieving enough comprehensiveness of membership to be able to represent effectively their respective sectors in the political process. They are either weak and incomplete or ineffectual. None can claim a quasi-monopolistic hegemony over a significant sector of socio-economic self-interest. The decentralisation of the US government and the existence of dispersed centres of authority allows individual business and small groups to lobby government and pursue their narrow interests outside the framework of peak associations. In addition, because of the large size and diversity of the US economy, it is hard for peak associations to represent a consensual view for business on most issues with the possible exception of macroeconomic policies. Moreover, monopolistic interest groups are regarded with deep

[65] D Voguel, *Fluctuating Fortunes: The Political Power of Business in America* (New York, Basic Books, 1989).

[66] D Voguel, "Why Businessmen Distrust their State: The Political Consciousness of American Corporate Executives" (1978) 8 *British J. Pol'y Science* 45–78, 67.

[67] See <http://www.uschamber.org>.

[68] See <http://www.nam.org>.

[69] R Salisbury, "Why no Corporativism in America" in P Schmitter and G Lembruch (eds.), *Trends Toward Corporativist Intermediation* (Beverly Hills, Sage Publications, 1979), 213–230, 214.

suspicion in American political culture and, thus, there is virtually no official incorporation of formal groups as participants in policy discussion. Therefore, US bureaucrats deal directly with individual firms or groups with narrow interests rather than peak associations representing the interests of nation-wide industrial sectors.

The pluralism of the business community has been institutionalised by US antitrust enforcement which has been stronger than in most other countries. Antitrust law is the US government's attempt to limit somewhat the economic and political power of business. Whereas co-operation has been the cornerstone of public policy in Europe and Japan, antitrust is the epitome of the adversarial relation between government and private business in the United States.[70] Instead of planning and limiting the autonomy of business, the American government has divided it through a plethora of antitrust laws such as the Sherman Act of 1890, the Federal Trade Commission Act of 1914 and the Clayton Act of 1919.

The fact that US industrialisation resulted from private efforts supported by the availability of large capital markets in which the state did not participate has been instrumental in the absence of strong links between American banks and business. The American financial-industrial relations system is one of the most market-oriented of all capitalist systems.[71] Business is largely dependent on capital obtained through the medium of capital markets and market intermediaries, in the form of high-risk capital such as equities or long-term marketable debt. Similarly, banks are notably absent as business equity holders. A series of federal laws limit the possibility of any links between banks and non-financial institutions. Thus, the Glass-Steagall Act of 1933 prohibits banks from owning stock in other companies, directly or indirectly, through affiliations with investment banks. The Bank Holding Company Act of 1956 prohibits banks from owning more than 5% of the voting stock in any non-bank company or from otherwise controlling any industrial firm. In addition, the US tax code encourages diversification of bank management trust holdings so that no more than 10% of a bank's trust funds are invested in any single corporation.[72]

America's market-oriented financial system implies a strong separation between business ownership and corporate management. Equity investors are a distinct, separate and largely dispersed class of claimants as against their corporations.[73] Consequently, in the case of bad economic performance, instead of selective intervention by equity owning banks such as that taking place in

[70] See D B. Audretsch, *The Market and the State: Government Policy Towards Business in Europe, Japan and the United States* (New York, Harvester Wheatsheaf, 1989), 30.

[71] On the American banking system, see Wolfgang H. Reinicke, *Banking, Politics and Global Finance: American Commercial Banks and Regulatory Change 1980–1990* (Aldershot, Edward Elgar, 1995), 23–38.

[72] W Kester, "American and Japanese Corporate Governance: Convergence to Best Practice?" in S Berger and R Dore (eds.), *National Diversity and Global Capitalism* (Ithaca, Cornell University Press, 1996), 107–137, 130.

[73] See "A Survey of Capitalism: Punters or Proprietors?", *The Economist*, 5 May 1990.

Germany or Japan, a change of ownership through take-over activity of equity on the market is the method to alter the control of business and introduce different patterns of investment and business practices. This implies that corporate management is always under the constant threat of being changed; and thus the need to look for short term profits which can be reported back to shareholders on an annual basis rather than focusing on long term business strategies. The market-oriented financial system also means that in times of economic crisis there is no sense of solidarity nor reciprocal responsibility: everybody is on their own. Although this may imply a much more dynamic economy and improve the competitiveness of individual firms, it is questionable that the inability to achieve collective responses in economic downturns will allow, in the long run, a smooth cohabitation with globalisation.

America's industrial relations reflect the country's overall pluralism, individualism and radical liberalism. US trade unions are weak, fragmented, traditionally politically uncommitted and are viewed with hostility by management. Unlike business, American trade unions are amongst the weakest of their kind of all developed countries. In 1990, the US ranked second last (after France) in union density of the 18 most advanced capitalist democracies.[74] Since the New Deal period when labour mobilised, took the political initiative and reached its peak at around 33% of the labour force, trade union density has decreased dramatically. While in 1977, 24% of the non-agricultural labour force were members of union or employee associations, this rate fell to 19% by 1984, to 16% by 1991 and roughly 15% in 1995.[75] In 1995, only 10% of the labour force in the private sector was unionised.

The dramatic decrease of union membership in the US may be due to several reasons. First, America's values of individualism, meritocracy, populism and *laissez faire* imply an hostile environment for the development of unionisation.[76] Second, the fall could be due also to shifts in the demographic, industrial and occupational positions of the labour force away from traditional heavily unionised types of workers and sectors to the services sector, where strong unionisation has traditionally been more unlikely. However, America's low unionisation rates are, most of all, the result of business resistance to trade unions. In no other advanced industrial Western country has management been as hostile to unions as in the United States, especially since the 1980s.[77] Business resistance to unionisation can take the form of outright hostility to unions or the

[74] J Visser, "The Strength of Union Movements in Advanced Capitalist Democracies: Social and Organizational Variations" in M Regini (ed.), *The Future of Labour Movements* (Beverly Hills, Sage Publications, 1992), 17–52, 19.

[75] See H Farber and A Krueger, "Union Membership in the United States: The Decline Continues", *National Bureau of Economic Research, Working Paper No 4216* (1992); see also S Liptset, *supra* n. 28, at 89.

[76] See H Farber, "The Decline of Unionization in the United States: What Can Be Learned from Recent Experience?" (1990) 8(1) *J. Labour Economics* S75–S105.

[77] See D Moberg, "Union Busting, Past and Present: Charting an Old American Tradition" (1992) 39 *Dissent* 73–80.

improvement of wages and working conditions so that workers will not feel the need for unions. Business may hire labour-management consultants whose hallmark is defeating union representation elections. Consultants may try to improve the working environment and emphasise positive labour relations which exclude trade unions, conduct a legal campaign that includes much communication with workers regarding the management's view of what unionisation will mean for the workforce or simply conduct an illegal election campaign by committing unfair labour practices. Furthermore, courts have been inclined to assert the primacy of vague common law rights of private property over the new collective rights of workers. Such judicial assumptions include the overriding importance of continued production, the need to control workers to prevent irresponsible action and the deference of workers to management's rights to run the workplace.[78] Moreover, federal laws like the Taft-Hartley Act of 1947 give managers the right to persuade their employees not to join unions and take from the latter many essential weapons including secondary boycott.[79]

Unions are not only weak but are also highly fragmented. The most important peak association for labour is, theoretically, the American Federation of Labour—Congress of Industrial Relations;[80] a federation within which the largest union is the Teamsters Union followed by the United States Auto Workers. Yet, American trade unions have pursued a more fragmented, decentralised and job-oriented unionism than their European counterparts. This has been partly due to the fact that they have had no united capital as a counterpart with whom to negotiate on an industry-wide basis.

The weakness of the US trade unions and the lack of national industry wide co-operation between labour and business implies that the latter may nearly always have its way. But while the overwhelming power of business may improve profits and economic performance, it increases the social tensions and sense of instability resulting from globalisation as even if the latter is at its best there will always be winners and losers.

2.B.4. The Way the US Socio-Economic Structures Affect American Trade Policy

Capitalism in the United States is characterised by a decentralised government incapable of developing coherent and co-ordinated economic or social polices which may imply wealth redistribution or limiting the autonomy of business and by a pluralist market where a fragmented business can override a weak

[78] In *National Labor Relations BD* v. *Mackay Radio & Telegraph Co*, 304 U.S. 333 (1938), the Supreme Court observed that employers could hire permanently staff to replace strikers in order to maintain production. See also *N.L.R.B.* v. *Fleetwood Trailer, Co*, 389 U.S. 375 (1969); *Belknap, Inc.* v. *Hale*, 463 U.S. 491 (1983); and *TWA, Inc* v. *Flight Attendants*, 489 U.S. 426 (1989).

[79] Moberg, *supra* n. 77, at 76.

[80] See <http://www.aflcir.org>.

labour. This pattern of divided government and interest group fragmentation applies both at federal as well as state level.[81]

America's unique radical liberalism implies an active and at many times aggressive, unilateral trade policy; reflecting an intolerance towards other political and economic systems as a result of the fact that domestically it has never been seriously contested.[82] The government's inability to develop domestically coherent and co-ordinated economic redistributive policies either in the form of industrial policy or social adjustment together with the lack of any concertation between its market actors leading to collective approaches to competitiveness, industrial crisis or globalisation, tends to generate reactive responses in the form of an aggressive trade policy. Trade policy becomes the *ad hoc* alternative to the lack of adequate domestic instruments to deal with international competition.[83] Having to leave the economy to the forces of a plural market, the United States government is trapped in a dichotomy between free trade and protectionism. But even if free trade is the preferred alternative, such a policy will be complemented by *ad hoc* protectionism as an exception to market openness in order to deal with specific domestic problems or industrial crises, as well as by an active approach in the international trading system trying to benefit its industries by imposing an international system which reflects its own.[84] America, with no domestic tools to meet the challenge of international trade, will either close itself in the form of protectionism or define the rules under which such trade takes place. No matter how many names we may give to the phenomenon of globalisation it is, in essence, nothing other than the internationalisation of the local uncontested American system.

Within America's trade policy, unfair trade instruments enjoy a privileged place. They provide protection on an exceptional basis to confront domestic problems. Protection is granted to the domestic industry either in the form of duties, simply chasing away foreign firms or by guaranteeing specified market shares.[85] As a result, unfair trade instruments are a form of indirect targeting of resources to specific threatened American industries and of government intervention in the domestic market structure.

[81] S Hansen, "Industrial Policy and Corporativism in the American States" (1989) 2(2) *Governance* 172–197, 191.

[82] On the argument of American liberalism not being able to live in comfort yet side by side with different foreign attitudes, see L Hartz, *supra* n. 29, at 286.

[83] L Tyson and J Zysman, "American Industry in International Competition", in J Zysman and L Tyson (eds.), *American Industry in International Competition: Government Policies and Corporate Strategies* (Ithaca, Cornell University Press, 1983), 15–59.

[84] M Brown and Jerel A Rosati, "The Reagan Administration and Economic Interdependence: Turbulent Relations with the EC" (1987) 42 *Int'l L.* 438–470, 469.

[85] On the protectionist effects of anti-dumping and countervailing duties other than the imposition of duties, see R Staiger and F Wolak, "The Effect of Import Source on the Determinants and Impacts of Antidumping Suit Activity", in A Krueger (ed.), *The Political Economy of Trade Protection* (Chicago, The University of Chicago Press, 1996), 85–93. On the protectionism of trade instruments in general, see Chapter I, Section B.

The legalistic process of such instruments fits into a system characterised by the concept of government acting as an open and neutral agent between the conflictual interests of plural and disorganised market actors.[86] The quasi-judicial nature of the trade remedy laws means that although in many cases economic and political strength are major determinants of protection, small and, most importantly, individual firms with narrow interests may still force government to pursue their market objectives.[87] One of the most striking features of America's trade instruments is the extent to which they compel the national government to serve the narrow interests of a few or individual businesses.

Unfair trade instruments also meet the imperative requirement of providing *ad hoc* protection while protecting the autonomy of business against any attempt from government to intervene and plan the economy. Protection by means of unfair trade instrument is granted only on the basis of whether or not foreign industries are doing business under the American domestic system and whether the domestic industry is losing market share, no economic restructuring plan being required. Unfair trade instruments reflect the absolute predominance of business in the American political system. In fact they do very little to improve the economic performance of the domestic industry as a whole.[88]

Finally, it is characteristic of the ideology of US trade policy to focus on the issue of fair competition.[89] The concept of fairness has two faces. On the one hand, focusing on the debate of fair trade becomes a tactic of appealing political resonance for US industry. In a system where pluralism, individualism and meritocracy are fundamental values, granting protection on the basis of fair competition seems to be undeniable. But in fact, the fair trade rhetoric with which to safeguard free trade and the plural market, serves the purpose of protecting an uncompetitive domestic industry.[90] On the other hand, the notion of fair trade has a determinative, normative meaning which delimits the range of acceptable economic behaviour for both foreign governments and market actors, prerequisite for entering the American market. Behind the US emphasis on fairness there is an insistence that other nations must not play the international trading game on the basis of principles other than those within which the American economy is institutionally constrained to play. The standards of fair trade instruments reflect nothing other than the principles on which the American capitalist system is based. The huge American market provides the economic muscle with which to impose the rules of the international trading

[86] T Howell, "Trade Protection: Rethinking the American Perspective" (1992) 25 *N.Y. U. J. Int'l L. & Pol'y* 251–262.

[87] See M Moore, "The Rise and Fall of Big Steel's Influence on US Trade Policy" in A Krueger (ed.), *supra* n. 85, 15–34, 31.

[88] See J Greenwald, "Protectionism and US Economic Policy" (1987) 23 *Stanford J. Int'l L.* 233–261.

[89] M Barrus, "The Politics of Competitive Erosion in the US Steel Industry" in J Zysman and L Tyson (eds.), *supra* n. 83, 60–105, 81.

[90] On how the rhetoric of fair trade influences the US government in granting protection, see E Kraus and S Reich, "Ideology, Interests and the American Executive: Towards a Theory of Foreign Competition and Manufacturing Trade Policy" (1994) 46(4) *Int'l Org.* 857–897.

system in order, in turn, to improve the competitive position of the American domestic industry.[91] Despite all its rhetoric, the fair trade argument is only an attempt to solve at the international level what historically rooted constraints have not allowed to occur in the first place in the domestic sphere. Thus, the irony is that fair trade serves to preserve and internationalise a domestic system characterised by a weak government and plural market actors which itself is handicapped in its attempts to develop domestic collective responses to meet the challenge of globalisation. Fair trade serves to internationalise the absolute dominance of corporate America in the US's decentralised and plural system. The result of this, of course, is the world-wide increase of unfair trade instruments and of trade conflict.

The analysis of the domestic structures of the United States and the basic features of its trade policy may serve as the context from which to view the legal elements of American trade policy. First, it can help us to understand what are the forces moving the constitutional actors involved in the policy process and the development of unfair trade instruments. In short: why constitutional actors act as they do. Second, it can illustrate the political background to the arguments evidenced in the different constitutional trade controversies and, thus, improve the legal discussion. Finally, it can serve as an approach to analyse the elements of unfair trade instruments and verify to what extent these reflect nothing other than America's domestic system.

2.C. THE CONSTITUTIONAL FRAMEWORK OF UNITED STATES' TRADE POLICY

2.C.1. Principal Constitutional Features of the United States' International Trade Policy

The United States has a much more complex international trade law framework than any other single developed country. This complexity results from the following, often conflicting, features:

(1) The United States Constitution became the basic instrument of government in America in 1788. This implies that the concerns of the founding fathers were not necessarily the same as those of the American people at the beginning of the twenty first century. While the Constitution of 1788 created a Republic, the American people have moved to a Democracy.[92] The framers' will was to create a system with a weak and partial representation, indirect election and, consequently, weak responsibility, weak accountability and virtually no popular participation. Contemporary US democracy in turn implies universal

[91] S Gill, "Neo-Liberalism and the Shift Towards a US-Centered Transnational Hegemony" in H Overbeek (ed.), *Restructuring Hegemony in the Global Political Economy: The Rise of Transnational Neo-Liberalism in the 1980s* (London, Routledge, 1993), 246–282, at 271.

[92] See L Henkin, *Constitutionalism, Democracy and Foreign Affairs* (New York, Columbia University Press, 1990), 12.

suffrage and hence a need for stronger representation, responsiveness, participation and accountability. However, the Constitution has not been amended to modify the framework of government or the distribution of powers among the different branches. Instead, most changes and redistribution of power have been made by the reinterpretation of the Constitution in response to political forces operating in a constantly spreading, growing and changing country.[93] As a result, in practice, the powers of the different actors in trade policy making do not necessarily reflect those written into the Constitution. Moreover, analysing the constitutionality and democratic legitimacy of the behaviour of the different actors may require taking into account, at least to a certain extent, the changes which have taken place during the last two hundred years.

Furthermore, the founding fathers' vision and concerns on the role of the United States in the world do not correspond with the contemporary reality of America leading the globalisation process.[94] On the one hand, at the Constitutional Convention, the foreign policy of the United States was perceived in a rather naive way. The constitutional drafters envisioned the US as a medium world power rather insulated from the problems of the rest of the world and concluding a limited number of relations with a few other world powers. On the other hand, the real constitutional debate in the convention of 1787 concerned the distribution of powers between the federal government and the states.[95] Under the Articles of the Confederation of 1777, Congress lacked the exclusive power to regulate foreign trade and external relations with third countries. This division of powers resulted in an inability to regulate foreign trade in an adequate manner and, in turn, to conflicts between the different states. Consequently, the Constitutional Convention was characterised by a large consensus on the need to remove the power over foreign trade from the states to the federal level. However, due to the limited vision of America's role in the world, there was no big concern over the distribution of powers as between the Executive and Congress at the federal level.

(2) The regulation of international trade is both a foreign relations and a domestic affair.[96] From the political point of view, this implies that foreign trade policy operates in an environment consisting of different domestic as well as external economic and political forces. But from the constitutional point of view, the symbiosis between international trade and international affairs implies that international trade law is also international law and conversely, that international law, to a certain, extent encompasses international trade affairs. Whereas the power to regulate domestically foreign trade is settled

[93] L Henkin, *Constitutionalism, Democracy and Foreign Affairs* (New York, Columbia University Press, 1990) 13

[94] J Rakove, "Making Foreign Policy—The View from 1787" in R Goldwin and R Licht (eds.), *Foreign Policy and the Constitution* (Washington, The AEI Press, 1990), 1–40, 6.

[95] J Gorlin, "Foreign Trade and the Constitution" in R Goldwin and R Licht (eds.), *supra* n. 94, 54–71, 56.

[96] S Cohen, *The Making of United States International Economic Policy* (New York, Praeger Publishers, 1977), 15.

clearly in favour of Congress, the entire framework is confused by the need to take into account the distribution of powers in foreign affairs. To a greater extent than in any other area, foreign affairs do not fall within the exclusive power of any branch and, thus, such interdependence implies both a stronger need for co-operation as well as a greater tendency towards conflict.[97] Indeed, the absence of a comprehensive and natural division in foreign affairs excluding the other branch is a strong invitation to compete for power and to claim concurrent authority. As a result, actors in the United States' international trade policy-making process have powers which they would not otherwise enjoy. Whereas Article I of the Constitution grants plenary power to Congress to regulate foreign trade, Article II vests in the President the powers to conduct foreign relations and these, in fact, encompass the foreign commerce of the United States.[98] In this respect, the increase of Presidential power in foreign affairs, due to the requirements of international relations, has reflected itself in the regulation of foreign trade.

(3) As a consequence of the previous features, the constitutional framework of United States international trade law does not necessarily draw a parallelism between the regulation of the domestic sphere and the regulation of the external sphere. The US system is characterised by the existence of a domestic democracy and an international democracy which are not totally parallel.[99] The US may be characterised domestically by a plural democracy; however internationally there is a tendency towards unity and single representation. As Denenberg says, "when threatened with external dangers the complex system of checks and balances reverts to a tribal dependence on the warrior chief."[100] Thus, the powers to regulate foreign trade domestically do not necessarily imply corresponding powers to negotiate international trade agreements. While enhancing efficiency this also implies a stronger conflict. Furthermore, as we shall see, to a certain degree, the lack of parallelism has an important impact on the relation between international trade law and federal law.

(4) Taking into account the decentralisation of American political institutions is essential when analysing the constitutional framework of the international trade policy of the United States and its democratic legitimacy. The fact that both the Executive and Congress are characterised by centrifugal forces suggests that reducing trade policy to a tension between these two branches is not completely useful. In analysing the changes in trade policy the issue should not be simply whether Congress or the Executive assert their powers but rather which sub-units within these two actors win as a consequence of the changes. Having this in mind is important to understand the democratic legitimacy argument in

[97] L Henkin, *Foreign Affairs and the Constitution* (New York, Norton & Company, 1975), 92.

[98] P Feller and A Wilson, "United States Tariff and Trade Law: Constitutional Sources and Constraints" (1976) *L. & Pol'y Int'l Bus.* 105–123, 107.

[99] See L Henkin, "Foreign Affairs and the Constitution" (1987/88) 66(2) *Foreign Affairs* 284–309, 309.

[100] R Denenberg, *supra* n. 34, at 80.

the US trade policy process. The legitimacy discussion should not be limited to whether the process is formally democratic but extended to a substantial approach, which enquires into which interests are emphasised in the trade policy process.

(5) Among the developed nations, the United States is unique due to the fact that the legislature plays a major role in the development and enunciation of international trade policy.[101] Though the Presidency has grown considerably stronger in foreign affairs than originally envisioned, Congress can always point to its express constitutional powers to regulate commerce with foreign nations and require the President, and foreign nations, to treat it as a major co-partner in international trade relations.[102] Yet this has to be made compatible with the developments of the international trading system where a national, uniform and strong voice is required to influence the developments of the multilateral trading system. The American response to the global challenge has been the delegation of powers from Congress to the Executive. Anti-dumping, countervailing duties, Section 301 and fast track are nothing other than a congressional delegation of powers to the administration to deal with international trade matters.

The delegation of powers from Congress to the President in foreign trade in itself implies four characteristics of the foreign trade law framework of the United States. First, delegation means control. Delegation is a two-way deal. Whereas delegation enhances the powers of the President in international trade, it also allows Congress to keep tight control of such policy. By delegating powers, Congress does not lock itself out of foreign trade policy.[103] Rather, the delegation of powers is a move away from spelling out the details of foreign trade towards the business of regulating what the Executive can and cannot do in international trade.[104] In this respect, the delegation of powers does not imply only that Congress retains control but furthermore, to a certain extent, the *quid pro quo* implies that it gains control over what the Presidency would be able to do on its own. Moreover, Congress often does not simply delegate powers to the President or the Executive in general but to independent agencies or units within the administration that are themselves created by, and thus politically responsive to, the legislature. Hence, by delegating powers, Congress can change the

[101] J Garten, *supra* n. 7 at 19.

[102] J H Jackson, "United States Law and Implementation of the Tokyo Round Negotiations", in J H Jackson, J V Louis and M Matsushita (eds.), *Implementing the Tokyo Round: National Constitutions and International Economic Rules* (Ann Arbor, University of Michigan Press, 1984), 139–197, 140; see also H Koh, "The Legal Markets of International Trade: A Perspective on the Proposed United States-Canada Free Trade Agreement" (1987) 12(2) *Yale J. Int'l L.* 193–249, 215.

[103] R Carter and L Eden, "Who Makes US Trade Policy" (1999) 13(1) *Int'l Trade J.* 53, at 92. But see I Destler, *American Trade Politics* (Washington, Institute for International Economics, 2nd ed., 1992), 15; (but it is also true that Destler refers to the delegation of powers that Congress made until the 1970s, before radical changes affecting international trade took place both at the international and domestic levels).

[104] See S O'Halloran, *Politics, Process and American Trade Policy* (Ann Arbor, The University of Michigan Press, 4th ed., 1997), 77.

internal debate within the administration and influence the trade policy outcome.[105]

Second, delegation reflects consensus. The delegation of powers to the administration, or to independent agencies, presupposes an agreement within Congress on the basic principles which govern US international trade policy. Taking into account the American Constitution's strong division of powers and the likelihood of divided government, co-operation between the different branches requires a consensus encompassing all parties. Delegation in trade policy entails consensus on the role that the United States must play in the international trading system. Delegation of powers was possible because it was backed by a broad national agreement, which reflected its socio-economic structures, on increasing the welfare of the country by adopting a free trade policy and providing for *ad hoc* protectionism in exceptional cases. Thus, unfair trade laws, while instrumental in the pursuit of a world-wide free trade system reflecting the American way, also provide *ad hoc* and limited protection to the American domestic industry. Furthermore, because of decentralisation, delegation of powers from Congress to the Executive can also enable Congress to adopt specified legislation that otherwise, as a centrifugal institution, it would not be able to implement. Delegating powers to the administration requires an agreement between the different forces of Congress and the President; thus it enhances the chances for Congress to adopt legislation, such as unfair trade instruments, which otherwise would not have the necessary support or the achievement of which would be much more burdensome.

Finally, from a technical point of view, the delegation of powers as a means of control and consensus suggests detailed rules concerning unfair trade instruments. The will of Congress to control trade policy through delegation results in United States' unfair trade instruments being much more detailed than those of its European counterpart. The increasing assertiveness of Congress in trade policy, as a result of the increasing impact of international trade in the American domestic system, is reflected in tighter rules on the Executive when implementing unfair trade laws.[106]

(6) United States' international trade law is further complicated by the political implications of federalism. From the constitutional point of view, in regard of international economic matters there appears to be no significant limitation on the powers of federal government.[107] The supremacy of federal international

[105] Thus in the Trade Agreements Act of 1979 implementing the Tokyo Round agreements, with regard to Anti-Dumping and Countervailing Duties, the most important change was the shift of the responsibility from the Treasury to the Department of Commerce which was considered to be much more sympathetic to the interests of the domestic industry. This institutional change, among other developments, favoured the growth of unfair trade cases.

[106] See E Stewart, "Existing Remedies and the Trade Deficit: The Promise of Reform Through Judicial Review" (1986) 18 *N.Y. U. J. Int'l L. & Pol'y* 1165–1189.

[107] See J H Jackson, "Constitutional Law Principles and Foreign Trade Law and Policy", in M Hilf and E U Petersmann (eds.), *National Constitutions and International Economic Law* (Deventer, Kluwer Law and Taxation Publishers, Studies in Transnational Economic Law, 1993), 65–89, 67.

trade law over state law is based on the supremacy of federal international law over State law and the prohibition on States from entering into any treaties with foreign nations, on the one hand, and the supremacy of the commerce clause and the prohibition on States imposing any duties on foreign imports, on the other hand.

First, Article VI, clause 2 of the Constitution reads:

> "This Constitution, and the Laws of the United States which shall be made in Pursuance thereof; and all Treaties made, or which shall be made, under the Authority of the United States, shall be the supreme Law of the Land; and the Judges in every State shall be bound thereby, any Thing in the Constitution or Laws of any State to the Contrary notwithstanding"

Furthermore, Article I, Section 10, clause 1 reads:

> "No State shall enter into any Treaty, Alliance or Confederation, grant Letters of Marque and Reprisal, coin Money; emit Bills of Credit; make any Thing but gold and silver Coin a Tender in Payment of Debts; pass any Bill or Attainder, ex post facto Law, or Law impairing the Obligation of Contracts, or grant any Title of Nobility."[108]

The treaty power, as expressed in the Constitution, is unlimited other than by those restraints, found in the Constitution itself, against the action of the government or its departments, and those arising from the nature of government itself and of that of the States.[109] This power extends to all proper subjects of negotiations between the US government and other nations but does not extend so far as to authorise what the Constitution forbids.[110] But it is the declared will of the people of the United States that every treaty made by the authority of the US shall be superior to the constitution and laws of any individual State.[111] In respect of rights reserved to the States, the treaty making power is not limited to what may be done by an unaided act of Congress.[112] Valid treaties are binding within the territorial limits of the States as they are throughout the dominion of the United States. Thus, the federal government has the power to do what is necessary and proper to implement a treaty; even if its action is not within other domestic powers. Furthermore, a provision of a treaty cannot be rendered nugatory in any part of the United States by either municipal ordinances or State laws; even if these do not have clear international implications but only merely local effects.[113] For the purpose of the supremacy of treaties over State law, the

[108] The prohibition on States entering into Treaties or Alliances is qualified by Article I, Section 10, clause 3 which forbids States from entering into any Agreement or Compact without the consent of Congress.

[109] *Geoffrey* v. *Riggs*, 133 U.S. 258; 10 S. Ct. 295; 1890 LEXIS 1907 (1889).

[110] *Reid, Superintendent, District of Columbia Jail*, v. *Covert*, 354 U.S. 1, 15; 77 S. Ct. 1222; 1957 U.S. LEXIS 729 (1957); see also *Asakura* v. *City of Seattle et al.*, 265 U.S. 332, 341; 44 S. Ct. 515; 1924 U.S. LEXIS 22611 (1924).

[111] *Hauenstein* v. *Lynham*, 100 U.S. 483, 489; 1879 U.S. LEXIS 1841 (1879).

[112] *State of Missouri* v. *Holland, United States Game Warden*, 252 U.S. 416; 40 S. Ct. 382; 1920 U.S. LEXIS 1520 (1920).

[113] *Asakura* v. *City of Seattle et al., supra* n. 110.

concept of treaty includes all international agreements validly entered into by the federal government.[114]

Second, Article I, Section 8, clause 3 of the Constitution reads:

> "[The Congress shall have the Power] To regulate Commerce with foreign Nations, and among the several States, and with the Indian Tribes."[115]

Moreover, Article I, Section 10, clause 2 reads:

> "No State shall, without the Consent of the Congress, lay any Imposts or Duties on Imports or Exports, except what may be absolutely necessary for executing its inspection Laws: and the net Produce of all Duties and Imposts, laid by any State, on Imports or Exports, shall be for the Use of the Treasury of the United States; and all such Laws shall be subject of the Revision and Control of the Congress."

Consequently, the States of the Union have no competence regarding commerce with foreign nations. The prohibition on States' interference with foreign trade must be interpreted much more strongly than that in relation to interstate commerce.[116] The prohibition on States imposing duties on the importation of goods also applies to taxes which are imposed on goods on the basis that they are imported, even once they are in the territory of the State.[117] Only when the importer has so acted upon the thing imported that it has become incorporated and mixed up with the mass of property of the country, the imported good may lose its distinctive character as an import and become subject to the taxing power of the State. While it remains the property of the importer, in his warehouse, in the original form or package in which it was imported, a tax upon it is too plainly a duty on imports to escape the prohibition in the Constitution.[118] Likewise, a State act may not discriminate between State and foreign products.[119]

This exemption of foreign commerce from State regulation does not prevent States from taxing the property of those engaged in such commerce located within the State as the property of other citizens is taxed, nor from regulating matters of local concern which may incidentally affect commerce.[120] Thus, States play an important role in many policies and activities that bear on the flow of goods, services and investment across national borders.[121] In this

[114] *United States* v. *Belmont et al., Executors*, 301 U.S. 324, 330; 57 S. Ct. 758; 1937 U.S. LEXIS 293 (1937); see also *United States* v. *Pink, Superintendent of Insurance of the State of New York, et al.*, 315 U.S. 203, 230; 62 S. Ct. 552; 1942 U.S. LEXIS 1060 (1942).

[115] However, the Constitution also establishes express limitations on Congressional power, intended to protect States. Import duties must be geographically uniform, and Congress may not override any State prohibition against the import of liquor. See Article I, Section 9, clause 6; see also 21st Amendment, Section 2.

[116] *Japan Line Ltd., et al.* v. *County of Los Angeles et al.*, 441 U.S. 434; 99 S. Ct. 1813; 1979 U.S. LEXIS 20 (1979).

[117] *Brown* v. *Maryland*, 25 U.S. 419; 1827 U.S. LEXIS 398 (1827).

[118] *Low et al.* v. *Austin*, 80 U.S. 29; 1871 U.S. LEXIS 1306 (1871).

[119] *Tiernan* v. *Rinker*, 102 U.S. 123; 1880 U.S. LEXIS 2010 (1880).

[120] *Leloup* v. *Port Mobile*, 127 U.S. 640, 648; 8 S. Ct. 1380; 1988 U.S. LEXIS 2028 (1888).

[121] R Poster, "The President, Congress and Trade Policy" (1988) 15(2) *Congress & The Presidency* 165–184, 166.

respect, as globalisation blurs the lines between the domestic and the external sphere, State regulations increasingly affect international trade and thus are themselves subject to the changes of international trade law. This situation, though in constitutional terms limiting very little the powers of the federal government to override State law through the regulation of international trade, has important political implications.[122] As Congressmen struggle to keep a balance between their State and constituencies' interests and those of the nation as a whole, the federal government needs the support of State officials to negotiate and enter into international trade agreements which may affect State laws.

An example of the political implications of federalism for US foreign trade law are the provisions of the Uruguay Round Agreements Act [URAA] dealing with State law. In order to implement the Uruguay Round Agreements the URAA needed to provide for a political compromise between the Executive and the States that, while trying to respect formally the international agreements, also attempted to protect the States' sovereignty.[123] This political deal between the Executive and the States leaves the former in a very uncomfortable position. The Executive must defend, in the WTO, a law which only applies in one State and with which it might not agree. Furthermore, if the WTO decides against such law, the Executive will need to decide whether to confront the WTO and jeopardise its international trade strategy or challenge the law in a federal court, and thereby confront a State, thus risking the support of Congress in future trade agreements.[124] The political implications of federalism have an important impact on the debate concerning the future of the trade policy making process and the procedure for the conclusion of international trade agreements.

(7) A final striking feature of the constitutional framework of United States' international trade law is the important role that private parties play in the policy-making process. Due to the decentralisation of the US government and the radical liberalism of its political culture, individuals play a much stronger role in the American trade policy making process than in any other Western political system. Private parties, not necessarily nation-wide associations but groups that may have narrow interests, can influence the system by two means. First,

[122] M Shaefer, "Twenty First Century Trade Negotiations, the US Constitution and the Elimination of US State-Level Protectionism" (1999) *J. Int'l Economic L.* 71.

[123] J O'Reilly, "Stop the World, We Want Our Own Labels, Treaties, State Voter Initiative Laws and Federal Pre-Emption"(1997) 18(2) *U. Pa. J. Int'l Econ. L.* 617–653; see also Section 102 Uruguay Round Agreements Act, 103 P.L. 465; 108 Stat. 4809 (1994); and the "Statement of Administrative Action", in *Message from the President of the United States Transmitting the Uruguay Round Trade Agreements, Texts of Agreements, Implementing Bill, Statement of Administrative Action and Required Supporting Statements*, 670–675, 103rd Congress, 2nd Session, House Document 103–316, Volume 1 (27 September 1994).

[124] Examples of this are the WTO disputes over several State laws. See *United States Measures Affecting Government Procurement* (WT/0588/1) (concerning an act enacted by the state of Massachusetts regarding State contracts with companies doing business with Burma); see also *United States, Certain Measures Affecting the Import of Cattle, Swine and Grain from Canada* (WT/DS/144/1) (concerning certain measures imposed by the State of South Dakota, and others, prohibiting entry or transit to Canadian trucks carrying cattle, swine and grain), available at <http://www.wto. int/wto/dispute>.

private parties can interfere in the process by influencing Congress as political or economic constituents. Congress' increased involvement in foreign trade is, at least in part, a function of the increasing pressures from the private sector.[125] Second, as a result of the division of powers between Congress and the Executive in foreign trade, individuals may exert their influence within the Executive through the Congressional instrument of delegation. Congress views individuals as a way of controlling the Executive in the trade policy matters.[126] Through the instrument of delegation, Congress establishes rights for individuals in the trade process in order to influence the final trade policy outcome. Thus, to a larger extent than other governments, the US government is bound to act in the international trading system for the pursuit of what may be the narrow interests of private parties. The important role of individuals is fundamental to understanding the debate on the democratic legitimacy of the trade policy making process and to determine how the nation-wide consensus on trade policy issues has been constructed. The question should be which individuals and which interests have been predominantly represented in the process.

2.C.2. Congress in the United States' International Trade Policy Making Process

2.C.2.a. The Powers of Congress in International Trade

Congress has absolute and plenary powers to regulate foreign trade. Such authority derives from three constitutional sources. First, Congress has the power to tax. Article I, Section 8, clause 1, reads:

> "The Congress shall have the Power To lay and collect Taxes, Duties, Imposts and Excises, to pay the Debts and provide for the Common Defence and general Welfare of the United States; but all Duties, Imposts and Excises shall be uniform throughout the United States;"

Second, the Constitution grants Congress the power to regulate commerce with foreign nations. Thus, Article I, Section 8, clause 3, reads:

> "[The Congress shall have the Power] To regulate Commerce with foreign Nations, and among the several States, and with the Indian Tribes"

The powers to tax and regulate commerce with foreign nations, though theoretically different, may complement each other and both apply to international trade. While the power of taxation can be used to regulate commerce with foreign nations, the power to regulate commerce with foreign nations may be exercised through, and as a form of, taxation.

[125] See Garten, *supra* n. 7, at 19.

[126] See D W. Leebron, Implementation of the Uruguay Round Results in the United States, in J H, Jackson and A Sykes (eds.), *Implementing the Uruguay Round* (Oxford, Clarendon Press, 1997), 175–242, 181.

Moreover, the Constitution provides for residual powers for Congress. Article I, Section 8, clause 18 reads:

> "[The Congress shall have the Power] To make all Laws which shall be necessary and proper for carrying into Execution the foregoing Powers, and all other Powers vested by this Constitution in the Government of the United States, or in any Department or Office thereof."

From the very beginning, United States foreign trade was the core of its foreign policy and the power to regulate commerce with foreign nations gave Congress a major voice in such. As the world and the United States have developed, the power to regulate commerce with foreign nations has enhanced the importance of Congress. Nevertheless, the power to regulate foreign commerce has been, in the main, the incidental beneficiary of the explosion of the power to regulate interstate commerce. A power which is nearly unlimited.[127]

The powers of Congress to regulate international trade are plenary. Congress has absolute and exclusive powers to regulate commerce with the Indian tribes, foreign nations and interstate commerce.[128] Such power is expressly conferred upon Congress, and by virtue of being an enumerated power, is complete in itself; acknowledging no limitations other than those prescribed in the Constitution.[129] It comprehends every species of commercial intercourse between the United States and foreign nations.[130]

As a result of the complete nature of Congressional power over foreign commerce it necessarily follows that no one has a vested right to engage in international trade by exporting or importing into the United States. No individual has a vested right to trade with foreign nations which is so broad in character as to limit and restrict the power of Congress to determine either what articles of merchandise may be imported into the United States and the terms upon which a right to import may be exercised.[131] Furthermore, no one has a legal right to the maintenance of an existing rate or duty. Neither the action of Congress, in fixing a new tariff, nor that of the President, in exercising his delegated power, is subject to impeachment, provided the prescribed forms of legislation have been regularly observed.[132]

Congress may implement any trade policy it wishes. The power of Congress to impose and collect duties and to regulate commerce with foreign nations is not limited to the purpose of raising revenue. Instead, Congress has the power to frame customs duties with a view to protecting and encouraging home indus-

[127] Henkin, *supra* n. 97, at 69.

[128] *United States* v. *Forty-Three Gallons of Whiskey, etc.*, 93 U.S. 188; 1876 U.S. LEXIS 1368 (1876).

[129] *Buttfield* v. *Stranahan*, 192 U.S. 470, 492; 24 S. Ct. 349; 1904 U.S. LEXIS 965 (1904).

[130] *Gibbons* v. *Ogden*, 9 Wheat. Rep. 1 (1824).

[131] *Buttfield* v. *Stranahan*, *supra* n. 129.

[132] *Norwegian Nitrogen Products Co.* v. *United States*, 288 U.S. 294, 318; 53 S. Ct. 350; 1933 U.S. LEXIS 958 (1933); see also *United States* v. *George S. Bush & Co., Inc.*, 310 U.S. 371; 60 S. Ct. 944; 1940 U.S. LEXIS 1085 (1940).

tries.[133] Thus it can decide to open totally the doors of America to foreign trade or it may chose to retreat into economic isolationism and autarky. When acting under the commerce clause, Congress can make whatever laws it may deem appropriate within the broad limits of the US Constitution.[134] Furthermore, the Constitution leaves to Congress a large discretion as to the means that may be employed in executing its commerce powers.[135] The United States government may regulate foreign trade unilaterally through the reduction or increase of tariffs or in the form of treaties with foreign nations.[136] Congress may decide to enact unilateral procedures to act in the international trading system, may permit the US government to enter into bilateral relations only or it may decide to participate in the multilateral trading system.

The powers of Congress in foreign trade are further enhanced by the relationship between domestic federal law and international law. An act of Congress ought never to be construed to violate the law of nations, if any other possible construction remains.[137] However, it is settled constitutional doctrine that Congress may nullify, in whole or in part, a treaty commitment or any other international agreement.[138] The power of Congress to override prior treaties or international agreements regulating foreign trade has been expressly upheld by the Supreme Court.[139]

The Supreme Court has perceived both treaties and statutes strictly as forms of legislation instead of regarding treaty law as an international act, as a source of independent international obligation for the United States.[140] This interpretation has been based on the fact that both treaties and federal laws appear in Article VI, Section 2 of the Constitution as the supreme law of the land neither predominating. The Court has also been influenced by the idea that the

[133] *J. W. Hampton, Jr., & Company* v. *United States*, 276 U.S. 394, 411; 48 S. Ct. 348; 1928 U.S. LEXIS 284 (1928).

[134] *Champion* v. *Ames*, 188 U.S. 321, 356; 23 S. Ct. 321; 1903 U.S. LEXIS 1283 (1903).

[135] *Champion*, at 354.

[136] *United States* v. *Forty-Three Gallons of Whiskey, etc., supra* n. 128.

[137] *Weinberger, Secretary of Defense, et al.* v. *Rossi et al.*, 456 U.S. 25, 31; 102 S. Ct. 1510; 1982 U.S. LEXIS 54 (1982); see also *Murray* v. *The Schooner Charming Betsy*, 6 U.S. (2 Cranch) 64; 2 L. Ed. 208 (1804).

[138] *James Foster and Pleasants Elam, Plaintiffs in Error* v. *David Neilson, Defendant in Error*, 27 U.S. 253; 7 L. Ed. 415 (1829); see also *Edye and Another* v. *Robertson*, 112 U.S. 580, 596; 28 L. Ed 798; 5 S. Ct. 247; 3 A.F.T.R. (P-H) 2473 (1884); see also *The Chinese Exclusion Case*; *Chae Chan Ping* v. *United States*, 130 U.S. 581, 600; 32 L. Ed. 1068; 9 Ct, 623 (1889); see also *Charles Coles Diggs et al. Appellants*, v. *George P. Shultz, Secretary of Treasury, et al.*, 470 F.2d 461, 465; 152 U.S. App. D.C. 313 (1972).

[139] *Whitney* v. *Robertson*, 124 U.S. 190; 31 L. Ed. 386; 8 S. Ct. 456 (1887). Moreover, it is probable that Executive acts adopted within the inherent powers of the President may also override public international law, as long as they are supported by some intent of Congress. See *The Paquete Habana*; *The Lola*, 175 U.S. 677; 44 L. Ed. 320; 20 S.Ct. 290 (1989); see also *Garcia-Mir* v. *Edwin Meese*, 788 F2d. 1446 (1986).

[140] Professor Henkin, however, considers that neither the text nor the history of the Constitution suggests that the framers intended that Congress have authority to disregard the international obligations of the United States. See L Henkin, "The Constitution and United States Sovereignty: A Century of Chinese Exclusion and its Progeny" (1987) 100 *Harvard L. Rev.* 853–886, 866–867.

constitutional division of powers between the three branches prevented it from interfering in other political branches in the regulation of international law.[141]

This relation reflects, on the one hand, the framers' intent to vest all legislative powers in Congress and, on the other, the lack of parallelism between the domestic power to regulate foreign trade and the distribution of powers in the negotiation and acceptance of international trade agreements. The courts' position of not placing too much emphasis on international law and thus considering that federal statutes (and maybe even Executive acts) may override prior international law, reflects not simply a reluctance to interfere in other political branches but rather the fear that judicial enforcement of internationally created rights will result in a bypassing of the domestic political process.[142]

Second, the fact that there is no parallelism in the division of powers between Congress' absolute powers to regulate foreign trade domestically and the conclusion of international agreements (either in the form of treaties, Executive agreements, or Congressional-Executive agreements through prior delegation or posterior approval through fast track that provide for a process where the powers of Congress are limited or non-existent) may also be an argument for maintaining the equality between federal law and binding international agreements.[143] In *Robertson*, the Supreme Court held:

> "A treaty is made by the President and the Senate. Statutes are made by the President, the Senate and the House of Representatives. The addition of the latter body to the other two in making a law certainly does not render it less entitled to respect in the matter of its repeal or modification than a treaty made by the other two . . ."[144]

Thus, while, from an international point of view, the United States is bound by international trade law, domestically Congress is sovereign. This relation between federal law and international law was as clearly reflected in the implementation of the Uruguay Round agreements as in all other trade conventions.[145] It has had an important impact on the United States' unfair trade instruments and on the way the US has acted in the international trading system.

The URAA evidences the inexorable struggle between the desire to maintain authority over domestic matters and the need to comply with international obligations.[146] Many provisions in the implementing legislation are aimed at limiting the status of the Uruguay Round agreements in domestic law and exercising close supervision over the new WTO.

141 *The Chinese Exclusion Case*; *Chae Chan Ping* v. *United States*, *supra* n. 138.

142 Note "Judicial Enforcement of International Law Against the Federal and State Governments" (1991) 104 *Harvard L. Rev.* 1269–1288, 1284.

143 J H Jackson, "Status of Treaties in Domestic Legal Systems: A Policy Analysis" (1992) 86 *Am. J. Int'l L.* 310–340, 323.

144 *Edye and Another* v. *Robertson*, 112 U.S. 580, 598; 28 L. Ed 798; 5 S. Ct. 247; 3 A.F.T.R. (P-H) 2473 (1884).

145 As to the relation between GATT 1947 and United States law, see J H Jackson, "The General Agreement on Tariffs and Trade in United States Law" (1967) 66 *Mich. L. Rev.* 250.

146 W Aceves, "Lost Sovereignty? The Implications of the Uruguay Round Agreements" (1995) 19 *Fordham Int'l L. J.* 427–474, 474.

First, Congress made absolutely clear that the Uruguay Round Agreements are not self executing and, thus, cannot be invoked against domestic law:

> "[No] provision of any of the Uruguay Round Agreements, nor the application of any such provision to any person or circumstance, that is inconsistent with any law of the United States shall have effect".[147]

The clause reflects the Congressional view that necessary changes in federal law, in order to conform with the WTO agreements, should be specifically approved and enacted by itself instead of provided for in a blank pre-emption of federal statutes by those agreements.[148]

Second, while authorising the Executive to issue regulations for the implementation of provisions of the URAA,[149] Congress limited any potential effects of the Act itself in US domestic law. The Act makes clear that nothing in it shall be construed to amend or modify any law of the United States, including any law relating to the protection of human, animal, or plant life or health; the protection of the environment; the protection of worker safety; or to limit any authority conferred under any law of the United States—including Section 301 of the Trade Act of 1974—unless specifically provided for in the URAA itself.[150] These limited effects of the WTO Agreements and the URAA upon domestic law of the United States are important because many federal laws which may violate international agreements are left unaffected by the implementing act.[151]

The URAA provisions also reflect congressional intent that the United States should adopt a unilateral trade policy, in violation of the international trade legal system, if necessary. Thus the preservation of its unfair trade instruments, such as Section 301 of the 1974 Trade Act, was perceived by Congress as a question of national sovereignty.[152] At the same time, such limits on the impact of WTO agreements on US domestic law ensure the opportunity for America to influence the international trading system. By allowing the violation of international law, if necessary, Congress provides the Executive with a powerful instrument whereby the United States may use its huge economic muscle to influence the development of the international trading system.

Third, Congress tried to guarantee its sovereignty by establishing strict rules on the policies which the United States should pursue in WTO *fora* and especially in the Dispute Settlement Mechanism.[153] Congress ensured that should

147 Section 102 (a)(1) URAA.

148 Statement of Administrative Action, *supra* n. 123, at 670.

149 Section 103(a) URAA.

150 Section 102(a)(2) URAA. The Statement of Administrative Action provides for an express list of federal environmental and health measures which, among others, are not amended or modified by the Act. See Statement of Administrative Action, *supra* n. 123, at 687.

151 In contrast, Article XVI (4) of the Agreement Establishing the WTO makes clear that each Contracting Party must ensure the conformity of its laws, regulations and administrative procedures with its obligations as provided in the WTO annexed agreements.

152 See J H Bello and A Holmer, "US Trade Law Policy Series No 24: Dispute Resolution in the New World Trade Organization, Concerns and Net Benefits" (1994) 28(4) *Int'l Law*. 1095–1104.

153 Sections 122, 123, 124, 125 and 126 URAA.

the Dispute Settlement Body find that a regulation or practice of the United States administration to be inconsistent with WTO law, such administrative actions may only be changed, if Congress is first consulted, a specific administrative procedure followed, and appropriate opportunity for public comment provided.[154]

Fourth, with regard to the issues that the URAA regulated, the United States took a minimalist approach. If the domestic provisions affected by the URAA were not in clear violation of the WTO agreements, as the US interpreted them, then Congress took no legislative action. Where Congress was unhappy with the international agreements, it generally took some measure to force Executive action or to narrow the scope of such provisions.[155]

Despite its broad powers, in the regulation of international trade, as in almost all other legislative issues, Congress acts as a decentralised institution. The implementation of the NAFTA in 1993 and the failure to re-enact fast track in 1997, when the Democratic party (the majority party in the NAFTA process) could not follow its own President, illustrate the limits to centralised leadership within Congress on matters concerning foreign trade.[156] Congressmen are often more concerned with their domestic demands than with following the main lead of their party. The opportunities to pass trade legislation on its own without making a political and institutional deal with the Executive are, in practice, low.[157] The enactment of foreign trade laws in Congress must go through the same burdensome procedure as any other domestic issue. This implies that by delegating powers to the President or in creating *ad hoc* procedures like fast track, Congress asserts its powers in international trade. Delegation has two faces. It reflects the reaching of a consensus within a decentralised Congress. Yet it also creates the political process to make possible such consensus.

2.C.2.b. The Trade Committees in Congress

As with any other legislative issue in Congress, foreign trade is dealt with mainly within committees. The most important committees for the regulation of international trade are the Ways and Means Committee of the House of Representatives and the Senate's Finance Committee, the so called College of

[154] Section 123(g) URAA. Special rules apply for the regulations and practices of the International Trade Commission. See Section 129(a) URAA; see also G N Horlick, "WTO Dispute Settlement and the Dole Commission" (1995) 29(6) *J. World Trade* 45. These provisions were complemented by the political compromise under the Dole Commission whereby a commission of federal appellate judges would monitor the WTO dispute settlement decisions. The agreement, however never became law.

[155] In this sense, see Chapter III, Section A, on the implementation of the R&D Subsidies provisions of the Agreement on Subsidies and Countervailing Measures.

[156] See B Loomis, *The Contemporary Congress* (New York, St. Martin's Press, 1996), 135.

[157] This is not to say, however, that Congress if left on its own, would be protectionist on the whole. See Carter and Eden, "Who Makes US Trade Policy", *supra* n. 103, at 93.

Cardinals.[158] Both Committees are considered to be extremely powerful and are high in the ranking of Congressmen's preferences.[159]

While both committees have specific subcommittees for foreign commerce, in the Senate, most of the international trade issues are dealt with at the full Finance Committee level. The jurisdiction of the Ways and Means and the Finance committees over foreign trade ranges from the regulation of tariff affairs, to the regulation of non-tariff barriers such as quotas and standards, regulation of unfair trade practices such as dumping, subsidisation, or counterfeiting, the provision of temporary relief from import competition and adjustment assistance, providing for bilateral and multilateral trade agreements with foreign trade partners, and the responsibility for authorising and overseeing the departments and agencies charged with the implementation of the trade laws and programs.[160]

The members of the Finance and the Ways and Means committees do not necessarily represent the views of their houses as a whole. Instead, as a result of the American electoral system, they tend to have close links with particular protectionist or free trade interests and favour those of their political or local constituencies. But as globalisation has tended to place a stronger emphasis on a wide variety of domestic issues, there has been an increasing conflict of jurisdictions between the international trade committees and the other committees of the House and the Senate.[161] This was made clear in the Uruguay Round implementation process where they had to compete with many different committees dealing with a wide range of domestic issues. Nevertheless, the House Ways and Means Committee and the Senate Finance Committee, and the interests they represent, continue to control most of the international trade policy-making process in Congress. This is particularly the case in the operation of the fast track procedure for the negotiation and implementation of international trade agreements.

2.C.2.c. Congress and Trade Policy

Congress is a stage where congressmen try to perform a trade drama in the hope that their proposals will most likely lose their force in the end. Congress is

[158] United States Senate, *GATT Implementation Legislation: Hearings on S. 2467 Before the Committee on Commerce, Science and Transportation*, 103rd Cong., 2nd Sess (1994).

[159] As to the allocation of seats within the Ways and Means Committee in the 106 Congress see <http://www.house.gov./ways-means/>. As to the allocation of seats in the Senate Finance Committee see <http://www.senate.gov/committee/finance.html>.

[160] See Committee on Ways and Means, US House of Representatives, *Overview and Compilation of US Trade Statutes*, 1997 Edition, 105th Congress 1st Session (Washington, US Government Printing Office, 25 June 1997), page V, available at <http://www.house.gov/ways-means/>.

[161] S Charnovitz, *supra* n. 20; see also *The Future of the President's Authority to Negotiate International Trade Agreements after NAFTA and the Uruguay Round: What Should Congress Delegate?, 293 Proceedings of the 88th Annual Meeting of the American Society of International Law*, Washington DC (6–9 April 1994).

characterised by a "cry and sigh" syndrome.[162] It is constantly sending out protectionist and unilateral threats in the hope that this will induce the Executive and foreign countries to take some action. Congress sees its trade bills as a way to send a message to the Executive and to the world.[163] This will sometimes imply that some protectionist or unilateral measure will pass. But, in fact, Congress has remained remarkably biased in favour of free trade and has, until now, accepted to delegate powers to the President with which to negotiate free trade agreements.[164]

However, legislative practice on trade shows that Congress considers unfair trade instruments as the price to be paid for trade openness.[165] Every time Congress has addressed the opening of the American market, the protectionist discourse has focused on unfair trade instruments. The American consensus on international trade has meant free trade complemented by *ad hoc* protectionism in the form of unfair trade instruments. The words of US International Trade Commissioner Bragg are illustrative:

> "In deciding how to deal with issues of import competition, our society has struck a balance in favour of open markets, while providing a limited safety valve in the form of the unfair trade laws, to allow domestic industries injured by unfair import practices to seek relief."[166]

Over the years, Congress has developed and worked on its historically rooted anti-dumping rules, countervailing laws and Presidential retaliation powers (Section 301) and accumulated an immense trade war arsenal. The pattern of implementing new features in unfair trade instruments is nearly always the same. It consists of groups of legislators starting by unfurling colourful excesses in order to gain the attention of both the Executive and foreign nations.[167] Meanwhile, the specialised aids and trade lawyers of the Congressional staff contrive less flashy technical changes and try to reach an agreement with the bureaucrats of the Executive by striking out the indelicacies. Thereafter, final agreements are reached behind closed doors in the committees and in the House and Senate conference.

[162] See R Pastor, "The Cry and Sigh Syndrome: Congress and Trade Policy" in Allen Schick (ed.), *supra* n. 17, 159–195, 61.

[163] Gorlin, *supra* n. 95, at 64.

[164] L Santos, "Trade Politics and the American Congress" (1995) 29(6) *J. World Trade* 74–78.

[165] As to the different US trade laws see Committee on Ways and Means, US House of Representatives, *Overview and Compilation of US Trade Statutes*, *supra* n. 160, pages 59–150, available at <http://www.house.gov/ways-means/>.

[166] See "Views of Commissioner Bragg", in International Trade Commission, *Economic Effects of Anti-dumping and Countervailing Duty Orders and Suspension Agreements* (Dissenting), Publication 2900 (1995) (Executive Summary [1]), available at <http://www.usitc.gov>.

[167] P Nivola, "Trade Policy: Refereeing the Playing Field" in Thomas E. Mann (ed.), *supra* n. 17, at 201–253, 239.

2.C.3. The Executive and the Independent Agencies in the United States' International Trade Policy Making Process

2.C.3.a. The Trade Powers of the President

The powers of the President to deal with international trade matters are diffuse and unclear. The best way to understand the abstraction of these powers is to start by following the classification of Presidential powers which Justice Jackson made in his concurring opinion in *Youngstown Sheet & Tube Co. v. Sawyer*, where the Supreme Court was asked to rule on the constitutionality of a Presidential seizure of steel mills; an action arguably based on the President's powers in foreign affairs. The Court held the Presidential seizure unconstitutional as it was an act against the express will of Congress. Further it considered that such domestic action could not be based on any express or implied exclusive Presidential powers in foreign affairs. In his concurring opinion, Justice Jackson sketched the possible constitutional basis of Presidential actions:

> "When the President acts pursuant to an express or implied authorisation of Congress, his authority is at its maximum, for it includes all that he possesses in his own right plus all that Congress can delegate. In these circumstances, and in these only, he may be said to personify the federal sovereignty. If the act is held unconstitutional under these circumstances, it usually means that the Federal Government as an undivided whole lacks power . . .
>
> When the President acts in absence of either a congressional grant or denial of authority, he can only rely upon his own independent powers, but there is a zone of twilight in which he and Congress may have concurrent authority, or in which its distribution is uncertain. Therefore, congressional inertia, indifference or quiescence may sometimes, at least as a practical matter, enable, if not invite measures on independent presidential responsibility. In this area, any actual test of power is likely to depend on the imperatives of events and contemporary imponderables rather than on abstract theories of law.
>
> When the President takes measures incompatible with the expressed or implied will of Congress his power is at its lowest ebb for he can rely only upon his own constitutional powers minus any constitutional powers of Congress over the matter. Courts can sustain exclusive presidential control in such a case only by disabling the Congress from acting upon the subject."[168]

The President may constitutionally execute the following acts. First, he may take a measure on the basis of his exclusive constitutional powers. In such case, the President may contradict the express will of Congress. Second, he may perform an act on the basis of concurrent powers with Congress. Third, he may take a measure in an area where the distribution of powers between the two branches is unclear. In the latter two categories, the silence or acquiescence of Congress may imply an authorisation to the President to act. But action

[168] *Youngstown Sheet & Tube Co. et al.* v. *Sawyer*, *supra* n. 46 (concurring opinion of Justice Jackson).

contrary to the express will of Congress will render the measure controversial. Fourth, he may take a measure on the basis not of his powers but of those delegated by Congress. Finally, he may hypothetically take a measure on the basis of both his powers and those delegated by Congress. In no case may the Executive take an action against the express prohibition of the Constitution.

The starting point is that the President has no inherent powers to regulate domestically international trade.[169] The powers of the President are dealt with in Article II of the US Constitution, which does not provide for any express Presidential powers to regulate domestically foreign trade. However, Article II, Section 1 of the US Constitution provides that the Executive power is vested in the President who must take care that the laws are faithfully executed. The Executive power is given in general terms, strengthened by specific terms where emphasis is regarded as appropriate, and limited by direct expression in the Constitution where limitation is needed.[170] This Executive power has been interpreted as resulting in shared responsibilities over matters of international trade.[171] The President's constitutional duty to take care that the law is fully executed would also be a source of Presidential powers in international trade, as such law may imply acts of Congress as well as trade treaties and international trade law. Furthermore, a long continued Executive practice, known to and acquiesced in by Congress, raises a presumption that a Presidential action has been taken pursuant to Congress' consent.[172] Thus, privileged by its capacity to take faster and more effective action than Congress, over the years, and especially since the Second World War, the Executive has gradually increased its powers in foreign trade as in many other areas.

The President plays a major role in foreign affairs: he is the Commander in Chief of the army and navy;[173] he has the power to make treaties, by and with the advice and consent of the Senate and provided two thirds of the Senators present concur;[174] he can nominate and appoint ambassadors, by and with the advice and consent of the Senate;[175] and receive ambassadors and other public ministers.[176] The President is the only voice of the nation in the external sphere and Congress is powerless to invade the field of international negotiations.[177]

[169] *Dooley* v. *United States*, 182 U.S. 222; 21 S. Ct. 762; 1901 U.S. LEXIS 1227 (1901); see also Lincoln v. *United States*; *Warner Barnes and Company* v. *United States*, 197 U.S. 419; 25 S. Ct. 455; 1905 U.S. LEXIS 1189 (1905); see also *United States* v. *Yoshida International, Inc.*, 63 C.C.P.A. 15, 22; 526 F. 2d. 560; 1975 CCPA LEXIS 119 (United States Court of Customs and Patents Appeals 1975).

[170] *Myers, Administratrix* v. *United States*, 272 U.S. 52; 47 S. Ct. 21; 1926 U.S. LEXIS 35 (1926).

[171] J Linearly, "International Trade Relations and the Separation of Powers Under the United States Constitution" (1995) *Dick. J. Int'l L.* 203–239, 224.

[172] *Dames & Moore* v. *Reagan, Secretary of Treasury, et al.*, 453 U.S. 654, 686; 101 S. Ct. 2972; 1981 U.S. LEXIS 44 (1981).

[173] Article II, Section 2, clause 1, US Constitution.

[174] Article II, Section 2, clause 2, ibid.

[175] Ibid.

[176] Article II, Section 2, clause 3, ibid.

[177] *United States* v. *Curtiss-Wright Export Corp. et al.*, 299 U.S. 304; 57 S. Ct. 216; 1936 U.S. LEXIS 968 (1936).

The President can negotiate with the government of foreign countries upon any subject at any time. He may also sign agreements, such signature meaning only that the compacts conform to what has been negotiated.[178] Furthermore, it is considered that the President has authority to administer and interpret the agreements, so long as he does not amend them, as well as to terminate, but not to abrogate, them.[179] As the regulation of foreign commerce cannot be exercised without relations with other countries and the President is the sole voice of the United States with regard to external relations, any regulation of foreign commerce through international agreement implies that Congress must share its commerce powers with the Executive. Thus, the move towards multilateralism in international trade enhances the powers of the Executive.[180]

The factual increase of Presidential powers in the regulation of foreign commerce has benefited from a parallel trend whereby the Executive has become more active in foreign affairs, with the acquiescence of Congress and the tolerance of the courts.[181] The President may enter into Executive agreements with foreign nations, without the advice and consent of the Senate, if the matters of the agreement fall within the scope of either his inherent or delegated powers.[182] The President has inherent powers to recognise, establish diplomatic relations and enter into agreements with foreign governments for the adjustment of the mutual claims of such governments and the United States as against one another, without the advice and consent of the Senate, as required in the case of treaties.[183] Provided they are within the inherent powers of the President, such Executive agreements may supersede prior domestic federal law, as well as state law.[184] In general, the President may have some powers to bind the United States in international trade matters through Executive agreements as long as such commitments do not contradict prior federal statutes and provided Congress is silent on them. Furthermore, the President has enhanced his power in foreign trade through legal subterfuge, such as voluntary restraint agreements. By these instruments, the Executive and foreign producers reach a gentlemen's compromise whereby the former promises that it will not, in principle, take any trade measures, such as anti-dumping and countervailing action, as long as the

[178] Jackson, *supra* n. 103, at 71.

[179] M Glennon, *Constitutional Diplomacy* (Princeton, Princeton University Press, 1990), mainly at 130–160.

[180] M Karns, "Multilateral Diplomacy and Trade Policy: The United States and the GATT" in M Karns and K Mingst (eds.), *The United States and Multilateral Institutions* (London, Unwin Hyman, 1990), 141–175.

[181] H Koh, "Why the President (Almost) Always Wins in Foreign Affairs: Lessons of the Iran-Contra Affair" (1988) 97(7) *Yale L. J.* 1255–1342; see also K Chapman, "Separation of Powers and Unilateral Executive Action: The Constitutionality of President Clinton's Mexican Loan Initiative" (1996) 26 *GA. J. Int'l & Comp. L.* 163–185.

[182] *Robert Dole* v. *Jimmy Carter, President of the United States of America*, 444 F. Supp. 1065; 1977 U.S. Dist. LEXIS 12090 (United States District Court for the District of Kansas 1977).

[183] *United States* v. *Belmont et al., Executors, supra* n. 114; see also *United States* v. *Pink, Superintendent of Insurance of the State of New York, et al., supra* n. 114.

[184] *Paul H. Coplin et al.* v. *United States*, 6 Cl. Ct. 115; 1984 U.S. Cl. Ct. LEXIS 1356 (United States Claims Court 1984).

producers do not export more than a certain quantity or do so above a specified price.[185] Since these instruments are only negotiations without binding legal force, in practice, they may be negotiated by the President without Congressional control.[186]

However, when administering international trade, the President cannot in any circumstances go against the express will of Congress, either unilaterally or through the acceptance international agreements of any kind.[187] The regulation of foreign commerce is a matter for Congress and when Congress has acted, the Executive may not enforce different regulations or enter into international agreements that contravene Congressional will.[188] In the same way that international trade agreements enhanced the powers of the Executive in foreign commerce, the increasing assertiveness of Congress—as a result of globalisation whereby the line between the external and domestic spheres has blurred—has limited the possibilities of Executive action in the external sphere.

2.C.3.b. Congressional Delegations of Powers: The US Trade Agencies

In practice, in foreign trade the Executive and the independent agencies act mostly on the basis of a Congressional delegation of powers. Through the mechanism of delegation, Congress tries to solve the dichotomy between the need for efficiency in the management of foreign commerce and the maintenance of its own constitutional prerogatives. The constitutionality of this delegation of powers in matters of foreign trade has been well established by the courts. Congress may delegate powers to the Executive or to other branches of government.[189] But delegation must fulfil two conditions. The powers delegated must be of a nature recognised as appropriate for delegation; as distinguished from a power that implicitly only Congress can exercise. Congress cannot delegate its legislative powers but can only authorise the Executive to develop regulations applying the basic standards of the law to the specific case. "This principle is vital to the integrity and maintenance of the system of government ordained by the Constitution."[190] It cannot be exempted, even by extraordinary conditions, because these neither create nor enlarge constitutional power, and, thus, they

[185] These agreements, however, are now prohibited by Paragraph 22(b) of the WTO Agreement on Safeguard Measures.

[186] *Consumers Union of US* v. *Henry Kissinger, Secretary of State, et al.*, 165 U.S. App. D.C. 75; 506 F.2d 136, 143; 1974 U.S. App. LEXIS 6537 (United States Court of Appeals for the District of Columbia 1974). But the President often, in fact, enters into such agreements as a result of Congressional pressures. See Note, "Voluntary Restraint Agreements and Democratic Decision-Making" (1991) 31 *Virginia J. Int'l L.* 281–319.

[187] *Youngstown Sheet & Tube Co. et al.* v. *Sawyer*, *supra* n. 46.

[188] *United States* v. *Guy W. Capps Inc*, 204 F.2d 655, 660; 1953 U.S. App. LEXIS 4020 (1953); see also *United States* v. *Guy Capps, Inc.*, 348 U.S. 296; 75 S. Ct. 326; 1955 U.S. LEXIS 1402 (1955) (affirmed but on different grounds).

[189] *Wayman and another* v. *Southard and another*, 23 U.S. 1; 1825 U.S. LEXIS 217 (1825), see also *Buttfield* v. *Stranahan*, *supra* n. 129.

[190] *Panama Refining Co. et al.* v. *Ryan et al*; *Amazon Corp et al.* v. *Ryan et al.*, 293 U.S. 388, 424; 55 S. Ct. 241; 1935 U.S. LEXIS 251 (1934).

cannot justify governmental action outside the sphere of constitutional authority.[191] Second, the delegation must set forth standards that are sufficiently clear to ensure that the delegate will carry out Congressional will.[192] Congress must tell the President what he can do by prescribing a standard which defines his discretion and guarantees that any authorised action he takes will tend to promote the legislative purpose.[193] The courts will look at the statute to see whether Congress has declared a policy with respect to the regulated subject, whether it has set up a standard for the President's action and whether it has required any finding by the President in the exercise of the authority to take a decision.[194]

While the President has maximum discretionary powers in international trade when he acts pursuant to an act of Congress, he must comply with the conditions and standards set forth in the delegation and show compliance in the grounds of his act.[195] The courts will look at whether the Presidential act falls within the Congressional delegated powers by trying to identify the intent of Congress.[196] But in practice the degree to which Congress allows the President or the administering agencies discretion, by defining more or less stringent standards, dictates, in large measure, the scope and threshold of judicial review in international trade.[197] Acquiescence by Congress in an administrative practice on the basis of the interpretation of a Congressional delegation may be inferred from Congressional silence during a period of years.[198]

The delegation of powers in international trade from Congress to the Executive goes back to the nineteenth century.[199] However its expansion occurred after 1934, starting with the Reciprocal Trade Agreements Act when Congress shifted its attention from individual tariffs to general trade policy. Despite the loss of Presidential prestige due to the Vietnam war, as well as other scandals and the increase of Congressional assertiveness in foreign commerce resulting from the pressures of globalisation, Congress has continued to delegate powers to the President. Countervailing duty law, anti-dumping law and

[191] *A. L. A. Schechter Poultry Corp. et al.* v. *United States*, 295 U.S. 495; 55 S. Ct. 837; 1935 U.S. LEXIS 1088 (1935).

[192] *Field* v. *Clark*; *Boyd* v. *United States*; *Sternbach* v. *United States*, 143 U.S. 649; 12 S. Ct. 495; 1982 U.S. LEXIS 2046 (1891); see also *J. W. Hampton, Jr., & Company* v. *United States*, 276 U.S. 394, 409; 48 S. Ct. 348; 1928 U.S. LEXIS 284 (1928) (where the Supreme Court upheld a Congressional delegation of power to the President whereby the latter could increase or reduce tariffs in order to equalise the costs of domestic production with the price of the imported product).

[193] E Eichmann and G Horlick, "Political Questions in International Trade: Judicial Review of Section 301" (1988) 10 *Mich. J. Int'l L.* 735, 737.

[194] *Panama Refining Co. et al.* v. *Ryan et al*; *Amazon Corp et al.* v. *Ryan et al.*, *supra* n. 190.

[195] *Dames & Moore* v. *Reagan, Secretary of Treasury, et al.*, *supra* n. 172.

[196] *United States* v. *Yoshida International, Inc.*, *supra* n. 169.

[197] F Morrison and R Hudec, "Judicial Protection of Individual Rights Under the Foreign Trade Laws of the United States", in M Hilf and E U Petersmann (eds.), *supra* n. 107, at 126; see also J Restani, "Judicial Review in International Trade: Its Role in the Balance Between Delegation by Congress and Limitation of Executive Discretion" (1988) 37 *Am. U. L Rev.* 1075–1086.

[198] *Norwegian Nitrogen Products Co.* v. *United States*, 288 U.S. 294, 314; 53 S. Ct. 350; 1933 U.S. LEXIS 958 (1933).

[199] For a detailed account of the history of this delegation, see *Field* v. *Clark*; *Boyd* v. *United States*; *Sternbach* v. *United States*, *supra* n. 192.

Section 301 are examples of Congressional delegation of powers in international trade to the Executive or to independent agencies.[200] These delegations have allowed the US to play a uniform and effective role in the international trading system.

However, delegation is a two way deal. By establishing the constitutionally required standards of Executive action Congress is actually controlling United States' trade policy. First, Congress does not lock itself out of the business of managing international trade law but has gone into the business of regulating what the Executive can and cannot do.[201] Moreover, by enhancing the rights of private parties to petition the administration and challenge decisions, Congress asserts its control over the Executive. American unfair trade laws are much more detailed and provide for greater private party rights, not simply because of the American legalistic culture but also because such laws reflect the tension between Congress and the Executive in their co-operation over regulating foreign trade.

Second, delegation allows Congress, a decentralised institution, to act. Delegation reflects a consensus in Congress. But the process of delegating power to the President sets in motion a mechanism which allows that wide consensus in international trade to actually crystallise. While no delegation would be possible were there not a consensus in Congress on the principles and basic framework on which the delegated power must be exercised, the process of delegation ensures both the availability and the taking into account of all legislative actors. Thus the process of delegation ensures that Congress can count on the President when it enacts the statute delegating powers. The President will not veto nor hinder a statute which gives him powers to act. Likewise, delegation implies that there will be a *quid pro quo* between the different interests in international trade. In practice, delegation has reflected a will for trade openness but with fair trade instruments as the price to pay.

Third, delegation allows Congress to control the creation and development of the Executive agencies and independent commissions dealing with international trade. Through delegation, Congress not only maintains control of its powers but, moreover, is capable of changing and monitoring the Executive's agenda by controlling the administrative agencies that take part in the policy-making process within the Executive. As a result, the International Trade Commission, the International Trade Administration of the Department of Commerce and the United States Trade Representative are dependent on Congress and, in fact, keep very close links with its Finance Committee and the Ways and Means Committee.

[200] R Baldwin and M Moore, "Political Aspects of the Administration of the Trade Remedy Laws" in Richard Boltuck and R Litan (eds.), *Down in the Dumps: Administration of the Unfair Trade Laws* (Washington, The Brookings Institution, 1991), 253–280.

[201] M Bailey, J Goldstein and B Weingast, "The Institutional Roots of American Trade Policy" (1997) 49 *World Politics* 309–338, 335.

The principal agency in international trade is the office of the United States Trade Representative.[202] It controls most of the trade policy process other than countervailing and anti-dumping duties which are within the jurisdiction of the Department of Commerce and the International Trade Commission.[203] It is a cabinet level agency within the Executive Office of the President.

The USTR is the most politically delicate of all the Presidential staff units. As a result of its close links with Congress, the different Presidents have viewed the USTR with some suspicion.[204] Its creation, the result of a political compromise between the President and Congress during the adoption of the 1962 Trade Expansion Act, was one of the earliest manifestations of Congress' will to limit the powers of the President in trade policy matters. Congress wished to transfer all delegation of powers from the State Department, which it considered to be too free-trade biased and concerned solely with the political implications of foreign trade, to the Department of Commerce, which was regarded as much more sympathetic to the concerns of domestic American industry. In the end, the creation by Presidential Executive Order of a Special Trade Representative (STR) as the main broker between the competing domestic, international, political and bureaucratic interests in foreign trade and responsive to both Congress and the Executive, was accepted as a political compromise.[205] As different Presidents tried to get rid or reduce the powers and budget of the STR, Congress, by means of the 1974 Trade Act, repealed President Kennedy's Executive Order and recreated the office as the United States Trade Representative (USTR), making it a statutorily based unit in the EOP and ensuring that the President would not be able to abolish it without the support of the legislature.[206] In 1980, by Executive Order 12188, President Carter authorised the USTR to set and administer overall trade policy.[207]

The USTR acts as the principal trade advisor, negotiator, and spokesperson for the President on trade and related investment matters. Its major areas of responsibility are all matters within the WTO, including the implementation of the Uruguay Round Agreements; trade commodity and direct investment matters dealt with by international institutions such as the OECD and the UNCTAD; export expansion policy; industrial and services trade policy; international commodity agreements and policy; bilateral and multilateral trade and investment issues; trade related intellectual property protection issues and import policy.[208] The agency also has administrative responsibility for the

[202] See <http://www.ustr.gov>.

[203] M Noland, "Chasing Phantoms: The Political Economy of USTR" (1997) 51(3) *Int'l Org.* 365–387, 366.

[204] Se I Destler, "United States Trade Policymaking in the Uruguay Round" in Henry R. Nau (ed.), *Domestic Trade Politics and the Uruguay Round* (New York, Columbia University Press, 1988), 191–208, 193.

[205] J Hart, *supra* n. 57.

[206] Section 141 of the Trade Act of 1974, P.L. 93–618, as amended (repealing Section 241 of the Trade Expansion Act of 1962, P.L. 87–794).

[207] See (http://www.ustr.gov/history/index.html).

[208] See (http://www.ustr.gov/mission/index.html).

Generalised System of Preferences and Section 301 complaints against foreign unfair trade practices, as well as Section 337,[209] and import relief cases under Section 201 (XIX of GATT).[210]

Through a formal inter-agency process, the USTR co-ordinates, and in practice controls, the formulation of the Executive's trade policies.[211] Inter-agency co-ordination is accomplished by the Trade Policy Review Group (TRPG), the Trade Policy Staff Committee (TPSC) and the Trade Policy Committee who are responsible for advising the USTR and the President on major trade policy issues.[212] This inter-agency organisation includes the USTR as chair, the Secretaries of Commerce, State, Treasury, Agriculture and Labour as well as any other agencies which the USTR may consider appropriate.[213] The first tier is the TPSC, which is composed of senior civil servants and supported by more than sixty subcommittees responsible for specialised areas as well as several task forces that work on particular issues. If agreement is not reached within the TPSC, or if particularly significant policy questions are being considered, then the issues are taken up by the TPRG. This is composed of assistant Secretary level officers and the Deputy USTR. Disagreements at the TPRG are referred to the Trade Policy Committee for cabinet level review. Finally, the inter-agency trade policy mechanism ends in the National Economic Council. This body is chaired by the President and composed of the Vice President, most of the Secretaries and the chairmen of the different Presidential staff units. Below the NEC are the NEC Deputies who consider the memoranda from the TPC as well as particularly important controversial trade-related issues. The officers of these committees try to establish a balance between acting as advocates for the interests and politics that their agencies represent, acting as members of the administration and being officials who must work with one another on a wide range of issues.[214]

Despite statutory requirements on the USTR to report to Congress and its political and economic dependence on the legislature,[215] the USTR will not contradict the will of the President who appoints the Representative.[216] However, one way for Congress to make sure that the USTR will not systematically follow the Executive, instead taking other interests into account, has been to require it to consult, on a systematic basis, the private sector. The President,

[209] Section 337 of the Tariff Act of 1930, P.L. 71–361, as amended.

[210] Section 201 of the Trade Act of 1974, P.L 93–618, as amended. The investigations of both Section 337 and Section 201 are carried out, however, by the International Trade Commission. The President with the advice of the USTR takes the final political decision.

[211] Noland, *supra* n. 203, at 366.

[212] Section 242 of the Trade Expansion Act of 1962, P.L. 87–794, as amended.

[213] See *Overview and Compilation of United States Statutes*, *supra* n. 160, at 222.

[214] D Tarullo, *supra* n. 24, 547–628, 596.

[215] Section 141 (c)(1)(F) of the Trade Act of 1974, P.L. 93–618, as amended; see also Section 141 (c)(1)(G) ibid.; Section 141(c)(1)(H) ibid. and Section 161 (c) ibid.

[216] The President appoints the USTR by and with the advice of the Senate. See Section 141 (b)(1) of the Trade Act of 1974, P.L. 93–618, as amended. This procedure follows Article II, Section 2, clause 2 of the Constitution.

through the USTR, must seek information and advice from representative elements of the private and non-federal government sectors in respect of the development, implementation and administration of the trade policy of the United States.[217]

The advisory committee is organised into three levels.[218] The most senior level is the Advisory Committee for Trade Policy and Negotiations (ACTPN); a forty-five member body composed of Presidentially appointed representatives of government, labour, industry, agriculture, small business, service industries, retailers, consumer interests and the general public.[219] The ACTPN meets at the request of the USTR and provides overall guidance on trade policy matters. The second level is composed of policy advisory committees representing overall sectors of the economy. The role of these committees is to advise the government on the impact of the different trade measures on their respective sectors. The lowest level is made up of sector advisory committees consisting of experts from different fields, appointed by the USTR and the Secretary of the relevant department or agency. These committees must provide specific technical information and advice on trade issues involving their particular sector.

The USTR is also required to seek the advice of appointed members of Congress. The Speaker of the House of Representatives and the President of the Senate, upon recommendation of the chairmen of the Ways and Means Committee and the Committee on Finance, must select five members from each of these committees to act as Congressional advisors on trade policy and negotiations.[220] The USTR must keep each advisor currently informed on matters affecting United States trade policy.[221]

Thus, through the USTR, Congress can influence the Executive's overall trade policy. Though the USTR will implement the agenda of the President with regard to international trade, it must, in practice, balance the interests of the different federal agencies, the private sector, Congress and the different States. But the entire structure also allows for the establishment of a broad agenda where different interests may be made compatible.

The International Trade Commission (ITC) was first established as the Tariff Commission with the original purpose of advising the President solely on the possible reduction or increase in tariffs with a view to equalising the price of foreign products with domestic costs of production.[222] Since its origin, the ITC

[217] Section 341 of the Trade Act of 1974, P.L. 93–618, as amended by Section 1631 of the Omnibus Trade and Competitiveness Act of 1988.

[218] See <http://www.ustr.gov/mission/index.html>.

[219] *Overview and Compilation of United States Statutes*, *supra* n. 160, at 229.

[220] Section 161 (a)(1) of the Trade Act of 1974, P.L. 93–618, as amended. Additional Congressional advisors may be appointed for specific trade negotiations. See Section 161(a)(2) ibid.

[221] Section 161(b) ibid.

[222] Title VII of the Omnibus Act to Increase the Revenue and for Other Purposes of 1916, 39 Stat. 795; see also J Dobson, "Two Centuries of Tariffs: The Background and Emergence of the US International Trade Commission" (Washington, *US ITC*, 1976), 85. In 1974, it was renamed the United States International Trade Commission. See Section 171 of the Trade Act of 1974, P.L. 93–618, as amended.

has developed into an independent, quasi-judicial agency headed by six commissioners who are nominated by the President and confirmed by the Senate.[223] No more than three commissioners may be members of the same political party.[224]

The ITC conducts studies, reports and investigations and makes recommendations to the President and Congress on a wide range of international trade issues.[225] It is in charge of making the injury determinations in anti-dumping and countervailing duty investigations.[226] It also assesses whether US industries are being seriously injured by trade imports and can recommend to the President that relief be provided, in the form of increase in tariffs or quotas or adjustment assistance to the domestic industry.[227] It also conducts unfair trade investigations with regard to the counterfeiting of goods.[228] Furthermore, it must advise the President on whether agricultural imports interfere with the price support programs of the US Department of Agriculture. Most importantly, the commission functions as the government's think tank on international trade, conducting objective studies on many trade issues, including nearly every commodity imported to, or exported from, the United States, as well as upon any topic requested by either the President or the Senate Committee on Finance and the House Ways and Means Committee.[229]

Finally, the International Trade Administration (ITA) is the agency of the United States Department of Commerce (DoC) with operational responsibility for the basic non-agricultural trade functions of the US government. It is responsible for export development, commercial representation abroad, the administration of the anti-dumping and countervailing duty laws, export controls, trade adjustment assistance to firms, research and analysis, as well as compliance with international trade agreements to which the United States is a party.[230]

Traditionally, the Treasury Department had been responsible for the administration of countervailing and anti-dumping law. However in 1980, as part of the political deal to implement the Tokyo Round agreements, Congress, in an example of its assertiveness and mistrust of the President in international trade issues, was able to obtain from the Executive a change in the anti-dumping and countervailing administering authority. The competence to administer these laws was taken from the Treasury Department, regarded by Congress as a free-trader, to the DoC which had traditionally defended the interests of domestic industry. This administrative change, together with the strengthening of the statutes and the increase of petitioner rights, resulted in the boom of anti-dumping and countervailing duty investigations during the 1980s.

223 See <http://www.usitc.gov>.

224 Section 330(a) of the Tariff Act of 1930, P.L. 71–361, as amended. See Section 330(c) ibid. As to the internal structure of the US International Trade Commission, see United State International Trade Commission, *Annual Report Fiscal Year 1992*, 30–31 (Washington, US ITC, 1993).

225 *Overview and Compilation of United States Statutes*, *supra* n. 160, at 226.

226 Title VII of the Tariff Act of 1930, P.L. 71–631, as amended.

227 Section 202 of the Trade Act of 1974 of 1974, P.L. 93–618, as amended.

228 337 of the Tariff Act of 1930, P.L. 71–361, as amended.

229 Section 332 ibid.

230 Executive Reorganisation Plan No 3 of 1979.

The Import Administration Department of the ITA deals with anti-dumping and countervailing investigations.[231] Within these investigations it is responsible for the determination of whether the imports are dumped or unfairly subsidised. In a typical year it initiates around 68 antidumping or countervailing investigations, completes approximately 54 preliminary and 33 final determinations, and issues 27 countervailing or anti-dumping duty orders. The investigations cover such products as steel, DRAMs, colour negative photographic paper, portable electronic typewriters, anti-friction bearings, tapered rolled bearings, televisions, cement, etc. In addition, the ITA. conducts numerous reviews, such as sunset, scope and anti-circumvention reviews, to ensure enforcement of the orders.

In its investigations, the ITA takes into account domestic politics and both its own trade policy agenda and that of Executive.[232] While the staff of the ITA have close contacts with the members of the Finance Committee and the Ways and Means Committee in Congress, and must report back to them from time to time, it is however able to pursue what it considers to be the United States' national interest. It will use its powers to administer the unfair trade laws to retaliate against and punish those countries which it considers to have high tariffs or non-tariff barriers. While emulating the protectionist pressures in Congress, the ITA, like the USTR, is able to establish the international trade agenda.[233] Indeed the ITA has historically been a source of international trade law, many of the concepts it created having been later adopted in the international trade arena.[234]

2.C.4. The Procedures to Conclude International Trade Agreements

2.C.4.a. The Treaty Procedure

Generally, there are five basic procedures through which the United States may negotiate and implement legally binding international trade agreements. First, the President may conclude sole Executive agreements, under his inherent powers, without the participation of Congress. Secondly, the United States may enter into an agreement through its constitutionally established treaty procedure. Third, the President may be authorised, pursuant to the terms of a prior agreement, to enter into additional agreements. Fourth, international agreements may be concluded as a Congressional-Executive agreement whereby, in

231 See <http://www.ita.doc.gov>.

232 W Hansen and K O Park, "Nation-State and Pluralistic Decision Making in Trade Policy: The Case of the International Trade Administration" (1995) 39 *Int'l Studies Quarterly* 181–211.

233 D Codevilla, "Discouraging the Practice of What We Preach: Saarstahl I, Inland Steel and the Implementation of the Uruguay Round of GATT 1994" (1995) 3 *Geo. Mason Indep. L. Rev.* 435–472, 445.

234 H Moyer, "How Will the Uruguay Round Change the Practice of Trade Law in the United States? US Institutions, Not the WTO, May Hold the Answer" (1996) 30(3) *J. World Trade* 63–85.

advance, Congress fully authorises the President to enter into certain agreements and those agreements thereafter become both binding international agreements and part of domestic law. Finally, the United States may use a Congressional-Executive agreement whereby any agreements negotiated by the President are subsequently implemented into domestic law by legislative action on the basis of majority approval of both houses in Congress.

The Constitution only provides expressly for the Treaty procedure as a means to enter into international agreements. Article II, Section 2, clause 2 of the US Constitution reads:

> "He [the President] shall have the Power, by and with the Advice and Consent of the Senate, to make Treaties, provided two thirds of the Senators present concur;"

The treaty clause is ambiguous. On the one hand, the phrase "advice and consent" suggests an important role for the Senate. On the other hand, the framers placed the treaty power in Article II of the Constitution; an article dealing with the powers of the President.[235] Though from an historical point of view, the issue is why the President was finally mentioned at all, many interpreters of the Constitution regard the placement of the treaty clause within Article II as the best evidence that the founding fathers intended to give the President a major role in foreign affairs.[236]

As originally conceived, the Senators were to play a major role in the treaty making process. It was to be a sort of senior council to the President providing him with advice on all aspects through the entire treaty making process.[237] But as from the very beginning Presidents found that system totally unworkable, the Senate was relegated to the controversial role of final approval of a treaty once it had been negotiated. Over the years, this often resulted in a lack of co-ordination between the President and the Senate; the latter refusing to accept a treaty that the Executive had negotiated for years. Despite the development of informal procedures of co-operation and co-optation, in practice, the Senate's high level of decentralisation and slow legislative process creates a graveyard for treaties.

In the treaty-making process, the President first negotiates and signs the agreements. The Senate decides thereafter whether to allow Presidential ratification of the treaty and finally the President, with the consent of two thirds of the Senators, ratifies the agreement. When the treaty arrives at the Senate, it can only accept or reject it. Strictly speaking, the Senate may not amend the treaty or impose conditional interpretations. In practice, it can consent to ratification by the President on condition that he amend the text or make a specific interpretation thereof.[238] Once the Senate has accepted the text, the President is free

235 H Sklamberg, "The Meaning of Advice and Consent: The Senate's Constitutional Role in Treatymaking" (1997) 18 *Michigan J. Int'l L.* 445–474, 455.

236 Rakove, *supra* n. 94 at 3.

237 Henkin, *supra* n. 92, at 43.

238 Glennon, *supra* n. 179, at 130.

to adopt, or not, the treaty but if he does adopt it, he must follow the Senators' conditions. In this respect, the legal effects of the Senate's conditions on the instrument of ratification depend upon the response of the other signatory as technically, the US' conditions imply a counter-offer. If the other party accepts the Senate's condition or amendment, both the treaty and the Senate's changes take effect internationally.[239] If the treaty is not self-executing, while Congress cannot refuse to implement it, Congress has often not actually delivered the implementation law which the President was seeking. [240]

Thus the treaty clause presents several problems for the conclusion of international trade agreements.[241] First, the President must obtain the support of two thirds of the Senate.[242] Second, the Senate has both the power and the inclination to amend treaties. Third, the Senate is very slow in approving treaties. Finally, if the treaty is not self-executing, the entire Congress must agree its implementation. This implies a conflict between a domestic democracy and an external democracy; between the powers of the House to legislate domestically and the sole powers of the Senate to accept international agreements.

2.C.4.b. Congressional-Executive Agreements

Congressional-Executive Agreements have been a means to avoid the problems posed by the treaty procedure. They may be achieved either through prior delegation to the President to negotiate and proclaim the results of an agreement, or through posterior Congressional approval of both an agreement and its implementation bill. Congressional-Executive agreements with prior delegation have been used for trade agreements concerning the reciprocal reduction of tariffs. Starting with the 1934 Reciprocal Trade Agreements Act,[243] Congress has continuously delegated the authority to negotiate, conclude and proclaim reciprocal tariff cutting agreements concluded with foreign nations.[244] The constitutional basis for such a process has been considered to be the delegation of powers from Congress to the President. Congress establishes specific guidelines and delegates powers to the President to reduce tariffs as a result of an international agreement where the parties are bound to reduce their tariffs on a reciprocal basis. Thus, although these agreements may have the force of law, it is

[239] Ibid.

[240] Henkin, *supra* n. 97, at 161.

[241] C V Grasstek, "Is the Fast Track Really Necessary?" (1997) 31(2) *J. World Trade* 97–119, 99.

[242] In practice, most trade agreements other than NAFTA, were voted affirmatively by more than two thirds of the Senate. But it is also true that such a vote followed the political deals allowed in the fast track implementation process.

[243] Reciprocal Trade Agreements Act of 1934, P.L. 73–316, 48 Stat. 493 (1934).

[244] The most recent grant of such authority was contained in Section 1102(a) of the Omnibus Trade and Competitiveness Act of 1988, P.L. 100–418. This authority has expired but there are different residual powers both to reduce or increase tariffs contained in several provisions of the Uruguay Round Agreements Act and the North American Free Trade Agreement Implementation Act. See Section 111 of the Uruguay Round Agreements Act, P.L. 103–465, 108 Stat. 4809 (1994); see also Section 201 of the North American Free Trade Agreement Implementation Act, P.L. 103–182.

the Presidential proclamation which changes the domestic law of the United States.[245]

Congress has refused to grant authority to the President to negotiate international agreements on non-tariff trade barriers on the basis of prior delegation Congressional-Executive agreements. This has been the result of the development of two phenomena. First, since the 1960s, Congress has increasingly reasserted its powers in international trade in response to what it considered a Presidency which was too biased toward free trade and lacking in prestige. Second, as globalisation has emphasised the impact of international trade on the American domestic sphere, Congress has become more and more concerned with international agreements which increasingly regulate not international but rather domestic issues. With the Trade Expansion Act of 1962,[246] Congress initiated a new trade regime with the delegation of powers to negotiate international agreements on non-tariff trade barriers through Congressional-Executive agreements which thereafter required a simple majority in both houses of Congress.[247] Though requiring a simple majority in both houses the procedure would be much easier, and for some more democratic, than the need for an affirmative vote of two thirds of the Senate.

The constitutionality of Congressional-Executive agreements is not clear, as the Constitution makes no reference to them. Understanding the debate on their constitutionality requires, first of all, distinguishing the debate on Congressional-Executive agreements with prior delegation, which mainly refer to the reduction or increase of tariffs, from those with posterior approval which refer to non-tariff trade barriers. Thereafter, it is important to take into account that the different arguments are based on two different, and to a certain extent contradictory features, of United States constitutional trade law. On the one hand, there is the argument concerning whether the Constitution of 1788 should be reinterpreted as to accommodate to America's democratic government at the beginning of the third millennium. On the other hand, there is the argument concerning whether the democracy for the governance of international trade issues should be parallel to that of domestic matters.

As regards Congressional-Executive Agreements with prior delegation, despite complaints over the lack of democratic legitimacy, from the very beginning neither the President, Congress nor the courts have questioned the constitutionality of such agreements.[248] The Supreme Court has refused to discuss the constitutionality of such procedures; instead holding that they are not treaties

245 *Sacilor, Acieries et Laminoirs de Lorraine, et al.* v. *United States et al.*; *Vallourec* v. *United States et al.*, 9 C.I.T. 280, 283; 613 F. Supp. 364; 1985 Ct. Int'l. Trade LEXIS 1567 (Court of International Trade 1985); see also *American Bitumuls & Asphalt Co. et al.* v. *United States*, 37 Cust. Ct. 58; 146 F. Supp. 703, 708; 1956 Cust. Ct. LEXIS 14 (1956).

246 Trade Expansion Act of 1962, P.L. 87–794.

247 H Koh, "Congressional Controls on Presidential Trade Policymaking after *I.N.S.* v. *Chadha*" (1986) 18 *N. Y. U. J. Int'l L. & Pol'y* 1191–1233, 1197.

248 D Tarullo, "Law and Politics in Twentieth Century Tariff History" (1986) 34 *UCLA L. Rev.* 285–370, 352.

for the purpose of requiring the advice and consent of two thirds of the Senate, though they are treaties for all other purposes.[249] Lower courts have upheld similar Congressional-Executive agreements, provided Congress has enunciated a policy or objective or given reasons for seeking the aid of the President and has specified when the powers conferred may be utilised by establishing a standard or intelligible principle which is sufficient to make it clear what action is proper.[250]

However, it could be argued that the previous case law refers only to tariff agreements or matters having a limited impact on the domestic sphere. Thus while Congress can delegate powers to reduce tariffs on the basis of reciprocal agreements, the regulation of non-tariff barriers through international agreements can only be accepted by two thirds of the Senate.[251] Those denying the constitutionality of Congressional-Executive agreements concerning non-tariff barriers divide their argument into two steps.[252] First, it is argued that such agreements can only be considered as treaties. If the constitutional drafters intended to give any meaning to a treaty that concept should at least include agreements with such political considerations, and implying such strong economic integration, as those evidenced by NAFTA and the WTO agreements.[253] While the US Constitution would allow for Congressional-Executive Agreements, it would distinguish these from treaties on the basis of the degree of constraint upon US sovereignty. International agreements that directly and significantly constrain the law-making authority of the US should be considered as treaties and therefore be submitted to the Senate for ratification on the basis of a two-thirds majority.[254] The treaty clause requirements would not disappear simply because we live in an era where almost anything can be called

[249] *B. Altman & Co.* v. *United States*, 224 U.S. 583; 32 S. Ct. 593; 1912 U.S. LEXIS 2328 (1912); see also *Weinberger, Secretary of Defense, et al.* v. *Rossi et al.*, *supra* n. 137; see also *Field* v. *Clark*; *Boyd* v. *United States*; *Sternbach* v. *United States*, *supra* n. 192.

[250] *Star-Kist Foods, Inc.* v. *United States (Bruno Scheidt, Inc., Party in Interest)*, 47 C.C.P.A. 52; 275 F.2d. 472; 1959 CCPA LEXIS 128 (United States Court of Customs and Patent Appeals 1959); see also *American Bitumuls & Asphalt Co. et al.* v. *United States*, *supra* n. 245.

[251] The issue has been decided by a District Federal Court in Alabama. See *Made in the USA Foundation* v. *US*, 56 F.Supp.2nd 1226 (1999) (upholding the use of a Congressional-Executive Agreement for the conclusion of NAFTA).

[252] *Complaint filed by the USA Foundation and the United Steelworkers of America in the United States District Court for the Northern District of Alabama*, available at <http://www.usawa.org>; see also Joel D Joseph, "Fast-Track Legislation is Unconstitutional", available at <http://www.madeusa.org/fast-track.htm)>

[253] L H Tribe, "Taking Text and Structure Seriously: Reflection on Free-Form Method in Constitutional Interpretation" (1995) 108 *Harvard L. Rev.* 1221–1303, 1266–1270.

[254] See Letter from Anne-Marie Slaughter, Professor of Law, Harvard Law School, in United States Senate, *GATT Implementing Legislation: Hearings on S. 2467 Before the Committee on Commerce, Science and Transportation, United States Senate*, 103rd Cong. 2nd Sess. 286–290, 286 (1994). Professor Slaughter suggests four factors on the basis of which it could be possible to determine whether an international agreement should be considered as a treaty in US domestic law: (1) the degree of constraint on US sovereignty; (2) the scope of the constraint; (3) the duration of the constraint; and (4) the solemnity and import of the agreement when viewed from the perspective of the international legal system.

commerce.[255] Second, treaties may only and exclusively be concluded through the treaty clause. Structural considerations outside Article I, Section 8 limit congressional authority.[256] The fact that Congress has the power to regulate commerce through Article I does not mean that it can make international trade agreements because there is a separate provision establishing detailed procedures for the conclusion of these treaties.[257] The possibility of Congress enacting all necessary and proper measures to regulate commerce should not imply that it can by-pass the treaty procedure.[258] Efficiency and past experience cannot change the meaning of the constitution.[259] Thus their main arguments are the denial of a parallelism between domestic powers and external powers and a refusal to accept a re-interpretation of the Constitution without an express constitutional amendment.

Those arguing in favour of the constitutionality of the Congressional-Executive procedure for the conclusion of international trade agreements base their arguments on completely opposite principles.[260] First, they argue the Constitution must be re-read in accordance with the new realities of the American democracy at the end of the twentieth century.[261] The processes that legitimised the Congressional-Executive agreement were merely variations on the institutional and doctrinal themes developed by the New Deal during the 1930s. It would be impossible to put into question these agreements without questioning the validity of many of the other modern interpretations and theories of the US Constitution, on which a great part of the modern US government is based. Even if neither Congress nor the President alone have authority to conclude international trade agreements, together they can embody the national sovereignty in international relations and can exercise all the powers inherent in such sovereignty; including the powers to make international agreements.[262] Put together, the powers of Congress and the President would be broad enough to deal with any issue in foreign affairs.[263] If neither the Senate nor the President exclude the possibility of using the Congressional-Executive procedure, such

[255] United States Senate, *GATT Implementing Legislation*, *supra* n. 254, *at* 317–339.

[256] The Supreme Court has held that the division of power between the three branches of government is violated where one branch of government invades the territory of another, regardless of whether the encroached upon branch approves the encroachment. See *New York* v. *United States*, 505 U.S. 144, 180–183; 112 S. Ct. 2408; 1992 U.S. LEXIS 3693 (1992).

[257] Tribe, *supra* n. 253, at 1250–1264.

[258] See Statement of Laurence Tribe, Professor of Law, Harvard Law School, in United States Senate, *GATT Implementing Legislation*, *supra* n. 254, at 290–312; see also E Borchard, "Treaties and Executive Agreements—A Reply" (1945) 54 *Yale L. J.* 611–664, 625.

[259] In this respect, see *Immigration and Naturalization Service* v. *Chadha et al.*, *supra* n. 46.

[260] Jackson, *supra* n. 103, at 74; see also Henkin, *supra* n. 92, at 60; see also J Lang, "The Operation of the Fast Track Implementation Process" in Baker and J Bialos (eds.), *The North American Free Trade Agreement: Issues, Options, Implications* (Washington, American Bar Association, 1992), 2–20, 4.

[261] B Ackerman and D Golove, "Is NAFTA Constitutional?" (1995) 108 *Harvard L. Rev.* 799–929.

[262] In this sense, see *United States* v. *Curtiss-Wright Export Corp. et al.*, *supra* n. 177.

[263] M McDougal and A Lans, "Treaties and Congressional-Executive or Presidential Agreements: Interchangeable Instruments of National Policy" (1945) 54(2) *Yale L. J.* 181–351, 260.

decision should be constitutionally and democratically valid.[264] Congressional-Executive agreements, they argue, meet a requirement for efficiency and are in accordance with the democratic principles of contemporary US government; allowing both Houses to decide on the acceptance of international agreements.

Furthermore, whereas there is no clear and explicit language in the Constitution that makes the treaty clause exclusive as to all international agreements, the commerce clause has been interpreted as being very broad and covering all commercial intercourse.[265] While there must be some issues that fall under the exclusive area of the treaty clause, matters that concern trade can be dealt with by Congress as Congressional-Executive Agreements, even if they have strong sovereignty implications.

The fact that neither the House of Representatives, the Senate nor the Executive have seriously challenged the validity of Congressional-Executive Agreements to conclude international trade agreements such as the WTO or NAFTA, despite this background of constitutional controversy, highlights the degree of consensus in US trade policy during the last two decades.[266]

2.C.4.c. Fast Track

However, during the last twenty-five years, US international trade policy has not been based solely on Congressional-Executive agreements. In the Kennedy Round implementation process such procedure proved to be inadequate for the implementation of international agreements on non-tariff barriers. Lack of co-ordination between the Executive and Congress ended in the former's international embarrassment when the latter refused to implement an anti-dumping code negotiated, and agreed to, by the President. Decentralisation of Congress, together with increasing reassertion of its powers in international trade, especially with regard to non-tariff trade barriers, removed from the President all credibility in international trade negotiations.

The solution was the fast track procedure; a re-elaboration of the Congressional-Executive agreements procedure. During the first years of the 1970s, the Executive sought full powers to modify US laws when needed to implement trade agreements on the basis of a Congressional-Executive agreement with prior delegation. An alternative proposal was the Congressional legislative veto mechanism whereby the President would negotiate and propose an

[264] See Statement of Bruce Ackerman, Professor of Law, Yale Law School, in United States Senate, *GATT Implementing Legislation*, *supra* n. 254, at 312–317 (1994). Professor Ackerman's reasoning differs from previous arguments in favour of Congressional-Executive Agreements in that he considers that this procedure developed in the New Deal as part of a new way of government in the US system.

[265] This was the reasoning of the Court in *Made in the USA Foundation*, *supra* n. 251, at 1319.

[266] Professor Jackson considers that the adoption of the WTO Agreement and annexes by means of fast track was another precedent in favour of Congressional-Executive agreements. See J H Jackson, "The Uruguay Round Results and National Sovereignty", in J Bhagwati and M Hirsh (eds.), *The Uruguay Round and Beyond: Essays in Honor of Arthur Dunkel* (New York, Springer 1998), 293–304.

implementing bill which would then become law unless the Congress vetoed it during a certain period.[267] Finally, as a compromise, Senator Talmadge proposed fast track to empower the President to negotiate without disempowering the Congress to legislate.[268]

Fast track was a compromise between Congress and the Executive with the purpose of dealing effectively with interdependence. It was created to increase and formalise the role of Congress while at the same time encouraging and facilitating negotiations with foreign countries. Its key feature was the Congressional assurance that it would make an up or down vote on the bill implementing and accepting the trade agreement, with no amendments and within a defined time period, in return for an Executive assurance that it would consult the legislature during the entire negotiation and implementation process.[269] Although fast track did not provide an absolute guarantee that the agreement would be implemented—because Congress could always vote down the bill or simply refuse to follow the procedure—it raised the comfort level for foreign negotiations. However, fast track was also designed to encourage domestic consensus on the objectives, priorities and strategies of US trade negotiations.[270] It was a deal between Congress, the President and the rest of the world on the principles of the international trading system. While its enactment reflects a commitment to free trade, its emphasis on non-tariff barriers reflects a concern that different domestic socio-economic structures in foreign countries may limit America's foreign trade interests. By means of fast track, Congress and the Executive agreed that entering into trade agreements with the United States—whereby it opened its huge market to foreign products—required foreign countries to adjust to America's way of doing business. This was more so since both the enactment of fast track and every implementation of a trade agreement implied the strengthening of US unfair trade instruments to protect and retaliate against different trading practices. Fast track and unfair trade instruments were fundamental features of the US domestic compromise to expand the domestic welfare pie by globalising the American system.

Fast track was first adopted in 1974, amended in 1979 and 1984, re-enacted in 1988 and extended in 1992. Following the fast track process, the United States has concluded the GATT Tokyo Round agreements, the United States-Israel Free Trade Agreement, the United States-Canada Free Trade Agreement, the

[267] On the legislative veto see J B Henry, "The Legislative Veto: In Search of Constitutional Limits" (1979) 16(3) *Harvard J. Legislation* 735–762. In 1983, the Supreme Court held the legislative veto unconstitutional on grounds that it violated the constitutional division of powers between the different branches of the United States government. See *Immigration and Naturalization Service* v. *Chadha et al.*, *supra* n. 46.

[268] Charnovitz, *supra* n. 20.

[269] H Koh "The Fast Track and United States Trade Policy" (1992) 18 (1) *Brooklyn J. Int'l L.* 143–180, 144; see also Leebron, *supra* n. 126, at 190. Lohmann and O'Halloran describe this deal as a "delegation and accommodation" game. See S Lohmann and S O'Halloran, "Divided Government and US Trade Policy: Theory and Evidence" (1994) 58(4) *Int'l Org.* 595–632.

[270] Lang, *supra* n. 260, at 3–5.

North American Free Trade Agreement and the WTO agreements.[271] Fast track was left to expire in 1994.[272]

The fast track procedure worked in the following way. First, Congress granted power to the President to enter into international trade agreements on non-tariff barriers, within a specified period of time, provided such agreements made progress in meeting specified objectives.[273] In the case of bilateral agreements, two additional requirements should be met. On the one hand, the foreign country should request the negotiation of the agreement.[274] On the other hand, the President should provide written notice to, and consult with, the Senate Finance Committee and the House Ways and Means Committee which could oppose the negotiations.[275] The granting of power to enter into international trade agreements was in fact linked to the creation and development of unfair trade laws. Thus, in the 1974 Trade Act, the US strengthened its countervailing duty and anti-dumping laws and created Section 301.[276] Similarly, in the 1988 re-enactment of fast track, Congress again strengthened Section 301 and created "special 301", "super 301" and "telecommunications 301" in addition to tightening its anti-dumping and countervailing duty laws.[277]

Second, during the negotiations, the Executive had to meet certain requirements. The Administration was required to consult on a constant basis with the appointed Congressional advisors from the Finance and the Ways and Means Committees as well as with the established committees representing the private sector.[278]

Third, ninety days before finally entering into the agreement, the President was required to consult the Finance Committee and the Ways and Means Committee and any other committees which may have had jurisdiction on the nature of the agreement, on how the agreement met the specified objectives and the legislative requirements which were necessary to implement such agreement.[279] Fourth, after entering into the agreement, the President should submit to the House and the Senate a final copy of the international agreement, a draft

[271] C O'Neal Taylor, "Fast Track, Trade Policy, and Free Trade Agreements: Why the NAFTA Turned into a Battle" (1992) 28 *Geo. Wash. J. Int'l L. & Econ.* 1–132, 12.

[272] However, the Executive still has some residual powers to enter into a limited number of international agreements.

[273] The agreements could be concluded until April 1993. See Section 1102(b) of the Omnibus Trade and Competitiveness Act, P.L. 100–418 (1988), expired. The objectives, specified in the 1988 Omnibus Trade and Competitiveness Act (OTCA) placed an emphasis on unfair trade practices. See Section 1101 ibid.

[274] Section 1102(c) OTCA, expired.

[275] Section 1102(c) ibid.; see also Section 1103(c)(2) ibid.

[276] See Sections of the 1974 Trade Act.

[277] See Sections of the OTCA. This also happened during the fast track extension of 1979 and 1984.

[278] Sections 135 and 161, Trade Act of 1974.

[279] Section 1102(d) OTCA, expired; see also Section 1103(a)(1)(A) OTCA, expired. Section 1102(e) provided a special extension for the negotiation of the Uruguay Round. If the agreement was not concluded before June 1993, the power to negotiate could be extended to the end of 1993 but then, the committee consultation should take place 120 rather than 90 days before finally entering into the agreement.

of the implementing bill, a statement of administrative action and supporting information on how the implementing bill changed the domestic legislation and made progress in achieving the specified objectives.[280]

Fifth, specified limitations applied. The fast track implementing process applied to implementing bills submitted with respect to trade agreements entered into before June 1991.[281] However, it could be extended up to June 1993 if the President required such extension and neither house of Congress adopted an extension disapproval resolution.[282] The extension disapproval could be introduced in either house and by any member but it should be referred to the Committees on Ways and Means and Rules in the House and the Committee on Finance in the Senate, and neither the House or the Senate could consider an extension disapproval resolution not reported by these committees.[283] Furthermore, all agreements were subject to a general disapproval resolution on the basis that the President had failed to consult with Congress on the trade negotiations.[284] The fast track procedures would not apply to the implementation of any agreement if both houses of Congress separately agreed to procedural disapproval resolutions within any sixty day period. But again, the House and Senate could only consider disapproval resolutions reported by the Committee on Ways and Means and Rules in the House and the Committee on Finance in the Senate.[285] Finally, all the rules on the fast track process were considered to be internal rules of procedure of each house. This was a full recognition of the constitutional right of either house to change its rules.[286] However, while either house could at any time refuse to follow the fast track procedure by changing its rules, the decentralisation of both houses made this possibility rather difficult.

Sixth, if all these requirements and limitations were met, Congress committed itself to adopt the implementing bill through an expedited process. Implementing bills were defined as those including the approval of the trade agreements, the statement of administrative action and the changes to law or new legislation which "were necessary or appropriate to implement the agreement."[287] Once the implementing bill was presented by the President no amendments were allowed.[288] The bill should be referred to any committees with jurisdiction, basically the Ways and Means Committee and the Finance Committee, and if these did not report back to their houses after forty-five days from referral, they would be discharged.[289] The debate on the floor of both

280 Section 1103(a)(1)(B) OTCA, expired.

281 One thing is the deadline to use the power to enter into international agreements and another is the deadline to take advantage of the fast track procedure to implement the bill in Congress. See Section 1103(b)(1)(A), OTCA, expired.

282 Section 1103(b)(1)(B), ibid.

283 Section 1103(b)(5), ibid.

284 As to the text of the resolution, see Section 1103(c)(1)(E) ibid.

285 Section 1103(c), ibid.

286 Section 151(a), Trade Act of 1974; see also Section 1103(d), OTCA, expired.

287 Section 151(b)(1), Trade Act of 1974.

288 Section 151(d), ibid.

289 Section 151(e), ibid.

houses was limited to no more than 20 hours,[290] and a up or down vote on the final passage of the bill should be made in the Senate and the House within fifteen days of the bill being reported by the committees.[291]

In practice, despite all its potential problems, if the President followed the advice of Congress and was able to broker between the positions of foreign countries, the legislative and the private sector, the fast track itself became invulnerable after it was granted.[292] But Congress kept a tight control on the Executive during the entire process.[293] It could establish the objectives of the negotiations when enacting fast track. Its Finance Committee and Ways and Means Committee could act as gate-keepers of any bilateral negotiations with foreign countries; refusing to grant fast track if the President did not follow their advice and meet their concerns. Members of these committees should be informed and consulted during the entire negotiations. Moreover, Congress made sure that the concerns of its constituencies would be taken into account through the private sector advice system. If the committees considered that the Executive did not take into account either their concerns or those of their constituencies they could threaten the entire process through a disapproval resolution. Alternatively, they could strengthen their control by making use of the extension requirements. Both houses could also change their own rules and amend fast track.

When the President concluded the negotiations, Congress could also influence the implementation bill. It could signal its concerns to the Executive when the latter consulted its committees ninety days before entering into the agreements. But most importantly, Congress influenced and actually drafted the implementation bill. The Ways and Means Committee and the Finance Committee drafted a proposal bill together with officers from the Executive in committee close door mock "mark up" sessions.[294] The President had to bargain carefully over the draft bill with both committees, as these controlled the entire implementation process. While the President was under no legal obligation to base its implementation bill on the language suggested by the committees, it would otherwise have no committee or Congressional support for the bill. It was during these mock mark up sessions that last minute changes to the bill would be introduced, depending on the influence of the Congressman and the constituency backing him.[295] Every fast track bill enacted to date contained

[290] Section 151(f), ibid; See also Section 151(g) ibid.

[291] Section 151(e)(2), ibid; see also Section 151(e)(1) ibid.

[292] E Sim, "Derailing the Fast Track for International Trade Agreements" (1990) 5 *Florida Int'l L. J.* 471–534, 506.

[293] A Holmer and J H Bello, "US Trade and Policy Series No 20: The Fast Track Debate: A Prescription for Pragmatism" (1992) 26 *Int'l Law.* 183–194.

[294] I Destler, *supra* n. 13, at 10.

[295] P J Kuypjer, "The EC's Common Commercial Policy: Which Way the Swing of the Pendulum?" in *The Future of the President's Authority to Negotiate International Trade Agreements After the NAFTA and the Uruguay Round: What Should Congress Delegate?, Proceedings of the 88th Annual Meeting of the American Society of International Law*, Washington DC., 6–9 April 1994, at 298.

provisions that were unnecessary to implement the agreement concerned, but were necessary to obtain the votes needed for passage.[296] The words "necessary or appropriate to implement the agreement" were used to provide all kinds of sweeteners to ensure the bill passed.[297] Many of these sweeteners have been concessions to Congress and the domestic industries in the form of strengthening US unfair trade laws, as well as limiting to a minimum the possible impact of the international agreements on such laws.[298] Every time fast track was granted or an agreement was implemented under this procedure, Congress extracted from both the Executive and foreign partners a new development of its unfair trade statutes.

The control that Congress exerted over the Executive during the negotiations and implementation of the international trade agreements does not necessarily imply that fast track was democratic. As the system is structured, in essence, fast track is democratic only if it clearly reflects a consensus in American politics. First, the control exerted by Congress was mainly through the Ways and Means Committee in the House, and the Finance Committee in the Senate. Fast track did not enhance the power of Congress as a whole, only that of a few selected committees whose interests were not necessarily the same as those reflected in the floor of the houses. At the end of the entire procedure, the floors were left only with the option of voting in favour or against it; thereby collapsing the entire work of long negotiations with the added risk of discrediting their President and the entire US government. Thus fast track could only be democratic if there was a broad consensus in the houses which was, more or less, reflected in those interests represented in the committees. Second, the private sector advisory system advantaged only the position of the interests which are represented in this system.[299] The issue should be the extent to which such an advisory system could represent all the interests of a plural and decentralised society. In fact, many consider that the system only benefited big business at the expense of other less obvious business interests such as labour and the environment.

Therefore, fast track was not only the reflection of a procedural development but rather the expression of a broad consensus. Fast track, as the pillar of United States' trade policy during the last quarter of the century, crystallised a wide consensus in American trade politics. It was a deal within and between Congress and the Executive, based on three basic principles: trade through multilateralism or regionalism; *ad hoc* and exceptional protectionism; and an international trade regime which reflected the American system.

[296] J H Bello and A Holmer, "The Post Uruguay Round Future of Section 301" (1994) *25 L. & Pol'y Int'l Bus.* 1297–1308, 1299.

[297] Section 151(b)(1), Trade Act of 1974.

[298] Codevilla, *supra* n. 233, at 435.

[299] P Goldmann, "The Democratization of the Development of United States Trade Policy" (1994) 27 *Cornell Int'l L.* J. 631–697, 650–660. But see R Hudec, "Circumventing 'Democracy'; The Political Morality of Trade Negotiations" (1992) 25 *N. Y. U. J. Int'l L. & Pol'y* 311–322 (arguing that fast track enhances democratic legitimacy because it allows international negotiations where all interests must be taken into account).

3

United States' Unfair Trade Instruments as a Reflection of its Domestic Sphere

3.A. THE UNITED STATES IMPLEMENTATION OF THE URUGUAY ROUND AGREEMENT ON RESEARCH AND DEVELOPMENT SUBSIDIES

3.A.1. Introduction

ONE OF THE most important compromises which made possible the WTO Agreement on Subsidies and Countervailing Measures was the green light provisions for research and development and regional and environmental subsidies. The agreement and its subsequent implementation in US domestic law and administrative practice, provide an example of the political theatre dimension of international trade law.[1] The wide divergences between the economic systems of the United States and other partners, as well as their respective constitutional constraints, implied the need to adopt a compromise which at first glance provided the appearance of a final legal solution, yet in fact left many issues unresolved, both at home and internationally.

The green light provisions of the Agreement on Subsidies and Countervailing Measures, together with the question of United States' sovereignty, were considered to be two of the most controversial issues for the US Uruguay Round implementation process. This process emphasised several characteristics of United States' trade law. First, it highlighted the control of Congress over foreign trade and the resulting need for the Executive to broker between the position of foreign partners and that of the legislative. Furthermore, it made clear the extent to which the Congressional standing committees on foreign trade, the Finance Committee in the Senate, and the Ways and Means Committee in the House, control the entire US international trade agenda. Despite the fact the United States' Executive had changed its position on research and development subsidies during the final days of the Uruguay Round—at the request of different federal agencies and departments as well of some members of Congress—it was compelled to adopt a narrow interpretation of the exceptions in its

[1] On the concept of the political dimension of international trade law, see R Hudec, "International Economic Law: The Political Theatre Dimension", (1996) 17(1) *U. Pa. J. Int'l Econ. L.* 9–15.

domestic countervailing duty law, in order to satisfy the trade interests represented in the Finance and Ways and Means committees.

From a substantial point of view, the implementation process sketches how Congress sees itself in the trade policy process. It exemplifies the extent to which, in Congress, the price to pay for broader free trade is tighter unfair trade statutes as a way of defending the American model. Protection was granted not simply because there is no happier consumer than one with a job but because the international trading system was characterised by different and competing trading systems and the United States should protect its interests by acting strongly unilaterally.

Finally, the implementation process shows how United States' trade policy has been the result of consensus. The process worked not simply because of the procedural mechanisms but because the majority in Congress knew that what it wanted was to increase domestic welfare by participating in a free trade system that reflected America's limited government and market plurality.

3.A.2. United States' Background on the R&D Subsidies Agreement

The US' long standing position on subsidies has been that all subsidies, whatever their form and purpose, are inherently distorting and should be prohibited.[2] This position has been reflected both in its countervailing duty law and its position in international trade negotiations. Therefore when, in 1988, Congress granted fast track authority to the Executive to negotiate the Uruguay Round, it established as one of the United States' basic negotiating objectives the improvement of the provisions of GATT and non-tariff measures agreements in order to define, deter and discourage (and otherwise discipline) the persistent use of unfair trade practices, including forms of subsidies, having adverse trade effects.[3]

Research and development subsidies were no exception to the United States' doctrinal position, as it considered that these subsidies were inherently subject to abuse. It made no economic sense to make an exception for research and development programs because, given the fungible nature of money, such subsidies would enable producers to shift the money they saved on research and development costs onto other areas. Neither could a distinction between basic and applied research be justified. Not only was it difficult to define the borderline between basic and applied research but, furthermore, what really counted in the industrial setting was whether the government concentrated its R&D

[2] G Depayre, "Subsidies and Countervailing Measures after the Uruguay Round: An Overview" in J Bourgeois, F Berrod and E Fournier (eds.), *The Uruguay Round Results: A European Lawyer's Perspective* (Brussels, European Interuniversity Press, 1996), 247–254, 247.

[3] Section 1101(b)(8)(A) of the Omnibus Trade and Competitiveness Act of 1988, P.L. 100–418 [OTCA].

effort in particular industries and whether it delayed the dissemination of the R&D findings to other firms.[4]

America's position towards research and development subsidies served to enhance both its export and protectionist interests. Both through negotiations and unilateral action, the US attempted to deter world-wide the use of R&D subsidies as well as to grant protection to its domestic industry.[5] The first countervailing duty against R&D subsidies was imposed in *Optic Level Sensing Systems from Canada*.[6] The Department of Treasury decided to take action against the foreign R&D subsidies only because it was pointed out that the company concerned had applied for a patent two years before applying for the R&D grant. Hence, it seemed obvious that the grant was not really to encourage research activities.

However, with time, the Department of Commerce (DoC), much more concerned with domestic industry than the Treasury, developed a methodology for imposing countervailing duties against foreign research and development programs. The countervailing nature of such subsidies was based on the argument that domestic countervailing duty law stated that a countervailing subsidy included the assumption of any costs or expenses of manufacture, production or export of a product.[7] As research and development were part of a private firm's costs, subsidies for such purposes were countervailing. In *Fresh Cut Roses from Israel*,[8] the International Trade Administration (ITA) set out the US position on research and development subsidies. It established a two-prong test to determine whether a foreign research and development subsidy was countervailing. A foreign subsidy was not countervailing, if the subsidy was generally available or the results of the program were publicly available, even for competing firms in the US.[9] Thus, the DoC would first apply its basic specificity test. Only R&D programs which were specific to certain industries would be considered as countervailing. In *Grain Oriented Electrical Steel from Italy*,[10] the ITA considered that the research and development funds obtained by Terni S.p.A. under an

[4] M Stein, "The Uruguay Round and the Trade Laws: Antidumping, Countervailing Duties, Commerce Provisions" in G Low (ed.), *The Commerce Department Speaks on International Trade and Investment 1994* (New York, Practicing Law Institute, 1994) 877–893, 886; see also Council of Competitiveness, *Road Map for Results: Trade Policy, Technology and American Competitiveness* (Washington, Council of Competitiveness, 1993), 78; see also P McDonough, "Subsidies and Countervailing Measures in The GATT Uruguay Round: A Negotiating History (1986–1992)" in T Stewart (ed.), *The GATT Uruguay Round: A Negotiating History (1986–1992)* (Deventer, Kluwer Law and Taxation Publishers, 1993), 94.

[5] See "EC, Canada Demand Changes in Subsidies Text; US Will Also Press Revisions", *Inside US Trade—Special Report*, 18 December 1992 at S4.

[6] *Optic Level Sensing Systems from Canada*, 44 Fed. Reg. 1728 (1979).

[7] Section 771 (5) (A) (ii) of the Tariff Act of 1930, P.L. 103–459, as amended; see also R Grey, "Some Notes on Subsidies and the International Rules" in D Wallace, F Loftus and V Krikorian (eds.), *Interface Three: Legal Treatment of Domestic Subsidies* (Washington, International Law Institute, 1984), 61.

[8] *Fresh Cut Roses from Israel*, 45 Fed.Reg. 58516 (1980).

[9] *International Trade Administration, Notice of Proposed Rulemaking and Request for Public Comments*, 54 Fed. Reg. 23366 (31 May 1989).

[10] *Grain Oriented Electrical Steel from Italy*, 59 Fed.Reg. 18357, 18364 (18 April 1994).

Italian National Research Plan were not countervailing because the plan had also benefited other industries or sectors and the steel industry had not, in fact, received a disproportionate share of the funds. The second part of the test was based on the argument that only those R&D results which were kept for the sole use of the subsidised industry provided a distortive benefit from the point of view of the market. Thus, in *Fresh Cut Roses from Israel*, the DoC considered that the R&D program was not countervailing because the results of the program conducted by the Hebrew University of Jerusalem were not restricted to Israeli firms but were available to the general public.[11] Thus, in one of the famous EC steel cases, *Certain Steel Products from France*, the ITA considered that research and development funds were countervailing because the program was industry specific and the results had not been publicly available.[12]

The US position towards research and development subsidies changed only during the final weeks of the Uruguay Round negotiations.[13] Such change of approach was the result of a clash in government between those with a more technology-oriented perspective and those concerned with international trade matters; between those who advocated an active US civil research and development policy and those who preferred to internationalise limited US government intervention. The Clinton Administration, which had arrived with an active R&D policy project, and some members of Congress, feared that the mention of research and development programs in the subsidies agreements would jeopardise US national defence programs.[14] Thus, Congressmen from the Democratic party urged US trade officials participating in the international negotiations to drop any reference to research and development subsidies from the "Dunkel draft" so as to protect US research programs.[15]

[11] This second test, however, was very much criticised by the US domestic industry. It was argued that from a commercial point of view the test did not make sense; what was important was the benefit the firm obtained by being the first to make use of the results before publishing them. See *Agrexco, Agricultural Export Co.* v. *United States*, 604 F. Supp. 1238, 1241 (CIT 1985).

[12] *Certain Steel Products from France*, 47 Fed. Reg. 39332 (1982); see also *Fuel Ethanol from Brazil*, 51 Fed. Reg. 3361 (1986); *Certain Carbon Steel Cases from Sweden*, 50 Fed. Reg. 33375 (1985); *Certain Steel Products from Belgium*, 47 Fed. Reg. 39304, 39319 (1982); *Fresh Cut Flowers from Kenya*, 52 Fed. Reg. 9522, 9523 (1987); *Pure Magnesium and Alloy Magnesium from Canada*, 57 Fed. Reg. 30946, 30950 (1992); *Miniature Carnations from Colombia*, 59 Fed. Reg. 10790 (1994); and *Certain Steel from Sweden*, 58 Fed. Reg. 61065 (1993).

[13] G Kleinfeld and D Kaye, "Red Light, Green Light? The 1994 Agreement on Subsidies and Countervailing Measures, Research and Development Assistance and US Policy" (1994) 28(6) *J. World Trade* 43–63; see also US Senate, *Hearings before the Committee of Finance of the United States Senate, Results of the Uruguay Round Trade Negotiations*, 103rd Cong. 2nd Session, 35 (1994); and US House of Representatives, *Hearings before the Subcommittee on Technology, Environment and Aviation of the Committee on Space and Technology of the United States House of Representatives, The GATT Subsidies Code and its Impact on R&D*, 103rd Cong. 2nd Session (1994).

[14] B Clinton and A Gore, "Technology for America's Economic Growth: A New Direction to Build Economic Strength", 22 February 1993 (Available in Lexis/Nexis, Executive Library, Clinton File); see also "Back to the Pork Barrel", *The Financial Times*, 4 May 1994, at 21.

[15] P Rosenthal, "Undermining the US Antidumping and Countervailing Duty Laws: The Undeniable Effect of the Dunkel Text" in W Willkie (ed.), *The Commerce Department Speaks 1992: Developments in Import Administration; Export and Investment Abroad* (New York, Practicing

The change of position by the United States trade representatives allowed for a final agreement on subsidies and countervailing measures and opened the way to the successful conclusion of the Uruguay Round.[16] US officials, finding themselves incapable of eliminating all the provisions on research and development subsidies, decided to negotiate with their European counterparts a broader exception for such programs, in order to be sure that US programs would be sheltered from GATT rules. Consequently the US and the EU representatives exchanged broader definitions of R&D for higher spending caps and the deletion of the requirement of prior notification.

3.A.3. The Uruguay Round R&D Subsidies Agreement

The final agreement on research and subsidies was drafted the following way: Article 8 of the Agreement on Subsidies and Countervailing Measures considered these subsidies, together with non-specific, regional and environmental subsidies, as non-actionable either under multilateral or unilateral countervailing duty laws. It distinguished further as between fundamental research, industrial research and pre-competitive development activity. Fundamental research was defined as an enlargement of general scientific and technical knowledge, not linked to industrial or commercial objectives. Fundamental research activities conducted independently by higher education or research establishments were not ruled by the agreement.[17] With regard to industrial research and pre-competitive development activity, the agreement expanded the stages of the research and development process which could be subsidised under the "Dunkel Draft" provisions. The latters definitions for basic industrial research and applied research seemed to have merged together to form the definition of industrial research.[18] Industrial research was therefore defined as planned research and critical investigation aimed at the discovery of new knowledge, with the objective that such knowledge may be useful in developing new products, processes or services or in bringing about a significant improvement in existing products, processes or services.[19] Pre-competitive development activity was considered as covering the translation of industrial research findings into a plan, blue-print or design of new, modified or improved products, processes or services, whether intended for sale or use. Such research included the creation of a first prototype

Law Institute, 1992), 117–147; see also Dunkel Draft from the GATT Secretariat, MTN. TNC/W/FA, I.

16 "US, EU Reach Deal on Research, Development Subsidies", *Inside US Trade*, 10 December 1993 at 1.

17 Footnote 24 of the 1994 Agreement on Subsidies and Countervailing Measure (ASCM).

18 Article 8(2) of The Agreement on Subsidies and Countervailing Measures of the Dunkel Draft from the GATT Secretariat, MTN. TNC/W/FA, I.

19 Footnote 27 of the ASCM.

which would not be capable of commercial use.[20] States could subsidise up to the creation of a first prototype in the R&D process.

Article 8(2) of the Agreement allowed government assistance for R&D if the assistance covered no more than 75% of the costs of industrial research or 50% of the costs of pre-competitive development activity. This was subsequent to the provision that the assistance be limited exclusively to personal costs, costs of instruments, equipment, land and buildings used exclusively and permanently for the research activity, costs of consultancy, additional overhead costs incurred directly as a result of the research activity and other running costs incurred directly or indirectly as a result of the research activity. Further, for R&D subsidies to be non-actionable they should comply with another requirement: they could not be contingent *de iure* or *de facto* on export performance or import substitution.[21] Notification of the subsidies was not required in order for these to become non-actionable, but only notified subsidies under the rules of article 8(3) automatically became non-actionable after the Subsidies Committee review.[22] Following notification, the Subsidies Committee should review the notification and determine whether the programs complied with the GATT rules.[23] Any challenge to this determination could be subject to the World Trade Organisation dispute settlement mechanism.[24] Subsidies which had been notified and were accepted by the Subsidies Committee could not be subject to countervailing duty investigations. R&D subsidies which had not been notified could be subject to countervailing duty investigations but if the investigation authority found that the program complied with the rules on R&D subsidies, it could not impose a countervailing duty against those programs. R&D subsidies which had been notified could only be subject to multilateral actions if they caused serious adverse effects to the domestic industry of the claimant member state.[25] These disputes were to be reviewed by the Subsidies Committee but they were not subject to the WTO dispute settlement rules. Thus, there was the danger of a contracting party blocking the resolution. In any case, the Committee could not order the subsidising country to remove the programs, but could only authorise the adversely affected party to impose adequate measures.[26]

The agreement on R&D subsidies was not final. First, no later than eighteen months after the date of entry into force of the Agreement Establishing the WTO, the Committee was bound to review the operation of the R&D provision along with the adequacy of the definitions.[27] Second, the non-actionability of R&D subsidies should last for five years after the entry into force of the WTO

[20] Footnote 28 ibid.

[21] Article 3 ibid.

[22] Footnote 33 ibid.

[23] Information on the notification of subsidies for research and development programs can be found at the World Trade Organisation's website. See <http://www.wto.int>.

[24] Article 8(5) of the ASCM.

[25] Article 9(1) ibid.

[26] Article 9(4) ibid.

[27] Footnote 24 ibid.

Agreement. No later than one hundred and eighty days before the end of this period, that is July 1999, the Committee was to review the operation of the provisions with a view to determining whether to extend their application, either as drafted or in a modified form, for a further period.[28] During the Ministerial Conference in Seattle, as there was disagreement between developed countries, notably the US which was pressed by Congress, and developing countries concerning the expansion of the exemptions for the benefit of the latter, the Subsidies Committee could not reach a consensus on the extension and thus the green light provisions automatically lapsed as of January 2000.

3.A.4. The Agreement's Implementation Process in the US

On 15 December 1993, President Clinton gave the required one hundred and twenty days prior notification of his intent to enter into the Uruguay Round Agreements as of 15 April of the following year. The notification contained a copy of all the agreements.[29]

Every time Congress approves an international trade agreement, it extracts some concession which is most likely to be related to its fair trade instruments. The Uruguay Round implementation process would be no exception to this. As Congress could not change the agreement's provisions, Congressmen, from the Finance and the Ways and Means Committees, and Executive officials engaged, during one full year, in a bargaining process which resulted in implementing legislation which, while allowing the United States to honour its commitments, laid down a strict interpretation of the agreement and thus both protected its domestic industries and pursued what were considered to be the country's interests in world trade.

The new R&D rules were considered to be a historical departure from America's long standing position on subsidies and to threaten its economic system of plurality and mistrust of government intervention. Not only would the new rules open important loopholes in United States' countervailing duty laws, but they would also push the United States government to develop a more interventionist R&D policy.[30] Thus, from the very beginning, the R&D subsidies agreement faced fierce opposition from both Congressmen and lobby groups.[31] In Congress, the main opponent to the agreement was Republican John

[28] Article 31 ibid.; see also *Joint Report of the US Trade Representative and the US Department of Commerce, Subsidies Enforcement Annual Report to the Congress* (February 2000), available at <ia.ita.doc.gov/esel/reports/seo2000/report2k.html>.

[29] Office of the US Trade Representative, Executive Office of the President, *Final Act Embodying the Results of the Uruguay Round of Multilateral Trade Negotiations (Version of 15 December 1993)* (Washington, US Government Printing Office, 1993).

[30] "Republican Senators Letter On Subsidies Code", *Inside US Trade*, 4 February 1994, at 16.

[31] K Bradsher, "Republican Senators Issue Complaint About Trade Pact", *The New York Times*, 1 February 1994, at 2; see also M Ebert, "Research Subsidies: Not So Fast", *Journal of Commerce*, 9 June 1994, at 8A.

Danforth, Senator from Missouri. The importance of his views was due to the fact that he was the ranking minority leader in the Finance Committee. Indeed, the Uruguay Round bill required the support of his committee in order to proceed through Congress as a fast track bill.

When, in March 1994, the Finance Committee held the required hearings before the Administration entered into the agreement, Senator Danforth together with other members of the Committee were able to raise the issue and express their strong opposition.[32] Senator Danforth argued that there was the danger of the US being faced with a dilemma: either weakening its countervailing duty laws and hence allowing foreign subsidies without doing anything—thus losing the trade game—or having to support an industrial policy. The latter implied "a major shift in the US trade policy from one promoting free market competition to one promoting government subsidies and industrial policy."[33] Senator Danforth's words reflected a long standing agreement on US trade policy. The agreement on research and development subsidies was considered to be a threat to the US system because it either required the country to change its economic system, by itself engaging in a coherent industrial policy, or it left it to compete against different economic models without the option of using countervailing duties as interface instruments. Furthermore, he linked the protection of US domestic industry, through the use of countervailing duties, with the promotion of a world-wide free competitive market which would benefit America's export interests. Indeed, Congress has traditionally believed that in using US economic muscle in the trading system, it should have an important role to play. Together with the US Administration, it believes that unfair trade instruments are not simply protectionist instruments but, more importantly, allow it to influence the trading system and to establish a world wide market based on plurality and non-government intervention which reflects its domestic system.

Hence, along with other Republican Senators, Danforth threatened to vote against any implementing bill which did not solve what he considered to be a serious problem for United States' trade policy.[34] He even suggested a parallel new agreement between the United States and the European Union on non-actionable subsidies.[35] However, in practice, Senator Danforth left open the possibility of closed-door negotiations between committee staff and Executive officials and offered to work with the Administration to resolve the differences over the subsidies provisions in order to clear the way for the Senate's approval of the accord.[36]

[32] *Hearings before the Committee of Finance of the United States Senate, Results of the Uruguay Round Trade Negotiations*, 103rd Cong. 2nd Session, 35 (1994).

[33] A Hazard, "Steel Firms Worry GATT Will Weaken Protection", *Chicago Tribune*, 14 February 1994, at 2.

[34] B Morris, "More Fight Left in the Uruguay Round", *The Independent*, 17 April 1994, at 7.

[35] J Danforth, "Trade Accord Should Be Renegotiated," *St. Louis Post-Dispatch*, 13 February 1994, at 3B.

[36] "Kantor Urges Passage This Year Of The Uruguay Round Legislation", *International Trade Reporter* Vol 11, No 11, 16 March 1994, at 416.

The Executive officials who were at the hearings argued that the US had no choice but to agree to an expansion of the "Dunkel Draft" provisions. They alleged that there would have been no other means to protect the US research and development programs because there was no way of convincing the EU trade representatives to drop the provisions.[37] However, the Administration promised US Senators that in the implementation bill it was willing to limit the provisions to five years and to set up a monitoring system to ensure compliance by the US and its foreign trading partners. It also promised that those foreign research and development programs which did not comply with the agreement would be countervailed in full.[38]

After the signature of the Uruguay Round Agreement at Marrakech, the US implementation procedure started formally. The process was characterised by bargaining between protectionist interests, free trade interests, Congressmen, the Executive and even foreign governments.[39] Domestic producers lobbied members of Congress for provisions in the Uruguay bill that would ensure they did not lose countervailing duty protection against foreign subsidies. Pressures came from the "Committee to Support US Trade Laws", the steel industry, the paper industry, the pork industry, etc.[40] In fact, many from the Washington international trade bar were mobilised in order to limit what was considered to be a weakening of America's unfair trade laws. They argued that the United States had opened its doors to unfairly subsidised imported products, threatening the survival of US domestic industry. The results were proposals from members of both the House and the Senate to include provisions in the Uruguay Round bill which tightened the definition of green light subsidies.[41]

Senators John Danforth and Max Baucus from the Finance Committee proposed that green light subsidies be subject to a process similar to that of Section 301 of the 1974 Act.[42] The proposal was intended to set up a process which would work in the context of Article 9 of the Subsidies Agreement; allowing US industries which were seriously injured by the green light subsidies to petition the Administration to take counter-measures. It required the US Administration to take retaliatory measures even if the Subsidies Committee procedure was blocked and draw up an annual list of foreign subsidies which surpassed the

[37] "US Trade Practices Defended by Kantor", *The Financial Times*, World Trade News Section, March 1994, at 6.

[38] *Hearings before the Committee on Finance of the United States Senate*, *Results of the Uruguay Round Trade Negotiations*, 103rd Cong. 2nd Session, 3 (1994); see also "Yerxa Sees Five Year Limit On Green Subsidies In Uruguay Round Bill", *Inside US Trade*, 11 March 1994 at 15.

[39] See "Canada Criticizes US Over GATT Implementing Proposals On Subsidies", *Inside US Trade*, 29 July 1994, at 16; see also "EC Praises US On Antidumping Legislation, Warns Against Additions", *Inside US Trade*, 1 July 1994, at 8.

[40] "Domestic Producers Seek Strong CVD Rules In GATT Implementation Bill", *Inside US Trade*, 6 May 1994, at 10; see also "US Agencies Wrestle Over Implementation Of New GATT AD/CVD Rules", *Inside US Trade*, 18 February 1994, at 4

[41] "Administration To Provide Language On AD/CVD Provision Of GATT Bill", *Inside US Trade*, 1 April 1994, at 7

[42] "Baucus, Danforth Offer Proposals To Implement GATT Trade Agreement", *International Trade Reporter*, Vol 11, No 26, 29 June 1994, at 1019.

serious prejudice threshold of the subsidies agreement. The Administration would be required to initiate a dispute settlement action for all eligible subsidies within thirty days of issuing the report. It also provided that if a foreign government sought green light status for a subsidy that did not meet the terms of the agreement, the United States Trade Representative would be forced to raise an objection in the Subsidies Committee. Furthermore, the Administration would not be allowed to extend the green light provisions beyond the five year period established in the Agreement without seeking the approval of Congress. The Senators warned that the provisions should be included in the Uruguay Round implementing legislation of the agreement if the latter was to be passed by Congress that year.[43] They knew that they could always block the Fast Track Procedure and turn the bill into an ordinary bill which would have had very little chance of being adopted.

On the other hand, the Administration argued that it could prevent the abuse of non-actionable subsidies by simply putting forward strict definitions and interpretations in the implementation bill. It considered that doing so would send a strong message to its trading partners about the tightly drawn meaning the US wanted to assign to the provisions. It proposed a monitoring system for foreign R&D subsidies, but did not consider that the termination of the agreement should be automatic. Rather, it argued that the Administration should be able to agree to renewal or modification without Congressional consent.[44]

As the ranking minority leader, Senator Danforth was able to obtain the support of the Senate Finance Committee for his proposals.[45] The Executive had to bargain with him over the rules on R&D subsidies which would be finally included in the final implementation proposal. Therefore, in a closed door non mark-up session, the Finance Committee introduced in the Executive's proposed draft bill, a procedure for non-actionable subsidies similar to that of Section 301 of the 1974 Trade Act, together with other provisions which severely tightened the Agreement on Subsidies and Countervailing Measures' green light subsidies provisions.[46] Furthermore, to ensure that the Executive's administration of the countervailing duty law would correspond with the committee's wishes, it negotiated with the Executive the latter's statement of administrative action which should be followed as an interpretative guide by both the Administration and the courts.

In its draft implementing proposal, in a non mark-up session, the House Ways and Means Committee incorporated the Finance Committee's propos-

[43] "Baucus, Danforth Offer Package To Beef Up Trade Laws In GATT Bill", *Inside US Trade*, 24 June 1994, at 3; see also "Danforth Pushes Administration For 301–Type Plan On Subsidies", *Inside Us Trade*, 27 May 1994, at 1

[44] "Administration Lays Out Curbs On Greenlighted Subsidies In GATT Deal", *Inside Us Trade*, 10 June 1994, at 13; see also "Memo Reveals Administration AD/CVD Provisions For GATT Bill", *Inside US Trade*, 17 June 1994, at 1.

[45] "Republican Concerns Threaten GATT Bill As Finance Committee Begins Mark Up", *International Trade Reporter* Vol 11, No 29, 20 July 1994, at 1124.

[46] "Senate Panel Backs Provision To Fight Abuse Of Green Subsidies", 5 August 1994, at 20.

als.[47] Thus, the Clinton Administration had to introduce most of these provisions in the final proposed bill. The final implementation bill was sent to Congress on 23 September 1994.[48] It contained the agreements, the implementation act as well as the statement of administration action to implement both the agreements and the act. After being approved formally by both the Finance Committee and the Ways and Means Committee, the bill was enacted by the House and the Senate in December 1994 with the up or down vote, which characterises the fast track procedure.[49]

3.A.5. The Final Legislation Implementing the R&D Agreement

The provisions dealing with research and development subsidies were a blow to foreign countries' expectations with regard to their programs. They can be divided into three groups. First there are those provisions which define a countervailing subsidy and grant non-actionability to R&D subsidies for countervailing duty investigation purposes. Second, there are those provisions introduced to enforce strongly the rights of the US in the WTO against any foreign abuse of R&D subsidies. Finally, there are some provisions which deal with notifications to Congress and the extension of the agreement after the five year period.

Section 251 of the Act provides that except for a subsidy granted on the manufacture, production, or export of civil aircraft, a subsidy for research activities conducted by a person, or by a higher education or research establishment on a contract basis with a person, must be treated as non-countervailing, if the subsidy covers not more than 75% of the costs of industrial research or not more than 50% of the costs of pre-competitive development activity, and if such subsidy is limited exclusively to those costs which were agreed in the Uruguay Round.[50] Civil aircraft subsidies are excluded because the US and the EU have concluded a special agreement for that industry. The definitions of industrial research and pre-competitive development and the allowed costs are a strict copy of those of the Subsidies and Countervailing Measures Agreement. However, the House Report establishes that the countervailing duty administering authority—the DoC—must establish a careful and sharp distinction between genuinely pre-competitive activity and later stage development and

[47] "Uruguay Round Trade Agreements Draft Implementing Proposal As Amended and Recommended by the Subcommittee on Trade, Committee on Ways and Means", H 782–15, 160, 29 June 1994.

[48] *Message from the President of the United States Transmitting the Uruguay Round Trade Agreements, Texts of Agreements Implementing Bill, Statement of Administrative Action and Required Supporting Statements*, 103rd Congress, 2nd Session, House Document 103–316, Vol. 1, 27 September 1994.

[49] "Senate Finance Approves GATT Bill, Dole Says He Will Not Block Vote", *Inside US Trade*, 30 September 1994, at 14.

[50] Section 251(a) Uruguay Round Implementation Act, Pub. L. 103–465, 108 Stat. 4809 (1994) (URAA).

production aid.[51] Both the House Report and the Statement of Administrative Action bound the Administration not to accord green light status to assistance for pre-competitive development activity unless the pre-competitive nature of the research is well established.[52] Under US law the term pre-competitive development activity must be strictly construed in order to prevent any circumvention.[53] All subsidies which are for production and not exclusively for R&D must be countervailed. In this sense, the US Administration committed itself to apply strict guidelines for claims that assistance is for pre-competitive development activity rather than for development or production support.[54] Thus, taking into account the difficulty of delimiting the different stages of the R&D process it seems that the administering authority and the Courts have a wide discretion to determine whether the subsidised program is intended for pre-competitive development or not.

The House Report also establishes that Congress intends the permitted research costs to be strictly construed. If the capital goods in which the government funds are invested are used for anything more than R&D, the subsidies must be countervailed in full. Moreover, it also states that the term "other operating costs" must be viewed as encompassing only those items which are directly consumed in the non-actionable research activity.[55]

Only Subsidies Agreement countries can obtain non-countervailing status.[56] The benefits of non-countervailing status are not available to those countries which have not also assumed the disciplines of the Subsidies Agreement and which are not otherwise entitled to unconditional MFN treatment. To benefit from the non-countervailing status, the ITA must make sure that all the criteria have been satisfied. Otherwise, the entire program must be countervailed in full. Furthermore, only subsidies which have been notified to the WTO Subsidies Committee will be exempt from the countervailing duty procedures. The Statement of Administrative Action states clearly that in a countervailing duty investigation or administrative review involving a subsidy program that has not been notified to the WTO, the respondent has the burden of adducing evidence demonstrating compliance with all the specific criteria for non-countervailing

[51] The House Report defines the legislative history of the bill and serves as a binding interpretative guide for the courts when applying the act. See House Report 103–826(I) at page 113.

[52] Ibid.; see also Statement of Administrative Action, in *Message from the President of the United States Transmitting the Uruguay Round Trade Agreements, Texts of Agreements Implementing Bill, Statement of Administrative Action and Required Supporting Statements*, 103rd Congress, 2d Session, House Document 103–316, Vol 1, 263, 27 September 1994.

[53] The distinction between the different stages of the R&D process has always been very fuzzy. Different texts give different concepts and thus a wider or narrower scope to the different stages. See Organisation for Economic Co-operation And Development, *The Measurement of Scientific and Technical Activities* (Paris, OECD, 1981) 25; compare with the *Community Framework for State Aids for Research and Development*, OJ 1986 C83/02; and the *Dunkel Draft from the GATT Secretariat*, MTN. TNC/W/FA, I.

[54] As to these guidelines, see *Statement of Administrative Action*, at 263.

[55] House Report at 113; see also *Statement of Administrative Action*, at 264.

[56] Section 251 (a) URAA.

status.[57] Moreover, in order to target countervailing subsidies as soon as possible, the United States Trade Representative (USTR) must notify the DoC that a notified subsidy has been considered by the Subsidies Committee as not complying with the provisions of the agreement. The DoC will thereafter be bound to initiate a CVD procedure against such a program. The implementing law further restricted the non countervailable status by stating, in Section 291, that the non-countervailing subsidy provisions would only apply to those investigation and review procedures initiated after the WTO enters into force in the US.[58]

Section 281 of the Act lays down the provisions regulating the "Enforcement of United States Rights Under the Subsidies Agreement". The Administration committed itself to use the green light challenge procedures in the Subsides Agreement aggressively in order to ensure that Article 8 is not abused.[59] The Act establishes a co-operative procedure between the DoC, the USTR, the International Trade Commission, private parties and industry advisory committees in order for the US to exercise its rights vigorously, intelligently and efficiently in the Subsidies Committee of the WTO.[60]

Generally speaking, the process has several interesting features. First, it gives standing to private parties who can petition the Administration to take action. Second, the DoC is required to assist the domestic industry in the monitoring of foreign subsidies.[61] Furthermore, by including the DoC and the ITA, Congress makes sure that there will be a co-ordinated agenda between United States' countervailing duty policy and its positions in the WTO *fora*. Finally, the Administration is expected to take into account the opinion of industry advisory committees. By establishing an inter-agency mechanism within the Executive and committing the latter to take into account the private sector, Congress has tried to make sure that neither the Executive nor an agency will follow its own independent agenda and disregard the legislative intent.

With regard to R&D subsidies, the enforcement procedure can be divided into two tracks. Section 281(e)(1) establishes the rules regulating the enforcement of the US rights under Article 8 of the Subsidies Agreement which refers to the notification of non actionable subsidies. Congress expects the Administration to use this procedure aggressively against all subsidy notifications which do

[57] *Statement of Administrative Action*, at 266. This seems to be in conflict with the GATT Dispute Settlement case law which considers Article VI of GATT as an exception. If Article VI is an exception to the basic principles of GATT, the government, in imposing a countervailing measure, should make sure that it complies with all the requirements established in the Agreement. Thus, the burden of proof should fall on the government of the complaining party. In this sense, footnote 1 to Article 10 of the Agreement on Subsidies and Countervailing Measures reads: ". . . In addition, in the case of a subsidy referred to in paragraph 2 of Article 8 conferred pursuant to a program which has not been notified in accordance with paragraph 3 of Article 8, the Provision of Part III or V [Countervailing Measures] may be invoked, but such subsidy shall be treated as non-actionable if it is found to conform to the standards set forth in paragraph 2 of Article 8."

[58] Section 291(a) URAA.

[59] *Statement of Administrative Action*, at 267.

[60] House Report at 123.

[61] House Report at 123.

not comply with the agreement. The standard of compliance which the US Administration must enforce is that of the US Act rather than that set out in the agreement.[62] The USTR and the DoC are required to maintain a co-operation system whereby the former must notify the latter of all notifications received by the Subsidies Committee. The DoC must then determine whether the foreign program complies with the Subsidies Agreement and notify its determination to the trade representative. Private parties may claim to DoC that a foreign subsidy program does not comply with the agreement. If the DoC determines that the program is inconsistent with the agreement, it must notify the USTR, who must oppose the program in the WTO.

Section 281(e)(2) of the Act establishes the procedure for enforcement of US rights under Article 9 of the Subsidies Agreement. It establishes a procedure similar to Section 301 of the 1974 Act whereby a private party may claim to DoC that a foreign green light subsidy is, in fact, causing serious adverse effects to the domestic industry. The DoC, in co-operation with the ITC, must then determine whether the foreign program is causing adverse effects to the domestic industry. If it considers that the foreign program does so, it must notify its determination to the USTR whom, unless the interested party objects, shall enforce US rights in the Subsidies Committee under Article 9 of that agreement. The US government has no intention of tolerating any unilateral foreign blockage of an Article 9 finding or remedy recommendation.[63] If the USTR determines that the Subsidies Committee is unable to make a determination because the procedure is blocked by another contracting party, or that the Subsidies Committee simply does not present its conclusions within 120 days after the date the matter was referred to it, it shall make a determination under Section 301 of the 1974 Trade Act.

Theoretically, the USTR *must* take action against the foreign subsidising country.[64] But both the process of Section 301 and that of Section 281 seem to have enough loopholes to allow for some discretion on the part of the Administration. But, again, this should be complemented by those provisions which deal with the extension of the agreement after the five years period and those which deal with the notification requirements to Congress. Section 281(f) requires the DoC to publish in the Federal Register and to notify Congress of all those foreign subsidy programs which have been notified to the Subsidies Committee. Section 282 of the Act establishes that the green light provisions shall cease to apply after five years from the date in which the WTO entered into force for the US, unless the Subsidies Committee extends or modifies those provisions and Congress gives its consent under a legislative procedure similar to that of the fast track procedure. Congress will decide again by July 2000. Hence, it is doubtful to what extent the USTR could have had any discretion if the Subsidies Committee were blocked.

[62] Section 281 (e)(1) (C)(ii).
[63] *Statement of Administrative Action*, at 281.
[64] Section 301 (a)(1)(a) of the 1974 Trade Act as amended.

3.A.6. The Post Uruguay Round Administrative Countervailing Duty Practice on R&D Subsidies

In the aftermath of the Uruguay Round, benefiting from the green subsidies list has been more difficult than anticipated by many of the United States' trading partners. Bound by its domestic Uruguay Round implementation laws and the change in mood towards R&D programs in Congress,[65] the effective and vigorous enforcement of the subsidies agreement has been a top priority of the United States.[66] Following Section 281 of the URAA, the DoC and the United States Representative have created the Subsidies Compliance Centre. It is charged with monitoring all foreign subsidisation programs, including research and development subsidies, and providing assistance to the private sector on these matters.[67] Within WTO *fora*, the United States has vigorously pushed for a restrictive interpretation of the non-actionable subsidies provisions. While not formally opposing research and development subsidies, the United States has attempted to make the achievement of green light status for subsidy programs as difficult as possible by demanding a large amount of detail for the notification of each green light subsidy.[68] This may have been one of the reasons why there were no notifications of R&D subsidies programs and no subsidies were granted multilateral green light status. Furthermore, while domestically US trade officials attempted to persuade Congress and their constituencies on the benefits of the green light provisions, in international *fora*, constrained by the possible reaction of Congress, they kept a dubious position and opposed any expansion of the exemptions.

With regard to countervailing duty investigations, the US has also followed an ambiguous practice. United States' trade officials have been trapped between the need to show their commitment to follow the will of Congress by tight enforcement of the R&D exceptions, in order to obtain an extension of the green light provisions, and maintaining fidelity to the United States' obligations within WTO.

In its new regulations on countervailing duty methodology, the ITA has expressed its intent to follow Congressional will and to limit, as much as

65 As a result of the 1994 Congressional elections, United States' politics suffered an impressive U-turn. The more conservative Congress which emerged from the elections, slashed many of the R&D programs with which President Clinton had enthusiastically arrived at Washington DC. Now, not even after the 1996 elections, does the President dare to talk of big government plans to encourage R&D.

66 *Subsidies Enforcement, Annual Report to the Congress: Joint Report of the Office of the United States Representative and the US Department of Commerce*, (February 1998), available at <http://www.ita.doc.gov/import_administration/>.

67 The Subsidies Compliance Centre has created an electronic database on foreign subsidies which is available at <http://www.ita.doc.gov>.

68 Interview at the Commission of the European Community, May 1997. US Department of Commerce, *Report to Congress: Review and Operation of the WTO Subsidies Agreement* (June 1999), available at <www.ita.doc.gov.import_admin/records/esel/scm-0699.htm>

possible, the research and development exceptions to its countervailing duty law.[69] Thus, it has reaffirmed its commitment to interpret the R&D provisions strictly by not limiting its investigation to a narrow review of the technical criteria, but instead analysing all aspects of the subsidy program and its implementation.[70] This seems to imply that stricter criteria apply for green light subsidies than for the application of other countervailing duty provisions.[71] Moreover, a determination that a particular subsidy received by a firm is a green light subsidy would not necessary mean that the ITA would find that the entire program under which the subsidy is provided satisfies all of the applicable green light criteria in all cases.

If a subsidy program has been notified under Article 8(3) of the Subsidies Agreement, the ITA will not challenge its eligibility for green light treatment in a countervailing duty investigation. However, the ITA may enter into consultations with the foreign government to determine whether the subsidy alleged in a petition is in fact one provided under the notified program. If the consultations do not resolve the question, the ITA will include the subsidy in the investigation until the party claiming the green light status demonstrates that the subsidy has been notified.[72]

The ITA will not consider claims for green light status if the merchandise under investigation did not benefit from the green light subsidies during the period of investigation or review. The green light status of a subsidy will be considered only in an investigation or review of a time period where the subject merchandise did benefit from the subsidy.[73]

Finally, following its intent to adopt a strict interpretation of the WTO and the URAA provisions, the DoC has dropped its previous public availability test whereby, provided the results of the government funded research and development were publicly available, no competitive benefit was considered to be conferred.[74] Despite claims that dropping the public availability test was not required by the Agreement on Subsidies or the URAA and was a U-turn compared to its previous practice,[75] the ITA has considered that such a test would

[69] Department of Commerce, International Trade Administration, Final Rule on 19 CFR Part 351, 63 Fed.Reg. 65348 (25 November 1998), text available at <http://www.ita.doc.gov/import_library/>. The rules on research and development subsidies are codified as 19 CFR Section 351.522 (b).

[70] Department of Commerce, International Trade Administration, Final Rule on 19 CFR Part 351, at 81.

[71] See *Comments submitted by the Delegation of the European Union to the United States*, available at <http://www.ita.doc.gov/import_library/>.

[72] Department of Commerce, International Trade Administration, Final Rule on 19 CFR Part 351, 82.

[73] Ibid., at 83.

[74] Canadian Embassy, *Government of Canada's Comments on US Department of Commerce Proposed Rules on Countervailing Duties US* Federal Register 26 February 1997, 23 May 1997, available at <http://www.ita.doc.gov/import_library/>.

[75] Up to the publication of the new rules on countervailing duty methodology on 25 November 1998, the International Trade Administration had consistently used the publicly available test. See *Live Swine from Canada: Final Results of Countervailing Duty Administrative Review*, 63 Fed.Reg. 2204, 2206 (1998); see also *Live Swine from Canada: Final Results of countervailing Duty Administrative Review*, 63 Fed.Reg. 47235, 47236 (1998).

be inconsistent with its concept of benefit: one which is conferred when a firm pays less for its inputs than it would otherwise do in the absence of the government provided input or earns more than it would otherwise do. The research and development subsidy would reduce the firm's input costs whether or not the results of the research are made publicly available.[76] This interpretation is too restrictive. By considering only whether the research and development subsidy reduces the costs of production of the firm, and not whether the research results are publicly available, the ITA totally refuses to give any consideration to a distortion test. The ITA looks simply at the input costs of the firm and does not stop to think whether the subsidy provides for an advantage to the firm by allowing it to keep for itself the results of the research. While a distortion test is not explicitly required under the Agreement on Subsidies and Countervailing Measures, the concept of benefit in Article 1 and Article 14 of the said Agreement could imply the requirement that an advantage in comparison to all other firms is given.

However, in practice, the ITA has tried to avoid taking a clear position when deciding upon foreign research and development subsidies in specific cases. The US will never accept a green light claim unless it absolutely has to; instead, it will always prefer to say that the subsidy is not non-specific or that it is too small to worry about.[77] The ITA will consider research and development subsidies as countervailing unless the defendant makes a successful claim that the programs are not actionable under the WTO agreement on subsidies.[78] But if the foreign country claims that the subsidy is not countervailing, the ITA will usually not analyse thoroughly the issue of whether the program qualifies as a green light subsidy; rather, it will simply allege that there is no need for such analysis as the subsidy is non-specific,[79] *de minimis*,[80] or, until the new regulations, since its results were publicly available.

As a result of the automatic lapse of the green light provisions in the ASCM, the US countervailing duty provisions on R&D subsidies will no longer have effect as of July 2000.

[76] Department of Commerce, International Trade Administration, Final Rule on 19 CFR Part 351, 83.

[77] Online interview with an official of the Commission of the European Community, November 1998.

[78] *Phosphoric Acid From Israel*; *Final Results of Countervailing Administrative Review*, 61 Fed.Reg. 53351 (1996).

[79] *Stainless Steel Sheet and Strip in Coils from Italy: Preliminary Affirmative Countervailing Duty Determination and Alignment of Final Countervailing Duty Determination with Final Anti-dumping Duty Determination*, 63 Fed.Reg. 63900, 63907 (1998); see also *Certain Pasta from Italy and Turkey: Final Affirmative Countervailing Duty Determination and Final Determination of Sales at Less than Fair Value*, 61 Fed.Reg. 30287, 30307 (1996).

[80] *Stainless Steel Sheet and Strip in Coils from France: Preliminary Affirmative Countervailing Duty Determination and Alignment of Final Countervailing Duty Determination with Final Anti-dumping Duty Determination*, 63 Fed.Reg. 63876, 63880 (1998); see also *Certain Hot-Rolled Lead and Bismuth Carbon Steel Products from the United Kingdom: Final Results of Countervailing Duty Administrative Review*, 63 Fed.Reg. 18367, 18370 (1998).

3.A.7. Some Remarks

The United States' implementation of the Uruguay Round agreement on R&D subsidies highlights several features of the relation between the domestic and external spheres. From an international point of view, it shows the extent to which international trade agreements are limited by the domestic structures of the major trading partners. The constitutional constraints, as well as the wide divergences between the different economic systems, of the European Union and the United States, required adopting a compromise which, while providing the appearance of a final legal solution, left many issues unsolved. Second, as the US domestic implementation and subsequent administrative practice proved, international law formally limited the policy of the governments of the trading partners, but it was incapable of changing fundamentally the domestic structures and expectations of each side. The great challenge of the WTO as an international legal system is that it brings together different economic systems.

From the US domestic perspective, the case highlights the consensus which has characterised US trade policy during the last quarter of a century. It makes clear the influence of Congress, especially that of the Finance and the Ways and Means committees, over US foreign trade; as well as the need for the Executive to broker between the demands of foreign partners and the legislature. From a substantial point of view, the case shows the relevance of unfair trade instruments in US trade policy. In Congress, the price to pay for broader trade are tighter unfair trade statutes. But unfair trade is not simply protectionism. Instead, it is also about defending the American model both at home and abroad. The countervailing duty provisions on R&D subsidies were aimed at ensuring that the United States government's long-term hands off policy would remain, and signalling America's policy abroad, thus enhancing its export interests.

3.B. UNITED STATES' COUNTERVAILING DUTY POLICY

3.B.1. Introduction

Between 1980 and 1999, the US ITA initiated 315 countervailing duty cases.[81] This impressive use of countervailing duties reflected not only the United States' domestic protectionist feelings, but was also part of a policy to safeguard its domestic structures. Through the use of countervailing duties, the United States actively pursues a policy of both unilaterally interfering in the domestic structures of its trading partners and multilaterally influencing and establishing the

[81] See <http://www.ita.doc.gov/import_admin/records/stats/cv8099.htm>.

rules of the international trading system to protect and advantage its own domestic organisation.[82]

3.B.2. The Legal Background of US Countervailing Duty Policy

The United States has taken advantage of the weaknesses in the original GATT rules in order to conduct its countervailing duty policy. Article XVI of GATT established very loose rules on the use of subsidies. It generally required all contracting parties to notify, and be willing to consult, with regard to all subsidisation programs.[83] Thereafter, it established different rules for export and domestic subsidies. With regard to export subsidies only those for non-primary products were strictly prohibited.[84] Surprisingly, the Agreement established very loose rules recommending the limitation of export subsidies for primary products.[85] Domestic subsidies were accepted as legitimate instruments of the contracting parties. The looseness of the subsidies' rules was emphasised by a lack of co-ordination between the regulation of subsidies and the authority to impose unilaterally countervailing duties against them. The contracting parties remained free to impose countervailing duties on all imported products which benefited from a foreign subsidisation program.[86]

The Tokyo Round was the first major GATT attempt to deal with non-tariff barriers. Subsidies and countervailing measures were considered to be one of the most controversial issues of all the round's negotiations.[87] Whereas the United States aimed at severely limiting the use of subsidies, the goal of most other contracting parties was to limit the use of countervailing duties and remain largely free to implement their subsidisation programmes. These differing goals reflected the varying views on the proper role of the government in economic affairs.[88]

The resulting Subsidies Code would leave all the parties free.[89] The contracting parties were incapable of reaching an agreement on the definition of an actionable subsidy. Furthermore, the Code proclaimed an asymmetric regulation

[82] Concerning the US specific policy towards Canada see G Gagne, "The Canada-US Softwood Lumber Dispute: An Assessment after 15 Years" (1999) 33(1) *J. World Trade* 67.

[83] Article XVI (I) of GATT.

[84] Article XVI (IV) of GATT.

[85] Article XVI (III) of GATT.

[86] Article VI of GATT; see also Chapter I, Section B.

[87] The Tokyo Round was the 8th Multilateral Trade Round under the auspices of GATT. See GATT BISD 26th Supp. 3 (1980); see also G Winham, *International Trade and the Tokyo Round Negotiations* (Princeton, Princeton University Press, 1986), 119.

[88] D Tarullo, "The MTN Subsidies Code: Agreement without Consensus" in S Rubin and G Hufbauer (eds.), *Emerging Standards of International Trade and Investment* (Totowa, Rowman & Allanheld Publishers, 1984), 63–99, 71–78.

[89] Agreement on the Implementation of Articles VI, XVI and XXIII of the General Agreement of Subsidies and Trade, done on 12 April 1979, in force on 1 January 1980; reported in GATT BISD 26th Supp. 56 (1980).

of subsidies and countervailing duties.[90] Whilst it only timidly introduced harsher rules deterring the use of subsidies, it gave freedom to the contracting parties to countervail all subsidies which caused injury to their domestic industry.[91] In implementing the Tokyo Round Agreements, Congress was determined to reassess its powers in international trade and to guarantee what it alleged would be a level playing field for its industry and, thus, to ensure the enforcement of its countervailing duty legislation. Congress' aim was to target as many foreign subsidisation programs as possible.[92] To this end, it adopted broad countervailing duty legislation which included a wide definition of a countervailing subsidy, while making the institutional and procedural changes necessary to facilitate both the filing of cases by private parties and the imposition of duties. Congress gave legal standing to domestic firms for court review, abolished all administrative discretion, established very strict time limits and made sure that private firms had full voice in the administrative process. Second, Congress pressured the Executive to move the administering authority from the Treasury Department, which traditionally had been considered as a free trader, to the DoC, seen generally as closer to the interests of US domestic firms. Finally, Congress improved the role of courts as reviewers of all administrative decisions in order to limit the discretion of the Administration.

United States' firms seeking protection were willing and able to take advantage of the legislative developments in countervailing duty law. The domestic industry would use countervailing duties as instruments of business strategy with which to harass foreign firms and discourage them from entering the US market.[93] The result was the development of an entire trade relief industry; able to create and develop an extremely elaborate methodology, which required more and more complexity and toughness in order to survive, and was ready to lobby against any limitations of US countervailing duty law. In turn, this unfair trade industry permitted the Executive to conduct its policy of deterring foreign subsidisation policies world-wide. Indeed, despite constitutional tensions between Congress and the Executive, there was a background agreement which made possible both the granting of protection at home and the establishment of the rules of the game abroad.

[90] But see F Benyon and J Bourgeois, "The EC-US Steel Arrangement" (1984) 21 C.M.L. Rev. 305–354, 327.

[91] R Rivers and J Greenwald, "The Negotiation of a Code on Subsidies and Countervailing Measures: Bridging Fundamental Policy Differences" (1979) 11 *L. Pol'y Int'l Bus*. 1447–1495.

[92] *Report of the Committee on Ways and Means, House of Representatives, to accompany H.R. 4537, Report No 96–317*, 96th Cong. 1st Sess. (1979); see also *Report of the Committee on Finance, United States Senate, to accompany H.R. 4527 to Approve and Implement the Trade Agreements Negotiations Under the Trade Act of 1974, Report No 249*, 96th Cong. 1st Sess. (1979).

[93] J Terry, "Sovereignty, Subsidies and Countervailing Duties in the Context of the Canada-US Trading Relationship", 46 *U. Toronto Faculty Rev*. 48.

3.B.3. US Countervailing Duty Practice Against Developing Countries

A good example of the US deterrence strategy would be its countervailing policy towards developing countries.

As a result of the Tokyo Round negotiations on subsidies, the United States had finally agreed to include an injury test in its countervailing duty law relating to dutiable imports in exchange for a limited strengthening of the subsidies rules both for developed and developing countries. During the negotiations, submitting developing countries to any regulation on subsidies had been considered a very important goal. These countries argued that the regulation of subsidies was fundamentally biased. Whereas the rules established only loose obligations on primary products on which they had a certain comparative advantage, they strictly prohibited export subsidisation programs for manufactured products. Consequently during most of the round, developing countries showed very little interest in the subsidies negotiations. Finally, after suffering certain countervailing duty actions by the United States, Brazil seriously began to participate in the negotiations. In order to obtain some restraint from the United States, Brazil was willing to talk, and furthermore, to bring other developing countries to the negotiation table.[94]

From the very beginning it was clear that developing countries should be subjected to less stringent rules. The issue was then what degree of commitment could be asked from developing countries. With the aim of obtaining a commitment from most developing countries,[95] Article XIV of the Subsidies Code finally established a discretionary clause encouraging developing countries to reduce or eliminate export subsidies when their use was inconsistent with their development needs.

However, the United States asked for the introduction of a clause by which it could refuse to accept a country as a Subsidies Code contracting party.[96] Thereafter, it announced that it would not consider as contracting parties to the Subsidies Code, and hence would not apply its injury test, to all those developing countries which rejected the Code and failed to make what the US considered to be a satisfactory commitment to phase out export subsidisation programs.[97] According to the US government, an acceptable commitment was one which contained a promise to phase out existing export subsidies and to refrain from increasing subsidies or adopting new ones. The US Administration

[94] D Tarullo, *supra* n. 88, at 77.

[95] Specifically, the contracting parties sought the commitment of Mexico and India. If these countries committed themselves, many other developing countries would follow.

[96] Article XIX of the Subsidies Code.

[97] B Hoekman and R Stern, "An Assessment of the Tokyo Round Agreements and Arrangements", in R Stern (ed.), *The Multilateral Trading System: Analysis and Options for Changes* (New York, Harvester Wheatsheaf, 1993), 70.

viewed the injury test and the Subsidies Code as a vehicle to affect changes in developing countries.[98]

As to be expected, US domestic industry was willing to collaborate with the Administration's policy. The lack of an injury test avoided what was considered to be a major obstacle in obtaining the imposition of countervailing duties on foreign products.[99] Indeed, half of the countervailing procedures initiated by the US Administration during the 1980s were against developing countries.

The United States' policy, however, was only partially successful.[100] The US was able to obtain a strong commitment from the Brazilian authorities to eliminate its export subsidisation programs. Thereafter, the US obtained commitments from Korea, Pakistan, India and Mexico.[101] These countries made progressively weaker commitments than the strong commitment obtained from the Brazilian authorities. Notably, the United States did not have any support from its major trading partners, the European Community and Japan, which considered export subsidies from developing countries as mere irritants and considered that the United States was unfairly discriminating between different countries with its injury test in order to use countervailing duties as punitive remedies.[102] Thus, the US negotiated alone to phase out commitments with many developing countries in order to provide the benefits of the Subsidies Code. It granted its injury test to those countries which signed the multilateral agreement and committed themselves to phase out export subsidies or to those countries which entered into an agreement similar to that of the Subsidies Code.[103] For the most part, these commitments were vague; and, in the short run, they did not seem to restrain developing countries from using export subsidies. However, the commitments may have had an effect in limiting the initiation of new programs. Together with other circumstances, the pressure from the United States influenced the change of political mood of developing countries

[98] *General Accounting Office Report to the Secretary of Commerce and the United States Trade Representative, Benefits of International Agreement on Trade-Distorting Subsidies not Yet Realized* (Washington, GAO/ NSIAD-83–10, August 15, 1983).

[99] See Congressional Budget Office, *A Review of US Antidumping and Countervailing Duty Law and Policy*, 6 (1994) (which argues: "In practice, the main hurdle to an industry seeking protection under Antidumping and countervailing duty laws is to demonstrate that it has been injured by the imports, not that the imports are dumped or subsidized").

[100] G Hufbauer, "Subsidy Issues After the Tokyo Round", in W Cline (ed.), *Trade Policy in the 1980s* (Washington, Institute for International Economics, 1983), 327–361, 341.

[101] Many of these commitments followed very difficult negotiations. India, for example, presented a GATT dispute resolution case against the United States arguing that its policy of denying her the injury test was coercive and violated article I of GATT. See *United States Countervailing Duties*, L/5192, 30 September 1981, BISD 28S/113. The harassment against Brazil also ended up in a later GATT panel. See *United States: Countervailing Duties on Non-Rubber Footwear from Brazil*, SCM/94 (4 October 1989).

[102] Interview at the Commission, May 1997.

[103] The United States obtained commitments from Brazil, India, Pakistan, Mexico, Taiwan, Venezuela, Honduras, Nepal, North Yemen, El Salvador, Paraguay, Liberia, Hong Kong, Indonesia, Israel, Korea, The Philippines, Turkey, Uruguay. See J H Jackson, *The World Trading System: Law and Policy of International Economic Relations* (Cambridge, The MIT Press, 1989), 260.

and their economic liberalisation programs. In the Uruguay Round negotiations, many developing countries actively participated in the establishment of rules aimed at limiting subsidisation programs.[104]

3.B.4. The Rationale for US Countervailing Policy

3.B.4.a. The Deterrence Approach

United States' policy against export subsidies from developing countries is an example of its general world-wide deterrence policy against subsidies.[105] Such policy was not simply a neutral policy with pure economic implications but rather it was a policy aimed at advantaging and protecting its domestic structures within international trade.[106]

Taking into account the possibility of countries having different markets with different social organisations (plural, organised) and different state traditions on intervention in the marketplace, the subsidies discussion goes far beyond pure economic issues and affects deeply the domestic structures of the different trading partners. In this context, the significant question is not whether or not to use subsidies, but under what conditions it is appropriate to do so. To pursue their objectives effectively, countries with strong market organisations will not need to subsidise as much as countries with strong states but plural markets. Limiting subsidisation would strongly affect the latter as their main way to achieve their society's goals—government intervention—could be seriously impaired. On the other hand, countries such as the United States, with weak governments and plural markets would lose very little as the result of the limitation on government intervention because, even if government intervention was allowed, their domestic structures would be a serious handicap to such a policy. Thus, limiting subsidisation would advantage, in relative terms, countries like the US with weak governments and plural markets while seriously affecting those countries with strong government and plural markets.

The fact that the United States was actually protecting and advancing its domestic structures when imposing countervailing duties can be seen when analysing its countervailing duty methodology. Starting with the steel cases against European countries in 1982, the ITA developed a highly complex

[104] P McDonough, "Subsidies and Countervailing Measures in The GATT Uruguay Round: A Negotiating History (1986–1992)" in T Stewart (ed.), *The GATT Uruguay Round: A Negotiating History (1986–1992)* (Deventer, Kluwer Law and Taxation Publishers, 1993).

[105] J H Jackson, "Perspectives on Countervailing Duties" (1989) 21 *L. & Pol'y Int'l Bus.* 739–761; see also J H Jackson, *supra* n. 103, at 255.

[106] R Mundheim and P Ehrenhaft, "What is a Subsidy? A Discussion Paper" in D Wallace, F Loftus and V Krikorian (eds.), *supra* n. 7, at 95; see also R Behboodi, *Industrial Subsidies in World Trade: Trade Policy or Trade Politics* (London, Routledge, 1994), 14.

methodology to identify and measure foreign countervailing subsidisation programs which it applied against imported products from all countries.[107]

It has been argued that countervailing duties are interface instruments.[108] The law should not be concerned with the national welfare derived from free trade but rather with the welfare of the firms and workers that compete with the subsidised products. It would be unfair for domestic firms and workers to have to compete with foreign subsidised products. Countervailing duties would be a means of preventing the distortive and distributional effects of country A's policies on country B's income distribution system when the subsidised goods were imported from country A to country B.

However, the ITA has followed a deterrence rather than an entitlement approach.[109] It has not been interested in the effects the subsidy could have on

[107] *Certain Steel Products from Belgium: Preliminary Affirmative Countervailing Duty Determinations*, 47 Fed.Reg. 26300 (1982); see also *Certain Steel Products from Belgium: Final Affirmative Countervailing Duty Determinations*, 47 Fed.Reg. 39307 (1982); and A Holmer, S Haggerty and W Hunter, "Identifying and Measuring Subsidies" in *The Commerce Department Speaks on Import and Export Administration 1984* (New York, Practising Law Institute, 1984), Volume I, 301. The US methodology used to identify and measure foreign countervailable subsidies can be found in Section 771 (5) of the Tariff Act of 1930, as amended; 19 U.S.C. 1677 (5); P.L. 71–361, as amended by P.L. 96–39, P.L. 98–573, P.L. 100–418, P.L. 100–449, P.L. 100–647, P.L. 101–382 and P.L. 103–465. See also *Notice of Proposed Rulemaking and Request for Public Comments*, 54 Fed.Reg. 23366 (1989); *Advance Notice of Proposed Rulemaking and Request for Public Comments*, 60 Fed. Reg. 80 (1995); and *Notice of Proposed Rulemaking and Request for Public Comments*, 61 Fed.Reg. 7307 (1996). The final rules on countervailing duty methodology have been codified as 19 CFR Part 351. See Department of Commerce, International Trade Administration, *Final Rule on 19 CFR Part 351*, 63 Fed.Reg. 65348 (25 November 1998), text available at <http://www.ita.doc.gov/import_library/>.

[108] S Marcuss, "Understanding Direct and Indirect Subsidies: Are the Problems Negotiable or Incurable?", in D Wallace, F Loftus and V Krikorian (eds.), *supra* n. 7, at 51; see also J Barcelo, "Subsidies, CVDs and Antidumping After the Tokyo Round" (1980) 13 (2) *Cornell Int'l L. J.* 257.

[109] C Goetz, L Granet and W Schawrtz, "The Meaning of Subsidy and Injury in the Countervailing Duty Law" (1986) 6 *Int'l Rev. L. & Econ.* 17–32; see also R Diamond, "Economic Foundations of Countervailing Duty Law" (1989) 29 *Virginia J. Int'l L.* 767; and R Diamond, "A search for Economic and Financial Principles in the Administration of US Countervailing Duty Law" (1990) 21 *L & Pol'y Int'l Bus.* 514. Prior to 1979, the United States tried to use a distortion test. It took into account the effects of government subsidies on the competitive position of the firm receiving such subsidies, and thus, it imposed only countervailing duties on those imported products which actually distorted the market place. It therefore recognised pre-existing market distortions and distinguished between efficient and inefficient subsidies. See *Float Glass from West Germany*, 41 Fed.Reg. 1244 (Dept Treasury 1976); see also *Float Glass from the United Kingdom*, 40 Fed.Reg. 54227 (Dept. Treasury 1975). However, in 1979, in implementing the Tokyo Round Agreements, Congress was determined to limit the Executive's discretion in the administration of CVD laws and thus it prohibited any distortion test. This prohibition was strictly interpreted by the US Courts. See *A.S.G. Industries Inc.* v. *United States*, 467 F.Supp. 1200 (C.C.P.A. 1979) (where the Court held that Congressional intent to tighten administration of countervailing duty law may not be frustrated by simply finding that, for purposes of the countervailing duty law there is no bounty or grant through the employment of a vague and undefined international trade distortion test). See also *British Steel Corporation* v. *United States*, 605 F.Supp. 286 (Ct. Int'l Trade 1985); and *Michelin Tire Corporation* v. *United States*, 6 CIT 320, 328 (1983). The US would thus not take an entitlement approach but rather would follow a deterrence policy against all foreign subsidies. The Uruguay Round Agreement on Subsidies and Countervailing Measures follows to a certain extent this deterrence approach. On the European Union's countervailing duty practice, see F Snyder, *International Trade Law and Customs Law of the European Union* (London, Butterworths, 1999), 229–234.

its domestic market, or in the market in general, but rather in comparing foreign government-market relations with its own government-market relations. The distortive effects of the subsidy depend basically on the production output of the recipient firm. The subsidy will distort the market if it actually enables the firm to produce more, and more cheaply, than prior to receiving the bounty. This will not depend simply on the amount of the subsidy received but also on both the characteristics of the recipient firm and its market context. But under United States' countervailing duty methodology, a countervailing subsidy is considered to be the difference in the recipient firm's cash flows. The US will countervail the full amount of the money received allocated adequately to the imported products instead of looking at the reality before and after the grant of the subsidy, and hence it does not look to the international effects of such program.[110] The law will only exceptionally allow for certain deductions from the gross amount received with the aim of determining the net amount.[111]

In the URAA, Congress confirmed the law's lack of interest in the actual effects of the subsidy. During the beginning of the 1990s, the relation between subsidisation programs and privatisation was an important issue of countervailing duty law. The question was what would happen if a national firm which had received government subsidies was privatised.[112] It could be argued that if the sale was an arms length transaction, the buyer was actually paying back the full amount of the subsidy. When the buyer made an offer for the company it would be taking into account the benefits which the subsidy would be providing to the firm. In his offer, the actual value of the subsidy would be included. Because the new owners would have paid for any continuing competitive benefits from prior subsidies, they would thereafter compete on exactly the same terms as any other company in the market.

However, a basic principle of US countervailing duty law is that the Administration should not be concerned with the actual effects of the subsidy but simply with the net amount received. Thus the ITA considered that only a part of the subsidies received are paid back in the privatisation process. To the extent that a portion of the price paid for a privatised company can reasonably be attributed to prior subsidies, that portion of the subsidies would be extinguished. Yet, the Administration did not look at the effects of the subsidy, at

[110] T Ehr, "Allocation of Countervailable Benefits over Time", in *The Commerce Department Speaks, 1990* (New York, Practising Law Institute, 1990) (Volume II), 261; see also G Horlick, "Comment", in R Boltuck and R Litan (eds.), *Down in the Dumps: Administration of the Unfair Trade Laws* (Washington, The Brookings Institution, 1991), 137; see also Section 251 (A) (C) URAA (which clearly states: "The administering authority is not required to consider the effect of the subsidy in determining whether a subsidy exists under this paragraph.")

[111] These are costs such as application fees and exports taxes. See 19 U.S.C. 1677 (6).

[112] R Nielsen, "Privatization and Subsidies", in G Low (ed.), *The Commerce Department Speaks on International Trade and Investment 1994* (New York, Practising Law Institute, 1994) (Volume II), 7–37; see also R Cunningham, "Countervailing Capital Subsidies: Commerce's Methodologies Approach: A Fundamental Breakdown", *The Georgetown University Law Center's Annual International Trade Update*, Washington DC, 24 June 1994.

what actually happened to the subsidies but only to their value.[113] This approach was overruled by the courts which considered that in an arms length transaction all subsidies were necessarily paid back.[114] But in the Uruguay Round implementation process, Congress insisted that the countervailing duty law was not concerned with what happened with the subsidy but only with its amount. It included a special provision in URAA that made clear that "privatisation does not by itself require a determination by the administrative authority that a past countervailing subsidy received by the enterprise no longer continues to be countervailing even if the change of ownership is accomplished through an arms length transaction."[115]

The ITA's privatisation methodology is consistent with its general approach towards subsidies.[116] It does not distinguish between efficient and inefficient

[113] In attempting to estimate that portion of the purchase price attributable to prior subsidies, the most reasonable approach is to look at the following proportion—the privatised company's subsidies to the company's net worth during the period from the earliest point at which subsidies with benefits remaining countervailable in the investigation could have been bestowed until the date of privatisation. The ITA computes this by taking the simple average of the ratio of allocable subsidies received by the company in each year over the company's net worth. The simple average of the rations of subsidies to net worth serves as a reasonable historic surrogate of the percentage that subsidies constitute of the net worth of the company. Then it multiplies the average ratio by the purchase price to derive the portion of the purchase price attributable to repayment of prior subsidies. Finally it deduces the benefit stream of prior subsidies by the ratio of repayment amount to the net present value of all remaining benefits at the time of privatisation. Thus the US Administration fails to take into account the effects of the subsidy; it looks only to its amount. See *Privatization. General Issues Appendix*, 58 Fed.Reg. 37259 (1993).

[114] *Saarstahl AG* v. *United States*, 858 F. Supp 1871 (CIT 1994); reversed by *Saarstahl* v. *US* v. *Inland Steel Bar Corporation*, Slip op. 94–1457–1475 (Court of Appeals Federal District 1996) (the Court of Appeals reversed the case taking into account Congress' implementation of the Uruguay Round); see also *Inland Steel Bar Corporation* v. *United States*, 858 F.Supp. 179 (CIT 1994) (where the Court held that the purpose of CVD law was to capture the benefit provided by the subsidy and thus where the shareholder is the government and the company is sold totally in an arms length transaction, the subsidy reverts to the state).

[115] See Section 251 (a)(F) URAA. An arms length transaction means a transaction negotiated between unrelated parties, each acting in its own interest, or between related parties such that the terms of the transaction are those that would exist if the transaction had been negotiated between unrelated parties. See Legislative History, House Report No 103–826, at 10. In this sense, the *Statement of Administrative Action* makes clear that the section was introduced to "clarify that the sale of a firm at arm's length does not automatically, and in all cases extinguish any prior subsidies conferred." See *Message from the President of the United States transmitting the Uruguay Round Trade Agreements, Text of Agreements Implementing Bill, Statement of Administrative Action and Required Supporting Statements*, 103rd Congress, 2nd Session, House Document 103–316, Vol 1, 258. As to ITA's current practice on privatisation, see Department of Commerce, International Trade Administration, *Final Rule on 19 CFR Part 351*, 9–15 (pages refer to the text format available at the ITA web site and not to the Fed. Reg. format). The United States' approach to privatisation was seriously put into question in *United States: Imposition of Countervailing Duties on Certain Hot-Rolled Lead and Bismuth Carbon Steel Products Originating in France, Germany and the United Kingdom*, SCM/185, 15 November 1994, paragraphs 420–427. However, this panel report was never adopted as it was analysed under the GATT dispute settlement rules prior to the WTO Understanding on Rules and Procedures Governing the Settlement of Disputes, and thus the panel decision was blocked. Thus the issue has been discussed again in *United States Imposition of Countervailing Duties on Certain Hot-Rolled Lead and Bismurth Carbon Steel Products Originating in the UK* WTO/DS 138/R (23 December 1999).

[116] But see D A Codevilla, "Discouraging the Practice of What We Preach: *Saarstahl I*, *Inland Steel* and the Implementation of the Uruguay Round of GATT 1994" (1995) 3 *Geo Mason Indep. L.*

subsidies; rather it considers all subsidies to be a *per se* distortion of the market.[117] The market plays a very important role in its methodology. ITA analyses the foreign market and punishes those states which have a government-market relation different to that of the United States.

3.B.4.b. Comparing Market Systems

United States' methodology focuses on the jurisdiction, the market and the government of the foreign country. It is interested in what happens in such jurisdiction. This was made clear in its methodology with regard to foreign subsidisation programs by which a government provided goods or services to a firm or acquired them at preferential price.[118] In *Carbon Black from Mexico*,[119] the ITA insisted that it continued to believe that comparisons within a jurisdiction were the most appropriate measure of whether preferentiality existed. In fact, it considered as the least preferable standard to determine the existence of preferentiality whether the price of the government was inconsistent with world wide prices. The ITA was interested in the domestic market and not in the international market.

The ITA's interest in the foreign country's domestic market could also be seen in its approach towards non-market economies. The ITA excluded non-market economies from countervailing duty law because these countries had no markets. There was no market to distort by the subsidisation programs. A tax rebate on export given in a non-market economy did not confer a subsidy. The Administration did not focus on the international trade distorting effects

Rev. 435–472, 436 (arguing that the URAA amendment embeds a pernicious contradiction in US countervailing duty law as it in fact discourages privatisation and economic reform world-wide).

[117] M Trebilock, "Is the Game Worth a Candle? Comments on A Search for Economic and Financial Principles in the Administration of Countervailing Duty Law" (1990) 21 *Law & Pol'y Int'l Bus.* 723–733, 724. The ITA thus adopts the anti-distortion school approach towards subsidies, which considers that all subsidies distort the market and thus that countervailing duties should target all subsidies regardless of their cause. This approach is the opposite to that which the European Community has held for many years, which considers that subsidies are not distortive *per se* and that they should be controlled only in order to limit their possible adverse international trade effects. See General Agreement on Tariffs and Trade. Committee on Subsidies and Countervailing Measures, *EEC Memorandum on US Final Countervailing Duty Determinations on European Steel Products*, SCM/35 (1982); see also J Bourgeois, "The GATT Rules for Industrial Subsidies and the New GATT Round" in E U Petersmann and M Hilf (eds.), *The New GATT Round of Multilateral Trade Negotiations, Legal and Economic Problems* (Deventer, Kluwer Law and Taxation Publishers, 1991), 219–236. The European Community has followed the same approach with regards to intra-Community state aids. See A Evans and S Martin, "Socially Acceptable Distortion of Competition: Community Policy on State Aids" (1991) 16 *Euro. L. Rev.* 79–111; see also Commission of the European Communities, *Third Survey on State Aids in the European Community in the Manufacturing and Certain Other Sectors* (Luxembourg, Office for the Official Publications, 1992).

[118] The preferentiality methodology was changed as a consequence of the Uruguay Round agreement. However, for our purposes its principles are still useful.

[119] See *Carbon Black from Mexico. Preferentiality Appendix*, 51 Fed.Reg. 13269, 13271 (1986).

of the programs but rather on what happened in the market of the foreign country.[120]

The aim of the US countervailing duty methodology is to determine both the existence and the amount of a countervailing subsidy.[121] In order to identify and measure a foreign countervailing subsidy the ITA applies two standards. First, the ITA applies a test of administrative convenience. The subsidy program must provide a favourable treatment to some firms with respect to other and thus be given *de iure* or *de facto* to a limited number of firms within a certain jurisdiction.[122]

Second, the basic test of United States' countervailing duty law is whether there is a benefit to the recipient. Such a test asks whether a government's action is inconsistent with commercial considerations. The subsidy is considered to be a market phenomenon. The law will analyse whether a government loan, or an equity infusion, or a loan guarantee or any government program is consistent with the market benchmark.[123] The subsidy will be the difference between the government price and the market price.[124] If a government provides a loan to a

[120] J Greenwald, "United States Law and Practice", in J Bourgeois (ed.), *Subsidies and International Trade: A European Lawyer's Perspective* 33–41, 35 (Deventer, Kluwer Law and Taxation Publishers, 1991).

[121] W Hunter and S Kuhbach, "Subsidies and CVD: Highlights Since 1984" in *The Commerce Department Speaks 1987* (New York, Practising Law Institute, 1987), 491; see also P Jamerson, "The Administration Of US Countervailing Duty Laws with Regard to Domestic Subsidies: Where it's Been, Where it Stands and Where it May Go" (1985) 12 *Syracuse J. Int'l L. & Com.* 549–124. The identification and measurement are steps theoretically different, but many times both processes will overlap. See G Depayre and R Petriccione, "Definition of a Subsidy", in J Bourgeois (ed.), *supra* n. 120.

[122] W Lay, "Redefining Actionable Subsidies under US Countervailing Duty Law" (1991) 91(6) *Columbia L. Rev.* 1495–1518. The Administration deducted the specificity test from the wording of the law: "The term subsidy has the same meaning as the term 'bounty or grant' as that term is used in section 303, and includes, but it is not limited to, the following:

(i) Any export subsidy (. . .)

(ii) The following domestic subsidies, if provided or required by government action to a specific enterprise or industry or group of enterprises or industry." See 19 U.S.C. 1677 (5)(A). The Administration considered that such an interpretation also followed Article 11(3) of the Subsidies Code. See G Horlick, "Subsidies and Suspension Agreements in Countervailing Duty Cases" in *Commerce Department Speaks on Dumping and Countervailing Duties* (New York, Practising Law Institute, 1982), 31–51. The Administration's interpretation was upheld in *Carlise Tire and Rubber Co.* v. *United States*, 564 F.Supp. 834 (CIT 1983). Following *Cabot Corp.* v. *United States*, 620 F.Supp. 722 (CIT 1985), the ITA has applied both a *de iure* and a *de facto* specificity test. In establishing the *de facto* test, the ITA weights three different standards. See Section 355.43 (b)(2) of the proposed regulations. This specificity test has been adopted by the Uruguay Round's Agreement on Subsidies and Countervailing Measures in Article 2.

[123] M Malmrose, "Interest Rate Benchmarks in Countervailing Proceedings", in *Commerce Department Speaks, 1990* (New York, Practising Law Institute (1990) (Volume II), 201; see also *Certain Softwood Lumber Products from Canada. Final Affirmative Countervailing Duty Determination*, 57 Fed.Reg. 22570 (1992); and *Michelin Tire Corp.* v. *United States*, 2 CIT 143 (1981).

[124] Until the Uruguay Round Implementation Act there was, however, one exception to this standard. Government-provided services or products would only be preferential if the government actually discriminated in prices. The subsidy would be the difference between what the government charged to the preferred firm and what it charged to all other firms. Following the Uruguay Round Subsidies Agreement, Congress defined preferential treatment as that which is less than adequate

firm at an interest rate of 8% whereas the market would charge a 10% interest rate, the subsidy would be the difference, that is, 2%. The benefit to the recipient standard, however, raises two fundamental issues. First, it is important to look at the market. The subsidy is a market phenomenon and the market is the background from which the subsidy can be identified. Second, it is necessary to analyse the government conduct which is prohibited. A government cannot act inconsistently with a market.

US methodology requires the existence of a domestic market. A good example of this is its methodology towards communist countries.[125] Because a subsidy is, by definition, any action that distorts or subverts the market process and results in a misallocation of resources, without a market it is considered meaningless to look for a misallocation of resources caused by subsidies. In non-market economies prices are set by central planners; losses suffered by production and foreign trade enterprises are routinely covered by government transfers; and investment decisions are considered to be controlled by the state. Thus in these countries, there is simply no market in which to interfere and thus it is impossible to determine a subsidy.[126]

The ITA's methodology would recognise the existence of mixed economies. It will accept the government as an actor in the market and will acknowledge some inter-relationships between the market and the government.[127] However, in mixed economies, private property still remains and price is still ruled by the forces of supply and demand. In mixed economies, governments do not try to supplant the market as the allocator of resources. Under the ITA's methodology, even in mixed economies there is still a market economy. Such systems are considered to be economically rational. In the absence of government intervention, prices are determined through the interaction of supply and demand. In response to these prices, resources flow to their most profitable and efficient uses. Profits drive market economy systems and guide capitalists to invest

remuneration, which shall be determined in relation to the prevailing market conditions for the good or service being provided or the goods being purchased in the country which is subject to the investigation or review. See F Tougas, "Softwood Lumber from Canada: Natural Resources and the Search of a Definition of a Domestic Countervailable Subsidy" (1989) 24 *Gonzaga L. Rev.* 135; see also Section 251 (A)(E)(iv) URAA.

125 For countries in transition to market economies, the ITA applies a market oriented industry test. See *Oscillating Fans from China*, 56 Fed.Reg. 10011 (1991); see also D W Richardson and R Nielsen, "Recent Developments in the Treatment of Non-market Economies under the AD/CVD Laws" in W Willkie (ed.), *The Commerce Department Speaks 1992: Developments in Import Administration; Export and Investment Abroad* (New York, Practising Law Institute, 1992), 149.

126 *Carbon Steel Wire Rod from Czechoslovakia: Final Negative Countervailing Duty Determination*, 49 Fed. Reg. 19370 (1984); see also *Carbons Steel Wire Rod from Poland. Final Countervailing Duty Determination*, 49 Fed.Reg. 19374 (1984). This approach was upheld in *Georgetown Steel Corporation* v. *United States*, 81 F.2d 1308 (Fed. Cir. 1986).

127 Thus, in the 1989 proposed rules, it would accept government loans as a market benchmark as long a such loans were not limited to a specific firm. See Section 355.44 (7) of the Proposed Rules. Under the new codified rules, the ITA will no longer consider such loans as commercial benchmarks but it will accept a government-owned bank loan as a commercial loan benchmark unless it is clear that the loan is provided on non-commercial terms or at the direction of the government. See 19 CFR 351.505(a)(2)(ii).

resources where they earn the highest possible return. This profit maximisation leads the capitalist to produce goods that are in demand at the least cost.

Despite theoretically accepting the existence of mixed economies, the market of the ITA's methodology is a perfect market. In the absence of the subsidy, the firm would experience market-determined costs of its inputs and receive a market-determined price for its output. Furthermore, it is not only a perfect market but also a plural market, ruled by individualistic economic actors. It is a market in which individuals purely seek profit. It is not a market in which banks may organise themselves and sacrifice short term profits in order to save industries. It is not a system in which trade unions and capital will reach agreements and rule their relations by consensus. It is not a market in which firms will establish long term relationships and sacrifice profits and limit competition in order to obtain long term economic growth. The market of the ITA's methodology is not necessarily an efficient market which guarantees economic growth, but it is one characterised by plurality and individualism. It is an ideal market which is close to the United States' market. A system ruled by extreme individualism in which market actors are incapable of organising and developing a concerted action. ITA's methodology punishes those systems which are different from the US market.

For example, in determining whether a government loan is inconsistent with market considerations, the ITA will try to discover the price which a private lender would have charged. But the US Administration assumes a certain rationale for a lender. The lender will not be a bank with a long term relationship with the firm and which will have a strong interest in the welfare of its client and therefore willing sometimes to risk heavily. Instead, it will be one which is purely ruled by profit. The interest loan will depend simply on the riskiness of the transaction.[128] In determining the short term loan benchmark, the ITA will look at the national average benchmark interest rate because short term loans are less risky than long term loans. However, with regard to long term loans, the ITA will look at the company-specific benchmark because such standard will enable it "to capture the fact that certain companies are more or less risky than average, and that commercial lenders will take these risk characteristics into account in setting the conditions of the loan."[129] But even though the ITA is assuming that the conditions of the loan will depend on the risk of the transaction, by using a company specific benchmark it is not taking into account that the loan which such a firm could have obtained in the market may have better or worse conditions than those of other firms dependent on the links that such a firm may have with the lenders. A private firm may not go simply to a loan market; instead it may obtain the loan at better conditions, from its housebank. The ITA's assumptions are, in fact, based on a parochial view of the financial

[128] 355.44(b) of the 1989 Proposed Regulations. The new rules are codified as 19 CFR 351.505 (a)(2).

[129] Background of the 1989 Proposed Regulations; see also 255.44 (b)(4) of the Proposed Regulations; and 19 CFR 351.505(a)(2)(iii).

system. It assumes, that like US firms, foreign corporations will borrow money from the bond and equity markets and not from housebanks with which they may share tight economic interests. Likewise, the Administration will distinguish between creditworthy and uncreditworthy firms.[130] The ITA again assumes that the private lender will require a premium interest rate from the uncreditworthy firm. But its blindness towards financial systems other than the American, leads it to believe that the existence of a private long term loan provided without an explicit government guarantee will be an indicator that a firm was creditworthy.[131]

In general, these same principles and rationales apply to all sort of subsidies. The US Administration will look for the market benchmark to determine whether the government intervention is consistent with commercial considerations. However, the market benchmark will be that determined by a plural market. The ITA will assume that private market actors will behave in a certain "rational" way. Thus, the market background would be one which is similar to the United States' market. This is important because the behaviour which is prohibited will depend on what type of market is involved. If the market were one different to that assumed by the US Administration, the government behaviour allowed would be different.

The second element of the ITA's "consistent with market considerations" test is what kind of behaviour is permitted by the government. The government may act in the market but it must do so in conformity with how the market would behave. This implies taking a political position with regard to the role of government in society. Because the ITA's test is not concerned with the actual effects of the subsidy, when applying its test it is in fact interfering in the domestic structures of the foreign country. Any government action in the market which is not consistent with the rational behaviour of a market actor in a plural and individualist market will be considered as a countervailing subsidy. Assuming a plural market and requiring a policy of government intervention in accordance with such a market it is not simply requiring a policy of low domestic government intervention but one which is in accordance with America's own hands off policy. Through its CVD methodology, the US Administration is globalising the American model.

3.B.5. An Illustration of the US Rationale: The GATT 1994 Steel Cases

The incapability of the United States to understand market behaviour different to its own and hence its tendency to punish market differences, was highlighted in 1994's fascinating GATT dispute regarding US countervailing duties on steel products from France, Germany and the United Kingdom.[132]

130 Se 355.44 (b)(6) of 1989 Proposed Regulations; see also 19 CFR 351.505(a)(3)(iii).

131 355.44 (b)(6)(ii) of 1989 Proposed Regulations; see also 19 CFR 351.505(a)(4)(ii).

132 *United States: Imposition of Countervailing Duties on Certain Hot-Rolled Lead and Bismuth*

The ITA's decision regarding steel from Germany illustrates the United States' concept of the market and how such an ideal is reflected in its methodology. In its administrative decision, the ITA had determined that countervailing subsidies were provided to the German steel firm Saarstahl through debt forgiveness by the governments of Germany and the Saarland, debt forgiveness by private banks, and the Worker Assistance Program. The most controversial question was whether the debt forgiveness by private banks constituted a countervailing subsidy. The US Administration had determined that as part of a restructuring program in 1986, private banks had agreed to forgive some debt owed to them by Saarstahl, if the governments of Germany and Saarland would forgive all debt owed to the governments by Saarstahl and if the government of Saarland would assure the future liquidity of Saarstahl.[133] The ITA considered the banks' forgiveness as a countervailing subsidy. It considered that:

> "The talks on the forgiveness of Saarstahl's debt were based on the common notion that all participants, including private and public creditors, would have contributed to the restructuring of Saarstahl if this restructuring was to be successful. The Governments of Germany and Saarland made their forgiveness dependent on private creditors also forgiving a portion of their claims against Saarstahl. The private creditors laid down the same condition with regard to the claims of the Governments of Germany and Saarland. [Thus] . . . we determine that the subsequent forgiveness of principal was countervailable because it was required by the governments as part of a government led debt reduction package for Saarstahl and because the two governments guaranteed the future liquidity of Saarstahl, thereby implicitly assuring the private banks that the remaining portion of Saarstahl's outstanding loans would be repaid."[134]

It is important to note that the ITA considered as countervailing not simply the government's forgiveness of debt or its assurance of liquidity but also the private banks' forgiveness of debt. The US Administration considered that:

> "Given the government's extensive role in bringing about the private banks' debt forgiveness and the absence of any document to support respondent's claim that the banks' actions were commercially sound, we find the forgiveness to be countervailable."

Thus, the two fundamental factors for the United States' decision were the government's involvement in the restructuring operation and what it considered to be a lack of commercial soundness on the part of the banks in forgiving the debt.

Carbon Steel Products Originating in France, Germany and the United Kingdom, SCM/185, 15 November 1994. This GATT Panel report reviewed the International Trade Administration's decision to impose countervailing duties on certain hot-rolled lead and bismuth carbon steel products. See *Final Affirmative Countervailing Duty Determination: Certain Hot Rolled Lead and Bismuth Carbon Steel Products from France*, 58 Fed.Reg. 6221 (1993); *Final Affirmative Countervailing Duty Determination: Certain Hot Rolled Led and Bismuth Carbon Steel Products from Germany*, 58 Fed. Reg. 6233 (1993); and *Final Affirmative Countervailing Duty Determination: Certain Hot Rolled Lead and Bismuth Steel Products from the United Kingdom*, 58 Fed.Reg. 6237 (1993).

133 paragraphs 12–15 of the GATT Panel.

134 58 Fed.Reg. 6233 (1993), at 6234–6235, as cited in the GATT Panel, paragraph 374.

In the GATT dispute, the United States and the European Community did not disagree on whether the action of a private party may result in a countervailing subsidy by reason of government involvement in such action, but rather on the conditions under which the action of a private party can be treated as a subsidy by reason of the interrelationship between actions of governments and the action of the private party.

The EC argued that an action of a private party could result in a subsidy to a third party only if public authorities, directly or indirectly, channelled public funds through a private party to a third party, or if the public authorities compelled or mandated a private party to provide funds to a third party. The EC considered the ITA's statement that the debt forgiveness by the private banks was required by the governments of Germany and Saarland as part of the debt reduction package did not provide a valid basis for qualifying the debt forgiveness by private banks as a subsidy. The provisions of the Agreement on Subsidies and Countervailing Measures required government intervention before any action could be construed to be subsidy. Discussions between government officials and private banks did not amount to government intervention. The governments did not channel funds through banks to Saarstahl, nor did they provide compensation to the banks for their debt forgiveness to Saarstahl. The governments did not exercise any control over the private banks' activities, nor did they direct or impose a legal obligation upon the banks to provide funds to Saarstahl. The mere fact that the government initiated a debt forgiveness package did not mean that the banks were required to participate in the plan. Parallel action by Saarstahl's major creditors, public and private, was necessary if the company was to survive. In any major crisis concerning the survival of a company, the major creditors had an interest to act in concert whilst pursuing their best interests. The fact that the action was beneficial to their debtor could not alter this. The banks, as the governments, had acted in parallel to preserve their own, distinct interests: "*Conscious parallelism between the actions of the banks and the governments as major creditors, even if the governments initiated the debt reduction package, was not a sufficient basis to treat the debt forgiveness by the private banks as a subsidy.*"

Concerning the statement whereby the governments assured the future liquidity of the company, the European Community considered that it was an insufficient basis for treating the debt forgiveness by the private banks as a countervailable subsidy. First, the assurance was neither enforceable nor quantifiable, it did not involve a financial contribution by the public authorities and did not amount to more than a statement of the common interest which was shared with the banks in ensuring the future commercial viability of Saarstahl. The assurance was in no way enforceable under domestic law. The government of Saarland was a majority shareholder in Saarstahl and the statements concerning the future liquidity of the company were entirely in keeping with the government's status and role as a majority shareholder. The purpose of the statements was to confirm to the private banks that the government would continue to participate in the restructuring plan designed to assure Saarstahl's survival and would not withdraw from its position as a shareholder. But even if the assurance made the debt reduction package commercially viable for the banks, the United States should have countervailed this assurance of liquidity instead of the debt forgiveness by the private banks.[135]

The United States argued that the banks had agreed to forgive the debt *only on the condition* that the government forgive its debt to Saarstahl and guarantee its debt to Saarstahl. The US considered that it was left to the signatories to reasonably interpret what constituted a subsidy. If a government action directly or indirectly bestowed a benefit, that benefit should be considered as a countervailable subsidy. A subsidy would be provided indirectly when the government's action set in motion the events that resulted in a benefit to the firm. For a subsidy to exist the Agreement required government action which was more than minor, insignificant or incidental and which resulted in a clearly identifiable benefit to the firm. There was in this sense a need for a government action but not a financial contribution in order to determine the existence of a subsidy. Furthermore, the Agreement did not require that there be a legal compulsion in order for a subsidy to be provided indirectly as a result of a government acting through a private party. The banks' forgiveness of debt was conditional on the fact that the governments forgave their debts and guaranteed the liquidity of the firm because, in the United States' opinion, it would had been irrational for the banks to forgive the debt had the government not intervened.

With regard to the alleged loan guarantee, the United States argued that it was much more than a mere statement from the government. Even if it was not legally binding, this commitment would be kept for other reasons. Legal enforceability was not the real issue. Rather it was the fact that the banks obviously believed the government's guarantee was a meaningful commitment that would permit them to forgive the loans.[136]

The substantial background of the whole dispute was, in fact, the concerted action between government and private capital which is so characteristic of corporative societies ruled by consensus, such as the Federal Republic of Germany.[137] In such markets, characterised by strong market cohesion, the government is an enabling actor capable of acting in the market through means other than direct government intervention. The strong relations between industry and banks through mutual equity participation and the ability of the state to enter in a continuous dialogue with business, allow the government to find solutions to economic and industrial problems without either adopting an interventionist policy which would imply a cost to the budget, or requiring compulsory action. Whether such government behaviour can be considered as a subsidy is questionable. Considering all government action as a subsidy even if such intervention did not involve a financial contribution nor a compulsory act would

[135] See paragraphs 109–136 of the GATT Panel.
[136] Ibid.
[137] Chapter 4.B (3), on the domestic structures of Germany.

imply having a system where there is a total separation of the plural market from the state. This, is in fact, the model which the US was thinking about when it countervailed the banks' action. The United States, a country in which there is a confrontation between the market and the state and where there is no long term commitment between market actors, could not conceive that concerted action between the banks, the government and the firm was not unfair.[138]

The United States' approach to the market, its idea of how market actors should behave and the impact which this has in its countervailing duty methodology, was also reflected in a different matter of the 1994 Panel Report. The United States and the European Community strongly disagreed on the behaviour of market actors and on whether all market actors should act in the same way. In its administrative decisions, the ITA had decided to consider as countervailing the provision of equity capital to certain firms by the governments of France and the United Kingdom, which already had an equity participation in such companies. The US Administration had determined that in cases where there was no market-determined price, such as the stock market price which could serve as a market benchmark, the determination of whether or not an equity infusion constituted a subsidy involved an examination of whether the firm in question is equity worthy. In such an examination, the ITA had used a reasonable private investor standard. The test was whether, from the perspective of a reasonable private investor examining the firm at the time the government equity infusion was made, the firm showed an ability to generate a reasonable rate of return within a reasonable period of time.

The EC argued that the United States' test treated inside and outside investors the same way. For the United States, a reasonable investor was an outside investor. However, the EC argued that the rationale for investment decisions of an inside investor could be considerably different from those of an outside investor. The French and the British governments already had a stake in the steel companies and thus they could not be expected to behave as an outside investor. For an inside investor, who had a big stake in a company, it made commercial sense to continue to invest in such a company even when an outside investor would not do so. If the inside investor provided further investment and helped turn the company around, where an outside would not have done so, this could not be taken to mean that the capital infusion was unsound and that it was a

[138] The Panel on this issue adopted a purely formal approach. It noted that in footnote 4 to Article 1 the words "directly or indirectly" refer to the modalities by which a bounty or subsidy was provided, but not to the effects of a subsidy on the conduct of a third party. Under the Agreement a subsidy could be considered to be provided indirectly when a government provided assistance to the production, manufacture or export of a product by acting through a third party, on the condition that the relationship between the action of the private party and the government was such that the action of the private party could be qualified as a governmental measure. However, "where a government took measures to assist a firm, which measures arguably constituted direct subsidies to a firm, the notion in footnote 4 and Article 1 of a subsidy provided indirectly did not permit a signatory to treat as an indirect subsidy by action of a private party which resulted from the measures taken by the government and which provided an additional benefit to the firm." See paragraph 399 of the GATT Panel Report.

subsidy. Inside investors had sometimes to accept a negative return on their assets as long as over the longer term the net capitalised value of the stream of income from their assets would remain positive.

The United States argued that there was no such recognised class of investors as inside investors. It argued that it was an accepted proposition in economic analysis that the investment behaviour of all investors was based on the marginal return of investment. In any particular situation investors behaved in the same manner, whether they were inside or outside investors. Whenever it made commercial sense for an inside investor to invest, it would also make sense for an investment to be made by an outside investor. Whether it made sense for an investor to retain past investment, as opposed to whether it would be economically rational for that investor to make new investments in the same firm, it was basic economic philosophy that rational investment decisions were made at the margin without regard to previous investments.[139] Again the US was taking as the standard for fairness that of its domestic system. It was internationalising the plurality of its domestic market system.

3.B.6. Some Remarks

The United States' countervailing duty methodology implies a certain concept of both the market and the role which the government should play within it. It is a methodology which disregards and punishes any market organisation which is different from its own market system. Countervailing duties are not only protectionist instruments which were developed due to the constitutional interactions between Congress and the Executive but they are also a means by which the United States both establishes the agenda of the international trading system and interferes in the domestic structures of foreign countries in order to advantage its own domestic organisation. The ITA's 315 countervailing duty investigations were an example of United States' broad consensus on trade policy. The duties resulting from them were adopted both to protect domestic industry, which as a result of the American domestic structures was incapable of adapting to the new challenges of globalisation, and to promote the country's export interests by moulding an international trading system into a reflection of the American way.

[139] Paragraphs 163–213 of the Panel Report. The Panel on this issue, however, ruled in favour of the United States by again adopting a very formal approach to the problem. It considered that there could be differences between an inside and outside investor, it decided to solve the issue by simply considering that the United States had reasonably approached the problem in its administrative decisions: "The Panel found that the DOC had expressly addressed the issue of alleged need to distinguish between inside and outside investors and that the explanation provided by the DOC for its decision not to make such a distinction could not be said to be inadequately supported by rational analysis." See Paragraphs 505–508 of the GATT Panel Report.

3.C. SECTION 301 OF THE 1974 TRADE ACT: A METAPHOR OF UNITED STATES TRADE POLICY

3.C.1. Introduction

Section 301 of the Trade Act of 1974 is the primary United States' statute giving the Executive authority to enforce United States' rights under international trade agreements and to take action against foreign unfair trade practices which adversely affect US commerce.[140] It is an expansion of the authority that had been vested in President George Washington in 1794, and which the United States Congress has repeatedly affirmed for almost two centuries, to retaliate against discriminatory foreign trade practices that unduly burden US commerce.[141]

Section 301 has become an aggressive unilateral trade instrument by which the United States may build up the international trade regime even at the cost of violating WTO, previously GATT, rules.[142] Congress has extended the scope of the Executive's authority, to provide it with the necessary leverage, by means of threats, to establish a trade regime which reflects its domestic structures and to open foreign markets by imposing on foreign countries the rule of free trade under what it considers to be fair trade.[143]

Section 301 is a metaphor for US contemporary trade policy. On the one hand, it is a good example of the success of America in the world trading system. The development of Section 301 reflects both Congress' concern with the US trade deficit and a reassertion of its constitutional trade policy powers.[144]

[140] Section 301 of the Trade Act of 1974, Pub. L. No. 93–618, S 301, 88 Stat. 144 (1974), as amended by the Trade Act of 1979 Pub. L. 96–39, the Trade and Tariff Act of 1984, Pub L. 98–573, the Omnibus Trade and Competitiveness Act of 1988, Pub. L. 100–418, 102 Stat. 1107 (1988), and the Uruguay Round Agreements Act, Pub. L. 103–465, 108 Stat. 4809 (1994); 19 U.S.C. 2411 (1996). Up to August 1999, 119 cases were initiated and 31 petitions were rejected or withdrawn. A list of Section 301 cases is available at <http://www.ustr.gov/reports/>; see also T Bayard and K Elliot, "Aggressive Unilateralism and Section 301: Market Opening or Market Closing?" (1992) 15 (6) *World Economy* 685–706. Section 301 of the 1974 Trade Acts has been recently discussed in a WTO Dispute Settlement Panel Report finding that in principle it did not violate the provisions of the Agreement Establishing the WTO or its annexed agreement. See *Sections 301–310 of the Trade Act of 1974* WTO/DS 152/R (22 December 1999).

[141] B Fisher and R Steinhardt, "Section 301 of the Trade Act of 1974: Protection for US Exports of Goods, Services and Capital" (1982) 14 *L. & Pol'y Int'l Bus.* 569–690, 573. Its immediate predecessor was the Trade Expansion Act of 1962, Pub. L. No 87–794 S 252, 76 Stat. 872 (1962).

[142] J Bhagwati, "Aggressive Unilateralism: An Overview" in J Bhagwati and H Patrick (eds.), *Aggressive Unilateralism: America's 301 Trade Policy and the World Trade System* (New York, Harvester Wheatsheaf, 1991), 1–45, 3. On the situation of Section 301 under WTO, see J Bello and A Holmer, "The Post Uruguay Round Future of Section 301" (1994) 25 *L. & Pol'y Int'l Bus.* 1297–1308.

[143] K Abbot, "Defensive Unfairness: The Normative Structure of Section 301", in J N Bhagwati and R Hudec (eds.), *Fair Trade and Harmonization: Prerequisites for Free Trade?* (Cambridge, The MIT Press 1996), 415–469.

[144] P Stern, "Reaping the Wind and Sowing the Whirlwind: Section 301 as a Metaphor for Congressional Assertiveness in US Trade Policy" (1990) 8(1) *B. U. Int'l L. J.* 1–19.

The creation and strengthening of Section 301 have been parallel to the adoption of trade agreements and trade expansion. These developments resulted in an effective tool by which the US has been able to achieve a substantial part of its trade policy goals.[145] While bilateral trade imbalances got the attention of policy makers, formal actions were clearly correlated with what the United States perceived as the existence of barriers to trade.[146] Thus, it proves how the United States has been able to solve the paradox of world interdependence by means of creating adequate constitutional co-operation procedures which permit a reasonable input of constituency pressure while at the same time making possible an effective trade policy which allowed it to lead the international trading system. On the other hand, the use of Section 301 and insistence on dispute settlement may now suggest the beginning of U-turn in United States' trade policy.

3.C.2. The Concept of Unreasonableness in Section 301

Section 301 allows the United States Trade Representative (USTR), to take retaliatory measures against foreign practices, acts or policies which violate or are inconsistent with the provisions of or otherwise deny benefits to the US under any trade agreement; or are unjustifiable, unreasonable or discriminatory and burden or restrict US commerce.[147]

Up to the conclusion of the Uruguay Round, the concept of "unreasonableness" became a central feature of the United States' aggressive policy under Section 301.[148] Whereas cases in the first decade of Section 301—from 1974 to 1984—sought the enforcement of US trade rights under the GATT, the second decade—from 1984 to 1994—reveal the United States as using its economic power in an attempt to hold on to its position as the world's leading trading nation. It did so by using the concept of "unreasonableness" to tackle foreign barriers not regulated by GATT.[149] The "unreasonableness" standard was the principal means by which the United States was able to pursue an international trade system which reflected its own domestic structures. It was used to establish a world-wide regime on goods, services, intellectual property rights and telecommunications; one consistent with the United States' market consideration standards.

[145] J Bello and A F. Holmer, "US Trade Law and Policy Series No 24: Dispute Resolution in the New World Trade Organisation, Concerns and Net Benefits" (1994) 28 (4) *Int'l Law.* 1095–1104.

[146] M Noland, "Chasing Phantoms: The Political Economy of USTR" (1997) 51(3) *Int'l Org.* 365–387.

[147] 19 U.S.C. 2411 (a) (1996); See also 19 U.S.C.. 2411 (b) (1996).

[148] See P Hansen, "Defining Unreasonableness in International Trade: Section 301 of the Trade Act of 1974" (1987) 96 *Yale L. J.* 1122–1146.

[149] See C O'Neal Taylor, "The Limits of Economic Power: Section 301 and the World Trade Organisation Dispute Settlement System", 30 (1997) *Vanderbilt J. Transnational L.* 209–315, 212–223.

As the law now stands, an unreasonable act, policy or practice is defined as "an act, policy, or practice, [which] while not necessarily in violation of, or inconsistent with, the international legal rights of the United States, is otherwise unfair or inequitable."[150] Such a concept allows a purely subjective determination of what is unfair or inequitable; enabling the United States to impose its own standards of behaviour on other nations. It is intended to reflect Congress' ideas on specific reciprocity and fair trade. The US legislature firmly believes that if the United States allows access to its markets, its trading partners should allow free access to theirs. The foreign market should allow equal access to that in the United States.[151] This implies that the foreign market should be the same as that of the United States.[152] Under Congress' considerations there should be one world-wide global market which is the same for all. Any socio-political structures in which national markets are embedded should simply vanish. Or rather, there should be only one world-wide market embedded in a system which reflects United States domestic system. The leverage provided by Section 301 allowed the US to impose an international trading system characterised by negative integration and thus deregulation and liberalisation at the national domestic level.

Following the amendments of both the Omnibus Trade and Competitiveness Act and the Uruguay Round Implementation Act, the statute provides certain examples of practices which are considered unreasonable under United States' law.[153] Unreasonableness includes, but is not limited to, any act, policy, or practice, or any combination of acts, policies or practices, which:

(I) Denies fair and equitable opportunities for the establishment of an enterprise. The USTR has consistently used the concept of unreasonableness as a device to open foreign markets to United States' services.[154] It strategically used the threat of Section 301, targeting key countries, to establish the agenda on services of the Uruguay Round negotiations.[155]

(II) Denies fair and equitable provision of adequate and effective protection of intellectual property rights notwithstanding the fact that the foreign country may be in compliance with the specific obligations of the Agreement on Trade-Related Aspects of Intellectual Property Rights or non-discriminatory market access opportunities for United States persons that rely upon intellectual property protection. The USTR has given special importance to the protection of intellectual property rights and has threatened foreign countries in order to impose intellectual property rights which protected US firms. This also served

[150] 19 U.S.C. 2411 (d) (3)(A) (1996).

[151] 19 U.S.C. 2411 (d) (3) (D) (1996).

[152] S Phillips, "The New Section 301 of the Omnibus Trade and Competitiveness Act of 1988: Trade Wars or Open Markets?" (1989) 22 *Vanderbilt. J. Trans. L.* 491–579, 527.

[153] 19 U.S.C. 2411 (d) (3) (b) (1996).

[154] *Canadian Communications Practices*, 60 Fed.Reg. 8101 (1995); see also *Koran Insurance*, 51 Fed.Reg. 29443 (1986); See also Argentinean Air Couriers, 49 Fed.Reg. 45733 (1984).

[155] *India Investment*, 55 Fed.Reg.25765 (1990); see also *Indian Insurance* 55 Fed.Reg. 25766 (1990).

to establish the Uruguay Round negotiating agenda on intellectual property rights.[156] Even after the completion of the Uruguay Round, Congress continues to give great importance to the protection and further strengthening of the international intellectual property right rules.[157] This provision is reinforced by what is generally called Special 301.[158] On the basis of the National Trade Estimate Report[159], the USTR must identify and target countries which do not provide adequate protection of intellectual property rights; even if such country is in compliance with its international obligations under the TRIPs agreement of the WTO.

(III) Denies fair and equitable market opportunities, including the toleration by a foreign government of systematic anti-competitive activities by enterprises or among enterprises in the foreign country that have the effect of restricting, on a basis that is inconsistent with commercial considerations, access of the United States' goods or services to a foreign market. The United States has targeted Japan's market structures as inconsistent with commercial considerations.[160] The provision is a clear example of the United States' fair trade standards. Foreign practices are considered to be unreasonable because they are inconsistent with what it considers to be commercial considerations. Anything which limits the rule of the market will be considered to be inconsistent with commercial considerations. The United States, in this provision, is clearly targeting socio-political structures in foreign countries which relate to market organisation and not to government intervention. Therefore, this policy has been the least successful. The United States has not been able to tackle effectively and change the structures that make the Japanese market so different: the *keiretsu*, vertical and horizontal, the strong links between government and business, and the cultural tendency to prefer domestic products.[161] Whereas it is possible to limit government intervention in foreign countries by imposing or changing policies, it is much more difficult to eliminate socio-economic structures. The way a market is socially organised is historically determined.

(IV) Constitutes export targeting. The term export targeting refers to any government plan or scheme consisting of a combination of co-ordinated action within a specific enterprise, industry, or group thereof which has the effect of

[156] *Brazil Pharmaceuticals*, 55 Fed.Reg. 27324 (1990); see also *Argentinean Pharmaceuticals* 53 Fed. Reg. 37668 (1988); *Thailand Copyright Enforcement*, 56 Fed.Reg. 67114 (1991); *Thailand Pharmaceuticals*, 57 Fed.Reg. 5030 (1992); *India Intellectual Property*, 56 Fed.Reg. 61447 (1992); *PRC Intellectual Property Protection*, 56 Fed.Reg. 61447 (1992); *Taiwan Intellectual Property*, 57 Fed.Reg. 25091 (1992); *Brazil Intellectual Property Rights*, 58 Fed.Reg. 64351 (1994); and *PRC Intellectual Property Rights*, 61 Fed.Reg. 33147 (1996).

[157] Section 315 of the Uruguay Round Agreements Act, Pub. L. 103–465, 108 Stat. 4809 (1994).

[158] 19 U.S.C. 2242 (1996).

[159] 19 U.S.C. 2241 (1996).

[160] *Japan Auto Parts*, 60 Fed.Reg. 35253 (1995); see also *Japan Construction Services*, 56 Fed.Reg. 20057 (1991); *Barriers to Access the Japanese Market for Consumer Photographic Film and Paper*, 61 Fed. Reg. 30929 (1996); and *Japan Lawyers*, 52 Fed. Reg. 7362 (1987)(withdrawn).

[161] M Anchodoguy, "Japanese-American Trade Conflict and Supercomputers" (1994) 109(1) *Political Science Quarterly* 35–80. For a further analysis of the Japanese domestic market structures see Chapter V, Section B.

assisting that entity to become more competitive in the export of a class or kind of merchandise.[162]

(V) Constitutes a persistent pattern of conduct that denies workers the right of association, denies workers the right to organise and bargain collectively, permits any form of forced or compulsory labour, fails to provide a minimum age for the employment of children, or fails to provide standards of minimum wages, hours of work, and occupational safety and health for workers. The law however provides for certain exceptions under this provision. Whenever the USTR considers that the foreign country has taken, or is taking, action that demonstrates a significant and tangible overall advancement of workers' rights or, the standard of rights provided is not inconsistent with the level of economic development of the foreign country, such practices shall not be treated as unreasonable.[163]

3.C.3. Action under Section 301

USTR retaliatory action against those countries which fail to modify any action considered unreasonable or fail to enter into an agreement with the United States to eliminate such a practice, is only discretionary.[164] But such a diminished threat of retaliatory action must be limited by the fact that, following the Omnibus Trade and Competitiveness Act, the USTR is expected to take unilateral action. The Act transferred from the President to the USTR, the authority to decide whether or not to take any action and what action to take subject to the direction of the President, if any. Although at the end of the day the USTR depends on the President, the Executive is expected to take retaliatory action whenever necessary.[165] The foreign action, however, must burden or restrict US commerce.[166] While the standard is much lower than that of injury in anti-dumping law, there must be some material impact on the US economy.[167]

[162] Committee on Ways and Means, US House of Representatives, *Overview and Compilation of US Trade Statutes*, 105th Cong. 1st Session, 84 (1997), available at <http:www.house.gov/ways_means/>.

[163] Section 302 (a) (1) of the 1974 Trade Act as amended, 19 U.S.C. 2412 (a) (1) (1996). The United States, however, may have pursued the enforcement of basic labour standards through the use of its General System of Preferences laws with regard to Pakistan (child labour), Maldives (worker rights), Guatemala (worker rights), Thailand (worker rights). See United States Trade Representative, Identification of Trade Expansion Priorities (Super 301) Pursuant to Executive Order 12901 (1996), available at <http://www.ustr.reports/12901report.html>.

[164] Section 301 (b) of the 1974 Trade Act, 19 U.S.C. 2411 (b) (1996).

[165] J Bello and A Holmer, "The Heart of the 1988 Trade Act: A Legislative History of the Amendments to Section 301" (1988) 24 (1) *Stanford. J. Int'l L.* 1, 9.

[166] Section 301 (b) (1) of the 1974 Trade Act, as amended, 19 U.S.C. 2411 (b) (1) (1996). The concept of commerce includes, but it is not limited to, services and foreign investments. See 19 U.S.C. 2411 (d) (1) (1996); see also 19 U.S.C. 2411 (d) (2) (1996).

[167] *Indonesia Pencil Slats*, 58 Fed.Reg. 610 (1992) (where an investigation was closed because it was considered that the foreign practice neither restricted nor burdened United States' commerce).

The threat of retaliatory action against "unreasonable" practices is increased by what is popularly known as Super 301.[168] Following the National Trade Estimate Report of Section 181 of the Act,[169] the USTR must identify trade expansion priorities and priority foreign country practices, the elimination of which is likely to have the most significant potential to increase US exports.[170] Thereafter the USTR must self-initiate under Section 302(b)(1) investigations with respect to all priority foreign practices so identified.[171] Action against such practices is mandatory if the foreign country refuses to phase out such practices. The United States has effectively used Super 301 to increase the threat of retaliation in order to remove what it considers to be foreign obstacles to trade.[172]

Additionally, the USTR must take action against countries whose practices violate US legal rights.[173] These practices may violate or be inconsistent with provisions of or otherwise deny benefits to the US under any trade agreement. It may include a WTO agreement or any other international trade agreement. The United States need not be a signatory to the trade agreement as long as it has some right, however vague, under the agreement. While the challenged conduct can be directly prohibited by any trade agreement, the term "deny" implies that the foreign government need not violate a trade agreement but only deny a benefit under the agreement, such as by nullifying or impairing a concession.[174] Action is also mandatory against practices that are unjustifiable and burden or restrict US commerce. An act, policy or practice is unjustifiable if it is in violation of, or inconsistent with, the international legal rights of the United States.[175] Acts, policies and practices that are unjustifiable include, when appropriate, any act, policy, and practice which denies national or most favoured nation treatment to United States' goods, services or investment.[176]

Mandatory action generally refers to practices which are regulated by WTO or other international trade agreements. Such mandatory action is subject to a limited number of exceptions.[177] Furthermore, the USTR is required to enter

[168] Section 310 of the 1974 Trade Act, as amended; 19 U.S.C. 2420 (1996).

[169] 19 U.S.C. 2241 (1996); see USTR, *1998 National Trade Estimate Report on Foreign Trade Barriers*, available at <http://www.ustr.gov/reports/>.

[170] USTR, *Identification of Trade Expansion Priorities Pursuant to Executive Order 12901*, October 1997, available at <http://www.ustr.gov/reports/>.

[171] For example, following the identification of Korean barriers to auto imports, the USTR initiated an investigation regarding such barriers. See *Korea: Barriers to Auto Imports*, 62 Fed.Reg. 55843 (1997); see also *USTR Report to Congress on Section 301 Developments Required by Section 309(a)(3) of the Trade Act of 1974 (June 1996–January 1998)*, at 3, available at <http://www.ustr. gov/reports/>.

[172] *Japanese Satellites*, 55 Fed.Reg. 25761 (1990); see also *Brazil Import Licensing*, 54 Fed.Reg. 26135 (1989); *Japan Supercomputers*, 55 Fed.Reg. 25765 (1990); *Japan Forest Products*, 55 Fed.Reg. 25763 (1990); *Indian Investment*, 55 Fed.Reg. 25765 (1990); and *Indian Insurance*, 55 Fed.Reg. 25766 (1990).

[173] Section 301 (a) (1) of the Trade Act of 1974, as amended; 19 U.S.C. 2411 (a)(1) (1996).

[174] *EC Citrus*, 50 Fed. Reg. 26143 (1985); see also *EC Enlargement*, 55 Fed.Reg. 48197 (1990).

[175] Section 301(d)(4)(a) of the Trade Act of 1974, as amended, 19 U.S.C. 2411 (d)(4) (a) (1996).

[176] Section 301(d)(4)(b) of the Trade Act of 1974, as amended, 19 U.S.C. 2411 (d)(4)(b)(1996).

[177] Section 301 (a) (2) of the Trade Act of 1974, as amended, 19 U.S.C. 2411 (a) (2) (1996). There is an additional exception which is the discretion to initiate an investigation. See Section 302 of the 1974 Trade Act, as amended.

into negotiations and follow the WTO dispute settlement procedures if necessary. However, the US Congress expressed its frustration with the old GATT dispute settlement procedures by establishing strict deadlines which in fact the GATT organs were unable to meet.[178] As a result, the United States used its mandatory retaliation power to strengthen the GATT dispute settlement procedure and establish a more advocacy-based system; a rule-oriented, *versus* a diplomatic or negotiated-oriented approach.[179] It attempted, successfully, to strengthen the GATT even at the cost of violating the multilateral rules. By the middle of the Uruguay Round, United States' trading partners were asking what price there was to pay in order to stop such retaliatory action.[180] Thus, the states participating in the Uruguay Round agreed to a dispute system procedure which is not only based on a rule-oriented approach but, furthermore, lays down its deadlines in order to fit with those of Section 301.[181]

It would be extremely naive to think that this new approach is in any way neutral. It is not simply a question of the rule of law *versus* a negotiated approach, instead the key question should be *what* rule of law.[182] Law is not simply neutral, but reflects and protects certain interests.[183] The establishment of a dispute settlement procedure is an important step in the creation and enforcement of a regime that reflects the domestic structures of the United States. Once the rules of such a regime are created, it is important to enforce this system effectively under the so-called "rule of law". Furthermore, the establishment of a rule-oriented approach was also useful to the United States because of its spill-over effects. The new dispute settlement procedure encourages other trading partners to play the same game of challenging foreign trade practices and, thus, enforcing a WTO legal system which is in fact a reflection of the American system.

In the aftermath of the conclusion of the Uruguay Round, through the use of Section 301, the United States has become an active player in the new WTO Dispute Settlement Mechanism.[184] This activist policy within WTO dispute

[178] United States International Trade Commission, *Report to the Committee on Finance, US Senate, on Investigation No 332–212 Under Section 332(g) of the Tariff Act of 1930: Review of the Effectiveness of Trade Dispute Settlement under the GATT and the Tokyo Round Agreements*, USITC (1985); see also Section 303 of the Trade Act of 1974, as amended, 19 U.S.C. 2413 (1996); and Section 304 of the Trade Act of 1974, as amended, 19 U.S.C. 2414 (1996).

[179] J H Jackson, "The Jurisprudence of International Trade: The DISC Case in GATT" (1978) 72 *Am. J. Int'l L.* 747–781; see also J H Jackson, "The Crumbling Institutions of the Liberal Trading System" (1978) 12 (2) *J. World Trade* 93.

[180] R Hudec, "Dispute Settlement", in J Schott (ed.), *Completing the Uruguay Round* (Washington, Institute for International Economics, 1990), 180–204.

[181] E Vermulst and B Driessen, "An Overview of the WTO Dispute Settlement System and its Relationship with the Uruguay Round Agreements: Nice on Paper but Too Much Stress for the System?" (1995) 29 *J. World Trade* 131–163.

[182] P Trimble, "International Trade and the Rule of Law" (1985) 83 *Michigan L. Rev.* 1016–1032.

[183] C Sumner, *Reading Ideologies: An Investigation into the Marxist Theory of Ideology and Law* (London, Academic Press, 1979); see also F Snyder, *New Directions in Community Law* (London, Weidenfeld & Nicolson, 1990), 34–61.

[184] A substantial number of all the consultations requested within the Dispute Settlement Mechanism have the US as a complainant. However, this proportion may have fallen during the last year. See Overview of the State-of-play of WTO Disputes, available at <http://www.wto.org>.

settlement reflects two trends in US trade policy. First, it is an example of the success of American trade policy. As a result of the aggressive use of Section 301, most of the unreasonable cases the United States pursued during the late 1980s and early 1990s are now actionable as WTO violation cases. Almost all Section 301 cases initiated by the USTR since June 1994 have been framed as WTO violation cases.[185] The cases also reflect a commitment on the part of the United States, as the leader of the world trading system, to support the WTO procedures.[186] An example of such commitment would be the *Kodak* case, where the United States reframed an "unreasonable" case—anti-competitive practices—into one which involved claims of both WTO violation and nullification and impairment.[187]

However, as the *Kodak* case has also proven, such a political commitment to the WTO procedures can have only limited results. The problem for the US is that the WTO still comprises member countries with very different domestic structures.[188] International trade rules can constrain, to a certain extent, the behaviour of governments but they are limited to changing the domestic structures in which national markets are rooted. The WTO rules allow for very few possibilities to tackle new trade issues such as anti-competitive practices, labour laws or the environment. The non-violation approach, under the nullification and impairment clause, may have very little success.[189] This situation is related to the second trend of the trade policy of the United States whereby Section 301 would exemplify its probable U-turn. The emphasis on Section 301 and the WTO Dispute Settlement would seem to be the result of a lack of fast track powers needed to participate actively in the international trading system by effectively concluding and implementing international trade agreements.[190] By focusing on the WTO Dispute Settlement, Executive officers can attempt to limit the negative effects of a lack of fast track. But this policy can only lead to a dead end. Substituting fast track with the use of Section 301 within the WTO would not allow the American government to pursue its interests in new trade areas as the international rules leave very little scope for such changes.

185 A list of all the cases initiated by the USTR can be found at <http://www.ustr.gov/reports/>. As to the exceptions, see China, *Intellectual Property Rights*, 59 Fed.Reg. 35558 (1994); see also *Japan, Auto Parts*, 59 Fed.Reg. 52034 (1994).

186 M Shaefer, "Section 301 and the World Trade Organisation: A Largely Peaceful Coexistence to Date" (1998) 1 *J. Int'l Economic L.* 156–160, 159. On the US moral obligation to foster the development of the WTO, see J H Jackson, "US Threat to the New World Trade Order", *Financial Times* 23 May 1995, at 17.

187 W Barringer and J Durling, "Out of Focus: The Use of Section 301 to Address Anticompetitive Practices in Foreign Markets" (1996) 1(1) *UCLA J. Int'l L. & Foreign Affairs* 99–142; see also *Japan –Measures Affecting Consumer Photographic Film and Paper* WTO/DS 44/R.

188 For a similar argument, see A Puckett and W Reynolds, "Rules, Sanctions and Enforcement under Section 301: At Odds with the WTO?" (1996) 90 *American J. Int'l L.* 675–689, 689.

189 As to the analysis of the nullification and impairment clause and further details on the Kodak case, see chapter V.B, on the Trade Barriers Regulation.

190 F Bergsten, "American Politics, Global Trade", *The Economist*, 27 September 1997.

3.C.4. Some Remarks

After decades of imposing the rules of the game, US trade policy is trapped. Either it drops its commitment to the WTO, resuming its aggressive unilateral policy under the "unreasonableness clause" of Section 301 and thus jeopardising the entire trading system, or it continues to follow the limited WTO rules and loses the battle in new trade areas, as it cannot conclude new trade agreements.

The way out of America's trade policy trap is the re-enactment of fast track. The procedure would allow it to conclude new agreements in new areas such as competition and investment. At the same time Section 301, both within the WTO and occasionally unilaterally, would be a means to define the negotiations agenda. However, as the Democrats have made clear, there will be no fast track unless the US makes a strong commitment to enforce, both unilaterally and multilaterally, workers' and environmental rights. Yet, as they say, for each vote the US President gets from the Democrats by promising to enforce workers rights, he will lose one Republican.[191] The American trade policy consensus has collapsed.

The same domestic structures which allowed the United States to succeed in world trade and fashion an Americanised planet have now put the country on the edge of a U-turn. The decentralisation of the American government, together with the plurality of its market make any compromise to deal domestically with the external threat impossible.

Up to the mid-1990s, the US was capable of reaching a compromise by focusing on non-tariff trade barriers. Such a policy would allow for limited protection through the use of trade instruments while serving to shape the world by targeting the non-tariff barriers of foreign countries. The deal served both protectionist and export interests and American multinationals. But the dramatic increase of globalisation (an essentially American globalisation), compromised the trade policy agreement. Globalisation broke the American practice of increasing the pie for all, through free trade. On its own, even at its best, it creates losers and winners and deepens the differences between the rich and the poor. Thus, globalisation increases the pie of wealth but it systematically leaves some without a share. Living in the age of globalisation implies reaching a domestic agreement to cope with the external threat by establishing an adequate redistribution of the benefits of international trade and liberalisation. But, as we have seen, it is doubtful whether the United States' structures can allow for a sound policy of welfare redistribution. As the attempted health-care reforms proved, such policies are structurally doomed to fail.

America is thus left only with trade policy. America can do what it has always been able to do. It may retreat from free trade or it may reach a new trade deal

[191] E Frost, "Restarting Fast Track; Introduction and Summary", in J Schott (ed.), *Restarting Fast Track* (Washington, Institute for International Economics, 1998), 9–25.

whereby it tries to protect those American groups which lose the most from free trade by imposing labour standards world-wide. In this sense, it is inconceivable that American big business will give away its world hegemony by refusing to accept some changes in the international trading system.

Part II

The European Union's Common Commercial Policy

4

The Domestic Structures of the European Union

4.A. INTRODUCTION

THE EUROPEAN COMMUNITY is an economic super-power that cannot meet its expectations and be assertive in the international trading system.[1] Despite being the largest trading block, it is incapable of maximising its influence, and thus, unlike its trading partners, it does not succeed in establishing the rules of the global order. The globalisation struggle, between the different trading partners in order to shape the world economy, demands the European Community, more than ever, to speak with a single, coherent and uniform voice. Europe must act together in a strong and efficient way, multilaterally and unilaterally, in order to protect the European economic, political and social model. But globalisation, by blurring the distinction between the domestic and the external sphere and severely affecting the domestic systems of the Member States, has locked the Community into an apparently irresolvable dilemma. While both the Member States and the European institutions are increasingly demanding a voice in the external sphere, they are incapable of finding an efficient procedure which will balance the interests and expectations of all. Hopelessly, the Community continues to behave in the world trading system as a fragmented actor.

The Common Commercial Policy can be seen as a reflection of the nature of the European Community. Most of the literature agrees on the fact that within the European project there has been a move from supranationalism to intergovernmentalism; a move which has been reinforced over recent years.[2] Since the establishment of the European Communities, there has been a diffusion of the borders between Community competence and Member States' competence in external trade. Europe's Common Commercial Policy has shifted from a single representation to a concerted representation; Member States have slowly

[1] L Tsoukalis, *The New European Community: The Politics and Economics of Integration* (Oxford, Oxford University Press, 1991).

[2] J Weiler, *The Evolution of Mechanisms and Institutions for a European Foreign Policy: Reflections in the Interaction of Law and Politics* (EUI Working Paper No 85/202 1985); see also A Moravcsick, "Preferences and Power in the European Community: A Liberal Intergovernmentalist Approach" in S Bulmer and A Scott (eds.), *Economic and Political Integration in Europe: Internal Dynamics and Global Context* (Oxford, Blackwell Publishers, 1994), 29–80; and M Mason, "Elements of a Consensus: Europe's Response to the Japanese Automotive Challenge" (1994) 32 (4) *J. Common Market Studies* 433–453.

increased their influence even in those areas where the Community had exclusive competence in the external sphere.[3] Conversely, Member States have realised the benefits of acting together and using the Community as an instrument to cope with interdependence. Not only has the Community slowly expanded its competence in external trade, but furthermore, Member States have decided to act together, assisted by the Community institutions; even in those cases where they considered that the Community had no competence.[4] Member States have sought the benefits of acting together in the international trading system without being willing to pay the institutional price of losing control over the overall commercial policy outcome. They have denied the extension of the scope of article 113[5] which requires qualified majority voting; preferring other forms of co-operation where unanimity would assure the protection of their interests. By adopting this approach the Member States have achieved only second-best outcomes.

Member States' constant desire to influence the Common Commercial Policy and the resulting competence struggle between the Commission and the Member States are the main reasons for most of the Community's problems in the international trading system.[6] First, the decision-making procedures of the Community, which the Member States dominate, have been argued to result in minimum common denominator decisions, and thus, in a protectionist policy.[7] Second, the need to balance all the interests of the Member States makes the Community a more cumbersome negotiator than any other participant in the international trading system.[8] Third, as a result of its internal problems, it is argued, there is in the Community a systematic bias towards conservatism and

[3] F Alting Von Gesau distinguishes between four forms of representation of the European Member States in the external sphere. First, all Member States may through the Community speak with a single voice in the external sphere. This would imply a system where the Commission would have a leading voice as the institution which is capable of establishing what the Community is. Secondly. Member States can speak individually, each on its own, in the external sphere. In between those two situations Member States can speak in the external sphere through concerted action where the Member States co-ordinate their actions with the assistance of the Community institutions, and through a system of mixed agreements. The development of the Common Commercial Policy would imply a move towards the intermediate situations. See F Alting Von Gesau, "The External Representation of Plural Interests" (1967) 5 *J. Common Market Studies* 426–453,433.

[4] An example of this has been the Community's negotiation of the Uruguay Round. In fact, the Community has negotiated GATT as a single unit ever since the Dillon Round. See K Falkenberg, "The European Union's Position in the Uruguay Round Negotiations" in S Konstadinidis (ed.), *The Legal Regulation of the European Community's External Relations after the Completion of the Internal Market* (Aldershot, Dartmouth, 1996), 63–69.

[5] Renumbered as Article 133 by the Treaty of Amsterdam.

[6] H Paemen and A Bensch, *From the GATT to the WTO: The European Community in the Uruguay Round* (Leuven, Leuven University Press, 1995), 94.

[7] G Patterson, "The European Community as a Threat to the System", in W Cline (ed.), *Trade Policy in the 1980s* (Washington, Institute for International Economics, 1983), 223–242.

[8] P Van den Bossche, "The European Community and the Uruguay Round Agreements" in J H Jackson and A Sykes (eds.), *Implementing the Uruguay Round* (Oxford, Clarendon Press, 1997), 23–102.

inertia in trade policy.[9] The Community's internal problems have traditionally resulted in a certain attitude in GATT; one based on a rather diplomatic approach towards trade conflicts.[10] Fourth, the division within the Community results in a rather soft approach, and the inability to threaten and use its economic muscle to force changes in foreign countries.[11] The internal divisions of the Community jeopardise its efficient use of trade instruments such as the Trade Barriers Regulation or its anti-dumping regulation. Moreover, despite the efforts to achieve a successful conclusion of the Uruguay Round and the concessions the Community has had to make, the internal divisions will not allow the Community to take full advantage of the new WTO rules, either multilaterally or unilaterally. The internal structure of the European Community affects its capability to take full advantage of the new dispute settlement mechanism.[12]

From the point of view of the Community's trading partners, the Community's internal struggles are viewed with confusion as well as fear, and yet also as an opportunity for abuse. On the one hand, the Community's trading partners have had difficulties in understanding who were the competent authorities when dealing with specific trade policy issues, as well as the Community's behaviour. This has led to the Community having problems *vis-à-vis* third countries and multilaterally, and thus struggling to be accepted as a member of international organisations.[13] On the other hand, foreign trading partners have been able to weaken Europe's position by bargaining with both Community's institutions and the Member States.[14]

Much of the literature has focused on the procedural aspects of the Community's shortcomings in international trade. It has portrayed the Common Commercial Policy as being the result of inefficient intergovernmental procedures that should be changed. The solutions proposed have taken both political and judicial forms. Some authors, together with the Commission, have asked, unsuccessfully, in two consecutive intergovernmental conferences for both the extension of the scope of the Common Commercial Policy and the reinforcement of the Commission's role in external trade as a means of improving the Community's position in world trade. Following this approach, not only would the Community's competence cover all trade in goods, including export

[9] S Ostry, "Europe and the Evolution of the Multilateral Trading System" (1990) 22 *Case W. Res. J. Int'l L.* 311–329, 313.

[10] F Roeseler, "L'Attitude des États-Unis et the la CEE Devant le Droit du GATT" in J Bourrinet (ed.), *Les Relations Communauté Européenne États-Unis* (Paris, Economica, 1987), 43–52.

[11] "Red Carpet for Sir Leon, the Man Japan Likes to do Business With", *The Independent*, Saturday 11 May 1996, at 9.

[12] C Ni Chatain, "The European Community and the Member States in the Dispute Settlement Understanding of the WTO: United or Divided?" (1999) 5(4) *European L. J.* 461.

[13] E Denza, "The Community as a Member of International Organisations", in N Emiliou and D O'Keeffe (eds.), *The European Union and World Trade Law after the Uruguay Round* (Chichester, John Wiley & Sons, 1996), 3–15; see also J Sack, "The European Community's Membership of International Organisations" (1995) 32 *C.M.L. Rev.* 1227–1256.

[14] D Tarullo, "US-EC Trade Relationship and the Uruguay Round" (1987) 24 *C.M.L. Rev.* 411–426, 419.

credit and credit insurance, and all economic and commercial measures involving services, capital, intellectual property, investment, establishment and competition, but what is more, the Commission—as the champion of the Community's interest as a whole—would be given a much stronger role in the management of trade policy, to the detriment of Member States.[15] Secondly, it has been argued that for the Community to cope with the increasing problems of globalisation a much more supranationalist and democratic approach should be adopted; thus EC institutions such as the European Parliament should be given a stronger say in external trade.[16] By granting stronger powers to the European Parliament the Community's trade policy would attain democratic legitimacy and become a much-enhanced, genuinely European, efficient and transparent policy. From a different point of view, it has been argued that, regardless of whether the Community expands its powers or not, the European partners should create an *ad hoc* fast track procedure similar to that of the United States; allowing the Community negotiators to be both more flexible and dynamic when negotiating with trading partners.[17] Finally, some have focused more on the Community's trade instruments aspect and have demanded stronger co-ordination in order to develop a more aggressive trade policy.[18]

Parallel to these calls for political change, there have been calls for judicial action. The European Court of Justice has been put in the position of deciding whether it should improve Europe's trade policy by changing the Community's legal order. First, it has been asked to expand judicially the scope of the Community's exclusive competence. Despite previous case law, the Court has been unwilling to take a decision which is primarily a political one.[19] Secondly, it has been argued, blindly and legalistically, that the Court should give direct effect to the WTO within the domestic legal order of the Community in order to solve the internal divisions and problems of the latter.[20] But, again and again, the Court, unwilling to take such political responsibility, has refused to do so. Regulation by law cannot be removed from reality.

Adopting an approach which focuses only on the procedural aspects of the Common Commercial Policy and emphasises the predominance of intergovern-

[15] Commission of the European Communities, *Initial Contributions by the Commission to the Intergovernmental Conference on Political Union*, SEC (91) 500, Brussels 15 May 1991; see also Commission proposal for the 1996 Intergovernmental Conference.

[16] W De Clercq, "Closing Address", in J Bourgeois, F Berrond and E Fournier (eds.), *The Uruguay Round Results: A European Lawyer's Perspective* (Brussels, European Interuniversity Press, 1996), 511–517.

[17] J Schott, "Brussels Needs Fast Track Authority for Uruguay Round", *Financial Times* 12 June 1991.

[18] J Mallet, "Le Development des Relations Economiques Exterieures de la Communauté Européenne", in J Schwarze (ed.), *The External Relations of the European Community: In Particular the EC-US Relations* (Baden-Baden, Nomos, 1989), 51–59.

[19] See Case 1/94, *Opinion on the WTO* [1994] ECR I-5267.

[20] E U Petersmann, "The Transformation of the World Trading System through the 1994 Agreement Establishing the World Trade Organisation" (1995) 6 *Euro. J. Int'l L.* 161–221; see also K Kuilwijk, *The European Court of Justice and the GATT Dilemma: Public Interest versus Individual Rights?* (Beuningen, Nexed Editions, 1996).

mentalism as the cause of Europe's problems in world trade, is both limited and superficial. On the one hand, the main shortcoming of most approaches is that, by simply focusing on procedures and thus advocating a change in procedures and in the scope of the Common Commercial Policy, they are only taking a superficial and legalistic view of the Community's shortcomings in international trade. A more fruitful approach to the Community's Common Commercial Policy would start from the assumption that trade policy is the result of a constitutional culture composed not only of the formal constitutional provisions of a state but also of the social order which acts as its context.[21] States cope with globalisation in different ways as a result of the different socio-economic structures in which their market economies are embedded. They differ in the influence of the government in the economy, in the degree of cohesion of their private enterprises, in the role of labour and social dialogue, in the relations between finance and industry, etc. Many of these fundamental features of state organisation and of society are deeply rooted and not susceptible to change.[22] If trade policy is the result a country's domestic structures, we should start by analysing the nature of the Community's market economy.

During the last decade, the Commission believed that the reluctance of Member States' bureaucratic structures to relinquish influence over the Common Commercial Policy was a serious threat to the Community's internal market.[23] It believed that a liberal policy, based on negative integration both within the Community and with regard to the external world, would not only improve the living standards of European citizens but also boost European integration.[24] Thus the Single Market Initiative (SMI) has had the aim of creating a uniform economic space by simply eliminating trade barriers, but without sufficient emphasis on creating a European social order.[25] The SMI has mainly been a programme dominated by negative integration.[26] But negative integration could only superficially erode the different domestic structures within which the European national markets are rooted.[27] The program has not

[21] T Prosser, "The State, Constitutions and Implementing Economic Policy: Privatization and the United Kingdom, France and the United States" (1995) 4 *Social & Legal Studies* 507–516.

[22] P Hall, "The Political Economy of Europe in an Era of Interdependence", in H Kitschelt, P Lange, G Marks and J Stephens (eds.), *Continuity and Change in Contemporary Capitalism* (Cambridge, Cambridge University Press, 1999).

[23] Interview at the Commission, Brussels, October 1996.

[24] Sir Leon Brittan, "*Globalization v. Sovereignty*? The European Response", Rede Lecture, Cambridge University, 20 February 1997; see also T Howell, R Gwym and M Gadbow, "European Community" in T Howell, A Wolff, B Bartlet and M Gadbow (eds.), *Conflict Among Nations: Trade Policies in the 1990s* (Boulder, Westview Press, 1992), 389–467 at 392.

[25] J Grahl and P Teague, "The Cost of Neo-Liberal Europe" (1989) 174 *New Left Review* 33–50, 40; see also N Fligstein and I Mara-Drita, "How to Make a Market: Reflections on the Attempt to Create a Single Market in the European Union" (1996) 102 (1) *Am. J. Sociology* 1–33.

[26] M Streit and W Mussler, "The Economic Constitution of the European Community: From Rome to Maastricht" (1995) 1 (1) *Euro. L. J.* 5.

[27] B Dankbaar, "Sectoral Governance in the Automobile Industries of Germany, Great Britain and France", in Hollingsworth, Schmitter and Streeck (eds.), *Governing Capitalist Economies: Performance and Control of Economic Sectors* (Oxford, Oxford University Press, 1994), 159–182.

created a uniform market, but simply united 15 different ones with their own historical traditions.[28]

An analysis of the Common Commercial Policy which starts by acknowledging the reality of the heterogeneity of the Community will allow us to see that the origin of the Community's limitations in international trade lies in the conflicting interests between the different Member States.[29] As the ability of governments to cope with globalisation has been restrained, the different market structures of the European Member States have acquired greater importance in order to cope with globalisation.[30] In the same way that domestic structures determined the government interventionist policies of the European states during the 1960s, European Member States continue to be divided in the ways of coping with globalisation.[31] When different states face instability and the need to make choices under the constraints of globalisation, different economic and social cultures result in different priorities and interests. Thus it is not surprising that Member States try to maximise their influence in trade policy; both within the areas of Community competence and by limiting the scope of the Common Commercial Policy. Simply trying to extend the competences of the Community or to improve the powers of the Commission or the European Parliament will continue to be a frustrating process. Member States will continue to restrict the scope of the Common Commercial Policy in order to maximise those situations where they can act together under the rule of unanimity.

Therefore, understanding the Common Commercial Policy, and the role that the Community's unfair trade instruments play within it, implies emphasising the lower level in the Community multi-level domestic system; and thus analysing the domestic structures of different Member States.[32] Furthermore, analysing the domestic structures of Member States will allow us to enquire what is the model, if any, that Europe exports through its Common Commercial Policy. Globalisation is nothing other than a struggle between states which try to establish unilaterally and multilaterally the model, the rules of the game, of the trading system. The great challenge for the European Union is to deal efficiently with global diversity by creating legitimacy procedures on the basis of domestic heterogeneity.

On the other hand, simply concentrating on whether the Common Commercial Policy is the result of an intergovernmentalist or supranationalist system can only provide us with a limited view of the Community's limita-

[28] K Dyson, "Cultural Issues and the European Single Market: Barriers to Trade and Shifting Attitudes" (1993) 64 *Political Quarterly* 84–98.

[29] This was highlighted years ago by different authors. See U Everling, "Possibilities and Limits of European Integration" (1980) 18 *J. Common Market Studies* 217–228.

[30] C Crouch, *Industrial Relations and European State Traditions* (Oxford, Clarendon Press, 1993).

[31] On the different ways European states managed government intervention in the economy, see A Shonfield, *Modern Capitalism: The Changing Balance of Public and Private Power* 2nd ed. (Oxford, Oxford University Press, 1970).

[32] S Bulmer, "Domestic Politics and European Community Policy Making" (1983) 21 *J. Common Market Studies* 339–363.

tions.[33] First, the influence that intergovernmental or supranationalist forces have in the Common Commercial Policy depends very much on the level of policy.[34] Trade policy encompasses a very wide variety of multilateral and unilateral measures, and Member States will not be capable of controlling in the same way the conclusion of an international agreement, whether it falls under Community policy or not, as the adoption of a trade instrument or the imposition of measures under such instrument. Second, even if all measures should need the approval of the Council, where fifteen Member States sit, this does not imply that other supranational institutions will not be able to exert control. The very fact of conflicting interests between the different Member States may allow the Commission to introduce proposals which can benefit the Community as a whole. Even if measures sometimes need consensus among all Member States, the fact is that when a minority of states opposes a measure, such as concluding an international agreement or imposing unilateral measures against a foreign country, they are not only facing that foreign country but, what is worse, its European partners with whom they have to do business every day. Furthermore, the Commission can have a great influence on the policy outcome simply by controlling information, not only on the situation with the Community's trading partners, but also on the Member States' positions. Third, it is insufficient to observe that some EC institutions represent the Member States' interests, and others the Community's interests.[35] Instead, there is, in all institutions, a varying degree of national and Community, as well as free trade and protectionist interests. Rather, it is much more useful to consider the Common Commercial Policy as a struggle between different Community institutions, between the EC and its Member States and between the Member States.[36] The Community's trade policy is the result of a conflict between different actors where, although the conflicting interests of the Member States play a very important role, there is still an important scope for the input, as well as their struggle for influence, of other players.[37] The degree of influence that each actor may have depends on the level of policy, the sector of trade and the possibility that different procedures

[33] A M Sbragia, "The European Community: A Balancing Act", 2(1993) 3 *Publius* 23–38, 25; see also T Risse-Kappen, "Exploring the Nature of the Beast: International Relations Theory and Comparative Policy Analysis Meet the European Union" (1996) 34(1) *J. Common Market Studies* 53–80, 55–57.

[34] J Peterson, "Decision-making in the European Union: Towards a Framework of Analysis" (1995) 2 *J. European Public Pol'y* 69–93.

[35] K Armstrong and S Bulmer, *The Governance of the Single European Market* (Manchester, Manchester University Press, 1998), 42–64.

[36] J Bourgeois, "Trade Policy Institutions and Procedures in the European Community" in M Hilf and E U Petersmann (eds.), *National Constitutions and International Economic Law, Studies in Transnational Economic Law* 8 (Deventer, Kluwer Law and Taxation Publishers, 1993), 175–201.

[37] See G Marks, L Hooghe and K Blank, "European Integration from the 1980s: State-Centric *v.* Multi-level Governance" (1996) 34(3) *J. Common Market Studies* 341–378. On neo-functionalism, intergovernmentalism, multi-level governance and new institutionalism see P Craig, "The Nature of the Community: Integration, Democracy, and Legitimacy" in P Craig and G de Búrca (eds.), *The Evolution of EU Law* (Oxford, Oxford University Press, 1999), 1–51.

establishing varying degrees of influence for each actor may coexist within the same trade instrument.[38]

4.B. THE DOMESTIC STRUCTURES OF FRANCE AND GERMANY

4.B.1. Introduction

Traditionally, although the main motors of European integration, both France and Germany have represented very different approaches to trade within the Community's Common Commercial Policy.[39] Whereas Germany generally considers that the survival of the economy is possible only if an export-oriented free trade policy is pursued, the French government has traditionally regarded free trade as a system that benefits countries or sectors which are economically strong.[40]

As European continental states, the political economies of France and Germany have many things in common. First, in the terminology of Dyson, both countries are characterised by being state societies.[41] A state society is one that has an historical and intellectual tradition of the state as an institution that embodies public power. Such countries exhibit strongly non-economic, non-utilitarian attitudes towards political relations; attitudes which deny that the public interest is simply the sum of private interests and assert the notion of the inherent responsibilities of the state, and an active conception of the administrator's role. The state tradition rests upon the belief that it is important for the individual that collective action can be undertaken so as to effect purposive change in social and economic life. This tradition is not necessarily associated with bigger government or with fewer limits to collective action. Rather, it is characterised by a widespread sense of the legitimacy of public action, by the state or private institutions performing a public role, by a willingness to define public power as distinctive and to exercise it authoritatively.[42]

Second, as late industrial developers, France and Germany tended to create institutions and policies that assumed the need for the organised development of

[38] C Hofhansel, "The Harmonization of EU Export Control Policies" (1999) 32(2) *Comparative Political Studies* 229, at 231; see also S Collinson, "Issue-Systems, Multi-Level Games and the Analysis of the EU's External Commercial and Associated Policies: A Research Agenda" (1999) 6(2) *European Public Pol'y* 206, at 220.

[39] In general terms, on trade policy, Member States usually align into two different groups. On the one hand, Germany, The Netherlands, Denmark, Sweden, Finland, the United Kingdom, Luxembourg, Ireland and Austria tend to take a free trade approach. On the other, France, Spain, Portugal, Italy and Greece prefer a much more interventionist stance; with Belgium taking an intermediate approach.

[40] J Pearce and J Sutton, *Protection and Industrial Policy in Europe* (London, Routledge & Kegan Paul, 1985), 58. On the role of Germany and France in trade policy, see D Webber, "High Midnight in Brussels: An Analysis of the September 1993 Council Meeting on the GATT Uruguay Round" (1998) 5(4) *J. European Public Pol'y* 578–594.

[41] K Dyson, *The State Tradition in Western Europe* (Oxford, Martin Robertson, 1980), 19.

[42] Ibid., at 256.

firms in strategic sectors so as to tackle the problems of capital and industrial mobilisation.[43] The need to mobilise mass resources in order to catch up with the industrial revolution implied the need for collective action and the development of an organised capitalism. However, France and Germany both diverged in the way they organised this collective action and how they progressed from a feudal to an industrial society. In France there was a strong break with all previous social and political institutions and a great mistrust on the part of the state, as the main actor of the transformation process, of society and the church. The development of liberalism in Germany was characterised by the incorporation of pre-liberal institutions and the absence of contention between the liberal state and the church.[44] Later developments, such as those after the Second World War, would also contribute to the emergence of different market systems. While post-war Germany was basically able to resume its nineteenth-century system wherein the state simply established the framework within which a strong and self-regulating industry and financial sector would co-operate, in France, as a result of the developments during the war, business was mostly delegitimated and thus the state had to intervene in a market where there was no social consensus.

Thus, although France and Germany have traditionally put great emphasis on collective action, they differ in the assumptions underlying how such action should take place. Whereas in France there has traditionally been a tendency to emphasise the problem of market failure and a willingness to accept the government as a strategic actor in the economy, in Germany the government will seek to play a limited but enabling role within a market embedded in a framework of corporativist institutions providing for the participation of major social groups.[45] In brief, whilst France will put the emphasis for collective action on the state, the German state will encourage the collective organisation of private market actors to achieve public goals.

4.B.2. The Domestic Structures of France

The French political economy is characterised by the paternalistic relationship between the strong state and its plural and disorganised market. The distinguishing feature of the French model is the intervention of central government, exercising a permanent function with the object of guiding a modernisation

43 Se K Dyson, "The Cultural, Ideological and Structural Context", in Dyson and Wilks (eds.), *Industrial Crisis: A Comparative Study of State and Industry* (Oxford, Martin Robertson, 1983), 26–66, 42.

44 C Crouch, "Sharing Public Space: States and Organized Interests in Western Europe", in J Hall (ed.), *States in History* (Oxford, Basil Blackwell, 1986), 177–210.

45 B Dankbaar, "Sectoral Governance in the Automobile Industries of Germany, Great Britain and France", in Hollingsworth, Schmitter and Streeck (eds.), *supra* n. 27, at 156–182, 177.

program which rarely reflects a compromise actually achieved between its private market actors.[46]

The state interventionist and anti-market tradition of France has its origins in the late industrialisation of the French economy, in comparison with that of countries such as the United Kingdom or the United States.[47] In France, where a modern state with a centrally controlled bureaucracy existed before industrialisation, the roots of industrialisation were political.[48] The state inspired and supported the establishment of industries as a way of extending its own power and authority. It sought to reduce social conflict and preserve the *status quo* by restricting both foreign and domestic competition.[49]

In France it is possible to speak of the state as a powerful independent force in political life and as the unifying authority of society. The government is the guardian of the common purpose and arbitrator between individual interests.[50] It has traditionally been considered as superior to individual market entities when it comes to the determination of the public interest. It is seen as the necessary agent both for creating new wealth and for the protection of established positions. This cultural approach towards the state is reflected in the French constitution. The Fifth French Republic confers a degree of power on the executive which governments in many other countries do not enjoy. Under its Presidential system, competence over economic policy falls on the executive, with very little power of control vested in the parliament. If the President has the support of the parliament, he will monopolise economic policy. Otherwise, in the case of "cohabitation" the President will have to share powers with the Prime Minister.[51] Yet in both cases economic policy remains under the control of the executive's cohesive state bureaucracy; a bureaucracy which believes itself to be capable of developing an independent interpretation of the public interest, one that is more than the sum of political pressures.

Despite all predictions, state intervention was a huge success in France from 1945 to 1975. The government was capable of restructuring the country from an agricultural into a highly developed industrial economy.[52] Such success was

[46] R Boyer, "French Statism at a Crossroads", in C Crouch and W Streeck (eds.), *Political Economy of Modern Capitalism: Mapping Convergence and Diversity* (London, Sage, 1997), 71–101, 78.

[47] D Green, "The State, Finance and Industry in France", in A Cox (ed.), *State, Finance and Industry: A Comparative Analysis of Post-War Trends in Six Advanced Industrial Economies* (Brighton, Wheatsheaf Books, 1986), 80–117, 84.

[48] J Zysman, *Political Strategies of Industrial Order: State, Market and Industry in France* (Berkeley, University of California Press, 1977), 15.

[49] J Hayward, *The State and the Market Economy: Industrial Patriotism and Economic Intervention in France* (Brighton, Wheatsheaf Books, 1986), 25.

[50] P d'Iribarne, "A Check to Enlightened Capitalism" in C Crouch and W Streeck (eds.), *supra* n. 46, at 161–173.

[51] A Crawson, P Holmes and A Stevens, "The Interaction between Firms and the State in France: The Telecommunications and Consumer Electronic Sectors", in S Wilks and M Wright (eds.), *Comparative Government-Industry Relations: West Europe, the United States and Japan* (Oxford, Clarendon Press, 1987), 10–34,12.

[52] W Adams, *Restructuring the French Economy: Government and the Rise of Market Competition since World War II* (Washington, The Brookings Institution, 1989).

due, on the one hand, to the international system of embedded liberalism whereby there was a clear line between the domestic and the external arena and, on the other, to the weakness and plurality of the French domestic market. Internally, the success of French government interventionism was the result of concerted action between the central government and big business; to the exclusion of other market actors, such as trade unions and small business, other economic sectors (except agriculture for political reasons), and left wing political groups. The relationship between the French state and its market actors has led to a process of constant deadlock. The government, by exercising social control and monopolising the main economic resources, prevented the development of any market cohesion.[53] Whereas Germany can be characterised as a web of semi-public interrelations between private market actors with the government playing a secondary role of supervision and case by case intervention, the French market economy consists of a wide range of bilateral relations between a strong government and different private actors.

The strong link between the French state and big business is first of all the result of the key role played by the *Grand Corps* of the state bureaucracy. The centralised French bureaucracy is characterised by its strong hierarchy, with a few *Grand Corps*, such as the Council of State, the Court of Accounts and the Finance Inspectorate at the top. These corps of officials are distinguished by their small size, their close camaraderie and by the fact that their role implies more a control of other officials than actual administrative work. The ministers have some control over which of the top officials will staff their administration, but they will be able to select only from those already on certain career tracks and proposed by the corps controlling the position. Most of these officials are the best and brightest graduates of the *Grand Ecoles*, especially the *Ecole Polytechnique* and the *Ecole National d'Administration* (ENA). They form a coherent and homogenous social and political body which has traditionally being committed to maintaining and extending the power of the state.[54] The importance of this elite of managers and officials has been maintained despite political changes in government.[55] During the 1980s and 1990s, both the socialist and the conservative governments continued to trust their bureaucracies to the officials of the *Grand Corps*. Furthermore, some of these officials, at a certain point in their careers, will move to the private sector and occupy the most senior positions in big companies. In 1986, of the CEOs of the top 200 French firms, half were graduates of one of the *Grand Ecoles* and at least one third were

[53] G P Freeman, "Financial Crisis and Policy Continuity in the Welfare State", in P A Hall, J Hayward and H Machin (eds.), *Developments in French Politics* (London, Macmillan, 1990), 182–200, 190.

[54] See J Marceau, "France" in T Bottomore and R Brym (eds.), *The Capitalist Class: An International Study* (Hemel Hempstead, Harvester Wheatsheaf, 1989), 47.

[55] See V A Schmidt, "An End to French Economic Exceptionalism? The Transformation of Business under Mitterrand" in A Daley (ed.), *The Mitterrand Era: Policy Alternatives and Political Mobilization in France* (New York, New York University Press, 1996), 117–140, 125.

graduates of the *Polytechnique* or ENA.[56] For all firms other than those that are family owned or subsidiaries of foreign multinationals, managers' career paths are more likely to depend upon their elite education and previous membership to the *Grand Corps* than on their managerial accomplishments. Thus, through a sort of *pantouflage* process, the state has been able to shape the action of big business, while at the same time keeping governments sensitive to the demands of big business, to the exclusion of small firms.

State intervention has also been promoted through the influence and control of the financial system.[57] The French financial system is traditionally a credit based system in which market interrelations have been determined by government administered prices.[58] Capital markets have been weak as a result of French savers' preference for liquidity. But the commercial banking sector has not been characterised by universal or mixed banking as in Germany. As a result of a series of bank failures in the nineteenth century, French banks have followed a very cautious policy.[59] With regard to their relations with industry this has meant providing only short-term loans for specific projects and an unwillingness to become entangled in the affairs of their industrial clients. The state in turn has tried to compensate for the weakness in the private financial markets by regulation and public ownership.

The traditional French banking system may be divided into the commercial banks, the co-operative and mutual sector and the savings banks, such as the *Caisse de Depots*. Next to the banking sector there are the non-banking financial institutions which raise funds by means of soft loans and share capital. The main source of economic growth has been the co-operative and savings banks and the non-banking financial institutions. The Ministry of Finance has been able to control most of these by regulation or ownership. Such control has allowed the state to fulfil an entrepreneurial role by stimulating savings, extending credit and facilitating economic and industrial growth. During the Mitterrand years, the government attempted to move the French financial system towards a universal banking system in which banks were to provide long-term finance and play a central role in the national economy. The universal banking system never materialised, the result being only a relative move towards the financing of industry through equity. However, unlike the Anglo-Saxon system, many companies continue to be linked in one way or another to big financial groups controlled by the state, despite privatisation.[60]

[56] Schmidt, *supra* n. 55, at 127.

[57] D Green, "Strategic Management and the State: France" in Dyson and Wilks (eds.), *Industrial Crisis: A Comparative Study of the State and Industry* (Oxford, Martin Robertson Press, 1983), 161–192, 162.

[58] J Zysman, *Government, Market and Growth: Financial Systems and the Politics of Industrial Change* (Ithaca, Cornell University Press, 1983), 71.

[59] Green, *supra* n. 47, at 95.

[60] R Deeg and S Perez, *International Capital Mobility and Domestic Institutions: Corporate Finance and Governance in Four European Cases*, Paper Presented at the Conference on the Political Economy of Corporate Governance in Japan and Europe, RSC (European University Institute, 10–11 June 1999), at 8–9.

The French government's control of the economy has also been facilitated by the weakness of the country's industrial relations and the exclusion of its trade unions. Indeed, French industrial relations have traditionally been in a constant conflict; lacking an institutional collaborative bargaining system and with neither side recognising any gains as legitimate or durable.[61] The unwillingness of trade unions to participate in a collaborative industrial relations system has been due to two basic reasons. Having been treated for nearly a century as illegal conspiracies, trade unions have never totally abandoned their outlaw mentality.[62] Most of all, the trade unions' lack of collaboration has been due to their weakness and plurality.[63] Unionism in France is divided into five major representative confederations (CGT, CFDT, FO, CFTC, CFE-CGC) and many other smaller and autonomous organisations.[64] The average union density for most of the second half of the twentieth century was much lower than in most West European countries.[65] Furthermore, each trade union has been committed to keeping an image of independence from both government and other unions. As a result, management has believed that unions were unable to impose major economic losses on the firm and that the cost of conflict would be small compared to the probable cost of bargaining. Thus, during most of the post-war period, management has remained hostile to trade union demands and has been opposed to increasing workers' participation in decision-making within firms. The result has been an industrial relations system characterised by trade unions' *guerrilla* and wild cat strikes, in which industrial relations and politics have usually been mixed.

Due to the social movements at the end of the 1960s, the French government's "new society" program called for a more collaborative and organised industrial relations system.[66] Yet such a program had very little success outside the public sector, and in practice only increased the role of the government in the labour market. Thus, state intervention not only came to establish the rules of the game but it is also relied on by both management and unions in order to reach an acceptable compromise. At the same time, such intervention prevents any actual modernisation of the system and the development of a labour system based on collaboration and mutual trust. As a result of the socialist control of government during the 1980s, industrial relations moved, in part, towards a system of micro-corporativism, where collaboration and bargaining takes place at the individual firm level rather than on a national level. The Auraux law,

[61] C Howell, "French Socialism and the Transformation of Industrial Relations since 1981", in A Daley (ed.), *supra* n. 55, at 141–160, 143.

[62] Hayward, *supra* n. 49. at 56.

[63] D Segrestin, "Recent Changes in France", in G Baglioni and C Crouch (eds.), *European Industrial Relations: The Challenge of Flexibility* (London, Sage 1990), 97–126, 118.

[64] D Labbe, "Trade Unionism in France since the Second World War" (1994) 17 *West European Politics* 146–168; see also M Rhodes, "Whither Regulation? Disorganized Capitalism and the West European Labour Market", in Hancher and Moran (eds.), *Capitalism, Culture and Economic Regulation* (Oxford, Clarendon Press, 1989), 228–267.

[65] Howell, *supra* n. 61, at 142.

[66] Ibid., at 144.

introduced by the socialist government, attempted to advance a corporativist system by creating work councils within firms. However, because such changes were introduced in a context of weak trade unions, the laws resulted in a blurring of the difference between work councils and unions, thus further weakening the strength of the latter. Moreover, although capital's power was reinforced due to the changes in the international trading system and the weakening of trade unions, it continued to be divided and unable to adopt a common position. Hence, it preferred to negotiate on a individual firm basis instead of adopting a nation-wide compromise which would benefit all. In the medium-term, both parties continue to look to the government as a source of mediation and compromise.

State intervention in France implies a capacity for policy initiative, a potential for far-sighted planning and a propensity to impose government will when it is necessary to attain public objectives. It is pursued, both at home and abroad, to ensure acceptable socio-economic outcomes by political means if necessary; suppressing or restructuring the market when needed. State intervention has attempted to direct the pace of industrial change: restructuring declining industries and assisting those regions affected by structural adjustment, promoting a belated specialisation in advanced industries and products, encouraging mergers in key sectors to ensure the creation of national champions, and supporting the expansion of French industries beyond national boundaries.[67]

Intervention has taken different forms. First of all, the state has attempted to determine the pace of growth *via* economic planning.[68] Up to 1988, the French government implemented nine separate plans establishing both economic growth targets and the means to achieve them. In general, the plans could be divided in three basic phases. The first plans were aimed at encouraging the economic and industrial reconstruction of the country during the post-war years. Thereafter, during the De Gaulle years, government concerned itself with the promotion of national champions in order to preserve national independence. Finally, since the 1970s, planning has basically aimed at restructuring and adjusting to the changes in the international trading system. Government intervention has also taken place through both nationalisation and privatisation. Even before the 1980s' nationalisations, the government's participation in the capital of industry and banking was much higher than in most countries. The 1980s' nationalisations provided the government with the opportunity to reorganise the economy and avoid unnecessary competition between firms; focusing each firm's efforts on one kind of product.[69] The subsequent privatisation process was seen not so much as a neo-liberal imperative but as a way to allow firms to get sufficient capital in order to compete in international markets. Privatisation, as nationalisation, was a government-led policy aimed at achiev-

[67] Green, *supra* n. 47, at 101.

[68] P Hall, *Governing the Economy: The Politics of State Intervention in Britain and France* (London, Polity Press, 1986), 139–225.

[69] V Schmidt, *supra* n. 55, at 120.

ing governmental goals.[70] The state has also played an active role in the economy through costly subsidisation programs and by granting protection. It has subsidised and protected from foreign competition specific economic sectors and groups such as agriculture, poorer regions, national champions and declining industries. The state has had to act as the saviour of an industrial system which has been incapable of organising itself, collaborating or developing strong links with the financial actors.[71] From an external point of view, the French state, endowed with a unique cohesion and a strength that allowed it to impose its policies on a weak and plural market, has tried to meet the structural changes in the world economy by systematically making use, at least in the short- and medium-term, of protectionist policies.[72] Free trade has been seen as a theory which only favours the economically stronger countries and which should be followed solely in those economic sectors for which success can be guaranteed.

During the 1980s and 1990s, the French government had to face, on the one hand, the globalisation process, and on the other hand, stronger European integration in the form of market liberalisation.[73] France has had to accept restrictions of its main tool: government action in the economy.[74] Thus, France has looked to other economic models, such as those of Germany or the United States. Yet, as the Auriaux changes show, recognising the superiority of another capitalist model does not mean that it can be easy to import this, due to the very fact that capitalist models have a social context and are path dependent.[75] Although France has tried to copy the policies of corporativist countries, it has been incapable of developing either the market arrangements or the actors' expectations which could allow those policies to become successful.[76] Instead it has changed and modernised in its own way, one in which the role of the government is paramount.

Thus, as a result of its limitations in the domestic sphere, the French government will try to safeguard its society in the external arena. It will see the European institutions as a means to cope with globalisation and, together with Spain, Portugal, Greece and Italy, it will generally push for protectionism and trade aggressiveness to safeguard its domestic sphere.

[70] V Schmidt, *From State to Market: The Transformation of the French Business and Government* (Cambridge, Cambridge University Press, 1996), at 49.

[71] Hayward, *supra* n. 49, at 68–106.

[72] P J Katzenstein, *Small States in World Markets: Industrial Policy in Europe* (Ithaca, Cornell University Press, 1985), 23.

[73] P Hall, "The State and the Market" in P A Hall, J Hayward and Howard Machin (eds.), *supra* n. 53, at 171–187.

[74] V Schmidt, "Loosening the Ties that Bind: The Impact of European Integration on French Government and its Relationship to Business" (1996) 34(2) *J.C.M.S.* 223.

[75] B Hancke, *Modernisation Without Flexible Specialisation: How Large Firm Restructuring and Government Regional Policies Became the Step Parents of Autartic Production Systems in France* (Wissenschaftszentrum Berlin Fur Sozialforschung, FS 97–304 1997), at 25.

[76] A Boltho, "Has France Converged on Germany? Policies and Institutions since 1958", in S Berger and R Dore (eds.), *National Diversity and Global Capitalism* (Ithaca, Cornell University Press, 1996), 89–104, 103.

4.B.3. The Domestic Structures of Germany

The German market economy is characterised by the strategic interrelationship between an enabling state and a strong organised market. While its economic ideology emphasises a governmental hands off approach to the market, German officials and business people take for granted and encourage a degree of industrial and inter-firm co-operation which cannot be found in states such as the United States or France.[77] The most distinctive feature of the German market is a widespread organised cooperation among different market actors and bargaining between organised groups conducted through publicly enabled associations.[78]

The German state is characterised by its plurality and restraint. As a result of the United States' influence during the post-war years, the German constitution seems to establish a strong bias in favour of a free market economy and a non-interventionist government.[79] The German state is curtailed by the divisions between both the Federal government and the Landers and as within the Federal government itself. At the federal level, each minister is individually responsible within a framework of general policy guidelines determined by the Chancellor. While the latter can mediate, he cannot overrule the policy of a minister unless he takes the political step of deciding that such policy violates federal guidelines, thus confronting the ministers.

Changes in the German government's economic policies have merely been questions of emphasis. Both the Social Democrats and the Christian Democrats have agreed on a moderate economic policy in which government should keep a certain distance from market intervention. The government's economic ideology has been based on the ordoliberal and social market principles developed since the 1930s. Ordoliberalism emerged in the 1930s as a liberal alternative to the totalitarian economy of the Nazi regime.[80] It envisaged a liberal order of the economy, and of the society as a whole, where the state should adjust the economic and social order to the changing economic conditions, in general, and secure the freedom of markets in particular. Public intervention should have the major goals of guaranteeing a stable money supply, keeping an open international economic system and securing and increasing market competition and social security.[81] Ordoliberalism was never implemented in Germany. Instead, on its foundations, a more realistic social market theory which put a stronger

[77] T Howell and G Hume, "Germany", in Howell, Wolff, Bartlett and Gadbaw (eds.), *supra* n. 24, 145–203, 150.

[78] W Streeck, "German Capitalism: Does it Exist? Can it Survive?", in C Crouch and W Streeck (eds.), *supra* n. 46, at 33–54, 39.

[79] A Shonfield, *supra* n. 31, at 239–297, 240.

[80] E Horn, *Management of Industrial Change in Germany*, 7 Sussex European Papers No 13, Sussex European Research Centre (1982).

[81] P Kurzer and C Allen, "United Europe and Social Democracy: The EC, West Germany and its Three Small Neighbours", in C Lankovski (ed.), *Germany and the European Community: Beyond Hegemony and Containment?* (New York, St. Martin Press, 1993), 102–123.

emphasis on social policy was developed. The social market is a third way between Manchester capitalism and totalitarian central planning.[82] It attempts to provide a synthesis between personal economic freedom and the ideal of social security and social justice. It aims at the realisation of the highest possible economic welfare through competition, steady economic growth, free international economic relations, protection of an economically efficient monetary order to achieve price stability through independent central banking, and stability of the public budget and balance of payments equilibrium, together with social security and social justice through maximising the national product, full employment and redistribution of income and wealth.

The German state is actively present in shaping the economic environment by negotiating and making possible agreements between market actors, but it cannot impose its policy or direct the details of German economic life.[83] Government enforcement has been an rare policy choice, with the only exception being the monetary policy imposed by the Bundesbank in order to preserve economic stability.[84] If industrial policy is taken to mean a government actively shaping the industrial structure of a country and attempting to direct its permanent modernisation, then such an industrial policy has not existed in Germany.[85] Instead, the abstract theory of the social market economy has functioned as an ideological framework for a very complex corporativist system of banking and industrial relations that has not only enjoyed considerable freedom from public regulation, but furthermore, has been strengthened by the government.[86] In a corporativist order the key actors are associations defined by their common purpose of defending and promoting the defined interests of their members. These actors are strategically interdependent in such a way that the actions of the organised associations can have a predictable and determinant effect on the satisfaction of other collectivities' interests. This induces them to search for relatively stable pacts.[87] Corporativist associations will be able to mediate between the state and the market and delimit the extent to which the two can invade and enlarge their domain at the others expense. Consequently, a key feature of Germany's economic policy has been a constant faith in the possibility of a collaborative dialogue on the basis of intellectual rationality and an emphasis on technicality that has been rooted in, and expedited by, the idea of

82 Se S Broyer, *The Social Market Economy: Birth of an Economic Style* (Wisssenschaftszentrum Berlin fur Sozialforschung FS 96–318 1996), at 14.

83 P Kurzer and C Allen, *supra* n. 31, at 102–123, 105.

84 K Dyson, "West Germany: The Search for a Rational Consensus" in Jeremy Richardson (ed.), *Policy Styles in Western Europe* (London, George Allen & Unwin, 1982), 17–46, 23.

85 H Abromeit, "Government-Industry Relations in West Germany", in M Chick (ed.), *Governments, Industries and Markets: Aspects of Government-Industry Relations in the UK, Japan, West Germany and the USA since 1945* (Aldershot, Edward Elgar, 1990), 61–83, 61.

86 K Dyson, "The State, Banks and Industry: The West German Case" in Cox (ed.), *The State, Finance and Industry* (Brighton, Wheatsheaf, 1986), 118–141, 120.

87 W Streeck and P Schmitter, *Community, Market, State and Associations? The Prospective Contribution of Interest Governance to Social Order* (Florence, European University Institute Working Papers No 94, 1984), 11.

common interest and objectivity.[88] The German government has acted as an enabling state, developing an extraordinary ability to assist groups in the market into organising themselves and granting them governance functions that would otherwise have had to be either performed by the state or left to the market.[89] The German state has created institutions and programs to boost the banking sector's capacity to supply long-term finance; supported public saving banks and co-operative banks that focused on long-term lending to small and medium sized enterprises; encouraged stability in the financial system to foster long-term investment; adopted and encouraged public policies for a skilled labour force and provided funding for research and development.[90]

Germany's market corporativism has led to the commercialisation of politics, or a private interest government, where the main actors are the commercial banks, the industrial associations and the trade unions. The German financial system has traditionally been a credit system where a limited number of financial institutions dominate, without in themselves being dependent on state assistance. The banking system can be divided into three categories. The private national and regional commercial banks, especially the Big Banks—Deutsche Bank, Dresdner Bank and Commerzbank—have traditionally focused on large firm financing both in the form of loans and equity capital. The public saving banks and the private co-operative banks, both characterised by extensive inter-organisation co-operation, have focused on small and medium sized enterprises.[91] All these banks are universal banks combining deposit banking with acting as house banks to a large number of firms. Capital is provided by long-term borrowing. This implies exchanging impersonal arms length lending for the personal and institutional ties of banks and lending institutions. Long-term borrowing implies, for the borrower, a long-term relationship with an institution that will want to interfere in the business as a condition for permitting the continued use of money.[92] Furthermore banks have been able to control the equity of industrial firms due to the equity stocks they own, the shares deposited by their clients or the possibility of keeping shares on loan from other banks in order to control a company.[93] Thus banks have managed to be represented in the supervisory boards of the most important firms. Conversely, however, a great part of the capital of banks is controlled by the firms to which they lend; thus allowing a certain degree of reciprocity between the financial and the industrial sectors. This has allowed banks to act as major organisers of Germany's economic life by avoiding unnecessary competition between firms, acting as

[88] Dyson, *supra* n. 84, at 35.

[89] Streeck, *supra* n. 78, at 38.

[90] S Vitolis, *German Industrial Policy: An Overview* (Wisssenschaftszentrum Berlin fur Sozialforschung FS 96–321 1996).

[91] R Deeg, *German Banks and Industrial Finance in the 1990s* (Wisssenschaftszentrum Berlin fur Sozialforschung FS 96–323, 1996), at 4–6.

[92] J Zysman, *supra* n. 58, at 63).

[93] But see J Edwards and K Fisher, *Banks, Finance and Investment in Germany* (Cambridge, Cambridge University Press, 1994).

early warning systems in identifying weaknesses in industry, ensuring an export-oriented approach and establishing a policy based on objectivity and technicality which has kept industrial policy away from the general political arena.[94]

Industry itself has also been characterised by strong interrelationships, solidarity and a cartelisation which is alien to other countries. Industries are linked through a maze of interlocking directorates and cross-share holdings of stock. As early as the 1950s Germany had enacted its anti-trust legislation, a result of the Allies' attempt to break up all pre-war cartels, but the law was full of exceptions and did not have much success.[95] Thus, despite all its rhetoric, Germany's anti-trust policy has allowed a broad scope for action by industry.[96] In fact the government has on occasions encouraged industrial concentration under the rationale of encouraging national firms to be internationally competitive. Moreover, German industry is strongly organised into vertical associations which play a significant role in the formation of economic policy. The two main associations are the Federation of German Industry (BDI), which represents German manufacturers and the Association of German Chambers of Industry of Commerce (DIHT), which represents a much wider range of businesses. Both associations have been controlled by successful firms; ensuring the case export-oriented and pro-free trade approach.[97]

During the last decade, there have been important changes in the relationship between the big commercial banks and large industrial firms. The internationalisation of financial markets and the development of equity markets in Germany have provided large firms with alternative sources of finance not under the control of German banks. However, while German multinational firms have been able to finance themselves through international markets, they continue to be characterised by a dense web of corporate interlocks which prevent undesirable external interference with management as well as serving as a basis for inter-firm cooperation, to compete against intensified domestic and foreign competition. Furthermore, as a result of the loss of large firms, banks have increased their involvement and long-term financing of small and medium sized enterprises. Hence, rather than losing connections with the real economy, a large segment of the German banking sector is becoming even more firmly rooted in its relations with industrial firms.[98]

Despite changes in the international trading system, and the consequent need for national adjustment, Germany's industrial relations have maintained a

[94] K Dyson, "The Politics of European Recession in Western Germany" in A Cox (ed.), *Politics, Policy and the European Recession* (London, The Macmillan Press, 1982), 32–64, 35.

[95] Howell and Hume, *supra* n. 77, at 151.

[96] Abromeit, *supra* n. 85, at 68.

[97] F Weiss, "Domestic Dimension of the Uruguay Round: The Case of West Germany in the European Communities", in H Nau (ed.), *Domestic Trade Politics and the Uruguay Round* (New York, Columbia University Press, 1988), 69–89.

[98] R Deeg, *Finance Capitalism Unveiled: Banks and the German Political Economy* (Ann Arbor, The University of Michigan Press, 1999), at 73–122.

remarkable degree of cooperation.[99] While trade unions in other countries have been characterised by their weakness and diversity, Germany enjoys a labour system with a traditionally high degree of unionisation and cohesion. German labour unions are organised along industry lines; with the Federation of German Trade Unions, an umbrella organisation, overseeing the group's interest as a whole. Yet, despite their strength, trade unions have been unwilling to boycott the modernisation of the German economic apparatus. Thus they have generally maintained an approach of cooperation and willingness to compromise towards capital.[100] They have accepted social sacrifices in order to achieve long-run economic growth and wealth distribution, in exchange for participation in the formulation and implementation of industrial strategy through codetermination at the firm, sectoral and national levels.[101]

Germany's privileged domestic structures allow it the necessary capacity both to adapt to the changes of the international political system and to remain open to the international trading system.[102] Its strong market organisation has allowed its government to pursue a free trade, and hands off policy in the economy and concentrate, instead, on guaranteeing social security and welfare distribution. The interrelation of the different market actors, and their permanent predisposition to negotiate and achieve objective and rational solutions, has allowed for the creation of informal crisis cartels controlled totally by banks, industry, trade unions and, to a certain extent, regional governments; the federal government intervening only in extreme cases. Change has taken place through the interdependent governance of social actors under the general supervision of the state.[103]

Hence, free trade in Germany has assumed a strong legacy of dense market institutions capable of guaranteeing the privatisation of protectionism. Yet, while Germany is a successful trader, it is much more dependent on the international trading system than other countries. Free trade is considered to be essential in order to preserve the liberal domestic economy, which in turn is considered as a precondition for democracy. Free trade is further a guarantee of raw materials and a way of coping with Germany's deep national feeling of insecurity. As a result of this, Germany sees the European Community as an important negotiator in the international trading system; one which should work for global economic liberalisation. During the 1980s, in response to France's offer

[99] O Jacobi and W Muller-Jentsch, "West Germany: Continuity and Structural Change", in Guido Baglioni and C Crouch (eds.), *supra* n. 63, at 127–153.

[100] O Jacobi and W Muller-Jentsch, *supra* n. 99, at 132.

[101] J Esser, W Fach and K Dyson, "Social Market and Modernisation Policy: West Germany", in K Dyson and S Wilks (eds.), *Industrial Crisis: A Comparative Study of State and Industry* (Oxford, Martin Robertson 1983), 103–127, 106.

[102] Appleby and J Bessant, "Adapting to Decline: Organizational Structures and Government Policy in the UK and West German Foundry Sectors", in S Wilks and M Wright (eds.), *supra* n. 51, at 181–211, 205 .

[103] P Katzenstein, "Stability and Change in the Emerging Third Republic", in P Katzenstein (ed.), *Industrial Politics in West Germany: Towards the Third Regime* (Ithaca, Cornell University Press, 1989), 307–353.

to exchange greater liberalisation within the Community for some measure of protection against third countries, especially Japan and NICs, Germany defended free trade both within the Community and in its commercial relations with the outside world.

4.B.4. The Persistence of Differences in Europe

During recent years, as a result of the increasing impact of globalisation and the SMI at a regional level on the different domestic spheres of the European Member States, there have been discussions on whether the future of Europe may be characterised by the convergence or divergence of Member States' political economies.[104] Recognising that there might be some convergence should not prevent us from acknowledging the coexistence of different economic cultures within the European Community.[105] The assault on trade barriers without taking into account the social and economic structures within which markets are embedded was simply not enough to construct a uniform European market. The SMI was only the point of departure but not the destination.[106] To a large extent, the different Member States remain highly diverse in their political economies.[107]

Due to the fact that the SMI and globalisation have in general reduced the role of the state in the domestic sphere, these forces have impacted on the different Member States in diverse ways.[108] The process affected most those countries, like France, which have traditionally put great emphasis on the role of the state.[109] These in turn have attempted to copy the policies of corporativist countries in order to improve their economic performance and survive the impact of globalisation.[110] But as economic performance is not the only standard and as industrial organisation is nothing more than a reflection of society, it is not clear that such attempts to readjust will succeed. Instead, it is more likely that as a

[104] C Crouch and W Streeck, "Introduction: The Future of Capitalist Diversity" in C Crouch and W Streeck (eds.), *supra* n. 46; see also J Hollingsworth and R Boyer, "Coordination of Economic Actors and Social Systems of Production", in J Hollingsworth and R Boyer (eds.), *Contemporary Capitalism: The Embeddedness of Institutions* (Cambridge, Cambridge University Press, 1997), 1–48.

[105] K Dyson, "Cultural Issues and the European Single Market: Barriers to Trade and Shifting Attitudes" (1993) 64 *Political Quarterly* 84–98.

[106] L Hooghe and G Marks, "The Making of a Polity: The Struggle Over European Integration", in H Kitschelt, P Lange, G Marks and J Stephens (eds.), *Continuity and Change in Contemporary Capitalism* (Cambridge, Cambridge University Press, 1999), at 71.

[107] S Wilks, "Regulatory Compliance and Capitalist Diversity in Europe" (1996) 3(4) *J. European Public Pol'y* 536–559, 549.

[108] On the erosion of the effectiveness of national measures, see B Hanson, "What Happened to Fortress Europe? External Trade Policy Liberalization in the European Union" (1998) 52 (1) *Int'l Org.* 55–85, 67.

[109] See A Cox, "The World Economic Recession and European Political and Economic Responses", in A Cox (ed.), *supra* n. 94, at 1–31, 17.

[110] C Crouch, *Industrial Relations and European State Tradition* (Oxford, Clarendon Press, 1993), 345.

result of the liberalisation wave, all Member States will maintain certain differences while adopting a certain number of elements from the Anglo-Saxon market economies.[111]

The survival of different market economies within Europe and the consequent lack of a common European model results in a confused and second-best Common Commercial Policy. The dilemma for the Community will be to try to reap the benefits of dealing efficiently in the international trading system on the basis of this domestic heterogeneity. As Member States lose their capacity to control their national economies they will increasingly assert their influence in external matters.[112] When national economies are facing instability and the need to make fundamental choices, different market economies will establish and reassert diverse priorities and interests.[113] The existence of diverse priorities will generate a conflict between the different Member States which will in turn spill over into a conflict between the Member States and the Community institutions.[114] Member States, distrusting each other, will want to reap the benefits of joint action without losing control of their external spheres. Thus, on the one hand, Member States will challenge the Community powers since their ability to influence the Community's trade policy outcome, and hence protect their disparate interests, will vary depending on whether or not the Community has exclusive competence.[115] On the other hand, Member States will try to keep control over trade policy matters falling within the scope of Community competence and thus there will be a conflict at the Community's centre level between the Council and the Commission. This will result in the consequent development of comitology as a system of governance and the denial of any substantial powers to the European Parliament. Subsequently, trade policy will be constrained as a result of being the output of a series of complex checks and balances and the conflict of contradictory interests: between different Member States, between the Member States and the Community and between the different institutions of the Community.

[111] M Rhodes and B van Apeldoorn, "Capital Unbound? The Transformation of European Corporate Governance" (1998) 5(3) *J. European Public Pol'y* 406–427.

[112] W Streeck, "Public Power Beyond the Nation State: The Case of the European Community" in R Boyer and D Drache (eds.), *States Against Markets: The Limits of Globalization* (London, Routledge, 1996), 299–315.

[113] H Plaschke, "National Economy Cultures and Economic Integration" in Staffan Zetterholm (ed.), *National Cultures and European Integration: Exploratory Essays on Cultural Diversity and Common Policies* (Oxford, Berg, 1994), 113–143, 141.

[114] Meunier and Nicholaides argue that the Member States' willingness to grant exclusive competence to the Community institutions depends on their level of competitiveness in the international economy and their overall attitude towards the delegation of sovereignty. See S Meunier and K Nicholaides, "Who Speaks for Europe? The Delegation of Trade Authority in the EU" (1999) 37(3) *J.C.M.S.* 477.

[115] But see J Bourgeois, "Les Engagements Internationaux de la Communauté et Leurs Implications sur le Plan Interne", in P Demaret (ed.), *Relations Exteriueres de la Communauté Européenne et Marché Interieur: Aspects Juridiques et Fonctionnels* (Gent, Storia Scientia, 1986), 161–183,169 (who considers that Community procedures offer the Member States a sufficient built-in guarantee that their interests will be taken into account).

Thus, the existence of different, and sometimes opposing, trade interests will render it impossible to make any changes in the Common Commercial Policy, towards more efficient action in the trading system, without raising serious questions about its legitimacy.[116] A more efficient trade action, in the form of qualified majority voting, democracy or a technocratic decision-making process, would be impossible when there is no consensus between the parties on the basic principles and interests of the trade policy.[117] Furthermore, the lack of common trade principles and interests will lead to the tragedy of Europe lacking a common view on the international trading system and on its contribution to and role within it.

However, the lack of trust must be balanced against the challenges of globalisation. The international trading system demands that Member States work together in order to reap the benefits of unity. This balance between the absence of trust and the need to cope with globalisation results in a unique system of governance; one characterised by a constant dialogue between intergovernmental and supranational forces that aims to solve the problems which the external dimension raises.[118] Thus, the Community trade decision-making process involves layers of internal negotiations within the Commission, between the Commission and the Article 113 (now Article 133) Committee, and with and within the Member States in the Council. These are supplemented by the interventions of the European Parliament, the business and the labour communities.[119] The intensity of such dialogue and the mutual dependence between intergovernmental and supranational forces will blur the borderlines of their respective influence. Many times it will be impossible to determine who is responsible for a specific trade outcome, and thus the discussion on which is the dominating system of governance—intergovernmental or supranational—becomes irrelevant.

In this sense, the problems of the Common Commercial Policy are especially relevant to the Community's use of its unfair trade instruments. First, the substance and procedure of unfair trade instruments are intertwined with the entire Common Commercial Policy process. Second, these instruments involve serious issues concerning the role of the state in the economy and the concept of fairness that they carry with them. As unfair trade instruments imply the granting of protection to declining industries at the risk of creating trade tensions and disrupting the international trading system, they will be perceived very differently by the Member States in accordance with their diverse political economies. Moreover, because the instruments embody the notion of trade fairness and the

[116] F Scharpf, "Economic Integration, Democracy and the Welfare State" (1997) 4 (1) *J. European Public Pol'y* 18–36, 25.

[117] Horeth, "No Way Out of the Beast? The Unresolved Legitimacy Problem of European Governance" (1999) 6(2) *J. European Public Pol'y* 249.

[118] M Smith, The European Union, Foreign Economic Policy and the Changing World Arena (1994) 1(2) *J. European Public Pol'y* 283–302, 289.

[119] A Murphy, *The European Community and the International Trading System: The European Community and the Uruguay Round*, 118 Centre for European Policy Studies (1990).

vision of the Community on how the trading system should be, the lack of a common European model to be exported will lead to conflict in their administration.

4.C. THE CONSTITUTIONAL STRUCTURES OF THE COMMON COMMERCIAL POLICY

4.C.1. Legal Basis, Competence and Procedure in the Common Commercial Policy

Behind the concepts of legal basis, competence and procedure lies the fundamental question of the legitimacy of decision-making procedures to act efficiently in the external sphere when, domestically, there is no consensus over the common good or common interests. The concepts of legal basis, competence and procedure define the balance between the diverse interests of the Member States; and thus their concern to preserve the internal system of powers on the one hand, and the efficiency of Community action in the world trading system, on the other.

In *European Parliament v. Council of the European Communities*, the European Court of Justice held that: "The Treaties set up a system for distributing powers among the different Community institutions, assigning to each institution its own role in the institutional structure of the Community and the accomplishment of the tasks entrusted to the Community".[120] Thus: "The rules regarding the manner in which the Community institutions arrive at their decisions are laid down in the Treaty and are not at the disposal of the Member States or the institutions themselves".[121] The rule of law plays a fundamental role as a mediator between the different actors and: "It is for the Court to protect that institutional balance by ensuring the full application of the Treaty provisions concerning the distribution of powers".[122] But, in doing this, the Court has generally followed a pragmatic approach and struck a balance between the conflicting interests of the different Common Commercial Policy actors and the need to act in a united and strong way in the world trading system.[123]

The concept of legal basis is fundamental within the Community's legal structure. First, it determines when the European Community can act. Within the Community legal system, there is always the presumption that competence lies

[120] Case C-70/88, *European Parliament v. Council of the European Communities* [1990] ECR I-204, paragraph 21.

[121] Case 68/86 *United Kingdom of Great Britain and Northern Ireland v. Council of the European Communities* [1988] ECR 855, paragraph 38.

[122] Case 316/91, *European Parliament v. Council of the European Union* [1994] ECR I-625, paragraph 12.

[123] T Tridimas and P Eeckhout, "The External Competence of the Community and the Case Law of the Court of Justice: Principle versus Pragmatism" (1994) Y.B.E.L. 143–177.

within the Member States. Article 3B(1)[124] of the Treaty states clearly that: "The Community shall act within the limits of the powers conferred upon by this Treaty and the objectives assigned to it therein."[125] The Treaty does not allocate, in bulk, the powers to conduct foreign affairs. Instead it adopts the pattern of enumerated powers; allocating specific powers to the EC institutions, with non-allocated powers remaining with the Member States.[126]

The express legal bases of the Common Commercial Policy are: Article 113, the main provision on trade policy;[127] Article 28, on customs tariffs;[128] Article 235, granting the Community the power to achieve any of its objectives whenever the Treaty has not provided it the necessary powers;[129] the Common Agriculture Policy Chapter;[130] and the international implications of internal measures.[131] Also relevant for trade policy purposes are: the legal bases for external relations such as Article 113; Article 238 on association agreements;[132] Article 229 on relations with the United Nations, the World Trade Organisation and other international organisations;[133] Article 130g(b) on international

[124] Renumbered as Article 5 by the Treaty of Amsterdam.

[125] Furthermore, Article 7(1)(b) reads: "Each institution shall act within the limits of the powers conferred upon by this Treaty".

[126] E Stein, "External Relations of the European Community: Structure and Process", in *Collected Courses of the Academy of European Law* (Dordrecht, Martinus Nijhoff, 1990), Vol. I, Book 1.

[127] The Treaty of Amsterdam has re-numbered Article 113 as Article 133 which reads:

> "1. The common commercial policy shall be based on uniform principles, particularly in regard to changes in tariff rates, the conclusion of tariff and trade agreements, the achievement of uniformity in measures of liberalisation, export policy and measures to protect trade such as those to be taken in the event of dumping or subsidies.
> 2. The Commission shall submit proposals to the Council for implementing the common commercial policy.
> 3. Where agreements with one or more States or international organisations need to be negotiated, the Commission shall make recommendations to the Council, which shall authorise the Commission to open the necessary negotiations.
> The Commission shall conduct these negotiations in consultation with a special committee appointed by the Council to assist the Commission in this task and within the framework of such directives as the Council may issue to it.
> The relevant provisions of Article 228 shall apply.
> 4. In exercising the powers conferred upon it by this Article, the Council shall act by qualified majority.
> 5. The Council, acting unanimously on a proposal from the Commission and after consulting the European Parliament, may extend the application of paragraphs 1 to 4 to international negotiations and agreements on services and intellectual property insofar as they are not covered by these paragraphs."

[128] Article 28, now renumbered as Article 25 by the Treaty of Amsterdam.

[129] Article 235, now renumbered Article 308. However, Article 235 (308) cannot serve as a basis for widening the scope of Community powers beyond the general framework created by the provisions of the Treaty as a whole, and in particular by those that define the tasks and functions of the Community. Article 235 cannot be used as a basis for the adoption of provisions whose effect would in substance be to amend the Treaty without following the procedure which it provides for that purpose. See Opinion 2/94 (Accession by the Communities to the Convention for the Protection of Human Rights and Fundamental Freedoms) [1996] ECR I-1759, paragraph 30. On article 235, see *infra*.

[130] See Article 43 in particular. Now renumbered Article 37.

[131] Internal measures, such as Regulations or Directives may establish rules for the common market which can affect third country nationals or may also establish a provision allowing the Community to negotiate with third countries on a certain area. See F Snyder, *International Trade and Customs Law of the European Union* (London, Butterworths, 1998), 437–482.

[132] Now renumbered Article 310.

[133] Now renumbered Article 302.

co-operation on R&D;[134] Article 130r(4) providing for external relations in respect of the environment;[135] Article 130y on co-operation policy;[136] Article 109(4) on economic and monetary matters;[137] and generally, again, Article 235.[138]

Initially, in the sphere of external relations, the EEC Treaty vested express powers in the Community for a limited number of areas only. This resulted in a doctrinal dispute as to whether the Community had, in the area of external relations, only those powers expressly attributed to it—the principle of limited powers, the attribution of powers approach—or instead, whether the powers which it had for internal action necessarily implied powers for external action—particularly parallelism, and the *foro interno foro externo* approach.[139] The European Court of Justice avoided a restrictive approach and expanded the external powers of the Community by proclaiming the principle of implied powers. Taking as a reference the principle of Community legal personality in international affairs,[140] the Court considered that the Community should have powers in external affairs on the basis of those provisions which allowed it to take action in the internal sphere. Thus, in the *ERTA* case, the Court held that: "To determine in a particular case the Community's authority to enter into international agreements, regard must be had to the whole scheme of the Treaty no less than to its substantive provisions."[141] Following such reasoning, the Court considered that the external relations competence of the Community:

> ". . . Arises not only from an express conferment by the Treaty—as is the case with Articles 113 and 114 for tariff trade agreements and with Article 238 for association agreements—but may equally flow from other provisions of the Treaty and from measures adopted, within the framework of those provisions, by the Community institutions."[142]

It is important to bear in mind, however, that the principle of parallelism, or implied powers, is limited by that of conferred powers. The principle of implied powers must operate within the constraints of the powers and objectives established in the Treaty.[143] In order for the Community to have implied external

[134] Now renumbered Article 164(b).

[135] Now renumbered Article 174(4).

[136] Now renumbered Article 181.

[137] Now renumbered Article 111(4).

[138] See C Flaesch-Mougin, "Le Traité de Maastricht et les Competences Externes de la Communauté Européenne: A la Recherche d'une Politique Externe de l'Union" (1993) *C.D.E.* 351–398.

[139] Se P Pescatore, "External Relations in the Case Law of the Court of Justice of the European Communities" (1979) 16 *C. M. L. Rev.* 615–645, 618.

[140] Case 6/64, *Flaminio Costa* v. *ENEL* [1964] ECR 585.

[141] Case 22/70, *Commission of the European Communities* v. *Council of the European Communities* [1971] ECR 263, paragraph 15.

[142] Ibid, paragraph 16; see also Joined Cases 3, 4 and 6/76, *Cornelis Kramer and others* [1976] ECR 1279, paragraph 19–20.

[143] Opinion 2/94 (*Accession by the Communities to the Convention for the Protection of Human Rights and Fundamental Freedoms*) [1996] ECR I-1759, paragraphs 23–27; see also M Cremona, "External Relations and External Competence: The Emergence of an Integrated Policy" in P Craig

powers the subject matter under consideration must fall within the internal powers of the Community.[144]

The legal basis also determines whether the Community's competence is exclusive or not. Whenever the Community enjoys a competence, there is, in principle, a presumption that such competence is concurrent and not exclusive; unless there is an indication from the text or the context of a treaty provision otherwise.[145] Thus, where the Community has not acted in a given field by adopting legislation, the Member States may act in such field. Conversely, whenever the Community acts in a certain area or from the text or context of the Treaty it is clear that such competence is exclusive, the Member States—as a result of their obligation of solidarity and loyalty towards the Community—are pre-empted from taking any measures which could jeopardise, or limit, the measures adopted by the Community.[146]

In *Kramer* and Opinion 1/76, the Court made it clear that the Community could have exclusive competence under its implied powers.[147] Such exclusive competence can result either from Treaty provisions providing for virtual external powers or from the scope of the measure adopted internally. Moreover, the Community's exclusive competence is not limited to those areas where measures have been taken within the framework of a common policy. Rather

> "In all the areas corresponding to the objectives of the Treaty, Article 5 EEC requires Member States to facilitate the achievements of the Community's tasks and to abstain from any measure which could jeopardise the attainment of the objectives of the Treaty."[148]

Third, the legal basis determines how the Community should act in the international trading system. Thus, the legal basis determines the division of powers between the different EC institutions and how each Community institution should behave.

In practice, due to the need to act together, the legal basis does not simply resolve whether the Community should act and how it should do so. Implicitly it also determines how the Member States and the Community institutions should proceed in order to benefit from common action in the world trading system. Community exclusive competence implies following a Community

and G de Búrca (eds.), *The Evolution of EU Law* (Oxford, Oxford University Press, 1999), 137–174, 151; and A Dashwood, "The Limits of European Community Powers" (1996) 21 *European L. Rev.* 113–128, 125–126.

[144] Opinion 1/76 *Draft Agreement establishing a European laying-up fund for inland waterway vessels* [1976] ECR 741, paragraphs 30–33.

[145] Tridimas and Eeckhout, *supra* n. 123, at 153.

[146] Case 40/69, *Hauptzollamt Hamburg-Oberelbe* v. *Firma Paul Bollman* [1970] ECR 84, paragraph 4. On pre-emption, see M Waelbroeck, "The Emergent Doctrine of Community Pre-emption—Consent and Redelegation", in E Sandalow and E Stein (eds.), *Courts and Free Markets* (Oxford, Clarendon Press, 1982), Volume III, 540–580, 554.

[147] See Joined Cases 3, 4 and 6/76; see also Opinion 1/76, *Draft Agreement establishing a European laying-up fund for inland waterway vessels* [1976] ECR 741.

[148] Opinion 2/91, *ILO Convention 170 on Chemicals at Work* [1993] 3 C.M.L.R. 773, paragraphs 9 and 10.

procedure whereby the interests of all Member States are not fully taken into account as these are partly sacrificed in order to achieve a common interest. Under exclusive competence Member States lose part of their control over the trade outcome as a result of the different voting requirements and the role that institutions, other than the Council, play.[149] Thus, Member States will challenge the existence of a legal basis which may allow the Community exclusive action in the external sphere for certain matters. However, between Community exclusive competence procedures and no common action at all, Member States will search for joint action through mixed agreements or by coordinated action; even in areas where the Community has no competence whatsoever.[150]

The increased use of mixed agreements is the result of both developments in the internal sphere and of globalisation: whereby domestic issues are increasingly affected by the external sphere. They result in those cases where the Community competence does not cover all the matters which are dealt with in the international agreement or action.[151] These arise from the impossibility of splitting those matters which fall under the Community competence from those which fall under the Member States' competence. Yet mixed agreements do not imply that both the Community and the Member States have a concurrent power; rather that they have shared powers to conclude the agreements or take international measures.[152] By mixed agreements the Member States are assured of both a stronger control over trade negotiations, or on how the trade measures are taken, and the need for their unanimous consent to the trade outcome.[153] While both exclusivity and mixity require a certain degree of coordination and cooperation between the Community institutions and the Member States, mixity, the participation of Member States together with the Community, reassures the Member States that their interests will be taken into account.

In this respect, the European Court of Justice has followed a rather pragmatic approach. By not only allowing, but in effect encouraging, joint action, the Court has taken into account both the conflicting interests within the Community and the need for common action in the external sphere.[154] Despite allowing for

[149] N Neuwahl, "Shared Powers or Combined Incompetence? More on Mixity" (1996) 33(4) *C.M.L. Rev.* 667, 671.

[150] C Tomuschat, "How to Handle Parallel Treaty Making Powers of the Member States and their Political Territorial Subdivisions" in J. Bourgeois, J Dewost and A Gaiffe (eds.), *La Communauté Européenne et les Accords Mixtes: Quelles Perspectives?* (College of Europe, Presses Interuniversitaires Européennes, 1997), 65–76; see also J Weiler, "The External Relations of Non-Unitary Actors: Mixity and the Federal Principle", in O'Keeffe and Schermers (eds.), *Mixed Agreements* (Deventer, Kluwer Law and Taxation Publishers, 1983), 35–83.

[151] C Elhermann, "Mixed Agreements: A List of Problems", in O'Keeffe and Schermers (eds.), *supra* n. 150, at 3–21, 5; see also A Dashwood, "Why Continue to Have Mixed Agreements at all?" in J Bourgeois, J Dewost and A Gaiffe (eds.), *supra* n. 150, at 93–98.

[152] Pescatore *supra* n. 139, at 624.

[153] Bourgeois, however, considers that this politico-institutional approach is not justified as it jeopardises in a disproportionate way the efficiency of the Community in world trade. See J Bourgeois, "Mixed Agreements: A New Approach?", in J Bourgeois, J Dewost and A Gaiffe (eds.), *supra* n. 150, at 83–91.

[154] See Opinion 1/94, *Opinion pursuant to Article 228(6) of the EC Treaty on WTO* [1994] ECR I-5267, paragraphs 106–109.

shared competence, the Court has stressed the requirement of common joint action in the external sphere.[155] Member States and Community institutions must be able to exercise their powers in a joint manner which will be consistent with the common interests of the Community.[156] Furthermore, the codes of conduct regulating the joint action are binding on all Community actors[157] and both the Community and the Member States are jointly liable to third states for the fulfilment of every obligation arising from the commitments undertaken following such mechanisms[158] Moreover, the Court has expressly accepted that Member States may take common action in areas of no Community competence by drawing on the rules of the Community institutions.[159]

Thus, the concepts of legal basis and competence lead on to the concept of procedure. The legal basis determines the form of joint action by the Community institutions and the Member States in external trade. As the Court held in *Hellenic Republic v. Council of the European Communities*: "As regards the choice of legal basis it must first be pointed out that choice may influence the content of the contested measure in so far as the procedural requirements connected with the enabling provisions in question are not the same from one piece of legislation to the next."[160] The legal basis is only important as long as it determines the procedure to be followed.[161]

The fact of conflicting interests between the Member States leads to the constant need to compromise and bargain. Compromise is possible for most of the acts that the Community can take concerning external trade.[162] The need to reach compromise implies the existence of trade-offs and side-payments and the frequent recourse to postponing decisions which will require future bargaining.[163] The concept of procedure becomes fundamental because it determines the

[155] M Footer, "Participation of the European Communities in the World Trade Organization", in S V Konstadinidis (ed.), *supra* n. 4, at 71–105.

[156] See Joined Cases 3, 4 and 6/76, *Cornelis Kramer and others* [1976] ECR 1279; see also Opinion 1/76, *Draft Agreement establishing a European laying-up fund for inland waterway vessels* [1976] ECR 741, paragraph 12; Opinion 2/91, *ILO Convention 170 on Chemicals at Work* [1993] 3 C.M.L.R. 773, paragraph 36; and Case C-25/94, *Commission of the European Communities* v. *Council of the European Union* [1996] ECR I-1469, paragraph 48.

[157] Case C-25/94, *Commission of the European Communities* v. *Council of the European Union* [1996] ECR I-1469, paragraph 49.

[158] Case 316/91, *European Parliament* v. *Council of the European Union* [1994] ECR I-625, paragraph 29.

[159] Case 316/91, paragraph 41.

[160] Case 62/88, *Hellenic Republic* v. *Council of the European Communities* [1990] ECR 1546, paragraph 10; see also Case 68/86, *United Kingdom of Great Britain and Northern Ireland* v. *Council of the European Communities* [1988] ECR 855, paragraph 6.

[161] Case 165/87, *Commission of the European Communities* v. *Council of the European Communities* [1988] ECR 5545, paragraph 19; see also Case C-268/94, *Portuguese Republic* v. *Council of the European Union* [1996] ECR I-6177, paragraph 79.

[162] Thus, whereas the unfair trade statutes written down by the United States Congress allow for very little discretion and practically no possibilities for bargaining within the investigation, those of the Community allow a very wide discretion for the Community institutions in order to allow them the chance to bargain.

[163] Mortensen, "The Institutional Paradoxes of EU Governance in External Trade: Coping with the Challenges of the Post-Hegemonic Trading System and the Globalised World Economy", in

degree of influence that each Common Commercial Policy actor will have in the taking of each trade policy measure. The procedure deriving from a certain legal basis will determine the role played by each institution, the voting requirements within the Council and the degree of influence Member States will have, dependent on whether or not the legal basis provides for exclusive competence.[164]

Following the appropriate procedure will maintain the balance of interests between the different EC actors. Each of the institutions must exercise its powers with due regard to the powers of the other institutions.[165] Thus in external trade, as the Court held in *France v. Commission*,[166] the allocation of powers between the Community institutions cannot be altered even as a result of the powers that such institutions may have in the domestic sphere. Following the appropriate procedure is also important in order to maintain limits on the degree of influence of the Member States and that of supranational institutions. Therefore: "Although the Council may . . . decide in each case whether it is expedient to enter into an agreement with third countries, it does not enjoy a discretion to decide whether to proceed through intergovernmental or Community channels."[167] Internal rules of law of the Member States, even if of a constitutional nature, cannot alter the division of powers between the Member States and the Community as laid down in the Treaty.[168]

The procedure also determines what the outcome will be; and thus how the Community shall interact within the international trading system. The likelihood of the Community actors reaching an agreement acceptable to all will depend on the procedure to be followed. The internal problems and conflicts within the Community system are externalised by way of the procedures used. Thus, for example, the fact that the Council had to adopt the Uruguay Round Agreements under the rule of unanimity, due to the circumstance that the Community did not have exclusive competence under Article 113 (now 133) of the Treaty, gave a strong veto power to the French government to use against the WTO Agriculture Agreement, conclusion of which was delayed and constrained.[169]

A Cafruny and P Peters (eds.), *The Union and the World: The Political Economy of a Common Foreign Policy* (The Hague, Kluwer Law, 1997); see also M Smith, *supra* n. 118.

[164] D Elles, "The Role of the EU Institutions in External Trade Policy", in N. Emiliou and D O'Keeffe (eds.), *supra* n. 13, at 19–30, 24.

[165] Case C-70/88, *European Parliament* v. *Council of the European Communities* [1990] ECR I-2041, paragraph 22.

[166] Case C-327/91, *France* v. *Commission of the European Community* [1994] ECR I-3641; see also N Burrows, "No General External Relations Competence for the Commission" (1995) 20 *Eur. L. Rev.* 210.

[167] Case 22/70, *Commission of the European Communities* v. *Council of the European Communities* [1971] ECR 263, paragraph 70; see also Opinion 1/78, *International Agreement on Natural Rubber* [1979] ECR 2871.

[168] Opinion 1/94 (Competence of the Community to conclude international agreements concerning services and the protection of intellectual property) [1994] ECR I-5267, paragraph 20.

[169] Y Devuyst, "The European Community and the Conclusion of the Uruguay Round" in C Rhodes and S Mazey (eds.), *The State of the European Union: Building a European Polity?* (Boulder, Lynne Rienner, 1995), Volume III, 449–467.

This implies that there is a relationship, although not necessarily a systematic one, between the procedure to be followed and the kind and content of measures to be taken. The need for efficiency and fast action in certain areas can play a role in the procedure which is selected. Generally, the greater the need for fast and efficient action in a certain area, the less influence the Member States will allow themselves to have in such a sector.

As a result of this, the choice of legal basis and hence, the procedure deriving from it, can only be based on objective factors such as the aim and content of the measure.[170] As the Court held in *Commission of the European Communities v. Council of the European Communities*: "It must be observed that in the context of the organisation of the powers of the Community, the choice of the legal basis for a measure may not depend simply on the institution's conviction as to the objective pursued but must be based on objective factors which are amenable to judicial review".[171]

However, the procedures which the Community follows in order to develop its trade measures are also important due to the fact that, as a result of the constant necessity to bargain, all procedures are interrelated to a very high degree. It is only by being aware of the interrelation between the different procedures that it is possible to understand the Common Commercial Policy as a whole. First, the procedure followed for certain decisions can influence the development of other policy areas. Second, the procedure followed in a certain instrument may result from how another measure needs to be implemented. Thus, to a very large extent, the interrelation between the different procedures is due to the need to trade-off in order to arrive at an agreement in a certain area. Third, how a certain instrument is used may depend on the procedure which must be followed to use a different one.[172] Moreover, due to the need to take into account the difference in legal basis and thus balance the conflicting interests of the different actors with the need to act in an efficient way, several procedures can take place within the same instrument. The same unfair trade instruments may require different decision-making procedures ranging from mere consultation of the Commission, to the Council, to mixity and unanimity depending on the level and area of policy in which the specific decision must be taken. This implies that to understand the development of unfair trade instruments it is necessary to understand how other measures, such as international trade agreements, are decided and hence the division of powers between the Community

[170] Case C-300/89, *Commission of the European Communities* v. *Council of the European Communities* [1991] ECR I-2867, paragraph 10; see also Case 68/86, *United Kingdom of Great Britain and Northern Ireland* v. *Council of the European Communities* [1988] ECR 855, paragraph 21.

[171] Case 45/86, *Commission of the European Communities* v. *Council of the European Communities* [1987] ECR 1493, paragraph 11; see also Case C-268/94, *Portuguese Republic* v. *Council of the European Union* [1996] ECR I-6177, paragraph 22.

[172] In this sense, sometimes the Commission will try to use *quasi agreements* in order to avoid the EC's internal procedures. See M Bronckers, "A Legal Analysis of Protectionist Measures Affecting Japanese Imports into the European Community-Revisited", in E Volker (ed.), *Protectionism and the European Community* (Deventer, Kluwer Law and Taxation Publishers, 1987), 57–120.

institutions and between the Community and the Member States. The features and developments of the unfair trade instruments reflect the constitutional problems of the Community's Common Commercial Policy, and thus the conflicting interests between the Member States.

Within the Common Commercial Policy several procedures may be involved. First, there may be coordination or joint action procedures. These must be followed where the Community does not have exclusive competence and thus it is necessary for a mixed agreement or a joint common action. Furthermore, Member States can act together in cases where there is absolutely no Community competence. This form of action will also require unanimity within the Council. There may also be situations where the Community may have exclusive competence but due to international law requirements, Member States must act individually, protecting, however, the interests of the Community.[173] Secondly, there may be those measures which fall under the exclusive competence of the Community. These measures may first require unanimity. This would be the case in those situations where the measures are taken under implied powers deriving from internal measures, which themselves require unanimity,[174] or where the Council decides that it should conclude agreements on the basis of Article 113 (133) or Article 238 dealing with association agreements. The Court has held that where an institution's power is based on two or more provisions of the Treaty, it is bound to adopt the relevant measures on the basis of those relevant provisions.[175] Unanimity may also be required when the Council insists in taking measures on the basis of a certain provision, such as Article 113, together with the general powers provided by Article 235. The Court has emphasised that Article 235 authorises the Community institutions to take the necessary measures if action by the Community should prove necessary to achieve one of the objectives of the Community and the Treaty has not expressly, or implicitly, provided the necessary powers.[176] Thus whenever the measure comes within the scope of another legal basis Article 235 should be excluded.[177] Despite this case law on Article 235, the Council has tended to use Article 235, together with other provisions, in order to guarantee the requirement of unanimity and thereby safeguard the interests of Member States. The Member States have not only looked for ways to limit the Community powers but, furthermore, have tried to reassert their influence within areas of Community competence. As a result, the Council will in practice generally

[173] Opinion 2/91, *ILO Convention 170 on Chemicals at Work* [1993] 3 C.M.L.R. 773.

[174] See Article 228, renumbered as Article 300 by the Treaty of Amsterdam.

[175] Case 165/87, *Commission of the European Communities* v. *Council of the European Communities* [1988] ECR 5545, paragraph 11.

[176] Case 8/73, *Haptzollamt Bremerhaven* v. *Massey-Ferguson GmbH* [1973] ECR 897, paragraph 3; Case 45/86, *Commission of the European Communities* v. *Council of the European Communities* [1987] ECR 1493, paragraph 13; and Case 62/88, *Hellenic Republic* v. *Council of the European Communities* [1990] ECR 1546, paragraph 21.

[177] Case C-271/94, *Parliament* v. *Council* [1996] ECR I-1689, paragraph 13; see also Case 165/87, *Commission of the European Communities* v. *Council of the European Communities* [1988] ECR 5545.

follow the rule of unanimity whenever it enters into international trade agreements.[178]

The Community can also either take unilateral measures, such as secondary trade legislation, under the sole basis of Article 113 or take conventional measures, which fall within the strict concept of commercial policy, under the basis of article 113 and 228. Article 228 makes sure that trade agreements shall be adopted by qualified majority; as is the case with all other trade measures falling within the scope of Article 113 (now Article 133). The Council may also need to adopt unilateral measures by unanimity or qualified majority on the basis of trade instruments such as the Trade Barriers Regulation (TBR). Or it may only need to decide measures by simple majority, as in the Anti-Dumping Regulation. Finally, the Community can adopt trade measures by following the committee advisory procedure to initiate investigation or the safeguard committee procedure (guillotine); such as when it decides to enter into undertakings, to suspend or terminate procedures, to impose provisional measures or to utilise the WTO Dispute Settlement procedure under the TBR. In cases where the advisory comitology procedure is followed the Commission will simply inform the Member States. Where measures are taken under the safeguard committee procedure, the Commission, after consulting the Member States, is the institution in charge of deciding on the measure, although the Council may, by qualified majority and within a limited time period, reverse such a measure if a Member State expresses its opposition to the Commission's decision by a certain deadline.[179]

It is important to take into account that although it would seem, in most cases that it is the Member States who decide, all these different procedures create the possibility for other institutions to influence the outcome. The Commission in all instances, even in cases of co-ordination where the Community has no competence whatsoever,[180] can play an important role as the institution charged with making proposals. Furthermore there might be decisions, such as the initiation of the TBR investigation or of the Anti-Dumping investigation, where it is the Commission alone which must decide. In this sense, the mere initiation of an investigation is a trade measure which can impact on both the domestic and the external sphere. Moreover, in all cases the Commission controls the information; not only that on with which the Council decides, but also information as to the position of the different Member States. Thus the Commission will be able to act as a broker and pursue what it considers to be the Community interest. Therefore, no matter whether the agreement or trade measure is mixed or not, in practice the Commission will in any case conduct the negotiations in consultation with the responsible committees and working groups of the Council.

[178] G Nafilayan, "La Coordination Communautaire au Sein du GATT", in C Stephanou (ed.), *La Communauté Européenne et ses États Members dans le Enceintes Internationales* (Paris, PUF, 1985), 38–52, 41; see also Douglas Webber, *supra* n. 40.

[179] On the comitology procedures followed within the Community's trade instruments, see Council Decision 99/468, O.J. 17.7.1999 L184/23.

[180] Joined Cases C-181/91 and C-248/91, *European Parliament* v. *Council of the European Communities and Commission of the European Communities* [1993] ECR I-3685.

The difference between exclusive or shared competence lies only in the degree of influence which the Commission and the Member States shall be able to exert.

On the other hand, in many procedures, the Parliament may also be able to play some role, albeit a small one. Even in the case of mixed agreements the European Parliament will be able to play an important role. This is due to the fact that such agreements will often affect measures in whose decision-making the Parliament must participate. The European Parliament could in practice actually have more powers in procedures followed due to mixed agreements, than under Article 113. While the latter does not provide for any powers for the European Parliament, mixed agreements could affect measures which should be adopted with the European Parliament's consent.[181] Furthermore, even if the Parliament plays no role in the adoption of many trade measures, such as the adoption of the TBR or the Anti-Dumping Regulation, it may exert some influence through acting as a sounding board or by questioning the Commission officials.

4.C.2. The External Trade Powers of the European Community: Article 133

4.C.2.a. The Debate About Article 133

The external trade powers of the Community can be grounded on the express legal basis of Article 113 (now Article 133), other articles and on the implied powers which the Community can derive from its Treaty provisions or from secondary legislation dealing with its domestic sphere. Thus the discussion on the external trade powers of the Community is not so much about whether it has such powers, but rather on their legal basis and how this determines the degree of influence the different actors can have in the common commercial process.[182] Thus the focus of attention has been on the scope of Article 113 of the Treaty as it allows for effective and strong Community action in the international trading system by providing for the Community's exclusive competence, qualified majority voting within the Council and no participation by the European Parliament.[183]

[181] P J Kuipjer, "The Conclusion of the Uruguay Round Results by the European Community" (1995) 6 *E. J. Int'l L.* 222–244, 232–233; see also S V Konstadinidis, "The New Face of the Community's External Relations: Recent Developments on Certain Controversial Issues" in S V Konstadinidis (ed.), *supra* n. 4, at 19–49.

[182] P Vigneron and A Smith, "Le Fondament de la Competence Communautaire en Materie de Commerce International de Services" (1992) 28 *C.D.E.* 515–569.

[183] With regard to the Community's exclusive competence over matters falling within the scope of Article 113, see Opinion 1/75, *Local Cost Standard* [1975] ECR 1355; see also Case 41/76, *Suzanne Criel, nee Dockerwolcke and Henric Schou* v. *Procureur de la Republique au Tribunal de Grande Instance, Lille and Director General of Customs* [1976] ECR 1921; Case 242/84, *Tezi BV* v. *Minister of Economic Affairs* [1986] ECR 933; Case 174/84, *Bulk Oil (Zug) AG* v. *Sun International Limited and Sun Oil Trading Company* [1986] ECR 559; Case C-70/94, *Fritz Werner Industrie-Austrustungen GmbH* v. *Federal Republic of Germany* [1995] ECR I-3189; Case C-83/94, *Criminal Proceedings against Peter Leifer and Others* [1995] ECR I-3231 and Case C-124/95, *The Queen, ex parte Centro-Com Srl* v. *HM Treasury and Bank of England* [1997] ECR I-81.

As in the United States, the discussion on the scope of the Common Commercial Policy as envisaged in Article 113 (now Article 133) reminds us of a process whereby everything is gradually subjected to trade. The debate on the limits of the Common Commercial Policy has reflected a struggle, within the Community, to cope with the developments of the international trading system. As long as the international trading order was concerned with the reduction of custom tariffs on goods, the need to draw the borderlines of the Community's external trade powers was rather limited. It was only when the international trading system started to subject everything to the rule of trade, and thus began to focus on other issues related to trade in goods, such as subsidies and commodity arrangements, as well as expanding to other areas such as services and intellectual property which had traditionally been a domain of governments in their domestic sphere, that the limits of Article 113 were put into question.[184]

Thus, the problems during the conclusion of the Uruguay Round agreements, where the Member States refused to consider the agreements as falling within the exclusive competence of the Community, despite the latter's success in speaking with a unitary and consistent voice and the promises from the Commission to allow Member States to become founding members of the new World Trade Organisation together with the Community, must be seen as the latest development of the Community's struggle to cope with an expanding trading system. As a result of United States' political pressure, synchronised with the strategic use of its trade instruments,[185] the focus of attention during the Uruguay Round negotiations moved from trade-related matters in goods to services and the protection of intellectual property. Accordingly, the discussion on the scope of the Common Commercial Policy moved to consider whether Article 113 could provide a sufficient basis to deal with the international trade aspects of these new areas.

Within the Community system, there have traditionally been two main positions concerning the scope of Article 113 of the Treaty.[186] The Council, together with most Member States, has considered that the fundamental standard to determine the scope of Article 113 should be the aim, the purpose and the objective pursued. According to such an approach, Article 113 should cover only

[184] The scope of Article 113 had already been challenged during the Tokyo Round and in the context of other trade negotiations such as commodity arrangements and export credits. See J V Louis, "The European Economic Community and the Implementation of the GATT Tokyo Round Results", in J Jackson, J V Louis and M Matsushita (eds.), *Implementing the Tokyo Round: National Constitutions and International Economic Rules* (Ann Arbor, The University of Michigan Press 1984), 21–76, 36–42. As to the problems with trade and development, see Opinion 1/78, *International Agreement on Natural Rubber* [1979] ECR 2871. In relation to the problems in the OECD with export credits, see Opinion 1/75, *Local Cost Standard* [1975] ECR 1355.

[185] On the use of US trade instruments to bring trade in services and intellectual property rights into the international trading system agenda, see Chapter III.C of this book.

[186] C Elhermann, "The Scope of Article 113 of the EEC Treaty", in *Etudes de Droit Communautés Européennes: Melanges Offerts a Pierre Henry Teitgen* (Paris, Editions A. Pedone, 1984), 145–169, 148; see also P Gilsdorf, "Portee et Delimitations des Competences Communautaires en Materie de Politique Commerciale" (1989) *Revue Du Marche Commun* No 328, 196.

those measures which are intended to influence the volume or pattern of trade in goods. Such an interpretation has been based on a narrow reading of the Treaty, arguing that a literal and systematic interpretation of the Treaty leads to the conclusion that the Common Commercial Policy can refer only to trade in goods.[187] First, the Common Commercial Policy provisions not only do not mention trade in services or intellectual property rights but, what is more, Article 110 of the Treaty[188] introducing the Common Commercial Policy, links the Community's commercial policy to the customs union which can only be related to goods. Second, Article 3 of the Treaty introduces the Common Commercial Policy immediately after mentioning the internal free movement of goods.[189] Such textual and systematic interpretation is underlined by noting that an historical reading of the Treaty would suggest that the drafter's intention was to have a common trade policy with regard to those measures which affect the flow of trade in goods.[190] Furthermore, such an approach argues, the logic of the Common Commercial Policy provisions would be to avoid the distortions that a lack of common action could cause in the internal market of goods. To this end Article 9 of the Treaty[191] prohibits any customs duties or charges having equivalent effect on imports and exports between Member States, independently of whether the product originates or has been put into free circulation in a Member State. Accordingly, as it is considered that there is no possibility of such distortions with regard to trade in services and intellectual property rights, these should be excluded from the scope of Article 113.[192] Hence, from the point of view of the Council, the Community powers to deal in international trade aspects, other than those concerning goods, such as services and intellectual property rights should be based only, if at all, on the implied powers of the Community. The Community's external trade powers would be limited by the development of its internal legal system. This approach is, in fact, much more concerned to preserve the Community's internal balance of powers than with the efficiency of Community action in the world trading system. In the trade policy dilemma between efficiency and legitimacy, this perspective would view legitimacy as referring to the preservation of the existing system of representation within the Community. The Community is seen as a confederal system; a model characterised by the merging of distinct politically organised units in

[187] P Mengozzi, "Trade in Services and Commercial Policy", in M Maresceau (ed.), *The European Community's Commercial Policy After 1992: The Legal Dimension* (Dordrecht, Kluwer Academic Publishers, 1993), 223–247.

[188] Renumbered as Article 131 by the Treaty of Amsterdam.

[189] C Timmermans, "Common Commercial Policy (Article 113 EEC) and International Trade in Services" in F Capotorti *et al* (eds.), *Du Droit International au Droit de l'Integration, Liber Amicorum Pierre Pescatore* (Baden-Baden, Nomos, 1987), 675–689, 684.

[190] F Perrau de Pinninck, "Les Competences Communautaires dans les Negociations sur Le Commerce des Services" (1991) 27 *C.D.E.* 390.

[191] Renumbered as Article 23 by the Treaty of Amsterdam.

[192] D Chalmers, "Legal Base and the External Relations of the European Community", in N Emiliou and D O'Keeffe (eds.), *supra* n. 13, at 46–61; see also S Hyett, "The Uruguay Round of GATT: The United Kingdom Standpoint", in N Emiliou and D O'Keeffe, ibid.

some form of Union, with the goal of furthering certain ends, without either losing their sense of national identity or resigned to losing their individual sovereignty to a higher central authority, where the different territorial units that form the confederal association are each homogenous in their market values and culture.[193]

The Commission, and other supporters of a broad exclusive Community international trade competence, have maintained that the essential factor to determine whether a certain measure falls within the scope of Article 113 would be the nature of such a measure. Article 113 would apply to those measures which have the characteristic of being an instrument relating to international trade. As the agreements of the Uruguay Round were instruments designed to regulate international trade, the Community should have exclusive competence to enter into them even if these regulate international trade in services and the protection of intellectual property rights.

The Commission's argument is basically teleological; one which considers that the concept of the Common Commercial Policy should be extended to situations beyond those originally foreseen by the framers of the Treaty. The Common Commercial Policy should be the external face of the common market; encompassing all areas of trade to cope with the developments of the international trading system and, at the same time, protecting the Community's external sphere from the trade distortions which could otherwise take place.[194] Such an approach considers that although it is likely that the drafters of the Treaty linked the Common Commercial Policy to the customs union, and thus, to trade in goods, this was due to the fact that at the time of drafting, only trade in goods could be anticipated. The main objective of the drafters of the Treaty, however, was to establish an efficient Community trade policy in the international trading system. Hence, the drafters of the Treaty provided for the Commission to maintain all appropriate relations with the organs of the United Nations, its specialised agencies and the General Agreement on Tariffs and Trade.[195] Thus, the Commission's approach argues, if the trading system has moved its focus to areas other than trade in goods and mere regulation of tariff barriers, the Common Commercial Policy should be flexible enough to cope with the developments in such a system.

Moreover, Commission supporters consider that there is a need to distinguish between trade diversions and trade distortions.[196] Trade diversions could take

[193] D Chryssonchoou, "New Challenges to the Study of European Integration: Implications for Theory Building" (1997) 35(4) *J. Common Market Studies* 521–542, 525. Professor Dashwood seems to share this vision. See A Dashwood, "The Limits of European Community Powers" (1996) 21 *European L. Rev*. 113–128, 113–114.

[194] J Bourgeois, "The Uruguay Round of GATT: Some General Comments from an EC Standpoint", in N Emiliou and D O'Keeffe (eds.), *supra* n. 13, at 81–90; see also N Emiliou, "The Allocation of Competence Between the EC and its Member States in the Sphere of External Relations", in N Emiliou and D O'Keeffe, ibid.

[195] Article 229 of the Treaty, renumbered Article 302 by the Treaty of Amsterdam.

[196] K Leivo, *The Need for an Exclusive External Competence of the European Community with Regard to International Trade in Services* (Bruges, College of Europe Working Papers No 17, 1997).

place in the Community as a result of the prohibition, in Article 9, on imposing any customs duty or charges having equivalent effect on the export or import of goods, between Member States, after these have been put into free circulation in a Member State. The lack of a customs union and a common commercial policy related to goods could result in trade diversions because third country goods imported into a Member State at a lower duty than in other Member States could be exported freely anywhere within the Community. The Commission's approach recognises that, with regard to services, such diversions could only take place in a limited way. However trade distortions concerning services are very likely to happen in the Community, absent a common commercial policy in this area. Trade distortions take place due to the lower production costs in different Member States. The lack of a Common Commercial Policy in services could allow a Member State to impose fewer restrictions on services from third countries which could in turn reduce the production costs of its own goods or services. Furthermore, the lack of a common commercial policy could allow Member States to subsidise the export of their services and thus distort all Member States' trade in third markets.

The Commission's position found certain support in the limited case law of the European Court Justice concerning the scope of Article 113 (now Article 133), prior to its WTO Opinion. In Opinion 1/75, where no distinction between goods and services was drawn with regard to export credits, the Court held that such measures "constituted an important element of commercial policy, that concept having the same content whether it applied in the context of the international action of a state or that of the Community".[197] The Court, without defining the scope of Article 113, held: "A commercial policy is in fact made up by the combination and interaction of internal and external measures, without priority being taken by one over the others".[198] Thus, the Court seemed to support the efficiency argument of the Commission by stating:

> "The common commercial policy is above all the outcome of a progressive development based upon specific measures which may refer without distinction to autonomous and external aspects of that policy and which do not necessarily presuppose by the fact that they are linked to the field of the common commercial policy, the existence of a large body of rules but combine gradually to form that body."[199]

Following the same reasoning, the Court held that formulation of a Common Commercial Policy not granting exclusive competence to the Community would raise the risk of compromising the effective defence of the common interests of the Community.[200] In Opinion 1/75 the Court also seemed to provide some support for the trade distortions argument. The Court argued: "Any unilateral action on the part of the Member States would lead to disparities in the condi-

[197] Opinion 1/75, *Local Cost Standard* [1975] ECR 1355, 1362; see also J Steenberger, "The Common Commercial Policy" (1980) 17 *C.M.L. Rev.* 229; and P Pescatore, *supra* n. 139 at 643.

[198] Opinion 1/75, at 1363.

[199] Ibid.

[200] Opinion 1/75, at 1364.

tions for the grant of export credits calculated to distort competition between undertakings of the various Member States in external markets."[201]

A few years later, the Court would maintain the open nature of the Common Commercial Policy although without clearly defining its scope. In a case concerning a commodity arrangement, concluded within the context of the new international trading system's concern with development and trade, it seemed again to support the Commission's teleological argument. The Court held:

> ". . . It seems that it would no longer be possible to carry on any worthwhile common commercial policy if the Community were not in a position to avail itself also of more elaborate means devised with a view to furthering the development of international trade. It is therefore not possible to lay down, for article 113 of the EEC Treaty, an interpretation the effect of which would be to restrict the common commercial policy to the use of instruments intended to have an effect only on the traditional aspects of external trade to the exclusion of more highly developed mechanisms such as appear in the agreement envisaged. A commercial policy understood in that sense would be destined to become nugatory in the course of time.
>
> Although it may be thought that at the time when the Treaty was drafted liberalisation of trade was the dominant idea, the Treaty nevertheless does not form a barrier to the possibility of the Community's developing a commercial policy aiming at a regulation of the world market for certain products rather than at a mere liberalisation of trade."[202]

Furthermore, in this case, the Court again considered that a common commercial policy of an open nature and under the exclusive competence of the Community was necessary to avoid Community distortions of trade.[203]

Following its previous case law, the Court would reinforce the teleological argument of the Commission some years later in Case 45/86. This held: "Article 110 lists among the objectives of commercial policy the aim of contributing to the harmonious development of world trade, which presupposes that commercial policy will be adjusted in order to take into account of any changes of outlook in international relations".[204] Moreover, in Case 62/88, the Court would make clear that the fact that a trade agreement, or measure, included provisions dealing with measures ancillary to trade could not prevent such an instrument from falling within the scope of Article 113.[205]

The Commission's teleological argument should have some limits, however. First, a teleological interpretation of a provision is only possible within the limits imposed by its wording and context.[206] Second, even if the intentions of the drafters were legally relevant, it is not clear that this intention was to establish

201 Ibid.

202 See Opinion 1/78, *International Agreement on Natural Rubber* [1979] ECR 2871, paragraph 44.

203 Ibid., at paragraph 45.

204 Case 45/86, *Commission* v. *Council* [1987] ECR 1493, paragraph 19.

205 Case 62/88, *Hellenic Republic* v. *Council* [1990] ECR 1546; see also Case 165/87, *Commission* v. *Council* [1988] ECR 5545.

206 Case 26/62, *Van Gend & Loos* v. *Nederlandse Asministratie der Belastingen* [1963] ECR 1, 12.

an open commercial policy capable of adapting to all the developments of the international trading system. The conclusions of the Treaty of Rome should be put within the context of the world-wide social compromise of embedded liberalism: states would slowly open to international trade but at the same time would remain the sovereigns of their domestic spheres. Whilst it is true that the drafters could only foresee an international trading system concerned with the reduction of tariffs on goods, it could also be argued that the drafters only agreed to the existence of such a common commercial policy precisely because it was limited to trade in goods, and thus it could only affect their domestic spheres in a limited way. Third, Article 113 was conceived as reflecting, in the external sphere, the level of internal legal and economic integration decided at that time; and thus it was only by chance that both the internal integration, and therefore Article 113, matched the needs of the GATT negotiations underway. Finally, while it is important to take into account the intent of the Treaty drafters and their possible concern for an efficient Community trade policy, it is also legitimate to have regard to the intention of the Member States today, which is consistent with the legal and political structure of the Community.

The biggest limitation of the Commission's approach is that it seems to assume that the Common Commercial Policy should have the same content as that of a federal state; thus, suggesting that the Community is a politically indivisible unit. Such an approach considers that it could be possible to have an exclusive Common Commercial Policy while at the same time, as in some federal states, having a concurrent power in the internal sphere.[207] Therefore, under such an approach, the external sphere represented by Article 113 would not necessarily have to reflect the domestic sphere.

This conception of the Common Commercial Policy was reflected in the Commission's proposals at the intergovernmental conference which led to the Treaty on European Union.[208] The proposal aimed for an exclusive common policy in the field of external economic relations which, in addition to trade in goods, would explicitly include export credit insurance regimes, economic and trade measures related to services, capital, intellectual property rights, investment, establishment and competition.[209] The Commission's approach was, in fact, based on the idea of the Community as a state; establishing an osmosis between economic, social, financial and monetary policy on the one hand and foreign policy on the other.[210] Instead, the representatives of the Member States adopted a conservative approach against any proposal endangering the *status quo* in external trade.

[207] P Vigneron and A Smith, *supra* n. 182; see also J Bourgeois, "Mixed Agreements: A New Approach?", in J Bourgeois, J Dewost and A Gaiffe (eds.), *supra* n. 150, at 83–91.

[208] Commission of the European Communities, *Initial Contribution by the Commission to the Intergovernmental Conference on Political Union*, SEC (91) 500, Brussels 15 May 1991.

[209] Y Devuyst, "The EC's Common Commercial Policy and the Treaty of the European Union: An Overview of the Negotiations" (1992) 16 *World Trade Competition* 67–80.

[210] M Maresceau, "The Concept 'Common Commercial Policy' and the Difficult Road to Maastricht", in M Maresceau (ed.), *supra* n. 187, at 3–20, 6.

The Commission's approach suffers from two main shortcomings. First, from a formal point of view, a federal system implies that the federal institutions in charge of trade policy are ultimately responsible to the European people rather than to the different state executives.[211] Thus, from a formal point of view, this approach would require, first of all, an amendment of Article 113 (now Article 133) so that the European Parliament could play a fundamental role.

Second, uniform exclusive action in the international trading system can only be possible as long as there is a domestic sphere with a single market culture which would allow the trade interests of the different Member States to be similar. In this sense, there are some federal states, such as Belgium, which do not grant exclusive powers to their central governments; instead allowing for the participation of their local authorities. The Commission's approach, in fact, tries to solve a substantial problem of divergent international trade interests between the Community Member States by means of procedure to cope with the fast developments in the international trading system. The discussion on Article 113 is not on whether the Community should have competence in external trade, but on what procedures it should follow to manage its trade policy. The fact is that it is unfeasible to try to act uniformly in external trade, under the rule of exclusivity and by qualified majority, in spite of the existence of opposed interests in the domestic sphere.

Thus, from a substantive point of view, the Commission's approach also lacks democratic legitimacy. A decision taken by qualified majority in the Council can only be democratically legitimate as long as there is a notion of a common good and certain common interests.[212] When Member States have contradictory interests, as a result of globalisation and domestic liberalisation, decisions which are not taken under the requirement of consensus may in fact lack legitimacy. Even if the European Parliament plays a fundamental role, when Member States have such divergent trade interests, it is not clear whether the Commission's approach would meet a substantive requirement of democratic legitimacy. On the other hand, as there are great disparities in policy priorities and principles due to the diverse economic cultures in which the different national markets are embedded, the rule of technocracy cannot be a basis for legitimation. Such legitimacy would only arise where the measure adopted is the result of a package deal that ensures the interests of the minority. After all, non-exclusive competence, mixity and the need for unanimity, although complicating the Community's decision-making process and thus its position in the world trading system, is a guarantee of the Community's legitimacy and therefore, in the long run, of European integration.

Concerning the distortion of trade argument, it is questionable whether such an abstract concept should be taken into account in determining the scope of the Common Commercial Policy.[213] Unlike trade diversions, distortions of trade

[211] Chryssonchoou, *supra* n. 193, at 528.

[212] F Scharpf, *supra* n. 116, at 20.

[213] F Jacobs, "*The Completion of the Internal Market* v. *the Incomplete Common Commercial Policy*", in S Konstadinidis (ed.), *supra* n. 4, at 3–18, 9.

can be the result of many market conditions; conditions which can vary and are difficult to control or calculate.

4.C.2.b. Opinion 1/94 and its Aftermath

In Opinion 1/94, the European Court of Justice settled many of the issues relating to the scope of Article 113 and the external trade powers of the Community.[214] As the Maastricht intergovernmental conference failed to provide for the enlargement of the scope of Article 113, and the Member States did not drop their opposition towards Community exclusive action in external trade despite the success of the Uruguay Round negotiations, the Commission tried to achieve judicially what it had not achieved politically. In March 1994, before signing the Marrakech protocols, the Commission submitted to the European Court of Justice a request for an Article 228(6) (now Article 300(6)) Opinion of the Court as to whether the Community had exclusive competence to conclude the WTO Agreement and its annexed agreements; either on the basis of Article 113 or on the basis of the Community's implied powers.

However, in the WTO Opinion, the Court seemed to align far more with the interests and concerns of the Member States than in its own past case law. The Court strengthened the exclusive competence of the Community in the area of goods, its core competence, whilst remaining reluctant to recognise exclusive competence for trade in services and intellectual property rights.[215] But in the latter areas, although with many inconsistencies, the Court seemed to reach a compromise whereby Member States would not lose all the control in these areas, but at the same time the Community would have certain exclusive competence; furthermore, common action would be required in all areas.[216]

Between the two opposite positions, maintained respectively by the Commission and by the Council, the Court established a balance based on three different, and to a certain extent contradictory, principles. First, the Court reaffirmed the principle of the efficiency of the Common Commercial Policy, as stated in its prior case law. The ECJ took into account both the needs imposed by the external sphere—whereby there had been a move from developed to developing countries in the production of goods, with the former specialising in the provision of services—and the open nature of the Common Commercial Policy as a necessity for coping with the external sphere, as the basis for considering that, as a matter of principle, trade in services could not be excluded from the scope of Article 113.[217]

[214] Opinion 1/94 (*Competence of the Community to Conclude International Agreements Concerning Services and the Protection of Intellectual Property—Article 228(6) of the Treaty*) [1994] ECR I-5267; see also J M Zijlmans, "The Exclusive External Competence of the European Community" (1995) 2 *M. J.* 405–429.

[215] M Hilf, "The E.C.J.'s Opinion on the WTO—No Surprise but Wise?" (1995) 6 *European J. Int'l L.* 245–259, 255

[216] T Tridimas and P Eeckhout, *supra* n. 123.

[217] See Opinion 1/94, paragraph 41.

However, the teleological principle was strongly limited. The Court considered that the efficiency principle could be accepted only as long as the division of competences, as stated in the Treaty, was not jeopardised in any substantial manner.[218] According to the Court, the external sphere could not alter the domestic sphere in an unlimited way. Thus, concerning the problems of Community representation in the WTO, it held that:

> "... Any problem which may arise in the implementation of the WTO Agreement and its annexes as regards the co-ordination necessary to ensure unity of action where the Community and the Member States participate jointly cannot modify the answer to the question of competence, that being a prior issue ... resolution of the issue of allocation of competence cannot depend on problems which may possibly arise in administration of the agreements".[219]

Furthermore, with regard to the problem of distortions of trade, the Court considered that such concerns could not affect the internal division of powers. Responding to the Commission's concerns over the possible distortions of trade due to the lack of an exclusive Common Commercial Policy for services, the Court held: "There is nothing in the Treaty which prevents the institutions from arranging in the common rules laid down by them concerted action in relation to non-member countries or from prescribing the approach to be taken by the Member States in their external dealings."[220]

Thus, albeit with certain inconsistencies, the Court showed some sympathy for the preservation of the domestic legal sphere and the internal distribution of powers. To a certain extent it seemed that it was the domestic sphere which determined the powers in the external sphere. Disputes over the legal basis for a proposed act would be determined not by the substantive scope of the competing basis but by the procedural requirements they laid down.[221] Hence, concerning intellectual property, the Court showed a strong concern for the domestic procedure rules through which intellectual property law in the Community should be adopted. The Court held:

> "If the Community were to be recognized as having exclusive competence to enter into agreements with non member countries to harmonize the protection of intellectual property and at the same time, to achieve harmonization at Community level, the Community institutions would be able to escape the internal constraints to which they are subject in relation to procedures and to rules as to voting".[222]

[218] E Neframi, "Quelques Reflexions Sur la Reforme de la Politique Commerciale par le Traité D'Amsterdam: Le Maintien du Statu Quo et l'Unite de la Representation Internationale de la Communauté" (1998) 34 (1–2) *C.D.E.* 137–159, 138.

[219] See Opinion 1/94 (Competence of the Community to conclude international agreements concerning services and the protection of intellectual property) [1994] ECR I-5267, paragraph 197.

[220] See Opinion 1/94, paragraph 79.

[221] A Arnull, "The Scope of the Common Commercial Policy: A Coda on Opinion 1/94", in N Emiliou and D O'Keeffe (eds.), *supra* n. 13, at 343–360.

[222] See Opinion 1/94, paragraph 60.

The Court, however, did not always maintain such approach in a consistent way. Indeed, the Court was limited by its own case law on efficiency. With regard to cross-border services, which were held to fall within the scope of Article 113 as a result of the need for an open Common Commercial Policy and the similarity with goods, the Court's opinion resulted in an exclusive external competence for the Community in an area where it neither has exclusive internal powers nor a developed common policy.[223] Nevertheless, it does seem that the Court had a certain concern for the protection of the domestic legal sphere despite the needs imposed by the external sphere. The impact which the international regulation of trade in services would have on the domestic systems of the Member States would be much stronger than that of trade in goods or cross-border services.

Yet, the most important principles that influenced the Court's reasoning were those of common action and the co-ordination of the Common Commercial Policy actors in the external sphere. Following Opinion 2/91, the Court not only exhorted both Member States and Community institutions to pursue joint action, but furthermore, it established the division of powers in such way that the Community actors will, in practice, be bound to develop a system of common action in the international trading system via some sort of mixity. The Court, in response to concerns expressed by both the Commission and the Council, emphasised that:

> "Where it is apparent that the subject matter of an agreement or convention falls in part within the competence of the Community and in part within that of the Member States, it is essential to ensure close co-operation between the Member States and the Community institutions, both in the process of negotiations and conclusion and in the fulfilment of the commitments entered into."[224]

This requirement, which derives from the obligation of unity in the international representation of the Community, was considered by the Court as imperative with regard to the WTO agreements. This was due to the structures established in the dispute settlement system and the view of all WTO agreements as forming part of a single package.[225]

The need for common action is also due to the fact that the Court was unable to establish a clear demarcation between the exclusive powers of the Community and those of the Member States. Concerning the division of powers under Article 113 of the Treaty, the Court's distinction between cross-border services and the three other forms of service provision will necessary lead to the conclusion of international trade agreements concerning services on the basis of mixed agreements.[226] The Court's distinction is unfeasible for international trade negotiations as these are usually concerned with trade in services

223 F Jacobs, *supra* n. 213, at 3–18, 5–10.

224 See Opinion 1/94, paragraph 108.

225 Opinion 1/94, paragraph 109.

226 M Footer, "Participation of the European Communities in the World Trade Organization", in S Konstadinidis (ed.), *supra* n. 4, at 71–105, 79.

as a whole and generally most service transactions involve more than one form of supply. On the other hand, from the point of view of the implied external powers of the Community, the Court's restrictive interpretation of such powers tied to the evolutionary nature of the internal market, makes it very difficult to establish a clear demarcation between the powers of the Community and those of the Member States, and thus, suggests the need for some sort of common action in the external sphere in the form of mixity.

Nevertheless, the Court did not explain how such common action should take place.[227] A code of conduct should regulate both the negotiation and conclusion of international trade agreements as well as the participation of the Community and the Member States in international organisations and their dispute settlement procedures. Some have argued that a new provision should be included in the Treaty establishing the duty of co-operation between the Community and the Member States whenever they both have competence on matters dealt with by an international agreement in which either of them participates.[228] While in the WTO it has often been possible in day to day business to avoid disputes of competence between the Commission and the Member States, and to secure some unity of representation, the Community actors have not yet agreed to a general code of conduct to deal with external trade. Instead, they have only agreed on a provisional method of common action, concerning negotiations on trade in services. Under this arrangement, the Commission is entrusted to negotiate on behalf of the Community and the Member States but it can only express the positions reached on all issues in accordance with the relevant Community decision-making procedures.[229] In the area of dispute settlement within the WTO, the Community and the Member States have developed a non-binding system. The Commission represents the interests of the Community and the Member States in all disputes. The Community initiates disputes following the procedure of Article 113, but under the rule of unanimity. However this system has sometimes met with difficulties, especially in cases of defending Member States against actions from third countries.[230]

As a result of Opinion 1/94 and posterior cases, the Court has established the division of powers between the Community and the Member States in external

[227] T Flory and F-P Martin, "Remarques A Propos des Avis 1/94 et 2/92 de la Cour de Justice des Communautés Européennes au Regard de L'Evolution de la Notion de Politique Commerciale Commune" (1996) 32 (3–4) *C. D. E.* 379–400, 392–400.

[228] J Heliskoski, "Should There Be a New Article on External Relations?", in M Koskenniemi (ed.), *International Law Aspects of the European Union* (The Hague, Kluwer Law and Taxation, 1998), 237–287.

[229] T Flory, "L'Union Européenne et le Nouveau Systeme Commercial de l'OMC", in *Third ECSA-WORLD Conference: The European Union in a Changing World*, 101–105 ECSA Brussels 19–20 September 1996. In its proposal regarding the Community's position in the WTO Millennium Round, the Commission suggested that any authorisation from the Council to enter into negotiations would be without prejudice to the distribution of competence between the Community and the Member States. See Commission of the European Communities, *Communication from the Commission to the Council and to the European Parliament: The EU Approach to the WTO Millennium Round*, COM (1999) 331 final.

[230] C Ni Chatain, *supra* n. 12, at 472–476.

trade in the following way: With regard to Article 113 (now Article 133), the Court has established a distinction between trade in goods and trade in either services or intellectual property. Article 113 applies to all aspects of trade in goods. In Opinion 1/94, the Court held that all the agreements annexed to the Multilateral Agreement in Trade in Goods fell under the exclusive competence of the Community on the basis of Article 113.[231] The Court was able to clarify some issues. First, it made clear that the fact that an international agreement established an internal organisation with budgetary implications and that the Member States would bear some of the expenses could not, in itself, justify limiting the exclusive competence of the Community.[232] The Court distinguished Opinion 1/78 on the basis that, in that case, the agreement under consideration established a financial policy instrument. Second, the Court considered that as the EURATOM Treaty did not contain any external trade provision, nothing in that Treaty could prevent agreements concluded on the basis of Article 113 from extending to international trade in EURATOM products.[233] Third, as long as the international trade agreements do not deal exclusively with coal and steel products, Article 71 of the ECSC Treaty does not apply and, thus, Article 113 is an adequate legal provision to enter into such commitments.[234] Fourth, international trade agreements on agriculture may be concluded on the basis of Article 113 despite the fact that internal measures implementing those agreements must be adopted on the basis of Article 43 of the Treaty.[235] The Court supported its decision with the objective of the Agreement of Agriculture, which it argued to be the establishment, on a world-wide basis, of a fair, market-oriented agricultural trading system. However, it is important to note that both Article 43 and Article 113 confer exclusive competence on the Community and require qualified majority voting within the Council. Thus, the Court did seem to take into account the internal division of powers in the Community. Fifth, with regard to the Agreements on Sanitary and Phytosanitary Measures and on Technical Barriers to Trade, the Court again looked at the objective of such agreements and considered that they were ancillary measures to trade in goods; their purpose was said to be to avoid unnecessary obstacles to trade.[236] Thus Article 113 applies to all such measures dealing with trade in goods. Since Opinion 1/94, the Court has made clear that Article 113 (now Article 133) applies to all such measures, despite the fact they might contain provisions dealing with health,[237] development policy,[238] human

[231] Opinion 1/94, paragraph 34.

[232] Ibid., paragraph 21.

[233] Ibid., paragraph 24.

[234] Ibid., paragraph 27.

[235] Ibid., paragraph 29.

[236] Ibid., paragraphs 31–33.

[237] Case 62/88, *Hellenic Republic* v. *Council of the European Communities* [1990] ECR 1546, paragraph 18.

[238] Case 45/86, *Commission of the European Communities* v. *Council of the European Communities* [1987] ECR 1493, paragraphs 19–20.

rights,[239] or have foreign and security objectives.[240] Measures which are ancillary to the principal objective of dealing with trade in goods may be based on Article 113. The Court seems to have based its extensive interpretation of the Community powers in respect of the trade of goods on the need to avoid distortions of trade and the open nature of the Common Commercial Policy.

Such teleological arguments, however, apply to services and intellectual property only in a very limited way.[241] With regard to services, the Court considers that the scope of Article 113 encompasses only cross-border services. Their treatment is due to their similarity to trade in goods. Yet, services, the provision of which requires the movement of either natural or legal persons, do not fall within the scope of the Common Commercial Policy.[242] The Court based this decision on two grounds. First, the fact that Article 3 of the Treaty establishes two different objectives: the Common Commercial Policy, Article 3(b); and measures concerning the entry and movement of persons, Article 3(d). It could be argued, however, that Article 3(d) only refers to Article 100c which deals with the concession of visas, a subject which is not dealt with in the GATS.[243] Second, the Court considered that, as there was an specific chapter of the Treaty dealing with the movement of persons, agreements covering such matters could not fall within the scope of the Common Commercial Policy.[244] It could be argued, however, that the Court's reasoning is not convincing as the Treaty chapter on services only deals with the movement of Member States' nationals.[245] Concerning transport services, the Court held that the existence of a Treaty chapter on transport implied external trade powers for transport on the basis of such provisions; thus it excluded these services from the scope of the Common Commercial Policy.[246] Thus, the Court did not follow the same reasoning as it had used for the Agreement on Agriculture. There, it had considered that the fact that the internal measures adopted to implement this agreement should be

[239] Case C-268/94, *Portuguese Republic* v. *Council of the European Union* [1996] ECR I-6177, paragraphs 24–27.

[240] Case C-124/95, *The Queen, ex parte Centro-Com Srl* v. *HM Treasury and Bank of England* [1997] ECR I-81; Case C-70/94, *Fritz Werner Industrie-Austrustungen GmbH* v. *Federal Republic of Germany* [1995] ECR I-3189; and Case C-83/94, *Criminal Proceedings against Peter Leifer and Others* [1995] ECR I-3231.

[241] Pescatore argues that the Court has artificially split trade policy into a traditional compartment, that of goods, imposed on the Community like a straight jacket, and an extensible concept for the use of Member States. See P Pescatore, "Opinion 1/94 on the Conclusion of the WTO Agreement: Is There a Escape from a Programmed Disaster" (1999) 36 *C.M.L. Rev.*. 387, at 391.

[242] Opinion 1/94, paragraph 46; see also M Vereecken, "La Competenza della Comunita a Concludere Accordi Internationali in Materia di Servizi" (1996) 35 (1) *Diritto Comunitario e Degli Scambi Internationali* 87–106. The Court has confirmed its approach in Opinion 2/92, *Third Revised Decision of the OECD on National Treatment* [1995] ECR I-521, paragraphs 24–25; see also Case C-360/93, *European Parliament* v. *Council of the European Union* [1996] ECR I-1195, paragraphs 29–30.

[243] M Vereecken, *supra* n. 242.

[244] Opinion 1/94, paragraph 45.

[245] T Tridimas and P Eeckhout, *supra* n. 123.

[246] Opinion 1/94, paragraph 48. The Court has confirmed its position in Opinion 2/92, *Third Revised Decision of the OECD on National Treatment* [1995] ECR I-521, paragraph 27.

based on Article 43 did not imply that it could not be concluded under Article 113 (now Article 133).[247] Yet, the fact is that whereas Article 43 grants exclusive competence to the Community and requires qualified majority voting within the Council, the Treaty provisions dealing with transport do not necessarily provide for Community exclusive powers.

Concerning intellectual property, the Court has held that only those customs measures affecting counterfeit trade in goods fall within the scope of Article 113. The Court based its decision on two arguments. First, unlike that of the Agreement on Technical Barriers to Trade, the main objective of the TRIPs Agreement is to strengthen and harmonise the protection of intellectual property and not simply to regulate international trade.[248] Second, including the harmonisation and protection of intellectual property within the scope of Article 113 would distort the internal division of powers in the Community. However, ancillary provisions for the organisation of purely consultative procedures, or clauses calling on the other party to raise the level of protection of intellectual property, may be included in acts falling within the scope of Article 113.[249]

Thus, on the basis of Article 113 (now Article 133), the Community has exclusive powers to deal with all measures concerning international trade in goods, as long as the measures do not deal exclusively with ECSC products, all measures concerning cross-border services and all customs measures affecting trade in counterfeit goods. The fact that such measures may have ancillary provisions dealing with other issues, such as health, development policy and intellectual property or are of a foreign policy nature, may not constitute an obstacle to including the envisaged measures within the scope of Article 113.

Concerning the implied powers of the Community, in Opinion 1/94 and subsequent cases, the Court has defined restrictively its prior case law.[250] The main principle is that Member States are prevented from taking external action in a certain area whenever the Community has adopted measures which could be affected by such Member State action,[251] or when such measures include provisions relating to the treatment of nationals of non-member countries or expressly confer on its institutions powers to negotiate with non-member

[247] J Bourgeois, "The EC in the WTO and Advisory Opinion 1/94: An Echternach Procession" (1995) 32 *C.M.L. Rev.* 763–787, 776.

[248] See Opinion 1/94, paragraphs 57–58. However, the WTO agreements were concluded by the Community and ratified by its Member States without any allocation between the Member States as to their respective obligations towards the other contracting parties. Thus, where a provision of the TRIPs agreement can apply to both situations falling within the scope of national law and situations falling within the scope of the Community, it is clearly in the EC interest that such a provision be interpreted uniformly by the ECJ, whatever the circumstances in which it is to apply. See Case 53/96. *Hermes International* v. *FHT Marketing Choice BV* [1998] ECR I-3603, paragraph 32.

[249] See Opinion 1/68, paragraph 68; see also Case C-268/94, *Portuguese Republic* v. *Council of the European Union* [1996] ECR I-6177, paragraph 77.

[250] A Maunu, "The Implied External Competence of the European Community after the ECJ Opinion 1/94—Towards Coherence or Diversity?" (1995/2) *L.I.E.I.* 115–127; see also A Dashwood, "Implied External Competence of the EC", in M. Koskenniemi (ed.), *supra* n. 228.

[251] Opinion 1/94, paragraph 77; see also Opinion 2/92, *Third Revised Decision of the OECD on National Treatment* [1995] ECR I-521, paragraph 31.

countries.[252] The Community may also have exclusive virtual implied powers based solely on the provisions of the Treaty, if the adoption of such measures in the external sphere is inextricably linked to the adoption of domestic measures.[253] Thus, the Court distinguished Opinion 1/76[254] by arguing that in that case the adoption of internal measures was not possible without entering into the agreement under consideration. Furthermore, the Court held that the Community could have exclusive competence under its implied powers on the basis of its internal power to harmonise only if it achieved a complete harmonisation of rules and there is the possibility of interference with international Community law by the continuing authority of the Member States.[255] As most of the internal market is based on directives requiring minimum harmonisation, the exclusive implied powers in external trade are seriously limited.[256] The Court followed the same approach with regard to Article 235 whereby the Community may have exclusive powers in the external sphere only if the internal competence has been exercised previously.[257]

Thus, with regard to the implied powers of the Community to act in the external sphere, the Court allowed for no exceptions and made sure that the EC's external trade powers strictly reflected its domestic sphere. The Community may have exclusive implied powers to deal with services and intellectual property in the external sphere only in those cases where it has adopted secondary legislation which could be affected by Member States individual action, where it has adopted provisions which concern third country nationals, or where it is to provide for the Community institutions to negotiate with third countries.

The scope of Article 113 was an important issue for the 1997 intergovernmental conference which was concluded in Amsterdam. Although with lower hopes than at the Maastricht conference, the Commission tried again to broaden the scope of the Common Commercial Policy. During the negotiating process leading to the Amsterdam agreements, there were four basic positions concerning the scope of Article 113.[258] First, the Commission argued that Article 113 should be redrafted to include all measures involving liberalisation and protection of services, direct foreign investment and intellectual property

[252] Opinion 1/94, paragraph 95.

[253] Opinion 1/94, paragraph 86; see also Opinion 2/92, *Third Revised Decision of the OECD on National Treatment* [1995] ECR I-521, paragraph 32.

[254] Opinion 1/76, *Draft Agreement establishing a European laying-up fund for inland waterway vessels* [1977] ECR 741.

[255] Opinion 1/94, paragraph 88; see also M Hilf, *supra* n. 215, at 448.

[256] A Maunu, *supra* n. 250, at 121; see also M Cremona, *supra* n. 143, at 155, who argues: "Uniformity of external policy as between the Community and the Member States depends on Community legislative activity rather than the fiat of the Court on the nature of implied powers—in marked contrast to the Common Commercial Policy where the Court had stressed its exclusive character even where the Common Commercial Policy was manifestly incomplete". But this is normal if we take into account the international evolution of the concept of trade, and that trade in goods has a weaker impact on the domestic sphere than trade in services and intellectual property.

[257] Opinion 1/94, paragraph 89.

[258] The following is based on information obtained from reading the publicly accessible Commission files on the 1996 Intergovernmental Conference at the Commission's premises.

influencing or affecting trade with third countries. A second approach considered that Member States should transfer to the Community only exclusive competence for certain matters which would be clearly defined and limited in scope. The aim of such transfer would be to meet the requirements of international trade negotiations, particularly the WTO. A third approach was to make explicit, in Article 113, an obligation on both the Member States and the Community to take a single position in those areas where competence was shared. Article 113 would provide for procedures in order to insure such common action. Thus, the Commission would be the single negotiator but it would be mandated by the Council. The agreements would be concluded by unanimity but the mandates to the Commission would be decided on the basis of qualified majority. A final approach was to provide for no Treaty change and, alternatively, try to arrange a code of conduct.

The Commission was willing to reach a compromise, and to extend the scope of Article 113 only in a limited way. However, not only were many Member States opposed the extension of the Common Commercial Policy but others actually demanded exceptions. In this context, a *sine qua non* objective of the Commission was to preserve the powers which the Community already enjoyed either under Article 113 or *via* the implied powers. When the Commission became aware of some Member States' proposals intended to dilute the powers of the Community, it decided to withdraw its petition for a broader Common Commercial Policy. As a result, the Amsterdam arrangements only introduced a fifth paragraph in Article 113 (now Article 133) whereby:

> "The Council acting unanimously on a proposal from the Commission and after consulting the European Parliament, may extend the application of paragraphs 1 to 4 to international negotiations and agreements on services and intellectual property insofar as they are not covered by these paragraphs."

Although the new provision enables the Council to expand the scope of Article 113 (now Article 133) to services and intellectual property, but not foreign investment, without having to go through a formal modification of the constituent treaty, it is very unlikely, however, that in the short or medium term the Member States will be able to reach the necessary consensus to expand the external trade powers of the Community. The extension may only apply to the negotiation and conclusion of international agreements and not to the adoption of unilateral measures, other than measures taken under the TBR. The phrase "may extend the application of" could be interpreted, however, as not necessarily equivalent to including the new areas in the scope of Common Commercial Policy in the same way Article 113 covers trade in goods. Instead of being permanently subject to the provisions of Article 113, the extension could be made, on an *ad hoc* basis only, to certain types of services and intellectual property in a particular international forum.[259] An expansive interpretation

[259] The European Policy Centre, *Challenge Europe: Making Sense of the Amsterdam Treaty* (Brussels, The European Policy Centre, 1998), 98.

would argue that Article 113(5) (now Article 133(5)) should be read as recognising that international agreements on services and intellectual property come within the core of the Common Commercial Policy.[260] This would be the case as the provision is a new paragraph of Article 113, which appears under the Title of Common Commercial Policy, and if these agreements fell outside the scope of the Common Commercial Policy, the Council, even if acting by unanimity, would not be able to extend the scope of the Community powers. A narrower interpretation would consider that Article 113(5) does not give the Council the power to create, under Article 113, a general competence for the Community in the area of services and intellectual property rights but only to extend the application of Article 113 to international agreements on those matters.[261] This interpretation would imply that the Council, under Article 113(5), would not be able to create a legal basis for autonomous measures such as unfair trade instruments. It could also mean that every time the Council decides to extend Article 113 to an international agreement it would have to do so by unanimity and after consulting the European Parliament. Hence, the Community will continue to require the agreement of all Member States in order to act in the external sphere. This will affect the Community's autonomous and conventional action in the international trading system.

4.C.3. Actors and Process of the Common Commercial Policy

4.C.3.a. Introduction

The Community may act in the international trading system by means of conventional and unilateral measures. Both means are so strongly interrelated and complement each other to such an extent that it is often meaningless to distinguish one from the other. On the one hand, the Community simultaneously uses unilateral and conventional measures in attempting to impose the rules of the international trading system. Article 113 (now Article 133) of the Treaty is the main legal basis for the adoption of trade measures. Article 228 defines the procedure for the negotiation and conclusion of international trade agreements. On the other hand, the discussion concerning the scope and limits of Article 113 affects both the Community's participation in international agreements and its adoption of unilateral trade measures. Thus, issues of mixity can arise at conventional as well as unilateral level. Likewise, as external negotiations have always been related to internal developments, the procedure of Article 228 to negotiate and conclude conventional measures affects the adoption of unfair trade instruments.

[260] J Bourgeois, "External Relations Powers of the European Community", 22 *Fordham Int'l L. J.* 149, at 153.

[261] A Dashwood, "External Relations Provisions of the Amsterdam Treaty" (1998) 35 *C.M.L. Rev.*1019–1045, 1022.

4.C.3.b. The Commission

The Commission is the most important single player in the Community's trade policy. First, as in all other Community policies, it is in charge of making proposals under Articles 113 and 228 of the Treaty. Second, it has the power to oversee the implementation of domestic trade measures, conducting negotiations and representing the Community in general dealings with third countries.

The Commission is a unique body in a unique institutional set-up.[262] It is a hybrid creature somewhere between a bureaucratic and a political organisation.[263] It has a political role with initiative but also normative tasks, and a bureaucratic role with its administrative and mediative functions.[264] The Commission, more than any other institution, has to make compatible the administrative, technical, ideological and national positions when participating in the Community's trade policy decision-making.

The Commission has been keen to maintain the European Union as a leader in keeping an open multilateral trading system.[265] It has firmly believed that economic liberalisation and trade openness will improve the economy of the Community; and that this will consequently promote European integration. But this free trade position is not always maintained in a consistent way, since the Commission has to reconcile, on a day to day basis, economic liberalisation with European integration. As the champion of European integration, the Commission's ultimate aim is always to expand its powers by maximising the scope of its competence. Thus, much of its activity in trade policy can be interpreted as an attempt to expand the scope of the Union's trade powers, without alienating the Member States or other economic interests. To do this, the Commission will constantly create, or facilitate, the emergence of new areas or opportunities to expand the Community's trade powers. [266] This implies that the Commission must often have regard to the special interests of powerful Community industries or problems of certain Member States or their regions. In this context, however, it is questionable whether the Commission's approach is adequate, and thus whether economic liberalisation and openness without regard to the different social and political structures within which the different national markets are embedded, is a position compatible with European integration. The irony of the Commission's approach could be that the more it

262 D Rometesch and W Wessels, "The Commission and the Council of Ministers" in G Edwards and D Spence (eds.), *The European Commission* (London, Longman, 1994), 202–224, 221.

263 D Coombes, *Politics and Bureaucracy in the European Community: A Portrait of the Commission of the EEC* (London, George Allen & Unwin, 1970), 234.

264 As to the general functions of the Commission, see Article 155 of the Treaty (renumbered as Article 211 by the Treaty of Amsterdam).

265 T Howell, R Gwyn and M Gadbow, "European Community", in T Howell, A Wolff, B Bartlet and M Gadbow (eds.), *supra* n. 24, at 389–467, 391.

266 L Cram, "The European Commission as a Multi-Organisation: Social Policy and IT Policy in the European Union" (1994) 1 *J. European Public Pol'y* 195–217, 199.

opens the Community to the forces of free trade, the bigger the conflicts between Member States, and thus the challenges to the Community's trade powers. The Commission's approach can be likely to succeed only as long as economic liberalisation results in constant economic growth and stability. Furthermore, the Commission must not be viewed as a monolith. Rather, it is a plural organisation from which contradictory trade policies can result; mainly through the existence of different Commissioners representing diverse political and national interests; or from different Directorate-Generals with disparate constituencies, and a wide hierarchy of officials where personal relations can play an important role.

The Commission can be divided into the College of Commissioners and their cabinets, with a political role, and the Commission departments performing a bureaucratic task. The latter is subdivided into Directorates-General with vertical responsibilities corresponding to different policy areas and the horizontal services such as the Legal Service, the Spokesman service, or the General Secretariat, which co-ordinates the work of all other services. Directorates-General respond to bureaucratic and political needs, so that each Commissioner can be responsible for at least one Directorate, as well as Member States' interests.[267] Each Directorate-General is headed by a Director-General, a person usually of a different nationality from the Commissioner to which he reports. The Directorate-General is divided into Directions, headed by directors reporting to the Director-General or its deputy. Again, each Direction is composed of several divisions, subdivided into units. At the Commission departmental level, the real power brokers are the officials at the Director-General and director level who must make political and technical considerations compatible.

The most important Directorate-General in the Common Commercial Policy process is the Directorate-General for Trade.[268] But in order to back up its actions and to sustain its capacity to exercise its external trade competence, the Commission has created an enormous diplomatic network with more than one hundred and twenty missions around the world.[269] Thus, of great importance to the Community's trade policy are also the Directorate-General for External Relations, the Directorate-General for Development and the Directorate-General for Enlargement.

Increasing interdependence has resulted in almost every department of the Commission having an interest in external trade policy. Thus the Directorate-General for Trade (DGT) has very close contacts with the other departments including those dealing with Industry, Agriculture and, especially, the Internal market. The relations between DGT and the other Directorates depend on the objectives pursued by each. Hence, the department in charge of the welfare of

267 D Spence, "Structure, Functions and Procedures in the Commission", in G Edwards and D Spence (eds.), *supra* n. 262, at 97–116, 99.

268 See <http://europa.eu.int/comm/dgs/trade>.

269 M Smith, "The Commission and External Relations", in G Edwards and D Spence (eds.), *supra* n. 262, 249–286, 254.

Community industry, the Enterprise Directorate-General, will generally try to use DGT to both promote and protect its constituency. This will sometimes create controversy. While DGT likes to believe it follows strictly the Community's WTO commitments on anti-dumping measures as pure instruments against unfair trade, the Enterprise Directorate-General will think of such measures as strategic instruments to protect the Community industry.[270] However, both departments may also often complement each other in promoting European industry; as seen in the case of market access in foreign countries, where Enterprise officials will send their constituents to the DGT units dealing with the TBR and market access policy. On the other hand, both DGT and the Internal Market Directorate-General are immersed in a free trade spirit and believe they complement each other in the liberalisation of the Community. Whereas DGT seems to consider that the Internal Market Directorate-General legitimates its policies by liberalising the Community market, the latter needs DGT's policies to calm fears of third countries over the internal market process. DGT also has close contacts with other Directorates-General on specific issues. Thus, for example, it will consult the Directorate-General for Competition in the determinations of injury and Community interest for anti-dumping and anti-subsidy investigations.

DGT is the responsibility of one Commissioner.[271] Following the recent reorganisation of the Commission, DGT is organised the following way. As with all Directorates, it is headed by a Director-General who reports to the Commissioner and its cabinet. There are several units in the department dealing with general issues such as administration, analysis, relations with the Parliament and co-ordination, reporting directly to the Director-General. The department also has a Deputy Director-General, of a different nationality from his superior, who is in charge of some of the department's Directions as well as the negotiations on the new trade round. The Directorate is organised in such a way that its Director-General and Deputy can control and co-ordinate all measures which are developed therein. The senior officials, for example, will be able to monitor and co-ordinate the Community's market access strategy with its WTO negotiations and with the use of the TBR. They will be able to co-ordinate policy in order to use its unfair trade instruments to incentivise and complement its trade negotiations. While most officials are immersed in a very specific area and believe themselves to be following clear rules, senior posts will be able to co-ordinate and implement certain specific policies. This, in fact, will be further developed at the Commissioners' level.

[270] This has sometimes created problems and bitterness. An example of this was the termination of anti-dumping measures against ball bearings from Japan, where DGT decided to terminate the measures before the Enterprise Directorate-General had reached a market access agreement with the Japanese producers. Interview at the Commission, Brussels, April 1997. See *Ball Bearings with a Greatest External Diameter not Exceeding 30 mm Originating in Japan*, O.J. 7.5.97 L117/28 (termination); see also *Ball Bearings with a Greatest External Diameter not Exceeding 30 mm Originating in Japan*, O.J. 3.5.97 L115/1 (termination).

[271] As of March 2000, the Commissioner in charge is the French Socialist Pascal Lamy.

DGT is divided into Directions. Each Direction is headed by a director and is divided into units managed by the heads of unit. Directions C and E deal with trade instruments. From a bureaucratic and a resources point of view, anti-dumping practice dominates the Commission's unfair trade instruments policy. Direction C, with its three units, is in charge of anti-dumping investigations, specifically the calculation of the dumping margin. Direction E, however, deals specifically with injury and the Community interest determinations for anti-dumping investigations, countervailing investigations, safeguard measures and the Trade Barriers Regulation. The units of these Directions co-ordinate their policies with those of other Directions. Hence, although Unit 3 of Direction E is in charge of the TBR proceedings, it closely co-ordinates its actions with those of Unit 4 of Direction D which deals with the Commission's general market access policy and other units dealing with trade negotiations. Thus, the development of the Trade Barriers Regulation, and other trade instruments, follow DGT's and the Commission's policies as a whole.

Both Directions dealing with unfair trade instruments report directly to the Director-General. Instead, the deputy Director-General monitors Directions D, G and M. Direction D deals with sectoral commercial issues such as textiles, shipping, etc, and market access. Direction G deals with negotiations in the WTO, the OECD and commercial questions with respect to agriculture, fisheries, and export credit policy. Direction M is responsible for services, investment, dual-use goods, standards and certifications, external relations for research, science, nuclear energy and the environment. When the Community is involved in large international trade negotiations, the Commission will create special task forces and inter-service groups. Thus during the Uruguay Round negotiations it created a special inter-service group in charge of policy co-ordination within the negotiations which met at the directors and heads of division level from different Directorate-Generals with an interest in the negotiations and, in turn, reported to a limited number of Commissioners.[272] Within DGT a special steering group was also created to provide overall leadership to the Commission's position and to fine tune its proposals so as to take account of the interests of the European Union's negotiating partners. Special groups involving officials from different Directorates-Generals may also be created with the purpose of implementing specific trade policies affecting the competence of different departments.[273]

Above the Commission services is the College of the Commission with its 20 Commissioners.[274] All Commissioners must be European Community citizens

[272] A Murphy, *supra* n. 119; see also H Paemen and A Bensch, *From the GATT to the WTO: The European Community in the Uruguay Round* (Leuven, Leuven University Press, 1995).

[273] The Market Access Action Group is a good example of such a group. See Chapter V.B, of this book.

[274] As to the composition and election of the College of Commissioners, see Articles 157 to 161 of the Treaty, renumbered as Articles 213 to 217 by the Treaty of Amsterdam.

and there should be at least one Commissioner from each Member State.[275] The President has particular responsibility for coordinating the work of the Commission as a whole and preserving its collegiate nature.[276] All Commission measures are supposed to be taken in a collective manner.[277] This, in fact, guarantees that the acts of the Commission are taken having regard to a wide spectrum of political, technical and national interests.

Commissioners are supposed to represent the Community interest without seeking or taking instructions from any Member State government or any other body. But in practice, Commissioners, and their respective cabinets, represent not only their ideological positions but also their national constituencies with whom they maintain close contacts. This national element serves not only to take into account national interests in the Commission's policies and proposals but, furthermore, it allows the Commission to sell its work much better in the different Member States; enabling a dialogue between intergovernmental and supranational interests.[278] Thus, when deciding on a specific trade measure, such as the imposition of anti-dumping duties, the Commissioners will be careful enough to have special regard to protecting the interests of their country if these are strongly at stake.[279]

The decision-making mechanism of the Commission affects both its legislative proposals to the Council and its technical measures applying existing rules. All measures must go through the same general procedure where both the technical input and the political interests of the Commission as a whole are taken into account.[280] The Commission's procedures can be divided into six general phases: initiation, drafting, interservice co-ordination, agreement between specialised members of the Commissioners cabinets, agreement by the *Chefs* of Cabinet and agreement by the College of Commissioners.[281] Before any proposed measure reaches the College of Commissioners or their cabinets the draft will have gone through a thorough negotiating process between the different bureaucratic levels; one which takes into account the interests of other Directorates and the interests and sensibilities of the Member States. Once the draft measure reaches the political level, the General Secretariat will be in charge of circulating it between the different cabinets. Before the measure

[275] In fact, Germany, Italy, Spain, the United Kingdom and France nominate two Commissioners.

[276] S Nuttall and E Noel, "The Functioning of the Commission of the European Communities", in J Bates, W Finnie, J Usher and A Wildberg (eds.), *In Memoriam J.D.B. Mitchell* (London, Sweet & Maxwell, 1983), 107–117, 111.

[277] Article 1, Rules of Procedure of the Commission, O.J. 25.9.1999 L252/41.

[278] M Cini, *The European Commission: Leadership, Organisation and Culture in the EU Administration* (Manchester, Manchester University Press, 1996), 101–179, 111.

[279] "EU/Norway: EU Continues Deliberations on a Possible Anti-Dumping Duty on Norwegian Salmon", *Agence Europe*, No 6949, 7–8 April 1997; see also "EU/ Norway: Commission Approves Measures Agreed With Norwegians to reduce Effects of Dumping on Norwegian Salmon", *Agence Europe* No 6986, 2–3 June 1997, at 13.

[280] D Spence, *supra* n. 267, at 103.

[281] The Commission has developed its own rules of procedure on the basis of Article 162(2) of the Treaty.

reaches the College of Commissioners, it will be discussed at the *Chefs* de Cabinet meeting, where there will be the possibility of an agreement. This allows for the measure to be placed on the Commission's agenda as an agreed point, if so, no further discussion being needed. The Commissioners, however, will discuss all the major issues which are still unsettled during their weekly meetings.

The rules of procedure of the Commission allow for a written procedure and the granting of a habilitation in specified cases. A mandate will be given to a Commissioner to take measures in the name of the Commission in areas of a managerial or an administrative nature.[282] The written procedure, however, will be initiated by the General Secretariat at the request of a Commissioner for minor decisions if the relevant Directorates have agreed to the proposal and the Legal Services has given its approval. If no reservations are made by the Commissioners through their cabinets, the measure shall be considered to be approved by the College of Commissioners.[283]

In order to understand the Commission's internal decision-making procedures in trade policy, it can be useful to analyse how a simple decision such as the initiation of an unfair trade investigation is taken. Under the Community's anti-dumping, anti-subsidy and trade barriers regulations, the Commission must decide on the initiation of an investigation within 45 days from the lodging of a complaint by either a private party or a Member State.[284] Within such period, the Commission must follow an internal procedure, involving both bureaucratic and political forces, as well as taking into account the Member States' interests.

Immediately after the Commission services receive an unfair trade complaint they will take several steps. First, the complaint will be transmitted to the Member States through the Permanent Representations' contact persons to the different advisory committees and put onto the agenda of the next advisory committee meeting. Second, it will be transmitted to the Commissioner's cabinet in charge of DGT. Third, the services of DGT will make an informal transmission of the complaint to the other Directorate-Generals which may be affected by the case, such as Enterprise, Internal Market or Competition. Fourth, the services dealing with the complaint will start informal contacts with the Legal Service of the Commission. Indeed, no trade policy decision can be taken without their advice, on both Community and international trade law. Finally, they will send a note to the Commission's translation services with the purpose of ensuring an adequate translation planning.

[282] Article 13 Rules of Procedure of the Commission.

[283] Article 12 Rules of Procedure of the Commission.

[284] As to the initiation of an anti-dumping investigation, see Article 5(9) Council Regulation No 384/96, O.J. 6.3.96 L 56/1, as amended. Concerning the initiation of an anti-subsidy investigation, see Article 10(13) Council Regulation (EC) 2026/97, O.J. 21.10.97 L288/1. For the initiation of a TBR investigation, see Articles 5(4) and 6(5) Council Regulation (EC) 3286/94, O.J. 21.12.94, as amended by Council Regulation (EC) 356/95, O.J. 23.2.95 L41/3.

After the complaint has been analysed at the levels of unit and Direction, the Commission services will send to the cabinet of the Commissioner a draft note to which will be attached the note analysing the complaint and the draft notice of initiation.[285] The note, however, will only reach the Commissioner after it has been circulated through and approved by, the medium and high level positions of the Directorate-General.

Thereafter, the Commissioner's cabinet will give its agreement in principle to the initiation of the investigation. The Commissioner's cabinet will ensure that a balance is kept between the Commissioner's ideological and national interests and the possibility of achieving a consensus with both other Commissioners and Member States' positions.[286] Such an agreement will be conditional on the position of other Directorate-Generals, Commissioners' cabinets and Member States. DGT officials will thus first send a draft notice of initiation to the translation services. Second, they will transmit to the Member States' representatives in the advisory committees and the Article 113 Committee deputies, if necessary, their position on the facts of the complaint. Third, they will start the formal interservice consultation procedure, whereby the advice of the officials of the Legal Service, other Directorate-Generals concerned and the desks of the third countries involved in the case will be requested. Such interservice consultation must usually take place within a week of the request.

Once the services of DGT have received the advice of other Directorates, they will send a draft note to their Commissioner with the comments received and a written procedure file. Again, such a note will only reach the Commissioner's cabinet after being approved by the medium and high level positions of the Directorate. Thereafter, the written procedure file concerning the initiation of the investigation will be sent to the General Secretariat, which must distribute it through all the Commissioners' cabinets.

Before the Commission takes any decision, however, its services will inform the Member States of their proposal and allow them to express their own opinions in the advisory Committees.[287] Following such an advisory meeting, the services will both distribute through the Directorate's hierarchy and send to the General Secretariat a Fiche Committee (*Fiche Comite*) indicating the Member States' positions on the initiation of the investigation.

[285] Such a draft will usually be sent within a week of the complaint being lodged, due to the fact that, in practice, most of the complaints are filed upon the prior advice of the Commission's services.

[286] As to how the Commission changes its proposals on the basis on the Member States' reactions, see "Brussels Rethink on Cotton Dumping Duties", *Financial Times*, Thursday 10 October 1996, at 7.

[287] As to the Advisory Committee and the procedure to be followed in the anti-dumping proceedings, see Articles 5(9) and 15 Council Regulation No 384/96, O.J. 6.3.96 L 56/1, as amended. With regard to the Advisory Committee and the procedure followed under the anti-subsidy regulation, see Articles 10(13) and 25. See also Article 10(13) Council Regulation (EC) 2026/97, O.J. 21.10.97 L 288/1. Concerning the Advisory Committee and the procedure to be followed under the Trade Barriers Regulation, see Articles 8(1) and 7 Council Regulation (EC) 3286/94, O.J. 21.12.94 L349/71.

Within the College of the Commission, the cabinets of the different Commissioners will discuss, if necessary, the decision to initiate the investigation. Thereafter, under the written procedure, if no Commissioner makes any objection within a limited time period, the decision will be implicitly adopted.[288] However, there may be cases where a Commissioner disagrees with the initiation. In such a case, the issue will be put on the agenda of the next Commission meeting. Here it will be discussed and decided after a bargaining which would reflect the ideological positions of the Commissioners, as well as their policy and national constituencies.

Thus, by controlling the initiation of an unfair trade investigation and other important steps of the investigation, the Commission is able to threaten third countries and influence the development of the international trading system for the benefit of, what it considers to be, the interests of the Community as a whole. But even the Commission's simplest trade decisions such as the initiation of an unfair trade investigation, imply a variable degree of political and bureaucratic influence. From the very beginning the Commission will try to make sure that such Community interest does not oppose the special sensibilities and interests of particular Member States.

4.C.3.c. The Council and its Committees

No trade measure is adopted without accommodating the interests of the Member States as represented at every level of Community decision-making. Member States participate in the Community's trade decision-making mechanism through the Council of Ministers; which is, in fact, an entire structure divided into the Council of Ministers, the Committee of Permanent Representatives, the Article 113 (now Article 133) Committee and other working and advisory committees.

Within the Council of Ministers, it is the General Affairs Council which deals with foreign trade.[289] The Council, however, will usually discuss important Community trade measures, those having strong political and economic implications and those issues which lower committees have not been able to agree previously. It will be for the Committee of Permanent Representatives (COREPER) to prepare the work of the Council and to try to agree on as many issues as possible so that the latter can simply rubber stamp them as agreed "A points".[290] COREPER, in fact, adopts the conclusions and discusses those issues

[288] For the initiation of an investigation, the accelerated written procedure is generally used. Due to the increasing number of conflicts in the Community, both with Member States and within the Commission when dealing with anti-dumping and anti-subsidy investigations, in 1997 the Commission decided to strengthen its internal procedures with special regard to the written procedure, in order to allow all Commissioners to be fully informed in time of all investigations. See "EU/Anti-Dumping: Commission Approves Improvements in Anti-Dumping Procedures Proposed by Sir Leon Brittan", *Agence Europe* No 7050, 4 September 1997.

[289] As to the functions and composition of the Council, see Articles 145 to 154 of the Treaty, renumbered Articles 202 to 210 by the Amsterdam Treaty.

[290] Article 151 of the Treaty, renumbered 207 by the Amsterdam Treaty.

on which agreement has not proved possible for whatever reason at the lower levels of the pyramid of committees that it heads.[291] However, it has no autonomous decision-making power, and thus, it can in no way legally substitute for the Council of Ministers.[292]

Within COREPER, trade policy issues are dealt with in COREPER II, in which the heads of the Member States' representations sit. Such a Permanent Representative will be a career diplomat appointed for the post as a result of a political decision in each Member States' government.[293] The Member States' delegations, however, are composed of a mix of career diplomats and line department officers with technical expertise. These will try to keep a difficult balance between informing their capitals on Community developments, defending their national positions, and interpreting their government instructions so that the Community machinery can move forward. COREPER II has increasingly given great importance to trade policy, especially international trade agreements, creating its own trade groups and thus, in some way, displacing the Article 113 Committee. Yet, the main role of COREPER II in the area of trade is to monitor the work of the entire structure of Community's trade policy committees.

It could be argued that the creation of the committee machinery has led to intergovernmentalism and to curbs on the opportunities for European integration. Indeed, the whole trade policy comitology apparatus is a testament to a lack of trust in trade policy, a lack between the Member States themselves, and between these and the Commission.[294] But trade committees should not simply be seen as a space for representing intergovernmental interests in trade, but rather as a forum where supranational and intergovernmental forces work together to cope with globalisation.[295] The Community's trade policy committees represent the distrust of 15 Member States with different socio-economic structures, but they are also a clear effort to achieve a common position which can benefit the European Community as a whole. The committees' function is to achieve agreements whereby a balance is kept between adequate technical solutions to cope with globalisation, Member States' interests and the general Community interest.

One issue which frequently creates conflict between the Council and the Commission, especially in implementing trade legislation, is the question of which type of committee procedure should be followed.[296] Whereas the Commission will seek a weak committee wherein the Member States have pro-

[291] F H Renshaw and H Wallace, *The Council of Ministers* (London, Macmillan Press, The European Union Series, 1997), 78.

[292] Case C-25/94, *Commission* v. *Council* [1996] ECR I-1469.

[293] Hayes-Renshaw, Lequesne and Mayor Lopez, "The Permanent Representation of the Member States of the European Communities" (1989) 28 *J. Common Market Studies* 119–137.

[294] S Wilks, *supra* n. 107, at 549–551.

[295] C Joerges and J Neyer, "From Intergovernmental Bargaining to Deliberative Political Process: The Constitutionalisation of Comitology" (1997) 3(3) *European L. J.* 273–299, 279.

[296] D Romestech and W Wessels, *supra* n. 262 at 217.

cedural rights only, the Council will be more interested in having committees with strong powers of decision-making, which can keep a tight control on the Commission. Within the Community's trade policy, specifically the administration of its unfair trade instruments, the committee procedures most used are the advisory committee procedure, where Member States have limited power of control, and the safeguard committee procedure, where the Commission's decisions are subject to the guillotine power of the Council.[297] However, the comitology question is not simply an issue of conflict between intergovernmental and supranational forces. Instead, the issue is often one of confrontation between Member States. Whether or not the Community follows a certain committee procedure in order to take certain trade policy decisions will affect the likelihood of such measures being adopted, and thus, benefit or jeopardise the particular interests of Member States. This, in fact, shows the difficulty of distinguishing between Member States' interests and those considered to be of the Community as a whole.

Despite the controversy over the committee procedure to be followed, both Member States and the Commission are usually interested in obtaining substantial agreement and in adopting measures by consensus. Thus, the committees' work will be devoted mainly to bargaining in order to arrive at successful solutions, satisfactory to all. This is done in several ways. First, whilst the Commission will not chair all committees but only those devoted to trade legislation administration, it will, in fact, control the agenda of them all. Through having the exclusive right of proposal and by virtue of controlling, most of the time, the information on the trade problems or on negotiations and on the positions of all the Member States, the Commission will in practice control the work of the committee. The Commission will usually pursue long-term strategies aimed at consensual decision-making. Thus, it will try to anticipate problems and test the Member States with early proposals; quietly removing them if it does not foresee the necessary support for their adoption. But the Commission will not simply broker the interests of the different Member States. Instead, it will try to reconcile its own proposals with the national interests. So that the Commission can do this, the committee system allows for national input from the very beginning. Hence, in the administration of anti-dumping law, although it will be difficult to counter the Commission on some of its detailed findings, Member States will be able to express their opinion at various stages of the procedure; thus allowing the Commission both to reflect the different Member States' interests, and to draft proposals which can muster the necessary national support.[298]

Second, the officials and representatives of the Member States holding the Presidency of the Council of Ministers will make an important effort to ensure

[297] E Vos, The Rise of Committees (1997) 3(3) *European L. J.* 210–229, 217; see also Council Decision 99/468, O.J. 17.7.1999 L184/23.

[298] P Holmes and J Kepton, "EU Anti-Dumping Policy: A Regulatory Perspective" (1996) 3(4) *J. European Public Pol'y* 647–664, 653.

that successful agreements are achieved. The main role of the Presidency will be to guarantee the necessary Community legislation and the agreement between the different Community trade actors.[299] In order to do this, it will be able to control the agenda of the different committee meetings as well as play the role of a mediator. Thus, it will postpone difficult decisions until more favourable moments, wearing down the opposition and building as much consensus as possible, while reminding everyone of its ability to call a vote. Furthermore, it will issue-link and establish package deals of selected items, the sum total of which will be attractive to all Member States, but ensuring that acceptance of a deal will mean the approval of one or two measures which have long been resisted. Moreover, due to the fact that all Member States hold the Presidency at some point, there will be a certain sympathy towards the Presidency and a strong feeling of responsibility for a successful outcome.[300]

Third, the fact that there is a considerable continuity in the national officials who sit in committee allows them a sound knowledge of what is acceptable to their governments, to their colleagues and even makes them sympathetic to other Member States in certain situations. There is a long time-range bargaining between the Member States during which they will give up some issues, in the hope that other Member States will act likewise in the future.

Fourth, by establishing an entire committee pyramid, the system allows several instances where agreements can be reached. The Commission and the Member States will be able to postpone decisions and go all the way up to the Council in order to allow for more opportunities for reaching an agreement. With regard to anti-dumping measures, where no agreement is reached in the Advisory Committee, decisions will be taken to the Commercial Policy Questions group of the COREPER and then on to the Council, where the Member States and the Commission will try to solve the issue as a part of a political compromise.[301] This shows the extent to which anti-dumping measures adopted by the Community are not simply the result of following clear technical rules which can be submitted easily to a clear and precise judicial review, but rather, they often result from a political compromise between different Member States with diverse domestic structures, on the one hand, and the Commission's position on the Community's interest, on the other. Thus, to a great extent, the "Community interest" clause in anti-dumping and similar unfair trade law becomes irrelevant from a purely technical point of view. Such a clause can be seen as simply an insurmountable obstacle for those trying to challenge the Council's agreement. Any stricter and clearer definition of the Community's

[299] G de Bassompierre, *Changing the Guard in Brussels: An Insider's View of the EC Presidency* (New York, Praeger, 1988), 48.

[300] J Hayes, *Making Trade Policy in the European Community* (New York, St. Martin Press, 1993), 130.

[301] See "EU/Anti-Dumping: Last French Attempt to Save Unbleached Cotton Measures", *Agence Europe* No 6977, 20 May 1997, at 8; see also "EU/Anti-Dumping: Provisional Duties on Unbleached Cotton Expire and no Definitive Duty Imposed—Reflection on Anti-Dumping Policy", *Agence Europe* No 6978, 22 May 1997.

interest clause will imply the need for a political bargain within the Council; a bargaining between protectionist and free trade countries which would probably affect other elements of the instrument.[302] Anti-dumping measures, like other trade policy measures, externalise the Community's trade policy structure.

Finally, and probably most importantly, Member States and the Commission reach acceptable trade solutions because they need to arrive at a common position. All the trade policy actors know that any common Community position is better than no position at all. Coping with globalisation and defending the different national interests requires speaking with one strong voice. Thus, Member States will commonly give up on a certain issue in order not to impede progress in Community decision-making. When a Member State considers whether or not to oppose a certain trade measure towards a third country it knows that it may have to withstand both the third country and its European partners.

The COREPER II controls a large number of working groups and trade committees such as the anti-dumping committee, the anti-subsidy committee, the trade barriers committee, committees for customs co-operation and implementation etc. However, separate from all these committees, and with some independent powers of its own is the Article 113 (now Article 133) Committee.[303] This committee is, in fact, a broad range of specialised committees; with experts in specialised issues from the Member States who have the role of assisting and monitoring the Commission in international negotiations and in the administration of the overall Common Commercial Policy.[304] The 113 Committee submits the respective national positions and discusses them with the Commission in order to synthesise the different national positions and, thus, arrive at a common position in regard of world trade. As other committees, it will act both as a watchdog of the Commission for the Council as well as facilitate the tasks of the former by acting as a sounding board where the Commission can test the acceptability of its proposals and clarify the Council's mandate.[305] Since it is an advisory body with no power of decision, no formal voting takes place in it. Matters are discussed until there is a consensus or a clear majority has been reached. Yet the Commission is careful in following its advice; it knows that the Member States' representatives sitting in the committee have a good knowledge of what is, and, thus, what is not, politically acceptable for their governments.

[302] See "EU/ Anti-Dumping: Sir Leon Brittan's Guidelines on Community Interest in Anti-Dumping Procedures Will Be Discussed by Member States During a High Level Informal Meeting on 6 May 1997", *Agence Europe*, No 6945, 1–2 April 1997, at 7; see also "EU/Anti-Dumping: UNICE Asks Commission to Clarify the Approach it Intends to Take in Assessing the Community Interest in Anti-Dumping Investigations—Serious Concerns", *Agence Europe* No 6960, 23 April 1997, at 15.

[303] See Article 113(2) of the Treaty.

[304] G Nafilyan, "La Coordination Communautaire au Sein du GATT", in C Stephanou (ed.), *supra* n. 178, at 38–52.

[305] J Bourgeois, "The Tokyo Round on Technical Barriers and on Government Procurement in International and EEC Perspective" (1982) 19 *Common Market L. Rev.* 5–33, 20.

The Article 113 (now Article 133) Committee meets at different levels.[306] The full members committee meets once a month and deals with overall trade policy matters. It is composed of senior servants from the national ministries dealing with trade. The Commission is represented at this level by the Director-General of DGT who will be accompanied by the relevant officials from DGT and other Directorate-Generals depending on the points on the agenda.

There is also, however, a Deputies 113 Committee which meets every Friday and deals with specific trade policy issues. This committee is composed of expert officials from either the national capitals or the permanent representations and the different Directors from DGT and, again, other Directorates-General if necessary. Commission officials and, to a lesser degree, those of the Member States, will be coming in and out of the meeting depending on the issue on the agenda. The committee is a discussion forum where both Community trade issues and Member States trade concerns are dealt with.[307] Next to these two committees there are a series *ad hoc* groups established to deal with specialised matters such as textiles, trade and environment, etc.

Traditionally, the Article 113 Committee was in charge of the drafting of the Council's mandate to the Commission for representation in international negotiations. However, it is now COREPER which is in charge of those common positions; the 113 Committee assisting the Commission in following the Council's mandate. The Commission is free in its contacts with third countries and is, in practice, constantly dealing with third countries either in the form of unilateral measures or informal conventional acts. However, when such contacts assume the nature of exploratory discussions with the aim of concluding a formal international agreement, the Commission must ask for authorisation from the Council. Such authorisation of preliminary decisions will not bind the Community for future formal negotiations but only enable the Commission to get information. This will be used to make a proposal to the Council for formal negotiations. By controlling the information on the preliminary negotiations on which the Council must take a decision, the Commission will be able to enhance what it considers to be the Community's interest.

Thus, most of the negotiation directives will be prepared by the COREPER on the basis of the Commission's recommendation to the Council. The latter will adopt these directives as A points without any discussion. Achieving an agreement on authorisation and negotiation directives will require an intense

[306] R Gray, "How Does the EC Set Trade Policy: Article 113 Committee Plays Key Role in Determining Community Position", *EUROPE: Magazine of the European Community*, September-October 1985, at 24.

[307] An example of a Deputies 113 Committee agenda could be: 1) Transatlantic relations: Joint Studies with the USA and Canada; 2) Dispute with the USA concerning solid urea from the former German Democratic Republic; 3) Anti-Dumping proceedings in Israel against steel plates from Spain; 4) WTO aspects of EU's preferential trade agreements with third countries: preparation of draft report by the Council to the European Council; 5) USA: extraterritorial legislation at subfederal level—state of play; 6) Egypt: import restriction on tyres; 7) Trade Barriers Regulation: final Commission decision on resorting to the WTO on changes to US rules of origin; 8) Other business. This information has been obtained from attending the 113 Committee meetings.

bargaining between the Commission and the Member States in the COREPER and in other Council committees. One of the most important issues for agreement will be the legal basis of such an agreement. The Council, by authorising the negotiations, will try to establish whether or not the issue falls under Community competence and the legal basis. The Council must take all decisions concerning the international negotiations, and its resulting trade agreements, by qualified majority if the issue falls under the scope of Article 113 (now Article 133) or by unanimity if the agreements cover fields for which unanimity is required: for the adoption of internal rules and for association agreements.[308] However, the stronger the sensibilities of Member States towards the content of the future negotiations, the less willing they will be to allow a legal basis for the agreement which does not require their consensus. Thus, Member States will try to protect their special interests and challenge the Community's exclusive competence by denying that the issue falls within the scope of Article 113 (now Article 133) or the Community's implied powers, or arguing that it affects a policy field for which unanimity is required.

Once the Member States and the Commission have reached an agreement, both as to the content of the negotiating directives and its legal basis, the Council will authorise the Commission to initiate negotiations. The Council's mandate is not a cession of powers, *cession de pouvoir*, but only a general directive. The Commission will negotiate the agreement in the name of the Community and not in that of the Council, as it is not legally a *mandataire du Conseil*.[309] During the negotiations, the Commission must act in consultation with the Article 113 (now Article 133) Committee. Where difficulties arise within the 113 Committee and the Commission as to the interpretation and clarification of the negotiating directives it is the COREPER which decides, again after bargaining between the Member States and the Commission.[310] In the intergovernmental conference leading up to the Maastricht summit, the Commission, without challenging the existence of such committees, tried to achieve greater freedom from them and to require only prior consultation with them.[311] But contrary to the Commission's proposals, the Treaty on European Union reinforced the role of such committees; formally requiring them for all agreements.[312]

Theoretically, when negotiating mixed agreements, the Commission with the advice of the 113 Committee will negotiate the area which falls under the competence of the Community and the Member States will negotiate those areas falling under their powers. In practice, there are a series of *formulae* that will blur the distinction between the Member States and the Commissions' powers.[313] Most of

[308] Article 228(1); see also Article 228(2).

[309] G Nafilyan, *supra* n. 178, at 47.

[310] E Noel and H Ettiene, "The Permanent Representatives Committee and the Deepening of the Communities" (1971) 6 *Government & Opposition* 422–447, 435.

[311] C F Mougin, *supra* n 138, at 377.

[312] Article 228(1).

[313] C Elhermann, "Mixed Agreements A List of Problems", in D O'Keeffe and G Schermers (eds.), *supra* n. 150 at 3–21, 9.

the time, the negotiations will be conducted by a joint Commission/Member States delegation and the COREPER will intervene both to clarify the Council directives and to coordinate the position of the Member States.[314] Through mixed agreements, Member States will try to increase their control over the negotiation process and protect their special interests while at the same time benefiting from the muscle of common action.

Under Article 228, the Council is the only institution empowered to enter into international agreements. It must decide on the signature and the conclusion of the agreement. Again, such decisions will imply an intense bargaining process where formal issues such as the agreement's legal basis and the voting procedure to be followed will be of great relevance. The Council will first decide the signature of the agreements. The agreement will be signed in the name of the Council of the European Union. Important agreements will be signed by the President of the Commission and that of the Council. Following the Amsterdam European Council, the Council may decide that the signature be accompanied by a decision on provisional application before entry into force.[315] Once the agreement is signed, the Council will decide its conclusion and implementation. The Community will only ratify a mixed agreement after all its Member States have done so. Following the Treaty on European Union, the Council may authorise the Commission to approve modification of the international agreement on behalf of the Community where the agreements provides for them to be adopted by a simplified procedure or by a body set up by the agreement.[316]

4.C.3.d. The European Parliament

Formally, during the trade decision-making process concerning both unilateral measures as well as international agreements, the European Parliament plays a very limited role. Article 113 (now Article 133) grants no role to the European Parliament in trade matters. Article 228 of the Treaty does not grant the European Parliament an active role in trade agreements other than association agreements, agreements establishing specific institutional frameworks by organising cooperation procedures, agreements having important budgetary implications and those entailing amendment of an act adopted under the co-decision procedure, for which its full assent is required. In this respect, the concepts of "specific institutional framework" and "important budgetary implications" will certainly be an issue for dispute in the near future. Furthermore, the Treaty of Amsterdam introduced two exceptions to the involvement of the European Parliament.[317] The Council, on a proposal of the Commission, may decide to suspend the application

[314] E Noel and H Ettiene, *supra* n. 310, at 435; See also G Sojstedt, *The External Role of the European Community* (Farnborough, Saxon House, 1977), 88.

[315] Article 228(2).

[316] Article 228(4); see also S Konstadinidis, "The New Face of the Community's External Relations: Recent Developments on Certain Controversial Issues", in S Konstadinidis (ed.), *supra* n. 4, at 19–49.

[317] Article 228(2).

of an international agreement with the only requirement that it inform the Parliament immediately. The same exception applies in those cases where the Council, on a proposal of the Commission, decides on a position to be adopted on behalf of the Commission in a decision-making body set up by an international agreement. This latter exception applies only in the case of international agreements based on Article 238, ie association agreements. Thus, the need to balance the various national interests and the Community interest pursued by the Commission, and the difficulty of such, implies that once a bargain is struck it will not be changed because of the European Parliament.[318] Yet, during the last few years, the Parliament has slowly enhanced its influence in international trade and developed informal procedures to allow it to keep a dialogue on trade matters with the other Community institutions.[319]

Within the European Parliament, its committees are key actors.[320] Generally, all debates, motions and Commission proposals go through a committee before they are introduced into the Parliament plenary. Membership of committees is allocated in proportion to the relative strength of the Parliamentary groups and the size of the national representation in the Parliament. Concerning external trade, the Committee on Industry, External Trade, Research and Energy is the most relevant. It deals with international agreements governing economic and trade relations with third countries, the economic and trade aspects of the European Economic Area and relations with EFTA, matters concerning the OECD and regional economic and commercial integration organisations situated outside the Community, and agreements signed in that context, WTO and other international organisations especially relating to trade in goods, services, intellectual property and investment, the common external tariff and dumping by foreign countries, as well as economic cooperation.[321] Through this committee, the European Parliament tries to play a role in the Community's trade policy. The questioning of Commission officials, debating of Commission reports and the participation of the Committee members in international trade negotiations as observers allows for a permanent dialogue and mutual support between both institutions interested in enhancing the Community interest.

Moreover, as traditionally the Treaty did not recognise any formal powers to the European Parliament with respect to international trade agreements, in 1973, the Council adopted with the Parliament the Westerterp (Luns II) procedure which applies to negotiations undertaken on the basis of Articles 113 and 235. Under this procedure, the Parliament is involved at three separate stages. Before the negotiations start, the Council is to inform the Parliament officially

[318] J Weiler, "The Transnational Setting: The European Parliament and its Foreign Affairs Committees", in A Cassese (ed.), *Control of Foreign Policy in Western Democracies: A Comparative Study of Parliamentary Foreign Affairs Committees* (New York, Oceana Publications, 1982), Volume II, 28.

[319] D Elles, *supra* n. 164, at 19–30, 26 .

[320] Committees have been created on the basis of Article 142 of the Treaty which empowers the Parliament to decide on its own procedures.

[321] See <http://www.europarl.eu.int/committees>.

and confidentially of the negotiation directive given to the Commission. The Parliament is expected to give an opinion. During the negotiations, the Commission must keep the relevant Parliamentary committees informed of the developments. At the end of the negotiations but before the agreement has been signed, the Council is to inform the relevant Parliamentary committees of the final content of the agreement. At that moment, the Parliament may ask for a special meeting with the President of the Council to obtain more information and to ask it to reconsider the agreement. After the signature of the agreement but before its conclusion, the Council must inform the plenary of the Parliament, which will have the opportunity to debate and give its opinion. While the Westerterp code is not a legally binding agreement between the Council and the European Parliament, since the Solemn Declaration on European Union in Stuttgart in 1983, it has been applied to all significant international trade agreements entered into by the Community.

The European Parliament continues to claim full participation in the development of the Community's activities in the WTO. It considers that its stronger participation would entail a democratic control of the decision-making powers of the WTO and on its impact on the sovereignty of the Community.[322] But it is questionable whether such changes would be possible in the context of fundamental differences in the trade interests of the Member States. Thus, by denying powers to the European Parliament in areas falling within the scope of Article 113 (now Article 133) but at the same time granting it powers on all other areas including those affecting the internal rules, the Council has gained an ally against the Commission concerning the scope of Article 113 (now Article 133).[323] As a result of interdependence and the limited scope of Article 113, the European Parliament has in fact increased its limited powers in external trade. Its powers will not only affect the conclusion of international agreements, but furthermore, as such conclusions are frequently issue linked to the adoption of domestic measures, it will also increase to a certain extent its powers concerning unfair trade instruments. The Commission will have to take into account the opinion and concerns of European Parliament when proposing and implementing its trade policy.

The Community machinery, thus, seems to be designed to reflect domestic structures in the external sphere, rather than formally adjusting to the external threat. The European Parliament has no formal role in external trade but due to interdependence it will increasingly have a *de facto* influence where it has powers in the domestic sphere. Likewise, the Commission together with the Member States will be able to take special care in protecting the latter's special interests during the entire trade policy making process. The Community's common good must accommodate Europe's diverse reality. A common and strong position in

[322] European Parliament, Directorate-General for Research, *Working Paper: The World Trade Organisation and the European Community* (Luxembourg, The European Parliament, 1995), 39.

[323] P Kuipjer, *supra* n. 181, at 234.

the international trading system will only be likely as long as the Community is capable of accommodating national differences. But the stronger the impact of the external sphere on the domestic structure of Member States, the more difficult it will be for all Community actors to achieve this task. The price to pay is lack of efficiency and the real possibility of losing the battle of globalisation.

5

The Community's Unfair Trade Instruments as a Reflection of its Domestic Sphere

5.A. CONSTRUCTED NORMAL VALUE, THE AUDIO TAPES IN CASSETTES PANEL AND ITS AFTERSHOCK IN THE COMMUNITY

5.A.1. Introduction

BETWEEN 1980 AND 1999, the European Community initiated seven hundred and fifteen anti-dumping procedures.[1] The Community's anti-dumping practice reflects something more than its seizure by protectionist interests. First, it illustrates how the Member States' different perceptions of the world trading system, resulting from their different domestic structures, affect the Community's Common Commercial Policy in general and its unfair trade instruments in particular.[2] One the one hand, the absence of a single model for the common market economy results in anti-dumping methodologies which are not in the Community's interest. On the other hand, due to the conflict of trade interests between the different Member States, the Community has been using anti-dumping procedures as second-best instruments to target alien market economies and to influence the rules of the international trading system. Second, the Community's anti-dumping practice also highlights the need to analyse the Common Commercial Policy beyond pure intergovernmental or supranational perspectives.

[1] Each year the Commission publishes an annual report on the Community's anti-dumping and anti-subsidy activities. As to the latest report see Commission of the European Communities, *XVII Annual Report to the European Parliament on the Community's Anti-dumping and Anti-subsidy Activities (1998)*, COM (1999) 411 final, 8.9.1999. The actual anti-dumping regulation is Council Regulation (EC) No 384/96, O.J. 6.3.96 O.J. L 56/1 (1996), as amended by Council Regulation (EC) No 2331, O.J. 6.12.96 L317/1 and Council Regulation No 905/98, O.J. 30.4.98 L128/18. See F Snyder, *International Trade and Customs Law of the European Union* (London, Butterworths, 1998), 212–258.

[2] As to the controversy on anti-dumping policy between the Member States, see F Engering, H De Brabander and E Vermulst, "EC Antidumping Policy in a Globalized World: A Dutch Perspective" (1998) 32(6) *J. World Trade* 115–126, 126.

5.A.2. The Community's Constructed Normal Value Methodology

Unlike countervailing duties, which target foreign government-market relations, anti-dumping procedures focus on the behaviour of foreign private market actors. Anti-dumping law implies a standard for enterprises concerning their market conduct as well as, to a certain extent, their relations with other companies. This regulation of private parties is completely unilateral as GATT rules do not regulate in any way market organisation or competition, but only the behaviour of governments in international trade.[3] Attempts to deal with competition or market organisation issues within the multilateral trading system have not had much success, nor does it seem that they will have in the near future.[4]

Anti-dumping practice is not politically neutral. Instead it is biased against foreign countries with domestic structures where market actors behave in ways other than on an arms length basis, since they presuppose a standard of fairness based on ideal perfect markets. Anti-dumping duties can be seen not only as interface instruments between markets with different socio-political frameworks but, moreover, as deterrence instruments against highly cohesive markets. To a certain extent, they are a means to impose an international trade regime characterised by a plural market economy where market actors deal on a pure arms length basis.

A determination of dumping consists in a comparison between the price of the product as exported to the Community and the normal value of the like Community product.[5] Determination of dumping requires three basic calculations: the calculation of normal value, export price and a comparison between the export price and the normal value.

In the case of imports from a foreign market economy country, the normal value of the like product is preferably established on the basis of the comparable price actually paid, or payable, for the like product in the ordinary course of trade by independent customers in the exporting country.[6] To qualify as normal value, the sales in the domestic market of the exporting country in the ordinary

[3] GATT does not impose on the contracting parties the obligation to prevent enterprises from dumping. See GATT BISD 30 Supp. 140 (1984).

[4] W Pape, "Socio-Cultural Differences and International Competition Law" (1999) 5(4) *European L. J.* 438; see also E-U Petersmann, "International Competition Rules for Governments and for Private Business: The Case of Linking Future WTO Negotiations on Investment, Competition and Environmental Rules to Reforms of Anti-Dumping Laws" (1996) 30(3) *J. World Trade* 5–35; M Cartland, "Anti-dumping and Competition Policy" (1996) 28(1) *L. & Pol'y Int'l Bus.* 289–296; B Hoekman and P Mavroidis, "Dumping, Anti-Dumping and Antitrust" (1996) 30(1) *J. World Trade* 27–52; R Pitofsky, "Competition Policy in a Global Economy—Today and Tomorrow" (1994) *J. Int'l Economic L.* 403; and D Tarullo, "Competition Policy for Global Markets" (1994) *J. Int'l Economic L.* 445.

[5] Article 1(2) of Council Regulation (EC) 384/96, as amended.

[6] Article 2(1) ibid. As to non market economies, see Article 2(7) ibid. Special rules may apply for imports coming from the People's Republic of China and Russia. See article 2(7)(b) ibid.

course of trade must be at least a 5% of the exports to the Community.[7] The Commission does not consider domestic sales below the cost of production as sales done in the ordinary course of trade and, thus, it excludes them for the purposes of calculating whether domestic sales constitute at least 5% of the export sales.[8] If there are no sales of the like product in the domestic market of the exporting country or these sales are insufficient, or the market does not permit a proper comparison, the normal value must be based on either the constructed value of the like product or the prices of export of the like product to a third country, provided that such prices are representative.[9] In practice the Community authorities have disregarded, for various reasons, the export prices to third countries.[10]

Thus, the constructed value of the like product is a basic determination in order to establish the normal value of the like imported product. Constructed value is calculated to check whether the domestic sales have been in the ordinary course of trade or to establish the normal value of the like product itself. The purpose of constructing normal value is to determine the selling price of the product as it would be if that product were sold in its country of export or origin.[11] The Commission determines the constructed value on the basis of the cost of production including a reasonable amount for selling, general and administrative costs plus a reasonable amount for profit.[12] It includes in the costs of production all costs in the country of production or exportation, fixed or variable, without any discrimination. Thus, it includes, without distinction, labour, energy, raw materials, plant upkeep, the cost of capital, etc. The Commission calculates the costs on the basis of the records kept by the party under investigation; provided that such records are in accordance with the generally accepted accounting principles of the country concerned and that they reasonably reflect the costs associated with the production and sale of the product under consideration.[13] In the allocation of costs the Community authorities consider the

[7] Article 2(2) ibid.; see also Commission of the European Communities, *Proposal for a Council Regulation Imposing a Definitive Anti-Dumping Duties on Imports of Gas-Fuelled, Non-Refillable Pocket Flint Lighters Originating in Japan*, COM (1998) 619, Brussels, 29.10.1998 (paragraphs 22–23); see also Case C-105/90, *Goldstar Company Limited* v. *Council* [1992] ECR I-677.

[8] *Disodium Carbonate from the United States of America*, O.J. 13.4.95 L 83/8; see also *Bicycles from Indonesia, Malaysia and Thailand*, O.J. 14.10.95 L 248/12; and Joined Cases 277 & 300/85, *Canon* v. *Council* [1988] ECR 5731.

[9] Article 2(3) Council Regulation 384/96.

[10] *Electronic Typewriters from Japan*, O.J. 22.6.85 L 163/1; see also *Colour television receivers originating in Malaysia, the PRC, the Republic of Korea, Singapore and Thailand*, O.J. 1.4.95 L 73/3. In this respect, the new WTO Anti-dumping Code seems to put a stronger emphasis on the use of the export prices to third countries. See Article 2(2) of the Agreement on Implementation of Article VI of GATT 1994 (Anti-dumping Code); and P Waer and E Vermulst, "EC Anti-Dumping Law and Practice after the Uruguay Round—A New Lease of Life?" (1994) 28 *J. World Trade* 5–21, 10.

[11] See Joined Cases 277 & 300/85, *Canon* v. *Council* [1988] ECR 5731; Joined Cases 260/85 & 106/86, *TEC* v. *Council* [1988] ECR 5855; and Joined Cases 273/85 & 107/86, *Silver Seiko* v. *Council* [1988] ECR 5927.

[12] Article 2(3) Council Regulation 384/96, as amended.

[13] Article 2(5) ibid.

evidence submitted on the proper allocation of costs provided that it is shown that such allocations have historically been used. Otherwise, preference is given to the allocation of costs on the basis of turnover.[14] Costs must be adjusted appropriately for those non-recurring items of cost which benefit future and or current production.[15]

The determination of selling and general administrative expenses must be based on data pertaining to production and sales in the ordinary course of trade of the producer.[16] The selling and administrative expenses to be included in the cost of production are those incurred in the domestic market and not those incurred in the export country.[17] The Commission includes in the cost of production an amount corresponding to the sales and general administrative expenses incurred by the domestic sales organisation of the exporter. It does this even if the exporter has no sales in its domestic market.[18] If the selling and general expenses cannot be determined on the basis of the data relating to the production and sales in the ordinary course of trade of the producer, the Commission establishes those amounts on the basis of the weighted average of the actual amounts determined for other exporters or producers, subject to investigation in respect of production and sales of the like product in the domestic market of the country of the country of origin;[19] or on the basis of the actual amounts applicable to production and sales, in the ordinary course of trade, of the same category of products for the exporter or producer in question in the domestic market of the country of origin;[20] or under any other reasonable method.[21]

The margin of profit to be added to the cost of production will also be based on the production and sales in the domestic market, in the ordinary course of trade, of the like product by the exporter or producer under investigation.[22] The Commission will normally disregard non-profitable sales for the purpose of establishing the profit margin.[23] In the case of a producer with a subsidiary, the Community authorities may use the combined profit margins of the two

[14] Article 2(6) ibid.

[15] Ibid.

[16] Article 2(6).

[17] Article 2(6); see also Case 250/85, *Brother Industries* v. *Council* [1988] ECR 5683; Joined Cases 277 & 300/85, *Canon Inc.* v. *Council* [1988] ECR 5731; Joined Cases 260/85 & 106/86, *TEC* v. *Council* [1988] ECR 5855; and Joined Cases 273/85 & 107/86, *Silver Seiko* v. *Council* [1988] ECR 5927.

[18] See Joined Cases 260/85 & 106/86, *TEC* v. *Council* [1988] ECR 5855.

[19] Article 2(6) (a); see also *Disodium Carbonate from the United States of America*, O.J. 13.4.95 L 83/8.

[20] Article 2(6)(b) Council Regulation 384/96, as amended; see also *Colour television receivers originating in Malaysia, the PRC, the Republic of Korea, Singapore and Thailand*, O.J. 1.4.95 L 73/3 (definitive); see also Joined Cases 260/85 & 106/86, *TEC* v. *Council* [1988] ECR 5855 (upholding a restrictive interpretation of the concept "same category of products").

[21] Article 2(6)(c) Council Regulation 384/96, as amended; see also *Microwave ovens from the PRC, the Republic of Korea, Thailand and Malaysia*, O.J. 7.7.95 L 156/5.

[22] Article 2(6) Council Regulation 384/96, as amended.

[23] See *Bicycles from Indonesia, Malaysia and Thailand*, O.J. 14.10.95 L 248/12.

companies.[24] If such an amount cannot be determined, the profit margin is based on the weighted average of the actual amounts determined for other exporters or producers, subject to investigation in respect of production and sales of the like product in the domestic market of the country of origin;[25] or on the basis of the actual amounts applicable to production sales, in the ordinary course of trade, of the same category of products for the exporter or producer in question in the domestic market of the country of origin;[26] or any other reasonable method, provided that the amount of profit does not exceed that normally realised by other exporters or producers on sales of products of the same category in the domestic market of the country of origin.[27]

The European Community's anti-dumping Regulation provides certain exceptions to this approach. First, following the new Anti-dumping Code the Regulation provides for consideration of start-up phases.[28] A start-up phase exists where there is significant investment including, for example, new production facilities. This may cover both new products or new factories. When the costs for part of the period for cost recovery are affected by start-up operations which take place within and during part of the investigation period, the average costs of the start-up period are those applicable, under the allocation rules at the end of this phase, and are included at that level, for the period concerned, in the weighted average costs. The length of the start-up phase is left open. It is determined in relation to the circumstances of the producer or exporter concerned, but will not exceed an appropriate initial portion of the period for cost recovery.[29] Secondly, again as a result of the new Anti-Dumping Code,[30] when determining whether the domestic sales price should be considered as normal value, the Community must exclude such sales only if it determines that they are made within an extended period of time, in substantial quantities and at prices which do not provide for recovery.[31] Domestic sales shall not be considered as sales below cost if prices which are below cost at the time of sale are above weighted average costs for the period of investigation;[32] or the sales below costs are not in an extended period of time, considered to be of one year but in no case less than six months;[33] or the weighted average selling price is not below the

[24] See Joined Cases 273/85 & 107/86, *Silver Seiko* v. *Council* [1988] ECR 5927.

[25] Article 2(6)(a); see also *Disodium Carbonate from the United States of America*, O.J. L 83/8 (1995); *Microwave ovens from the PRC, the Republic of Korea, Thailand and Malaysia*, O.J. 13.4.95 L 156/5; and Joined Cases 260/85 & 106/86, *TEC* v. *Council* [1988] ECR 5855 (upholding this practice).

[26] Article 2(6)(b) Council Regulation 384/96.

[27] Article 2(6)(c) ibid.

[28] See Article 2(2)(1)(1) and footnote 6 of the Anti-dumping Code; see also Article 2(5) of Council Regulation (EC) 384/96; and I Van Bael, "The 1994 Anti-Dumping Code and the New EC Anti-Dumping Regulation", in J Bourgeois, F Berrod and E Fournier (eds.), *The Uruguay Round Results: A European Lawyer's Perspective* (Brussels, European Interuniversity Press, 1996), 233–246.

[29] Article 2(5).

[30] See Article 2 (2)(1) of the Anti-Dumping Code.

[31] Article 2(4) Council Regulation 384/96, as amended.

[32] Article 2(4)(a) ibid.

[33] Article 2(4) (b) ibid.

weighted average unit cost or the volume of sales below unit cost is less than 20% of sales being used to determine normal value.[34] However, these provisions provide only for very timid limitations to the Community's approach. The Community, in fact, continues to consider all costs the same without distinguishing between fixed and variable costs.

If we take into account the theoretical division between states on the basis of their market cohesion, whether they are plural or characterised by a tendency to concerted action and cohesiveness, the European Union's constructed normal value methodology raises some concerns. Imposing anti-dumping duties on the basis of such constructed normal values entails punishing countries characterised by cohesive markets. Bearing in mind the persistence of different market economies within the Union, the issue is whether it is efficient to favour some market economies and deter others.

Imagine two firms (firm A and firm B) each in a different country (country X and country Y).[35] Both firms may be equally efficient, they may have the same aggregate costs of production of a certain good. However, the costs of production may be divided into variable costs and fixed costs. Thus, whereas both companies may have the same aggregate costs, they may diverge in their cost structure. The organisation of the market in countries Y and X may diverge to the extent that their firms have different costs structures.

Both firms' costs are the sum of the variable and fixed costs. However, because of the market organisation of country X the fixed costs of firm A could be higher than the fixed costs of firm B; conversely, because of the market organisation of country Y, the variable costs of firm B would be higher than the variable costs of firm A. Thus, for example, whereas under country Y's business practices and labour law, labour could be considered to be a variable cost, in country X, the labour system could be characterised by worker tenure and thus, labour would be considered to be as a fixed cost.

In times of economic prosperity, there would be no difference between the systems. The producers of both countries would try to maximise profits by charging a price which is above all costs. But in the short run, in times of little demand or very strong competition, demand would be very elastic. A difference in price would make a very big difference in the demand. If the producer chose to charge a price above all costs it might not sell anything at all. Hence, economists consider that it is economically rational to sell below total costs but above variable costs.[36] As long as the producer is able to cover any additional variable costs it is sensible to continue producing below all costs because in the short-

[34] Ibid.; see also *Personal Fax Machines from the PRC, Japan, Republic of Korea, Malaysia, Singapore, Taiwan and Thailand*, O.J. 31.10.97 L297/61.

[35] J H Jackson, *The World Trading System: Law and Policy of International Economic Relations*, 6th ed. (Cambridge, The MIT Press, 1994), 218–223; see also J H Jackson, "Dumping in International Trade: Its Meaning and Context", in J H Jackson and E Vermulst (eds.), *Antidumping Law and Practice: A Comparative Study* (New York, Harvester Wheatsheaf 1990).

[36] P Victor, "Antidumping and Antitrust: Can the Inconsistencies Be Resolved?" (1983) 15 *N. Y. U. J. Int'l L. & Pol'y* 339–350.

medium run it will have the fixed costs anyway, whether it produces or not. Hence, in county X's market system where the variable costs are lower than in country Y, producer A will be much more willing to reduce its prices than producer B in country X.

By following a methodology which considers as dumping any sale below all costs, fixed and variable, the European Union is deterring country A type market economies; i.e. those with high fixed costs that are not necessarily less efficient in the long run, but are less flexible because they have high fixed costs such as long term relations between capital and labour. The European Union would be promoting an international trading system characterised by plural markets where their actors pursue their individual interests without any social cohesion or co-operation between them. But the irony is that, unlike the markets of other trading partners, such as the United States, the different market economies of the Community are far away from this ideal. Continental markets are characterised by the lack of flexibility; either because of the traditional dominant role of the state in the economy or because of market corporativism.

This issue shows the paradox of the Community Common Commercial Policy. The process of globalisation, harnessed to the domestic liberalisation of the Single Market Initiative, has pushed those European countries where the state has traditionally played a dominant role in the economy to call for protectionist measures against foreign imports. As GATT rules impose stringent standards for the imposition of safeguard measures, relating both to non-discrimination between foreign imports and serious injury to the domestic industry,[37] the Community attempts to satisfy the protectionist European states by imposing anti-dumping duties.[38] But the fact is that EC anti-dumping law, as well as all other EC unfair trade instruments, have been copied from those developed in the United States and enshrined in GATT rules. The Community is using an instrument which was never envisaged for continental market economies. By doing this, the Community would appear to be further promoting an international trading system characterised by the absence of concerted behaviour in the market and government intervention. This would further disembed both those market economies which have traditionally relied on the state and those which have relied on concerted behaviour in order to cope with free trade. If we were to see trade policy as a reflection of the domestic sphere, the

[37] The Community has traditionally argued in favour of the possibility of adopting safeguard measures on a discriminatory basis in GATT *fora*. See M Bronckers, "Reconsidering the Non Discrimination Principle as Applied to GATT Safeguard Measures, A Rejoinder", in *Selective Safeguard Measures in Multilateral Trade Relations* (Deventer, Kluwer Law and Taxation, 1985), 54–78; see also N Scott, "The Commercial Policy of the European Economic Community (EEC)" in D Salvatore (ed.), *National Trade Policies* (Amsterdam, North-Holland, 1992), 31–56, 39.

[38] C Norral, "New Trends in Anti-Dumping Practice in Brussels" (1987) WORLD ECONOMY 97. An analysis of the anti-dumping cases would show that the complaining industries are located predominantly in the southern Member States, such as France and Spain, whereas the importers of the foreign products are located to a great extent in northern states such as The Netherlands and Germany.

Community's anti-dumping policy would highlight the thin Anglo-Saxon homogenisation of the Community market.

5.A.3. Asymmetry, the Audio Tapes in Cassettes Panel and its Aftershock

5.A.3.a. The Background

Between 1980 and 1996, the Community imposed massive anti-dumping duties against Japanese exports of electronic products that changed radically the economic and political relations between the two partners.[39] One of the most important legal issues within the dumping determinations of these proceedings was the asymmetry issue, when comparing normal value and export price. This legal dispute illustrates the Community's inability to influence efficiently the rules of the international trading system. However, it also highlights the superficiality of analysing the Common Commercial Policy in pure intergovernmental or supranational terms.

To understand the asymmetry dispute it is necessary to take into account several issues. First, it is important to revise the concept of dumping. Article VI of GATT defines dumping as the process "by which products of one country are introduced into the commerce of another country at less than the normal value of the products".[40] Due allowance must be made in each case for differences in conditions and terms of sale, for differences in taxation and for other differences affecting price comparability. However, the 1979 GATT Anti-dumping Code considered a product as being dumped, i.e. introduced in the commerce of another country at less than its normal value, "if the export price of the product exported from one country to another, is less than the comparable price, in the ordinary course of trade, for the like product when destined for consumption in the exporting country."[41]

A main issue in the definition of dumping is whether it is profit discrimination i.e. selling at lower profits abroad than in the home market, or simply price discrimination, i.e. charging a higher price in one country than in another. While considering dumping as profit discrimination implies taking into account all the

[39] N Komuro, "EC Antidumping Measures vis-à-vis Japan", in *The European Union in a Changing World*, 107–120, 107 (Third ECSA-WORLD Conference, Brussels 19–20 September 1996).

[40] Under Article VI(1) of GATT. "A product is to be considered as being introduced into the commerce of an importing country at less than its normal value if the product exported from one country to another is less than the comparable price in the ordinary course of trade, for the like product when destined for consumption in the exporting country, or, in the absence of such domestic price, is less than either the highest comparable price for the like product for export to any third country in the ordinary course of trade or the cost of production in the country of origin plus a reasonable amount for selling cost and profit."

[41] See Article 2(1) of Agreement on Implementation of Article VI of the General Agreement on Tariffs and Trade, 1979 GATT BISD 26th Supp. 171 (1980). Article 2(1) of the WTO Antidumping Code repeats the 1979 Antidumping Code. See Article 2(1) of the Anti-Dumping Code.

differences in costs in each market, and thus, would equalise both markets, price discrimination only takes account of different costs of different markets as long as it can be proved that such costs clearly affect the different prices, and, thus, would penalise the existence of different markets.[42] The idea of dumping as price discrimination is based on the asymmetrical access of markets, i.e. dumping would be possible because the domestic markets are closed, thus, the costs do not necessarily affect the price. The international trade rules do not provide a clear definition.

Secondly, it is important to understand how the market distribution of a product works. Usually the producer does not sell directly to the consumer. Instead it sells to the distributor, who in turn sells to the wholesaler, who in turn sells to the dealer, who finally sells to the end-user. Each market actor will have its own costs and will wish to make a profit. Furthermore, if the producer can control the distribution chain of its products it might control its market sector.

Thirdly, we must understand the difference between direct costs and indirect costs (variable/fixed costs). Direct costs (variable costs) would be all those costs which directly influence the making of an economic transaction. Thus, they include transport, production, handling, taxes, etc. Indirect costs (fixed costs) are all those expenses which the economic agent has, independent of whether it makes the transaction. Indirect costs include the general, selling and administrative expenses of the producer.[43]

Finally, we should be aware of the market organisation of Japan. The Japanese market illustrates the extent to which international trade is based not only on exchange rates set by capital markets and legal barriers set by governments, but also by concrete relationships among the different market actors who actually make the buying and selling decisions.[44] The model of Japan as a cohesive market based on consensual ordering is reflected in the existence of complex networks of long-term contractual relationships and the persuasive reliance on relational contracting: the *keiretsu*.[45]

The word *keiretsu* literally means affiliated chain.[46] They are not formal organisations in a legal sense but instead are loosely organised alliances within

[42] For the argument that dumping can only be defined as profit discrimination, see P Waer and E Vermulst, "The GATT Panel Report on the EC Anti-Dumping Proceedings Concerning Audio Tapes in Cassettes: Back to Basics in the Concept of Dumping?" (1995) 29 (6) *J. World Trade* 31–44, 44. Compare W Muller, N Khan and H A Neumann, *EC Anti-Dumping Law—A Commentary on Regulation 384/96* (Chichester, John Wiley & Sons, 1998), 3–8.

[43] As we have observed, to a certain extent, whether a cost is variable or fixed depends on the market economy of the economic agent. See section A.1 of this chapter.

[44] M Gerlach, "Keiretsu Organisation in the Japanese Economy Analysis and Trade Implications" in C Johnson, L D'Andrea Tyson and J Zysman (eds.), *Politics and Productivity: How Japan's Development Strategy Works* (New York, Harper Business, 1989), 141–176, 141.

[45] J O Haley, "Luck, Law, Culture and Trade: The Intractability of United States-Japan Trade Conflict" (1989) 22 *Cornell Int'l L.* J. 403–423, 416; see also J McMillan, "Why Does Japan Resist Foreign Market-Opening Pressure?" in J Bhagwati and R Hudec (eds.), *Fair Trade and Harmonization: Prerequisites for Free Trade?* (Cambridge, The MIT Press, 1996), Volume I, 515–541.

[46] T Myerson, "Barriers to Trade in Japan: The Keiretsu System-Problems and Prospects" (1992) 24 *Int'l L. & Politics* 1107–1113, 1108.

the social world of the Japanese business community.[47] The relevance of these social and economic networks is highlighted by the fact that they take place in a system where the Japanese government delegates most of its regulatory power to private market actors.[48]

The historical predecessors of the *keiretsu* were the *zaibatsu* which developed during the Meiji Restoration as large family conglomerates with strong links with the imperial bureaucracy in an attempt to compensate for the late industrialisation of the Japanese economy.[49] Yet, the real binding force of the *zaibatsu* were not the holding companies or the family ties; but rather the extensive personal relationships and sense of loyalty to the corporate identities.[50] Thus, when the American troops left Japan after trying to bury forever the *zaibatsu* system, the new Japanese government, eager to develop its devastated economy, encouraged a market *keiretsification* by creating links other than family links on the basis of the old *zaibatsu* patterns. But as the new *keiretsu* tried to reproduce the old *zaibatsu* that had a stake in all sectors of the Japanese economy, they developed as heterogeneous entities; consisting of groups of companies from different sectors. As a result, the *keiretsu* must compete ferociously between themselves to survive in the Japanese market.

There are basically two types of *keiretsu*: horizontal *keiretsu* and vertical *keiretsu*. A horizontal *keiretsu* is like a corporate convoy where large groups of companies travel together and keep an eye on each other around an identity enterprise, usually a large city bank, next to a trading company and a few giant insurance and industrial firms. There are no formal structures within the groups. Instead they are organised by two processes. Whereas the core members of the group meet in informal councils, defining the overall interests of the group, the flow of resources affecting ownership, finance and trade are the manifestation of such defined interests.

Vertical *keiretsu* overlap usually with the horizontal groups. Most of the big companies of the horizontal group are heads of their own vertical *keiretsu*. These may be production *keiretsu*, consisting of a pyramid of suppliers and assemblers providing goods to the parent company, or distribution *keiretsu*, a pyramid of enterprises that market the goods of the main firm. Often, vertical groups are composed of both production and distribution *keiretsu*. As a result they look like two pyramids put together by their main points with the main firm in the intersection.

[47] G Bader, The Keiretsu System of Japan; Its Steadfast Existence Despite Heightened Foreign and Domestic Pressure for Dissolution" (1994) 27 *Cornell Int' L. J.* 365–386, 365.

[48] F Upham, "Privatized Regulation: Japanese Regulatory Style in Comparative and International Perspective" (1996) 20(2) *Fordham Int'l L. J.* 396–511. The great difference between Japan and the European corporativist systems is that whilst in the latter the role of market actors has a public sanction, in Japan regulation is privatised and is often secret. Ibid., at 495.

[49] J Fallows, *Looking at the Sun: The Rise of the New East Asian Economic and Political System* (New York, Pantheon Books, 1994), 72–116. See also K Miyashita and D Russell, *Keiretsu: Inside the Hidden Japanese Conglomerates* (New York, McGraw-Hill, 1994), 21.

[50] Ibid., at 33.

The overall benefit of the *keiretsu* is not short-term profit but rather security and long-term economic viability. However, whilst the *keiretsu* compete between themselves, such a set of cohesive structures is a strong barrier to the entrance of newcomers. Only those companies which are part of a group are able to survive economically. For our purposes the most problematic *keiretsu* are the vertical distribution *keiretsu*. During the 1960s the electronic and auto industries developed huge networks of affiliated distributors. The producers supplied the goods, the marketing tools and almost all the prestige, while the small dealers provided the shop and labour. Thus, the producer bore most of the marketing costs but in return the small leader had to be loyal to their brand names. The main advantage of the system was savings for the parent firm, since the affiliated firms forming part of the vertical *keiretsu* and distributing the goods to the dealers shared in the marketing costs. Because the producers controlled the entire retail network, they could control the price of the products and the entrance of newcomers. Therefore, competition from cheaper alien products became limited and, thus, the competition between the different *keiretsu* focused on the quality of the goods and on developing ever larger distribution networks, as close as possible to the consumers.

The result of this process is that whilst it is extremely difficult for foreigners to enter the Japanese market, Japanese producers have the necessary domestic economic support to compete in foreign markets. Whether this is fair or unfair depends on whether we consider fairness as strict market share reciprocity, and, thus, to a certain extent similar market organisation, or whether we take fairness to mean national treatment, i.e. treating foreigners the same way that Japanese firms are treated on their domestic market. Because Japanese producers themselves face equally severe restrictions in access to distribution networks and other prerequisites for new entry in their home Japanese market as foreign entrants, to ensure reciprocity of market share to foreign producers would in fact imply special favours for foreigners.[51] Indeed, the entire distribution structure does not necessarily provide more profits to the overall entity but rather security resulting from a very long-term investment, and a sense of mutual loyalty between firms. The entire distribution network involves huge costs which are in fact borne by the producer or its subsidiaries.

5.A.3.b. The Community's Asymmetry Methodology

The eagerness of the Community institutions to gain credibility and authority led them to develop an "asymmetrical" comparison methodology in order to deal with what was considered to be the "Japanese problem."[52] This concern was two sided. On the one hand, despite tariff reduction and government liberalisation, the Japanese electronics market continued to be closed to European

[51] J Haley, *supra* n. 45, at 420.

[52] B Hindley, "Dumping and the Far East Trade of the European Community" (1988) 11 *World Economy* 445–464, 446.

and third country products.[53] On the other hand, and for many as a result of this, Japan continued to gain European market share and to drive out European producers from the electronic sector. The panic concerned both the loss of employment opportunities and of the technology race, as European industries were losing out in the sun rising products. The Community institutions took advantage of the looseness of the Anti-dumping Code and the EC Anti-dumping Regulation; developing a series of methodologies whose result clearly discriminated against Japanese electronic producers.[54] The purpose was twofold. First, the Community attempted to stop the flow of Japanese products into the European market. Second, to a certain extent, the Community used its anti-dumping measures as a second best instrument to punish what it considered to be the domestic Japanese closed market system, and to break into this system. However, not only would the results of the approach be limited but, in the process, the Community as a whole would lose its international credibility and frictions would arise between its Member States.

In determining the normal value, the Community developed the concept of "economic single entity". For the purposes of establishing the normal value, "prices between parties which appear to be associated or to have a compensatory arrangement with each other may not be considered to be in the ordinary course of trade unless it is determined that they are unaffected by the relationship."[55] In the context of market distribution networks, the sales between the producers and distributors with whom they have an association or compensatory agreement are not used; instead, the Community takes as the domestic price that charged to the first independent buyer.[56] The normal value calculated at the level of the price charged to the independent buyer will normally be higher than that charged by the producer to the related distributor since the resale price charged by the related distributor will have to cover the extra cost which it has incurred.[57] The extra costs of the related distributor are in practice both direct and indirect.

The Community interprets the term "associated" in a functional manner by focusing on the existence of a single economic unit as opposed to a legal entity.[58]

[53] H Yamane, "EU Efforts to Open the Japanese Market: Government Structure and Private Practices" (1998) 3 *European Foreign Affairs Rev*. 481, at 501.

[54] E Vermulst and P Waer, *AC Anti-Dumping Law and Practice* (London, Sweet & Maxwell, 1996), 182.

[55] Article 2(1) Council Regulation 384/96, as amended.

[56] The GATT basis for this approach would be the emphasis of Article 2(1) of the Anti-dumping Code on "the ordinary course of trade" when determining the normal value. The Commission argues that sales between associated firms or those which have compensatory arrangements cannot be considered to be in the ordinary course of trade. See *Certain Thermal Paper Originating in Japan*, O.J. 26.9.91 L270/15; *Certain Compact Disc Players Originating in Japan*, O.J. 17.1.90 L12/21; and DRAMs from Japan, O.J. 25.7.90 L193/1. See also P Waer, "Constructed Normal Values in EC Dumping Margin Calculations—Fiction or Realistic Approach?" (1993) 27 J. *World Trade* 4.

[57] I Van Bael and J F Bellis, *Anti-Dumping and other Trade Protection Laws of the EC*, 3rd ed. (Bicester, CCH, 1996), 66.

[58] *Certain Electronic Scales Originating in Japan*, O.J. 16.10.85 L275/5 (recital 15); see also *Electronic Weighing Scales Originating in Japan*, O.J. 29.4.93 L104/4.

For the purpose of determining the existence of a single economic entity, the Community will not focus on the legal structure of such entity but instead it will make (a) a functional analysis, i.e. whether the function of the sales companies is to sell or facilitate the sale of the producer's goods, (b) an equity analysis, i.e. whether the producer controls the equity of the distributor; and (c) a management analysis, i.e. whether there are strong links between the companies with respect to management personnel and staff. In practice, the Community will treat parties as associated if there is at least a 5% of common shareholding.[59]

The Commission's rationale has been that only by taking into account the prices charged by the subsidiaries is it possible to ensure that costs which would be an integral part of the selling price, even if made by the exporter's internal sales department, are taken into account in cases where the selling activity is carried out by the company which, although a legal entity, is controlled by the manufacturer.[60] All costs (both direct and indirect) should be included because all such costs would be included in the selling price if the marketing had been carried out by the producer. This approach to the determination of normal value has been consistently upheld by the European Court of Justice.[61]

If the normal value must be constructed, the Community institutions will include all costs from both the producer and the related subsidiaries. The Commission includes the direct expenses as well as the selling, general and administrative expenses of both firms.[62] As the aim of constructing the normal value is to determine the selling price of the product as it was sold in the country of origin, the Community considers that all the expenses of the related subsidiary should be taken into account.

The Community has considered that the rules for the establishment of the export price are completely different. The export price is the price actually paid or payable for the product when sold for export from the exporting country to the Community.[63] The export price is the price of the product before entering the Community frontier. Where there is no export price or where it appears that the export price is unreliable because of an association or a compensatory arrangement between the exporter and the importer or a third party, the export price may be constructed on the basis of the price at which the imported products are first resold to an independent buyer, or if they are not resold in the condition in which they were imported, on any reasonable basis.[64] Unreliability is

[59] E Vermulst and P Waer, *supra* n. 54, at 182.

[60] W Muller, N Khan and H Neumann, *supra* n. 42, at 69.

[61] See Joined Cases 273/85 & 107/86, *Silver Seiko* v. *Council* [1988] ECR 5927; see also Joined Cases 277 & 300/85, *Canon* v. *Council* [1988] ECR 5731; Case 250/85, *Brother Industries* v. *Council* [1988[ECR 5683; Case 301/85, *Sharp* v. *Council* [1988] ECR 5813; and Case C-179/87, *Sharp Corporation* v. *Council* [1992] ECR I-1635.

[62] See *Certain Types of Electronic Microcircuits Known as DRAMs Originating in Japan*, O.J. 25.1.90 L20/5 (recitals 48–50).

[63] Article 2(8) Council Regulation 384/96, as amended.

[64] Article 2(8) ibid. This provision basically follows Article 2(5) of the Agreement on Implementation of Article VI of GATT, 26th Supp BISD 171 (1980), as well as Article 2(3) of the Anti-Dumping Code.

assumed from the mere fact that there is, or there appears to be, an association or compensatory arrangement.[65] Importers and exporters are usually considered to be associated if there are any links between them other than those which exist in a straight arm's length buyer-seller relationship. In such cases, the Community institutions will take the price to the first independent buyer and then deduct all expenses which have been incurred between the importation of the product and the final sale to the independent buyer. The purpose of this construction is to enable the establishment of a price at the Community frontier which is not influenced by the relationship between the producer/exporter and its associated importer.[66]

The Community institutions make adjustments for all costs, including duties and taxes, incurred between importation and resale, and for profits accruing, to establish a reliable price at the Community frontier level.[67] They deduct from the price to the first independent buyer all costs which would normally have been borne by an independent importer.[68] The Commission actually deducts both the direct and indirect costs (selling, general and administrative expenses) of the related importer plus profit.[69]

Once export price and normal value have been determined it is necessary to compare both prices. The problem with regard to Japanese imports was that whereas normal value was at the level of the sale from the related distributor to the first independent buyer, the export price was at a level corresponding to that prior to importation. Thus, whereas the normal value included all costs of the related distributor and producer, the export price included only the cost of the producer.

A fair comparison would require making adjustments so that both prices reflected the same level of trade and the same product.[70] Article VI of GATT required due allowance for differences in conditions and terms of sale, for differences in taxation, and for other differences affecting price comparability. Prior to the 1979 Anti-dumping Regulation, the Community maintained a flexible approach towards the possibility of making adjustments.[71] However, in

65 I Van Bael and J F Bellis, *supra* n. 57, at 107.

66 *Electronic Weighing Scales Originating in Singapore and the Republic of Korea*, O.J. 22.10.93 L263/1 (recital 6); see also *Ball Bearing Units Originating in Japan*, O.J. 6.2.87 L35/32 (recital 13); compare *Electronic Weighing Scales Originating in Japan*, O.J. 29.4.93 L104/4 (recital 21); see also *Certain Compact Disc Players Originating in Japan and South Korea*, O.J. 18.8.89 L205/5 (recital 13).

67 Article 2(9)(b) Council Regulation 384/96, as amended.

68 Note that under Community law, it is the importer who is supposed to pay all import duties and taxes.

69 As to the items for which adjustment is made see Article 2(9)(c) Council Regulation 384/96, as amended. In this context, the Community takes as profit that of an independent importer and not that of the related importer. See *Certain Hydraulic Excavators Originating in Japan*, O.J. 8.3.85 L68/13 (recital 11); see also *Certain Magnetic Disks from the United States, Mexico and Malaysia*, O.J. L 249/3 (1995); see also Joined Cases 273/85 & 107/86, *Silver Seiko* v. *Council* [1988] ECR 5927.

70 Sometimes, the constructed value and the export price could be based on like products which had some differences.

71 I Van Bael and J F Bellis, *supra* n. 57, at 114.

1979, when implementing the Tokyo Anti-dumping Code, the Community changed radically its approach and adopted the principle that no adjustments should be made for indirect costs.[72] Council Regulation 2423/88 established an exhaustive list of adjustments which, again, excluded the indirect costs of the domestic selling subsidiaries.[73]

The adjustment process, netting back, implied that the export price was established at the ex-factory level whereas the normal value included the indirect costs, i.e. selling, general and administrative expenses of the related subsidiaries plus the amount of profit which was supposed to correspond to such expenses. The Community put forward both an economic and a legal argument for this approach. First, it argued that the definition of dumping was based on price comparability, and thus only those costs which affected price could be adjusted. In an open market, prices were influenced by buyers, who were not concerned with the costs of selling overheads, and possibly by other suppliers whose selling overheads could be different.[74] Only if the producer were able to set the price without constraint, and thus in practice held a monopoly which the Community considers to be the basis of dumping, would the indirect costs affect the final price. Second, from a legal point of view, both the EC Regulation and the GATT established different rules for the calculation of the normal value, the export price, and the comparison. There was no reason to deviate from this principle merely because of formal structures such as the delegation of certain functions to one or more companies, the corporate structure of the group under company law or the handling of sales by the integrated company department or independent subsidiary.[75] In practice, the Community was comparing markets. By considering that the export price should be established on an arm's length basis, it was punishing those markets which were different from the "ideal market", which the Community was supposed to be. The Japanese producers were being punished because their market was not a plural market characterised by transactions between producers and the chain of distributors on an arm's

[72] Article 2(10)(c) and Article 2(10)(d) Council Regulation (EC) 3017/79, O.J. 31.12.79 L 339/1.

[73] The Regulation allowed adjustments for differences in physical characteristics, import charges and indirect taxes, selling expenses resulting from sales made at different levels of trade or in different quantities or under different conditions and terms of sale. But the selling expenses which could be adjusted were limited to transport, insurance, handling, and ancillary costs, packing, credit, warranties, guarantees, technical assistance and other after-sales services, personnel engaged in direct selling activities. See Article 2(9) Council Regulation 2423/88, O.J. 2.8.88 L209/1. The Court upheld the principle that such a list was exhaustive. See Case 204/84, *Toyo Bearing* v. *Council* [1987] ECR 1809; see also Joined Cases 294/86 & 77/87, *Technointorg* v. *Commission and Council* [1988] ECR 6077.

[74] J F Beseler and A N Williams, *Anti-Dumping and Anti-Subsidy Law: The European Communities* (London, Sweet & Maxwell, 1986), 105.

[75] *Certain Electronic Scales Originating in Japan*, O.J. 16.10.85 L275/5 (recital 25); see also *Certain Compact Disc Players Originating in Japan and South Korea*, O.J. 18.8.89 L205/5 (recital 59); see also Case 204/84, *Toyo Bearing* v. *Council* [1987] ECR 1809; Case 258/84, *Nippon Seiko* v. *Council* [1987] ECR 1923; Case 260/84 *Minebea* v. *Council* [1987] ECR 1975; Case 250/85, *Brother Industries* v. *Council* [1988]ECR 5683; Joined Cases 277 & 300/85, *Canon Inc.* v. *Council* [1988] ECR 5731; and also Joined Cases 273/85 & 107/86, *Silver Seiko* v. *Council* [1988] ECR 5927.

length basis; instead being cohesive groups which expanded from the manufacturer of the product's components to the final sale to the consumer.

The Community limited somewhat this approach by introducing the concept of "selective normal value."[76] If the producer could show that it sold both to related distributors as well as to unrelated distributors, the Community would take as normal value, the price of sale to the independent distributor. However, the application of this exception was in practice restricted as the producer had to show that it sold in its domestic market to both related and independent distributors.[77]

One of the most contentious issues of the Uruguay Round anti-dumping negotiations was the problem of fair comparison. Japan and other Asian countries pressed for an adjustment in indirect costs when making a fair comparison. The Community, on the other hand, refused, as it considered that a systematic adjustment would imply a redefinition of dumping from price discrimination to profit discrimination.[78] In the end, the contracting parties reached a loose compromise which, while maintaining the requirement of price comparability being affected, required a fair comparison to be made, such that where the export price had been constructed, the normal value should be established at the same level of trade and further, that authorities should indicate to the parties which information was necessary to ensure a fair comparison and should not impose an unreasonable burden of proof on those parties.[79] The new Code does not preclude making adjustments for indirect costs and related profits but it does not say that such adjustment should be made *per se*, as it always includes the requirement of affecting price comparability.

The Community institutions implemented the new Code by inserting an adjustment for level of trade where in relation to the distribution chain in both markets, it is shown that the export price is at a different level of trade to the normal value and that the difference has affected price comparability. This latter requirement must be demonstrated by consistent and distinct differences in functions and prices of the seller for the different levels of trade in the domestic market of the exporting country.[80] The Community continues to insist on defining dumping as price discrimination and to consider that not all costs affect price *per se*. As with the selective normal value methodology, the main obstacle is the fact that this provision presupposes that the producer sells at different levels of trade in its domestic market. Furthermore, it is very difficult to prove that prices at the different levels of trade are different from each other on a transaction by transaction basis; there may always be specific instances in which sales

[76] P Didier, "EEC Antidumping: The Level of Trade Issue After the Definitive CD Player Regulation: Japanese Proposal to GATT on the Level of Trade Issue" (1990) 24(2) *J. World Trade* 103–109, 104.

[77] *Electronic Weighing Scales Originating in Japan*, O.J. 29.4.93 L104/4 (recital 30); see also *Certain Compact Disc Players Originating in Japan*, O.J. 17.1.90 L12/21 (recitals 24–27).

[78] W Muller, N Khan and H A Neumann, *supra* n. 42, at 125.

[79] See Article 2(4) of the Anti-Dumping Code; see also P Waer and E Vermulst, *supra* n. 10.

[80] Article 2(10)(d) Council Regulation 384/96, as amended.

prices charged at one level of trade overlap with specific sales price at one or more other levels of trade.[81]

5.A.3.c. The Audio Tapes in Cassettes Panel

The asymmetry issue ended up before a GATT dispute settlement Panel.[82] Once again, the GATT dispute settlement had to deal with conflicts arising from the existence of different market structures within the international trading system. Japan brought a complaint against the Community's imposition of anti-dumping duties on audiocassettes originating in Japan in 1991.[83] Among the several claims brought by Japan, the most important one was the Community's asymmetric methodology.[84]

The arguments of the parties were those which had been put forward for more than a decade.[85] Japan insisted on the Anti-dumping Code's requirement of fairness when comparing normal value and export price. Article 2 of the Code had to be read as a whole, requiring a fair determination of dumping. Fairness implied comparing like with like. If adjustments were made to the export price, the same adjustments should be made to the domestic price used for normal value.

The Community argued that there was no such a symmetry requirement in the Code. The Agreement only established rules concerning the determination of normal value, export price and a comparison where adjustments should be made if these affected price comparability. The rules on the determination of export price and the determination of normal value had a different rationale. One set of rules was intended to establish the export price as if it had been based on an arm's length basis, the other set aimed at determining the price of the

[81] P V Schueren, "New Anti-Dumping Rules and Practice: Wide Discretion Held on a Tight Leash?" (1996) 33 *C.M.L. Rev.* 271–297, 284; see also E Vermulst and P Waer, "The Post Uruguay Round EC Anti-Dumping Regulation—After a Pit Stop, Back in the Race" (1995) 29(2) *J. World Trade* 53–76, 59; see also *Stainless Steel Fasteners and Parts Thereof Originating in the People's Republic of China, India, the Republic of Korea, Malaysia, Taiwan and Thailand*, O.J. 20.2.98 L50/1 (recital 38) (adjustment granted); compare *Advertising Matches Originating in Japan*, O.J. 17.6.97 L158/8 (recital 20) (adjustment rejected); see also *Personal Fax Machines Originating in the People's Republic of China, Japan, Republic of Korea, Malaysia, Singapore, Taiwan and Thailand*, O.J. 30.4.98 L128/1 (recital 33) (adjustment rejected); and *Bicycles Originating in Taiwan*, O.J. 26.8.98 L 10/26 (recital 36) (adjustment rejected).

[82] *EC-Anti-Duties on Audio Tapes in Cassettes Originating in Japan*, ASP/136, April 8, 1995. Although the Panel report was delivered in 1995, Japan had brought the case in 1993 and its claims referred to the Tokyo Anti-dumping Code. Thus, the dispute settlement procedure was ruled by that of the Tokyo Agreements and not by the new WTO dispute settlement agreement.

[83] *Audio Tapes in Cassettes Originating in Japan, the Republic of Korea and Hong Kong*, O.J. 13.11.90 L313/5 (provisional); see also *Audio Tapes in Cassettes Originating in Japan, the Republic of Korea and Hong Kong*, O.J. 5.5.91 L119/35 (definitive). These measures had been taken under Council Regulation 2423/88.

[84] Other claims concerned zeroing, calculation of constructed normal value, and the determination of injury.

[85] The arguments of the parties concerning asymmetry can be found in paragraphs 80–112 of the Panel report.

product destined for consumption in the domestic market. In making the comparison there could be no allowance for the indirect costs of the related subsidiaries because these, in an open market, did not affect price comparability.

The main argument was in fact the definition of dumping. Thus the parties' main difference rested on whether anti-dumping should be used as an instrument to compare markets and punish those different from an ideal perfect one based on an arm's length basis; whether determining dumping implied comparing markets and, thus, was based on price discrimination, or whether in determining dumping an adjustment should be made for all the differences in market structures so that dumping would only mean profit discrimination. In this context, the Community argued in one of its submissions to the Panel:

> "The purpose of dumping investigations is not to determine what economic conditions allow differential pricing between import and export price, but merely to establish that price discrimination exists. The differential costs (if any) may form part of the structure which allows market separation and dumping to be practiced. If dumping is found to exist, any allowance granted on the basis of indirect cost comparison would inevitably be flawed because the cost structure would be a reflection of two different markets with two different price structures. The basic purpose of anti-dumping actions which is recognized and permitted by the Code, would be nullified."[86]

The Panel's reasoning with regard to the asymmetry issue was extremely confusing. This was a result of the fact that there has never been an agreement between the different contracting parties on either the definition of dumping or which allowances to make when comparing normal value with export price.[87] Still, the Panel's main conclusion was that differences in costs and profit could affect price comparability. As the Community Regulation allowed only for an exhaustive list of adjustment items, which did not include the indirect costs of the distribution subsidiaries, it was held not to be in compliance with the Anti-dumping Code.

The Panel report could be interpreted in two ways. On the one hand, it could be interpreted as establishing an obligation on the investigating party to make adjustments for indirect costs without requiring the exporter to demonstrate that such costs affect the price. On the other hand, it could be construed that the report only considered that the Community was wrong in excluding *per se* indirect costs as an adjustment item. The Panel report should only be interpreted as allowing for the possibility of adjustments for indirect costs to be made. Otherwise, it would be establishing a definition of dumping as profit discrimination for which there has never been agreement between the contracting parties.

[86] Interview at the Commission, Brussels, May 1997.

[87] The Panel's reasoning with regard to asymmetry can be found in paragraphs 367–388 of the Report. Indeed the Community and other anti-dumping users raised the confusion within the report as one of the arguments not to implement it.

5.A.3.d. The Implementation of the Panel Report in the Community

The Panel's report was a shock for the Community. This was so even though it ruled against the Community only with regard to the asymmetry issue. The Panel threatened one of the Community's main strategies for dealing with what it considered to be the "Japanese problem." Furthermore, the report increased the tensions between the different Member States concerning the Community's anti-dumping policy. The way the Community reacted to the report reflected a balance between its intention to preserve anti-dumping as a trade weapon, the divisions between the different Member States, and the Community's official commitment to the new international trading system.

The first factor the Commission took into consideration when making its proposal to the Council on a Community reaction to the report, was the dissension between the Member States over anti-dumping. In the Anti-Dumping and Article 113 committees, it became clear that the Member States differences which had always been emblematic over their approach towards anti-dumping re-emerged in relation to the report. While Spain, Belgium, Italy, Portugal, Greece and France preferred to reject the Panel, the United Kingdom, The Netherlands and Sweden were positive about adopting it's conclusions. Germany kept its options open and Austria was inclined towards adoption, insisting that the whole issue should be seen within the context of the EC-Japanese relations.[88] Whereas southern countries with plural markets and a traditional reliance on the state pushed towards protection in order to cope with globalisation, the countries with markets characterised by concertation and co-operation preferred full commitment towards the international trading system.[89]

The Commission officials realised there were four possible basic alternatives. First, the Community could adopt the Panel report and implement the Regulation accordingly. This would prove the Community's commitment towards the new WTO rules and, thus, it would enhance its prestige in the international trading system. But such an approach entailed too many drawbacks. (a) The Community would risk the Panel report being interpreted as always requiring an adjustment for indirect costs and therefore adopting the definition of dumping as profit discrimination. This would mean losing a fundamental interface instrument to deal with different market economies. (b) Most importantly, there was no way the Commission would obtain the necessary votes in the Council to adopt such proposal, as the southern Member States opposed strongly the Panel report. (c) It was unlikely that the other contracting parties who were traditional users of anti-dumping law would support the Community.

Secondly, the Community could simply refuse the Panel's finding and make no changes to its basic Regulation, since the Panel had reached its decision under

[88] Interview at the Commission, Brussels, May 1997.

[89] The exception to this was the United Kingdom.

the old dispute settlement rules, prior to the WTO. By not adopting the Panel report, the Community would be sure to safeguard its anti-dumping strategy. But this met with very strong opposition from the northern states, as it would strongly affect the Community's standing in the multilateral trading system.

Thirdly, the Commission considered proposing the adoption of the report but with a reservation concerning the asymmetry issue and thereafter make some amendments to the Regulation. However, while basically preserving the commitment of the EC to the new trade rules, the reservation could not ensure that the Panel report would not threaten the Community's long standing position on anti-dumping. Furthermore, Commission officials realised that not even this proposal would obtain the necessary votes in the Council.

Finally, the Commission decided to make a proposal which was mainly based on its ability to obtain the necessary votes in the Council. The formula was to reject adoption of the Panel report, but to make some amendments to the basic Regulation which would reflect the Community's interpretation of the Panel's reasoning. By taking this approach, the Community would not lose completely its prestige, whilst being sure of preserving its anti-dumping strategy. Most importantly, this proposal would be a compromise between the different Member States' positions. Whereas the southern Member States were reassured that the Community would basically keep its methodology, the free trade states foresaw more restraint in the Community's future anti-dumping practice.[90]

In amending the Regulation, the Council first introduced an additional paragraph to Article 2(10)(d) of the Regulation whereby, when an existing difference in the level of trade cannot be quantified because of the absence of the relevant levels on the domestic market of the exporting countries, or where certain functions are clearly shown to relate to levels of trade other than the one which is to be used in the comparison, a special adjustment can be granted.[91] This amendment is a recognition that a level of trade cannot be refused simply on the grounds that the exporter is not in a position to quantify its claim.[92] However, the producer must show that it is performing certain functions which refer to levels of trade other than the one which is to be used in the comparison.[93]

[90] As to the Commission's official proposal, see Commission of the European Communities, *Proposal for a Council Regulation (EC) Amending Regulation (EC) No 384/96 on Protection Against Dumped Imports from Countries not Members of the European Community*, COM (96) 145 final, Brussels 10.4.96; see also "Japan in EU Cassette Row", *Financial Times*, Friday 20 September 1996.

[91] Article 2(10)(d) Council Regulation 384/96, as amended by Council regulation 2331/96, O.J. 6.12.96 L317/1. The amendment seems to be a bit more restrictive than the proposal. See COM (96) 145 final.

[92] W Muller, N Khan and H A Neumann, *supra* n. 42, at 132. See *Personal Fax Machines Originating in the People's Republic of China, Japan, Republic of Korea, Malaysia, Singapore, Taiwan and Thailand*, O.J. 30.4.98 L128/1 (recital 39) (adjustment granted).

[93] E Vermulst and B Driessen, "New Battle Lines in the Anti-Dumping War: Recent Developments on the European Front" (1997) 31(3) *J. World Trade* 135–157, 138; see also *Stainless Steel Wires with a Diameter of Less than 1 mm Originating in the Republic of Korea*, O.J. 24.3.99 L1/12 (recital 19) (adjustment denied); see also *Stainless Steel Wires with a Diameter of 1 mm or more Originating in India*, O.J. 24.3.99 L13/24 (recital 17) (adjustment denied); and *Sacks and Bags*

In order to avoid being criticised for having an exhaustive list of possible adjustments, the Community introduced a new Article 2(10)(k); whereby an adjustment may be made for differences in other factors not provided for under subparagraphs (a) to (j), if it is demonstrated that they affect price comparability. In particular that the customers consistently pay different prices on the domestic market because of the difference in such factors.[94] The new provision, however, insists on the principle that the different costs must affect price comparability. It must be shown that the customers consistently pay higher prices because of the difference in the other factors.[95]

5.A.4. Some Remarks

By developing a methodology concerning normal value, export price and the comparison for its anti-dumping procedures, the Community attempted to manage what it considered the "Japanese problem." It tried both to limit the flow of Japanese electronic goods into the Community market and to target the closed market nature of Japan. However, this policy was shaped by the persistence of different market economies within the Community.

From an institutional perspective, the Community's policy was strongly determined by the conflict of interests between the different Member States. Thus in the aftershock of the Panel report, Member States realigned again according to their trade interests. The European states were prisoners of their diverse domestic market structures and hence, the Commission had to broker between these diverse interests in order to salvage as much as possible the prestige and effectiveness of the Community in the international trading system. However, the case also highlights how despite the differences, the Commission was capable of promoting what it considered as the Community's interest.

From a substantial point of view the obvious question is why did the Community use its anti-dumping law as an aggressive instrument to target the Japanese market? After all, anti-dumping duties only indirectly put pressure for change on foreign markets.[96] If the Community intended to open the Japanese market the best and preferable option would be to do so by offensive means and not by imposing duties on imports into the Community.[97] The obvious answer

Made of Polyethylene Originating in India, Indonesia, and Thailand, O.J. 16.1.1999 L11/1 (adjustment denied)

[94] Article 2(10)(k) Council Regulation 384/96, O.J. 6.3.96 L56/6, as amended by Council Regulation 2331/96, O.J. 6.12.96 L 317/1.

[95] *Personal Fax Machines Originating in the People's Republic of China, Japan, Republic of Korea, Malaysia, Singapore, Taiwan and Thailand*, O.J. 30.4.98 L128/1 (recital 54) (adjustment denied).

[96] B Hoekman and P Mavroidis, "Dumping, Antidumping and Antitrust" (1996) 30(1) *J. World Trade* 27–52, 30.

[97] See F Engering, H De Brabander and E Vermulst, "EC Antidumping Policy in a Globalized World: A Dutch Perspective" (1998) 32(6) *J. World Trade* 115–126, 117.

is that, as we shall see in the next section, the Community, unlike the United States, did not have (nor does it now have) such an offensive instrument to attempt to break into the Japanese market. The Community was bound to use its anti-dumping regulation as a second best instrument to pursue its trade policy goals.

From a defensive point of view, the international trading system prevented the Community from making discriminatory use of safeguard measures which would have been both more effective and, probably, domestically less polemical. But as the Member States which had traditionally relied on government intervention demanded some form of protection to compensate for the changes resulting from integration, the Community institutions developed instead an "asymmetry" methodology which would guarantee a high level of dumping and, thus, grant protection in the form of anti-dumping duties or harassment. Yet, by taking an instrument allowed in the GATT agreements and developing its methodology to the maximum, they would achieve the Community's interest only to a certain extent. While discriminating against the Japanese market system could be argued to be in the interests of the Community as it safeguarded the European markets from an alien system, the irony is that such an approach required promoting an international trading system characterised by a plural market, which the Community has traditionally lacked. By playing the GATT game, the Community would be granting protection on the basis of a liberal instrument which reflects only partly its domestic system. The Community's policy reflected the thin Anglo-Saxon homogenisation of the Community's market. In doing this, the Community authorities were overlooking the persistence of market differences within the Community and, thus, allowing the controversies of the Common Commercial Policy, and the anti-dumping practice in particular, to continue.

5.B. THE COMMUNITY'S TRADE BARRIERS REGULATION: AN EXAMPLE OF THE COMMON COMMERCIAL POLICY

5.B.1. Introduction

In December 1994, the European Union adopted, as part of the Uruguay Round implementation package, Regulation (EC) No 3286/94,[98] the new "Trade

[98] Council Regulation 3286/94, O.J. 31.12.94 L 349/71, as amended for technical reasons by Council Regulation 356/95, O.J. 23.2.95 L41/3. Bronckers, "Private Participation in the Enforcement of WTO Law: The New EC Trade Barriers Regulation" (1996) 33(2) *C.M. L. Rev.* 299–318. This Regulation repeals Council Regulation 2641/84, O.J. 20.9.84 L252/1, as amended by Council Regulation 522/94, O.J. 10.3.94 L66/10, the so-called "New Commercial Policy Instrument". Cases initiated under Regulation 2641/84 were: *Unauthorised Sound Recordings in Indonesia*, O.J. 21.5.87 C136 /21; *Exclusion from the US Market of Certain Aramid Fibres*, O.J. 5.2.86 C25/2; *Port Charges in Japan on Cargoes and Shipping Companies*, O.J. 16.2.91 C40/18; *Pirate Sound Recordings in Thailand*, O.J. 20.7.91 C189/26; *Fund Levy and Customs Duty*

Barriers Regulation" (TBR). The TBR establishes procedures which are aimed at responding to obstacles to trade, which may have an effect on the market of the Community or in the market of a third country.[99]

The TBR can be seen as an example of the Common Commercial Policy by highlighting how the different trade interests of the Member States have led to the development of a second-best instrument. The persistence of different market systems within the Community, accentuated as a result of globalisation, have resulted in the limitation of the TBR's scope as well as strongly committing it to the strict standard of international trade law. As a result, the Community will be unable to use this strategic instrument to influence effectively the future rules of new sectors in international trade, such as services, intellectual property rights or foreign direct investment, or to target new emerging markets in the world, such as the People's Republic of China or Russia, or to push for new rules in important policy areas which affect trade, such as competition, labour standards or the protection of the environment. However, the TBR also shows how the Community's trade policy is the result of a conflict between different constitutional actors in which, despite the important role that the conflicting interests of the Member States play, there is still an important scope for the input of other players, as well as their struggle for influence.

5.B.2 The Intra-Community Bargaining

As with its predecessor, the adoption of the new TBR and its features was the result of a highly complex ideological and institutional bargaining process between different Community actors.[100] Its adoption was part of the negotiation and implementation process of the Uruguay Round whereby the external negotiations were linked to internal developments as an integral part of a Community package.

On 15 December 1993, the General Affairs Council approved the global package of the Uruguay Round unanimously. As the Council considered that the international agreement did not fall completely within the exclusive competence of the Community, arguing instead that it should be treated as a mixed agreement, its acceptance required the Member States' consensus. This unanimity was only possible after the Council had fulfilled two prior conditions set by

in Turkey, O.J. 31.8.93 C235/4. Known rejected complaints were *Deprivation of Patent Protection by Jordan for a New Polymorphus Substance*, O.J. 1.2.89 L30/67; Case 70/87, *FEDIOL* v. *Commission* [1989] ECR 1781. By 1964, the Commission had already proposed a unilateral trade instrument similar to that of Section 301. *Proposition d'un reglament du Conseil etablissant des principes communes et une procedure communautaire au sujet de la defense commerciale de la CEE, contre des pratiques anormales de la part des pays tier. Presentee par la Commission au Conseil le 26 novembre 1963*, Supplement au Bulletin de la Communauté Economique Européenne No 1–1964.

[99] Article 1 of the TBR.

[100] On the adoption of the New Commercial Policy Instrument, see Bronckers, "Private Response to Foreign Unfair Trade Practices: US and EEC Complaint Procedures" *in Safeguard Measures in Multilateral Trade Relations* (Deventer, Kluwer Law and Taxation, 1985), 157–250, 211–219.

some Member States. First, Portugal demanded the approval of Community support programmes for the modernising of its textile industry which, it alleged, would be severely damaged by the Uruguay Round deal. Second, certain Member States, led by France, had established as a precondition the strengthening of the Community's instruments for trade policy. Certain guidelines were agreed by qualified majority voting (the United Kingdom and the Netherlands voting against) with regard to the "New Commercial Policy Instrument" (NCPI) and anti-dumping and countervailing measures.[101] With this decision, France and its supporting countries had partially obtained a long-standing request.

By June 1992, as part of the completion of the Common Commercial Policy and the internal market, the Commission had made a proposal to strengthen the Community's trade instruments.[102] This proposal increased the powers of the Commission and made it easier to adopt retaliatory measures. With regard to countervailing, anti-dumping and the NCPI, it proposed a drastic change in the decision-making procedure by suggesting that all definitive measures should no longer be taken by qualified majority in the Council but by the Commission, following the management committee procedure.[103]

The 1992 Commission's proposal met very strong opposition from the five traditionally free trade oriented Member States: the United Kingdom, the Netherlands, Germany, Luxembourg and Denmark. They rejected the increase in the Commission's power, arguing that there was no need to alter the existing procedures. The controversy paralysed the Council for the whole year. The conflict was a clear example of the Community's common commercial policy struggle. Once again, there was confrontation between Member States that were able to cope with globalisation, due to the fact that they had social arrangements which controlled the market, and other Member States, led by France, whose only means to control globalisation and the market were the types of government intervention that both the Single Market Initiative and the Uruguay Round had strongly limited.

As with other issues regarding unfair trade instruments there seemed to be an alliance between the Commission and the more protectionist Member States. There were two reasons for this. First, the Commission, as a broker between the Member States, was conscious of the need to grant a certain amount of protection in order to counterbalance the opening of the European market. In the back of the

[101] "EC/Uruguay Round: Following Agreement on the Instruments for Trade Policy and Action Plan for Textiles for Portugal, the Council Unanimously Approves the Results of Negotiations in Geneva", *Agence Europe* No 6130, 16 December 1993, at 7.

[102] *Commission Proposal for a Council Regulation* (EEC) *on the harmonization and streamlining of decision making procedures for Community instruments of commercial defense and modification of the relevant Council regulations*, O.J. 17.7.92 C181/9; Interview at the Commission, Brussels, March 1997.

[103] The procedure was based on the "management committee procedure" as laid down in Article 4 Council Decision 87/373, establishing the procedures for the exercise of implementing powers conferred on the Commission, O.J. 18.7.87 L 197/33. This Decision has been replaced by Council Decision 99/468, O.J. 17.7.99 L184/23.

minds of the Commission officials was not only the fact that the Community would further open itself to foreign trade, and thus limit government intervention policies thanks to the Uruguay Round deals and the completion of the internal market, but also the increasing likelihood that the new Scandinavian countries with a strong free trade bias would enter the Community.[104] The Commission officials and the protectionist states were increasingly irritated by the difficulties of adopting retaliatory measures even in what they considered to be well justified cases. The entrance of the Scandinavian states and Austria, traditionally corporativist countries and mostly in favour of free trade, would make things worse.[105] Second, the use of unfair trade instruments results in an increase in the powers of the Commission. In implementing such instruments, the Commission has a certain degree of flexibility that allows it to follow certain policies. Indeed, such instruments are a way of opening a space for common European action and a way of reinforcing the links between the Commission, as the champion of European integration, and European industry.

As a result of the compromise of December 1993 (reached within the General Affairs Council), the Commission and the protectionist Member States did not wait until the final Uruguay Round implementation package to strengthen the Community's trade instruments and thus the Council enacted Council Regulation 522/94 on March 1994.[106] However, the compromise was very different from the Commission's proposal. With regard to anti-dumping and countervailing duties, the Regulation only reduced the Council's qualified majority vote to that of a simple majority requirement.[107] Concerning the NCPI, the

[104] Interview at the Commission, Brussels, 17 October 1996.

[105] Before the enlargement, the Council was divided into a group of protectionist states composed of France, Spain, Italy, Greece, Portugal and Belgium, and a group of free traders composed of Denmark, Ireland, the United Kingdom and The Netherlands. Germany and Luxembourg would vote in favour or against the measures depending on the case. After the enlargement, the balance of power changed dramatically. The Netherlands, Denmark, the United Kingdom and Ireland have been joined by Finland, Sweden and Austria, together with Germany and Luxembourg which seem to have changed their approach radically. Interview with an Official of a Member State's Permanent Representation to the European Union, Brussels, July 1997. See Vermulst and Driessen, "Commercial Defense Actions and Other International Trade Developments in the European Communities IX: 1 July 1994–31 December 1994" (1995) 6 *European J. Int' L.* 287–316; see also Maclean and Eccles, "A Change of Style Not Substance: The Community's New Approach Towards the Community Interest Test in Anti-Dumping and Anti-Subsidy Law" (1999) 36 *Common Market L. Rev.* 123–148, 129. In fact Sweden tends systematically to oppose the imposition of duties. Thus, the Council has dramatically changed its pattern of behaviour; now rejecting or approving the imposition of anti-dumping and countervailing duties by a very small margin. "Anti-Dumping: Bed Linen Imports Slapped with Duties Up to 27%", *European Reports* No 2233, 19 June 1997, at 2; "EU/Anti-Dumping: Council Decides by Small Majority to Introduce Definitive Anti-Dumping Duties on Certain Outdoor Shoes in Textiles Originating from China and Indonesia (With Some Exceptions)", *Agence Europe* No 7041, 31 October 1997, at 6–7; "Commission Losses Controversial Vote on Duties", *Financial Times*, Thursday, 17 September 1998, at 3.

[106] O.J. 10.3.94 L66/10. The Council Regulation was preceded by the European Parliament's approval. *European Parliament Session Documents: Second Report of the Committee on External Economic Relations*, 18 January 1994; Commission of the European Community, "Commission Welcomes Council Agreement in the EU Import Regime", *Informacion a la Prensa*, 8 February 1994.

[107] Article 1 of Council Regulation 522/94.

Regulation simply made it compatible with the WTO dispute settlement procedure and timidly enhanced the powers of the Commission.[108] In order to recompense the protectionist countries led by France, the Regulation conceded that commercial measures could be taken without a prior investigation when the factual and legal situation did not require it. The Regulation made it clear that Member States could ask the Commission to go to the WTO without a prior investigation if the case was clear. This was counterbalanced, however, by the introduction of a duty on the Commission to keep the 113 Committee informed of its investigations. Thus, although the Regulation enhanced the possibilities for taking measures under the anti-dumping and countervailing procedures and slightly increased the effectiveness of the new policy instrument, it did not meet the expectations of either the Commission or the more protectionist Member States.

Within this confrontation between free trade and protectionist Member States on 10 October 1994, the Commission made a proposal for the final amendment of the NCPI as part of the Uruguay Round implementation package.[109] The proposed new trade instrument was part of the masterminded new Market Access Strategy (MAS).[110] This policy is an inspired gamble that tries to broker between different Member States, institutions and interests. First, the MAS tries to find a solution to the constant confrontation between the protectionist and the free trade Member States. In order to solve the dichotomy of whether or not to adopt a defensive protectionist policy through the use of anti-dumping and countervailing measures, the Commission proposes to adopt a third way which consists of helping European business in foreign markets. Instead of protecting domestic industries against imports, the Community, by taking advantage of the new possibilities of the trading system and the Treaty's Article 13, would support European firms in exporting to foreign markets. Such a proposal is difficult to reject for both the free trade and protectionist Member States. For the protectionist states, it is a sort of aggressive trade policy which helps their industries. In a sense, such a policy is nothing more than a more modern form of government intervention. Behind these policies is the inability of some states to cope with globalisation domestically, and without recourse to foreign trade measures. For the free trade Member States, it is difficult to reject such a proposal because it is based on the idea of market openness. Second, the new MAS also brokers between the Member States and the Community. By adopting a proposal whereby the Commission would investigate and try to eliminate foreign trade barriers, the Community would be able to play a strong role in the trading system. Again, the proposal was intended to open a new

[108] Article 2 ibid.

[109] Commission of the European Community, *Uruguay Round Implementing Legislation*, COM (94) 414 final (1994).

[110] Commission of the European Communities, *The Global Challenge of International Trade: A Market Access Strategy for the European Union. Communication to the Council, the European Parliament, the Economic and Social Committee and the Committee of Regions*, COM (96) 53 final (1996).

window for Community action in the external sphere, as the policy is nothing more than the basics of European integration—working together with the purpose of confronting the problems of globalisation.[111] Third, the proposal is an attempt to promote its free trade political commitment by showing the business community that the Community's liberalisation efforts could pay off through pursing an active policy in the international trading system.

Following Article 113 of the Treaty, the MAS consists of a co-operation procedure between the Commission and the Member States. The Market Access Unit (MAU) of the Commission[112] must keep a database of all the foreign trade obstacles that may affect Community enterprises. The MAU is to be advised by the Market Access Action Group (MAAG), a Commission inter-service group where more than 50 officials from the Directorate-General for Trade and other Directorates-General concerned meet twice a month with the purpose of analysing the different trade barriers encountered and how to tackle them. The MAU has established a database of foreign trade barriers in different countries and their trade obstacles which affect most of the Community's foreign trade.[113] For each foreign obstacle to trade, the MAU, together with the MAAG, will make a report and decide whether or not it would be appropriate to take action against it. Once the Commission has decided that action is appropriate, it informs the Article 113 Deputies' Committee for approval to act. The programme, in fact, works in the same way as the negotiation and conclusion of an international agreement. The Commission may not start any action at international level, whether or not within the framework of the WTO, unless the Member States, through Article 113, give their consent under the rule of qualified majority. Thus, although the MAS increases the Community's action, especially that of the Commission, in the international trading system, the possibilities for quick and effective action by the Community are partly diluted as the entire procedure is under the strict control of the Member States.[114]

The Commission's new trade instrument proposal was an attempt to enhance the MAS under Article 113. It tried to strengthen the role of the Community in the international trading system by increasing both the availability of the instrument to European business and the possibility of retaliation. With its proposal, the Commission was trying to respond to the demands of the protectionist Member States and some Community industry associations for a tougher trade policy, while at the same time avoiding the opposition of the free trade Member States.[115]

[111] "EU/TRADE: Suggestions by 113 Committee to Guarantee Coherence of European Strategy for Access to Third Country Markets", *Agence Europe* No 7047, 30 August 1997, at 5.

[112] The Market Access Unit of the Commission is DGT-D4 was created in June 1996.

[113] The website of the market access database is available at <http://mkaccdb.eu.int>.

[114] Schuren and Luff, "The Trade Barriers Regulation and the Community's Market Access Policy" (1996) *European Foreign Affairs Rev.* 211–230, 222.

[115] France, with the support of Spain, Belgium, Greece, Italy, Portugal and Ireland continued to push for a more assertive EU trade policy as part of the Uruguay Round implementing legislation: "WTO Launch Celebrations Overshadowed by Outstanding Problems", *European Reports* No 2000, 10 December 1994 at V 5–6.

Furthermore, the Commission attempted to bypass the strict control of the MAS by the Article 113 Committee by means of enhancing its own powers in the instrument's decision-making procedures.

Basically the Commission's proposal introduced a three track approach with the aim of protecting the interests of the Community in the international trading system. First, as in the NCPI, it allowed complaints on behalf of Community industry.[116] Such complaints should contain sufficient evidence of the existence of both an illicit commercial practice and injury. Second, as in the NCPI it permitted the referral by a Member State.[117] Any Member State would be able to ask the Commission to initiate the procedure referred to in Article 1 with the purpose of:

1) Responding to any illicit commercial practices with a view to removing the injury resulting therefrom;

2) Responding to any commercial practice whether illicit or not with a view to removing the adverse trade effects resulting therefrom. Adverse trade effects were defined as those which were felt in respect of a product or service on the market of any non-member country and which could give rise to actions under relevant international rules (not international trade rules), whether as a result of an illicit commercial practice or otherwise, and which had a material impact, actual or potential, on the economy of the Community, in a region of the Community, or on a sector of economic activity therein.[118] Adverse trade effects would include cases where the trade flows of products or services were prevented or there was the threat of such. Thus, it could include the threat of measures.

3) Ensuring the full exercise of the Community rights with regard to the commercial practices of third countries. Community rights would be those international trade rights of which it could avail itself; either under international or under generally accepted rules.[119]

The greatest improvement of the Commission's proposal was the inclusion of a third track which allowed Community enterprises, and not only Community industry, to present a complaint which contained sufficient evidence of the existence of commercial practices, whether illicit or not, and of the adverse trade effects resulting therefrom.[120] This provision had been a long-standing demand of both the protectionist Member States and European business.[121] Under the old Regulation, it had been very difficult for Community business to prove the existence of injury to a domestic industry as a result of a third state's practice which had its effects outside the Community. Due to this problem, the

116 Article 3 of the Commission proposal.

117 Article 4 of the Commission Proposal.

118 Article 2(5) ibid.

119 Article 2(2) ibid.

120 Article 3 ibid.

121 Arnold and Bronkers, "The EEC New Trade Policy Instrument: Some Comments on its Application" (1988) 22(6) *J. World Trade* 19–38, 21.

Commission in at least one case had to interpret the concept of Community industry in a very broad way.[122]

An illicit commercial practice was defined as any international trade practice attributable to a third country which was incompatible with international law and with generally-accepted rules.[123] Likewise, a right of action against non-illicit practices could result from relevant international rules or generally accepted rules. Hence, the Commission proposed the same broad and ambiguous standards as the previous NCPI. Despite the EC's general commitment to its international obligations,[124] it had been argued that the NCPI's standard gave the Community a very similar right of unilateral action to that of the United States under Section 301 of the 1974 Trade Act.[125] First, the scope of the term "international law" was unclear. It was no doubt intended to include at least the GATT and GATT side-agreements.[126] However, in *Unauthorised Recordings in Indonesia*,[127] the Commission made it clear that the concept of international law could also refer to other bilateral and multilateral agreements to which the Community was a party. International law could even include customary international law. Second, the term "generally accepted rules" was considered to be the most controversial. It seemed to be as ambiguous as the concept of unreasonableness in Section 301, a provision which extended the scope of action beyond international law.[128] It was argued that the term referred to objectively predetermined criteria which could include soft law and those rules of international trade law that were generally accepted.[129] However, although the term implied legal qualities, it entailed the possibility of the Community imposing standards included in agreements to which the targeted country was not a party.[130] It was argued that this was all a *faux debat*, as what was important was the requirement that all Community measures be in accordance with international law.[131] But this argument failed to take two important issues into account. First, the scope of the measures allowed by international law is extremely broad. Second, the strategic value of unfair trade instruments is based on the threat, and not on the actual imposition of the measures. The

122 *Port Charges in Japan on Cargoes and Shipping Companies*, O.J. 16.2.91 C40/18.

123 Article 2(1) of the Commission Proposal.

124 Article 2(2) Council Regulation 2641/84.

125 Zoller, "Remedies for Unfair Trade: European and US Views" (1985) 18 *Cornell Int'l L. J.* 227–245.

126 C de la Torre, "The EEC New Instrument of Trade Policy: Some Comments in the Light of the Latest Developments" (1993) 30(4) *C.M.tL. Rev.* 687–719, 697.

127 *Unauthorised Sound Recordings in Indonesia*, O.J. 21.5.87 C136/21.

128 Schonoveld, "The European Community Reaction to the Illicit Commercial Trade Practices of Other Countries" (1992) 26(2) *J. World Trade* 17–34, 21.

129 J Bourgeois, "EC Rules Against 'Illicit Trade Practices' – Policy Cosmetics or International Law Enforcement?" (1988) *Annual Proceedings of the Fordham Corporate Law Institute: Europe/America Antitrust and Trade Law*, Chapter 6, at 12–13.

130 This is what in fact happened in *Unauthorised Recordings in Indonesia*, O.J. 21.5.87 C136/21.

131 J Bourgeois, *supra* n. 129, at 14–15.

Community would be able to obtain unilateral trade concessions from third countries without violating international law.[132]

Thus, the Commission's proposal, though intended to limit the possibilities of any aggressive unilateral action, left some loopholes which could allow for a more flexible trade policy instrument. As expected, the proposal faced the strong opposition of Germany, the Netherlands, Luxembourg, Denmark and the United Kingdom. Their main concern was with the Commission's proposal to introduce the third track for Community enterprises. They considered that such a proposal would allow the Commission to pursue indiscriminate attacks on trade policy practices, making the instrument dangerously similar to Section 301, whilst only coming under the limited control of the Member States.[133]

The Commission tried to convince both protectionists and free traders that its proposal was adequate. It promised that, in the future, its trade policy would respond to the demands of European industry while, at the same time, it insisted that Europe would not take the law in into its own hands.[134]

The adoption of the new trade instrument as part of the Uruguay Round implementation package was further complicated by the European Court of Justice's Opinion on the scope of Article 113 of the Treaty and the division of powers in external economic relations between the Community and the Member States.[135] First, it would control the bargaining process leading to the adoption of the instrument. As the instrument was part of a package aimed at implementing the Uruguay Round agreements, its adoption would require unanimity in the Council and the assent of the European Parliament. This would affect both the substantial and procedural provisions of the instrument. Second, the Member States would seriously limit the scope of the instrument on the basis of the Opinion.

Third, as a result of Opinion 1/94 and the fact that the Uruguay Round agreements established a specific institutional framework by organising co-operation procedures, the European Parliament was able to express its opinion on the proposed market access instrument. The Parliament supported the Commission's proposal. On 12 December 1994, the Committee on Economics, Monetary Affairs and Industrial Policy unanimously approved its opinion on the implementation of the Uruguay Round for the Committee on External Economic Relations. The opinion considered the Commission's proposal to be necessary

[132] An example of this could have been *Port Charges in Japan Cargoes and Shipping Companies*, O.J. 16.2.91 C40/18 (where the case referred to services which at that time were not under the rule of GATT law). In another case, Bulgaria refrained from exporting whisky with the Scotch Whisky label when the Community producers threatened to file a complaint under the instrument.

[133] "Definition of Community Legislation Implementing Marrakech Accords Still Poses Difficulties Between Member States—Reservations in Principle on New Commercial Instrument—Other Differences", *Agence Europe*, 12 December 1994, at 8; "New EU Trade Weapon May Hold Deadly Firepower", *European Reports* No 1998, 12 December 1994, at V9.

[134] "Sir Leon Outlines Future Priorities and Defends Quotas", *European Reports* No 1986, 22 October 1994, at V 10; "New EU Trade Weapon May Hold Deadly Firepower", *European Reports* No 1998, 3 December 1994, at V 9.

[135] See Chapter IV.C.2 of this book.

to allow the EU to undertake the removal of technical barriers not regulated by the WTO agreements. It also considered as necessary the Commission's third track proposal, in order to allow access to third country markets which was equivalent to the one allowed by the EU to the exports of third countries.[136] Hence, the Committee seemed to be in favour of a more aggressive and flexible trade policy instrument which could allow the Community to influence the future rules of the international trading system. Three days later, on 15 December, the European Parliament, under Article 228(3) of the Treaty, approved the Commission's legislative proposal as part of the GATT 94 package by simple majority.[137]

On 19 December, the Council of Ministers adopted the "Trade Barriers Regulation" as part of the Uruguay Round package only after it had reached an overall political compromise both amongst the Member States and with the Commission.[138] However, before enacting the TBR, it carefully amended some features of the Commission's proposal in order to make sure that the instrument would not go beyond the WTO and so that it would not lose control over the procedure. The free trade Member States allowed for no flexibility and made sure that the TBR would be in strict compliance with the standard of international trade law as contained in international agreements.[139] Furthermore, the Council introduced Article 2(8) of the TBR and thus made it clear that the term "services" should only be taken to mean those services in respect of which international trade agreements can be concluded by the Community on the basis of Article 113 of the Treaty.

5.B.3. The TBR's Strict Commitment to the Standard of International Trade Law

The new Regulation aims to tackle foreign obstacles to trade against which the Community may have a right of action under international trade rules.[140] International trade rules are strictly those contained in international agreements to which the Community is a party and which have an impact on international trade.[141] Article 1(1) of the TBR makes it clear that the basic purpose of the TBR

[136] European Parliament Session Documents, Opinion for the Committee on External Relations of the Committee on Economics, Monetary Affairs and Industrial Policy, 12 December 1994.

[137] "European Parliament Plenary Session, GATT Trade Agreements. Parliament Gives Assent", *European Reports* No 2006 Supplement, 11 January, 1995, at 14–15; "With its Assent on the Marrakech Agreements, the European Parliament Approves the Changes to Community Trade Regulations", *Agence Europe* No 6380, 16 December, 1994, at 4.

[138] "Political Agreement by Council on Results and Implementation of Uruguay Round", *Agence Europe* No 6380, 19–20 December 1994, at 6.

[139] C Norall, "Some Thoughts on the New Community Trade Barriers Regulation" (1995) 3 *International Trade Law Reporter* 67.

[140] Articles 2 (1) and 2(2) of the TBR.

[141] Article 2(2) ibid.

is to exercise the Community's rights in the WTO. With this purpose, the TBR establishes three tracks:

First, the Regulation allows for complaints to be brought on behalf of Community industry when they contain sufficient evidence of injury as a result of obstacles to trade in third countries that have an effect on the Community market. The characteristic feature of this track is that the foreign obstacle must have an effect on the Community's domestic market. Theoretically speaking, the action need not only refer to imports but may also affect exports. The defensive action of the TBR is, thereby, residually maintained. Although the TBR, as part of the new MAS, was intended to tackle foreign trade measures having an effect on foreign markets, it would not have been politically acceptable to the more protectionist Member States to delete the provision referring to the protection of the Community market.[142] Under this track, it will be possible to allege the infringement of any international agreement, be it bilateral or multilateral, which sets out rules applicable to trade. This defensive right of action could be an alternative to the use of Community's Countervailing Duty Regulation.[143] However, this defensive action is seriously limited by the requirement to act on behalf of the domestic industry and by the requirement to prove the existence of injury.[144] Up to now, only one case has been initiated under this defensive track and this was in combination with an offensive right of action under Article 4 of the TBR.[145]

The main improvement of the Regulation is to require the Community institutions to act after receiving, on behalf of Community enterprises, complaints containing sufficient evidence of obstacles to trade which have an effect on the market of a third country and which result in adverse effects for Community business.[146] Following Article 58(2) of the Treaty, a Community enterprise is considered to be a company or firm formed in accordance with the law of a Member State and having its registered office, central administration or principal place of business within the Community, and directly concerned in the production of goods or services which are the subject of the obstacle to trade.[147]

[142] Interview at the Commission, Brussels, April 1997.

[143] Council Regulation 2026/97, O.J. 21.10.97 L288/1. From an international viewpoint the TBR's defensive action could be used in parallel to a countervailing duty investigation as footnote 33 of the *Agreement on Subsidies and Countervailing Measures*, O.J. 23.12.94 L335/156 allows for the parallel invocation of both a domestic countervailing investigation and the dispute settlement procedures provided for prohibited and actionable subsidies. However, Article 15 of the TBR states that the instrument will not apply in cases covered by other existing rules in the common commercial policy field.

[144] The concepts of domestic industry and injury are basically the same as those contained in the anti-dumping and countervailing duty regulations. Articles 2(3) and 2(5) of the TBR. Compare Article 3 and Article 4 of Council Regulation 384/96, O.J. 6.3.96 L56/1 as amended by Council Regulation 2331/96, O.J. 6.12.96 L317/1, and Council Regulation 905/98, O.J. 30.4.98 L128/18. Compare Article 8 and Article 9 of Council Regulation 2026/97, O.J. 21.10.97 L288/1.

[145] *Brazilian Export Financing Programme*, O.J. 17.4.99 C108/33.

[146] Article 4(1) of the TBR; see McNelis, "The European Union Trade Barriers Regulation: A More Effective Instrument" (1998) 1 *Journal International Economic Law* 149–155, 149.

[147] Article 2(6) of the TBR. In fact, it seems that most of the complaints received have been filed not by individual enterprises but by associations of enterprises. See *United States Antidumping Act*

Both public and private sector Community enterprises may file a complaint. Sole practitioners are not covered by the TBR unless they set up an undertaking under the conditions laid down by the law of the Member State in which they are established. Under the TBR, Community institutions should accept complaints from the subsidiaries of foreign enterprises which are incorporated in an EC Member State. Thus, the TBR may be combined with the retaliatory instrument of a different trading partner. Large multinationals may be capable of increasing the pressure on third countries by compelling the European Union and other trading partners to open cases against a certain third country. Furthermore, the Commission has interpreted Article 2(6) broadly, by accepting cases from enterprises which do not actually produce the goods in the Community but trade therein with goods from foreign countries.[148] Naturally, enterprises or groups of enterprises which, in practice, represent the Community industry can also request this type of action.[149]

Action on behalf of Community enterprises requires a right of action which is based on the international trade rules contained in multilateral or plurilateral trade agreements, specifically, but not necessarily limited to, the WTO Agreement and its annexed Agreements. As a result of the political trade off, the Regulation strictly limits offensive action on behalf of Community enterprises to multilateral or plurilateral trade agreements.[150] Bilateral agreements and all agreements which are not exclusively trade agreements should be excluded.[151]

of 1916, O.J. 25.2.97 C 58/14 (where the complaint was filed by EUROFER); *Trade Obstacles to Leather in Argentina*, O.J. 26.2.97 C59/6 (COTANCE); *Import Licensing for Steel Plates in Brazil*, O.J. 27.6.97 C 197/5 (EUROFER); *Trade Obstacles to Cognac in Brazil*, O.J. 2.4.97 C 103/3 (BNIC); *Trade Obstacles to Copper Scrap in Korea and India*, O.J. 22.5.96 C 148 (EUROMETAUX); *Trade Barriers to the Leather Sector in Japan*, O.J. 9.4.97 C 110/2 (COTANCE); *Rules of Origin for Textiles in the United States*, O.J. 4.3.97 L 62/43 (FEDERTESSILE); *Protection of Sound Recordings in Thailand*, O.J. 16.1.96 L 11/7 (IFPI); *Music Licensing Practices in the United States*, O.J. 11.6.97 C 177/2 (IMRO); *Brazilian Import Licensing Regime for Steel Plates*, O.J. 27.6.97 C 197/2 (EUROFER); *Brazilian Import Licensing Regime for Textile Products*, O.J. 27.2.98 C 63/2 (FEBELTEX); *Trade Practices Maintained by Canada in Relation to Imports of Prosciutto di Parma*, O.J. 22.6.99 C176/6 (Il Consorzio del Prosciutto di Parma); *Measures Imposed by the Republic of Korea Affecting Trade in Pharmaceutical Products*, O.J. 30.7.99 C218/3 (EFPIA).This might be due to the fact that in practice it is very difficult for a medium or small sized enterprise to handle a TBR complaint. For small and medium sized enterprises it might be a problem to appear publicly to attack trade practices which take place in the market where it intends to do business. The TBR does not allow the Commission to keep the name of the complainant confidential. The Commission services, however, will keep confidential the name of those enterprises which are represented by the association filing the case. Interview at the Commission, Brussels, May 1997. Exceptions to this trend are *Brazilian Trade Barriers to Sorbirtol*, O.J. 24.11.98 C 361/13 (Cerestar Holding BV); *Brazilian Export Financing Programme*, O.J. 17.4.99 C108/33 (Dornier Luftfahrt GmbH).

[148] *United States Antidumping Act of 1916*, O.J. 25.2.97 C 58/14.

[149] *Brazilian Export Financing Programme*, O.J. 17.4.99 C108/33 (where the complaining enterprise was de facto the only Community producer of the product in question); *Measures Imposed by the Republic of Korea Affecting Trade in Pharmaceutical Products*, O.J. 30.7.99 C218/3 (where EFPIA represented the entire Community pharmaceutical industry).

[150] Article 4(1). The Community institutions, however, made a very limited exception to this principle. *In Mass Housing Levy in Turkey*, O.J. 17.12.96 L 326/71 (initiated under the NCPI).

[151] Unlike article 1(2) applying generally to all actions and which reads: ". . . But they can also be those laid down in any other agreement to which the Community is a party and which sets out rules

While the most common multilateral or plurilateral trade agreements will be the WTO Agreements, they could also include the Shipbuilding Agreements or the OECD Export Credit Agreement.

It has been argued that the targeted country need not be a party to the agreement.[152] However, taking Article 2(2) of the Regulation into account,[153] it should be considered that both the Community and the targeted country must be contracting parties. An offensive action on behalf of Community enterprises is not possible against countries such as the People's Republic of China or Russia.[154] The Community will have to wait until these countries become a party to the WTO before being able to tackle their obstacles to trade under the offensive action on behalf of Community enterprises. This is a serious handicap for the effectiveness of the Community's trade policy towards these countries as it has lost an effective tool to influence their transition towards a market economy.

The Regulation considers that obstacles to trade shall be any trade practice adopted or maintained by a third country.[155] The trade obstacle must be created by a trade practice of the country in question. There must be some sort of government relation with the practice. Government may be considered to be both federal and sub-federal levels of public authority. The Commission has considered, as obstacles to trade, trading practices adopted by foreign enterprises which are caused by the lack of adequate laws or the failure by the foreign country's public authorities to enforce such existing laws.[156] Obstacles to trade have

applicable to trade between the Community and third countries," Article 4(1), which specifically applies to offensive actions on behalf of Community enterprises, reads: "... Such a complaint however, shall only be admissible if the obstacle to trade alleged therein is the subject of a right of action established under international trade rules laid down in multilateral or plurilateral trade agreements."

152 Beekmann, "The 1994 Revised Commercial Policy Instrument of the European Union" (1995) 19 *World Competition* 53–75, 65.

153 Article 2(2) TBR reads:

> "For the purposes of this Regulation and subject to paragraph 8, the Community rights shall be those international trade rights of which it may avail itself under international trade rules. In this context, international trade rules are primarily those established under the auspices of WTO and laid down in the Annexes to the WTO Agreement, but they can also be those laid down in any other agreement to which the Community is a party and which sets out rules applicable to trade between the Community and third countries."

154 Gunther and Prost, "Le Reglement Communautaire sur les Obstacles au Commerce", *Les Echos*, 11 July 1996. Thus while Sir Leon Brittan has rightly maintained in the European Parliament that action against the People's Republic of China was possible under the Trade Barriers Regulation, his statements disguise the fact that such action would not be possible at the request of a Community enterprise but only on behalf of a Member State and mostly in regard to bilateral agreement with such country. See *Written Question No 1970/96 by Wolfgang Nubbaumer to the Commission. Trade Relations with China*, O.J. 4.12.96 C365/56; *Written Question No 0680/96 by Viviane Roding to the Commission. Import Quotas of Ceramics from China*, O.J. 25.6.96 C185/78.

155 Article 2(1) of the TBR.

156 *Protection of Sound Recordings in Thailand*, O.J. 16.1.96 L 11/7 (where the alleged practice was the lack of adequate enforcement of laws protecting intellectual property rights); *Trade Barriers to the Leather Sector in Japan*, O.J. 9.4.97 C 110/2 (where one of the alleged practices was the toleration by the Japanese government of restrictive business practices in the leather sector).

not only been interpreted as encompassing such practices which are actually taking place, but also the existence of laws or regulations which may result in the imposition of illegal obstacles to trade.[157] Furthermore, the legal measures need not be in force but only part of the foreign country's legal order.[158] This interpretation is based on the idea that such laws or regulations imply a threat and, thus, deter European enterprises from doing business in such countries. Furthermore, the Commission has considered that the concept of obstacles to trade may encompass both obstacles to the import into, or the export from, the foreign country.[159]

An action on behalf of Community enterprises must allege the existence of a foreign obstacle to trade which has an impact on the market of a third country. However, the third country need not be the same as that which adopts or maintains the trade practice.[160]

The Community enterprise or Member State claiming an offensive right of action must provide *prima facie* evidence of the existence of adverse trade effects as well as a material impact on the Community market as a result of the foreign obstacle to trade. The concept of adverse trade effects seems to be rather loose. It is a threshold which may have been borrowed from Article 5 of the Agreement on Subsidies and Countervailing Measures.[161] It can include both the actual or the threat of adverse effects.[162] It is important to bear in mind that Article XXIII of the GATT does not protect trade flows but rather competitive opportunities to trade.[163] Hence, adverse effects could include the halt to exports, the loss of sales or market share, failure to increase market share in contrast to what could be expected under normal circumstances, increased competition in the

[157] *United States Antidumping Act of 1916*, O.J. 25.2.97 C 58/14 (where the alleged trade practice is the existence of the United States Antidumping Act of 1916 which if applied would impose treble damages against foreign companies not in accordance with the rules of WTO). The Commission's interpretation has been supported by WTO Dispute Settlement. See United States—Antidumping Act of 1916, (WT/OS136); *United States: Definition of Industry Concerning Wine and Grape Products*, SCM/71 (24 March 1986) adopted by the Committee on Subsidies and Countervailing Measures on 28 April 1992 BISD 39S/436, paragraph 4.1; see Article XVI (4)of the Agreement of WTO which reads: "Each Member shall ensure the conformity of its laws, regulations and administrative procedures with its obligations as provided in the annexed Agreements."

[158] *Music Licensing Practices in the United States*, O.J. 22.12.98 L346/60 (where the Commission considered that a bill signed by the United States President which had not yet entered into force could be the object of a WTO dispute settlement procedure and, thus, of TBR action).

[159] *Trade Obstacles to Leather in Argentina*, O.J. 26.2.97 C 59/6 (where one of the alleged obstacles is Argentinean practices restricting exports of hides); *Trade Obstacles to Copper Scrap in Korea and India*, O.J. 22.5.96 C 148.

[160] *Brazilian Export Financing Programme*, O.J. 17.14.99 C108/33 (where the practice is allegedly being adopted by the Brazilian government but it has an effect on the market of the United States in the form of a loss of sales of the Community producer).

[161] Article 5 of the Agreement on Subsidies includes in the concept of adverse effects injury in the sense of that of Anti-Dumping and Countervailing actions, nullification or impairment as interpreted by GATT case law and serious prejudice or threat of serious prejudice. Article 5 of the *Agreement on Subsidies and Countervailing Measures*, MTN/FA II-13.

[162] Article 2(4) of the TBR.

[163] P Cottier, "Dispute Settlement in the World Trade Organisation: Characteristics and Structural Implications for the European Union" (1998) 35 *C.M.L. Rev*. 325–378, 361.

Community market as a result of loss of foreign market share, increased costs, etc. The Commission has interpreted adverse trade effects to include even the loss of image of a European enterprise.[164] But to weed out any frivolous complaints, the Community enterprises must provide sufficient evidence of the existence of a material impact on the Community market or on a Community region.[165] Evidence of material impact could be, for example, the fact that the trade obstacles may affect companies, products or services other than those concerned in the complaint, jobs that are at risk, the fact that the production, the enterprise or the industry is localised in certain specific regions, the fact that the production or the enterprise is localised in disadvantaged regions, the fact that Community enterprises are dependent on the world market for the supply of certain raw materials, the possibility of using the trade obstacle as a precedent to discourage all European exports, the fact that the complainant represents the entire Community industry of the like product, etc. Material impact must not be interpreted as an independent element but rather as one which should be weighed together with adverse trade effects in order to ensure that the Community has an actual reason to be concerned by the foreign obstacle to trade.

Finally, the TBR allows Member States to request the Commission to both start a procedure against obstacles to trade that have an effect on the markets of the Community, with a view to removing the injury resulting therefrom, and to respond to obstacles to trade which have an effect on the market of a third country, with a view to removing the adverse effects resulting therefrom.[166] Member States may ask for action to tackle obstacles to trade against which the Community has a right of action arising from any international agreement to which it is a party. Thus, unlike Community enterprises, Member States could ask the Community institutions to take action under bilateral agreements. However, Member States, suspicious of the TBR as an instrument which actually enhances the powers of the Commission in external trade, prefer to use the general Article 113 procedure to tackle problems in foreign trade.[167] By doing so, the Community institutions miss the chance of tackling effectively foreign obstacles in important rising markets which are not subject to major multilateral trade agreements. The different domestic structures and resulting conflicting trade interest between the Member States leads them to mistrust the Community institutions and consequently to slowly lose the battle over globalisation.

[164] *Rules of Origin for Textiles in the United States*, O.J. 4.3.97 L 62/43 (where it was considered that the changes to rules of origin in the United States, which resulted in products which had traditionally been labelled as Made in Italy being labelled as Made in China had the adverse trade effect of a loss of image for the Community enterprises trading with such products).

[165] Article 2(4) of the TBR.

[166] Articles 1 and 6, ibid.

[167] In fact, there has never been, either under the NCPI or the TBR, any case filed by a Member State.

All decisions taken under any of the three tracks must be in the interest of the Community.[168] The Commission has tended to interpret the Community interests in a very broad way. It has considered as Community interests the need to ensure that WTO partners fully comply with their international obligations, the need to protect and enforce intellectual property rights, and in particular, geographical indications, the need to safeguard the access of the Community's top quality products in the agricultural sector to third country markets, the fact that the trade practice affects a wide range of products and could also affect other Community industries, the fact that the complainant is a major industry and employer in the Community, the need to ensure a market for exports in certain industrial sectors, the possibility that other countries may engage in similar trade practices increasing the harm to the Community, etc.

The Commission might attempt to investigate facts not alleged in the complaint, provided such facts are related to the main issue of it. During the investigation, the Commission will also take into account eventual possible violations of international trade rules, other than those alleged in the complaint.[169] It may also investigate products other than those referred to in the complaint, particularly those which interested parties who make themselves known within the time limits, show to be affected by the alleged practices which result in a obstacle to trade.[170] Furthermore, the Commission may try to analyse legal provisions other than those alleged in the complaint, even if such provisions are not part of an agreement which give a right of action for a complaining party who is not a Member State.[171] However, despite any broad interpretations that the Community institutions may try to adopt, the fact is that the TBR severely limits any action to that within the rule of international law. There must be a right of action which is derived from an international agreement.

A right of action exists when international trade rules either prohibit a practice outright, or give another party affected by the practice the right to seek the elimination of the effects of the practice in question.[172] Thus, the TBR may be used against practices which violate international agreements or which, though not prohibited, cause injury to the domestic industry of the Community or serious prejudice to the interests of the Community,[173] or simply nullify or impair the benefits arising from such agreements. In this sense, it could be argued that the nullification and impairment provisions of Article XXIII (1)(b) of GATT and the *Understanding on the Rules and Procedures Governing the Settlement*

[168] Articles 8, 11 and 12 TBR.

[169] *Trade Practices Maintained by Canada in Relation to Imports of Prosciutto di Parma*, O.J. 22.6.99 C176/6.

[170] *Measures Imposed by the Republic of Korea Affecting Trade in Pharmaceutical Products*, O.J. 30.7.99 C218/3.

[171] Interview at the Commission, June 1997.

[172] Article 2(1) TBR.

[173] In this context, see Article 5 of *The Agreement on Subsidies and Countervailing Measures*; see also *Brazilian Export Financing Programme*, O.J. 17.4.99 C108/33.

of Disputes[174] could be used to allow the Community some flexibility and to try to influence the agenda in new areas of trade.[175] Traditionally, the GATT/WTO case law has considered the benefits protected to be the assurance of better market access through the improved market competition derived from a tariff binding or the promise of a tariff binding.[176] Nevertheless, some GATT/WTO Panels reveal a certain tendency to consider, under special circumstances, a broader range of areas in which the tariff bindings are of little or no importance.[177] This approach could improve the possibility of using the nullification and impairment provisions to develop new rules in new areas of trade.[178] However, taking into account the GATT/WTO precedent on non-violation cases, and the *Kodak* Panel report in particular, such an approach would be extremely difficult.[179] A complaining party bringing a non-violation case before a WTO Panel must prove that it had a reasonable expectation that the benefits deriving from the agreement it was entering into would not be nullified or impaired by measures taking place in the foreign country.[180] First, a non-

[174] Article 26 of the Understanding.

[175] In this context, there have been two TBR cases against practices which, although they did not violate international trade agreement were alleged to nullify or impair their benefits. *Trade Obstacles to Copper Scrap in Korea and India*, O.J. 22.5.96 C 148; *Trade Barriers to the Leather Sector in Japan*, O.J. 9.4.97 C 110/2 (where one of the obstacles to trade alleged were certain restrictive business practices which nullified or impaired the benefits of GATT). The Commission considered however that these allegations had not been proven. *Trade Barriers to the Leather Sector in Japan*, O.J. 3.6.98 L159/65. It is important to note that the European Community had already filed a non-violation case in the GATT Dispute Settlement Mechanism against Japanese restrictive business practices which were considered to nullify or impair the benefits arising from GATT. Communication from the European Communities, *Japan: Nullification or Impairment of the Benefits Accruing to the EEC under the General Agreement and Impediment to the Attainment of GATT Objectives*, L/5479, 8 April 1983.

[176] Von Bogdandy, "The Non-Violation Procedure of Article XXIII: 2, GATT: Its Operational Rationale" (1992) 26 (4) *J. World Trade* 95–111, 98.

[177] *EC Tariff Treatment of Citrus Products from Certain Countries in the Mediterranean Region*, *L/5776* (1985); *United States Measures Affecting Nicaragua*, L/6053 (1986); see also Chua, "Reasonable Expectation and Non-Violation Complaints in GATT/WTO Jurisprudence" (1998) 32(2) *J. World Trade* 27–50, 39.

[178] Cho, "GATT Non-Violation Issues in the WTO Framework: Are They the Achilles' Heel of the Dispute Settlement Process" (1998) 39(2) *Harvard Int'l L. J.* 311–355 (arguing that the use of non-violation cases should be limited and reframed into violation cases within the context of the WTO or the other multilateral organisations).

[179] *Japan—Measures Affecting Consumer Photographic Film and Paper*, WT/DS44/R.

[180] Petersmann, "Violation-Complaints and Non-Violation Complaints in Public International Trade Law" (1991) 34 *G. Y. B. Int'l L.* 175 (1991); P. Pescatore, "Drafting and Analyzing Decisions on Dispute Settlement, in P Pescatore, W Davey and A Lowenfeld (eds.), *Handbook of WTO/GATT Dispute Settlement* (New York, Transnational Juris Publications Inc, 5th ed., 1995), Volume I. For the GATT case law on non violation cases see *Australian Subsidy on Ammonium Sulphate*, 6 November 1950, GATT BISD 7 Supp. 68; *European Economic Community: Production Aids Granted on Canned Peaches, Canned Pears, Canned Fruit Cocktail and Dried Grapes*, L/5778, 20 November 1985; *German Import Duties on Starch and Potato Flour*, GATT BISD 3 Supp. 78 (1955); *Treatment by Germany of Imports of Sardines*, G/26, 31 October 1952, GATT BISD 1 Supp. 53; *Italian Discrimination Against Imported Agricultural Machinery*, L/833, 23 October 1958, GATT BISD 7 Supp. 68; *Japan, Trade in Semi-Conductors*, L 6309, 24 March 1988, BISD 35 Supp. 116; *Uruguayan Recourse to Article XXIII*, L/1923, 16 November 1962, GATT BISD 11 Supp. 95; *United States: Restrictions on the Importation of Sugar and Sugar-Containing Products Applied*

violation case would require a positive measure by a government.[181] Private action may be considered as a government measure if there is sufficient government involvement in it. It is unlikely that governmental tolerance of private practices would be considered as a non-violation case; unless such action is reflected in a positive measure such as the granting of an exemption by the competition authorities or the failure to fulfil legal obligations.[182] The benefits may refer to the agreements of GATT 1947 as well as those of the WTO agreements. However, the contracting party must not have been able to foresee the nullifying or impairing event. If the measure existed before the GATT concession, there would be a strong presumption that the complainant should have anticipated the measure. Moreover, it is the complaining party that has the burden of proving the nullification or impairment of benefits in non-violation cases.[183] It must be proven that the measure had more than a *de minimis* contribution to nullification or impairment. Whenever the complaint refers to a trade obstacle other than a clear trade barrier such as a quota or a tariff, the complaining party has the heavy burden of proving the existence of adverse effects. In any case, the Panel cannot ask the contracting party to remove the nullifying or impairing measure but only allow for compensatory measures.[184] Thus, the opportunities for using the non-violation provisions to influence the future developments of the international trading system are seriously limited.

It could be argued that the Community institutions could initiate TBR investigations against obstacles in cases where it is not clear whether or not there is a legitimate right of action arising from an international trade agreement. The Commission will initiate investigations whenever there is simple *prima facie* evidence of a right of action arising from international agreements.[185] The Commission could use the threat that the initiation of an investigation implies to change foreign trade practices even if they were not clear-cut cases. Thus, the formality of the procedure, with its strict deadlines, could intimidate foreign countries.[186] However, the provisions of the TBR jeopardise the credibility of

under the 1955 Waiver and under the Headnote to the Schedule of Tariff Concessions, L/6631, 22 June 1990; *Panel on Vitamins*, L/5331, 18 June 1982, GATT BISD 29 Supp. 110.

[181] The only time a government's negative measure has been considered as giving rise to a non-violation case was in *German Import Duties on Starch and Potato Flour*, GATT BISD 3 Supp. 78 (1955) (where the non-fulfilment of a promise was considered as nullifying the reasonable expectations of the claiming party).

[182] Komuro, "Kodak-Fuji Film Dispute and the WTO Panel Ruling" (1998) 32(5) *J. World Trade* 161–217, 215–217.

[183] *Uruguayan Recourse to Article XXIII*, L/1923, 16 November 1962, GATT BISD 11 Supp. 95, paragraph 15; *United States: Restrictions on the Importation of Sugar and Sugar-Containing Products Applied under the 1955 Waiver and under the Headnote to the Schedule of Tariff Concessions*, L/6631, 22 June 1990, paragraph 5.20; *Japan, Trade in Semi-Conductors*, L 6309, 24 March 1988, GATT BISD 35 Supp. 116, paragraph 131.

[184] *Australian Subsidy on Ammonium Sulphate*, 6 November 1950, GATT BISD 7 Supp. 68, paragraph 16.

[185] *United States Antidumping Act of 1916*, O.J. 25.2.97 C 58/14.

[186] In fact there have been several cases in which the mere threat of initiating a case has removed the foreign obstacle to trade.

such threats. Article 12(2) of the Regulation makes clear that the Community must follow the dispute settlement commitment whenever this is required by its international commitments. The possibility of threatening third countries in unclear cases is limited by the fact that, in most cases, it will be a WTO Panel which will decide on the issue. Secondly, even after the whole procedure has been followed, and the WTO Dispute Settlement Mechanism has allowed for the adoption of retaliatory measures, the Council must decide to retaliate by qualified majority. It is doubtful whether the majority of Member States would support retaliation in non clear-cut cases. Thus, from a strategic point of view, the best thing that the foreign country should do is to wait until the very last moment before removing the measures.

The TBR's commitment to international trade law could be relativised; it could be argued that the instrument adds very little to the Community powers of retaliation because the Community can always take measures under the general Article 113 (now Article 133) of the Treaty.[187] Indeed, the Community could always follow the general market access strategy procedure and adopt, if necessary, measures under Article 113 of the Treaty. However, while this interpretation is legally correct, it is undeniable that this instrument creates a mechanism which makes retaliation much easier and thus increases the threat against the foreign country in order to change its trade practice.[188] The foreign country will certainly not perceive in the same manner a threat of measures taken following a detailed mechanism and after a whole procedure has been adopted, as opposed to that under a general constitutional power.

Thus, the political bargaining which preceded the implementation of the TBR strongly limited the flexibility of the previous Regulation. The strict and inflexible commitment to international trade law has become the most important feature of the TBR.[189] Indeed, the basic principle of the Commission is "never try to imagine any unilateral TBR action which can not be compatible with the Community's international obligations under the WTO."[190] This approach does not necessarily reflect a stronger devotion to the multilateral trading system. Instead, the commitment to international trade law in the TBR is the point of equilibrium between the different constitutional powers of the Community. The free trade Member States had allowed for a more active market access instrument only on condition that it was strictly committed to the standards of international trade law as contained in international agreements.

The TBR's commitment to international trade law may explain why the Commission seems to be so interested in an efficient WTO Dispute Settlement

[187] J Bourgeois, *supra* n. 129, at 2.

[188] An example of this is *Rules of Origin for Textiles in the United States*, O.J. 4.3.97 L62/43 (where the United States did not take seriously the requests of the European Union until a TBR procedure was initiated).

[189] But see Beekmann, "The 1994 Revised Commercial Policy Instrument of the European Union" (1995) 19 *World Competition* 53–75.

[190] Sourmelis, "Seminar on the Trade Barriers Regulation", Commission of the European Community, Brussels, March 1997.

Mechanism, and, thus, calls on Member States to keep their faith in the WTO.[191] But this approach might not always be useful. First, strong trading partners may need some flexibility in order to influence the system. The world trading system is a game in which the rules are in permanent development. The construction of a common European market model implies, to a certain extent, its protection at an international level.

Second, over-emphasising the element of international trade law can lead to blind reliance on the international trading legal system and to lead us to consider the enforcement of international trade law as always being in the interest of the Community. In the notices of initiation in all TBR cases, the Commission has stated that ensuring that third countries fully comply with their commitments under the WTO Agreements is a priority for the European Community. The Commission believes that the United States has successfully played the role of the international trade law enforcer and the European Union should start to play the same game.[192] But what the Commission seems to overlook is the fact that the WTO agreements simply enshrine an Anglo-Saxon market model which does not reflect the variety of systems within the European market. In a game it is not only important how well the actors play, but what the rules are. In a casino, no matter how good the players are, the house always wins. Enforcing the rules of the international trading system might not be in the interests of the Community because possibly such an international legal system is not always in the Community's interests. Moreover, imposing the rules of the system on other parties implies accepting the possibility of having those same rules enforced against oneself. Thus, if the Community cannot effectively influence the rules of such a system, it is playing a game which it can never win.

5.B.4. The Procedure and Scope of the TBR

The bargaining process which led to the inflexible commitment to international trade law also affected the procedural features of the regulation. Although devised in a more limited way than the Commission's 1992 proposal, the TBR was intended both to revitalise the role of the European Union in world trade and to enhance the powers of the Commission against the Member States. However, the latter's lack of trust in the Community, and their constant reassertion of power, severely limited the Commission's initial objectives. Nevertheless, the procedures of the TBR illustrate, first, how the Common Commercial Policy is based on the need to keep a shifting balance between the advantages of acting together to pursue common goals and the need to ensure that the interests of all the Member States are not jeopardised to an unacceptable extent.

[191] "EU/WTO: Sir Leon Brittan Explains Why it is in the EU's Interest to Accept and Support WTO Dispute Settlement Procedures and Conclusion—Procedures in Progress", *Agence Europe* No 7076, 10 October 1997, at 8.

[192] Interview at the Commission, Brussels, March 1997.

Second, they highlight the extent to which the ability of the different trade policy actors to influence the decision-making process varies depending on the level of policy, the step of the procedure at which the decision has to be taken, and the area of international trade. Third, the mechanism of the TBR shows how, despite the control of Member States and the limitations on the scope of the instrument, the Commission is sometimes able to achieve what it considers to be a common goal.

The strict control of the Member States over the Commission's MAS was to be bypassed by the TBR. The alliance between the Commission and Community enterprises, through the new third track which allowed action on behalf of the latter, was intended to result in an improvement in the powers of the Commission. This enhancement was based both on how the decisions were to be taken and on the basic feature of market access trade instruments: the threat of retaliation. The division of power between the Commission and the Council, with regard to decisions to be taken during the procedure, implies a serious threat of retaliation in clear-cut cases of violation of international trade law which should compel the foreign government to take the Commission seriously.

Within forty five days of the complaint being filed, the Commission must decide whether or not to initiate an investigation procedure.[193] Even if the Article 113 (now Article 133) Committee decided not to take action at the request of an enterprise or industry under the MAS, the latter would still be able to ask the Commission to start a TBR investigation. During this period, the Commission must make a determination of whether there is *prima facie* evidence of the facts alleged in the complaint. In practice, most of the initial analysis will have been done in the meetings between the Commission officials and private business before the case is officially filed. Furthermore, Commission officials will even invite the private business to file a complaint after the case has been discussed within the Market Access Action Group and has been considered as "TBR interesting." Thus, most of the forty five day period is used to make sure that there is enough support within the Commission to launch the case and that there is no overriding opposition within the Member States.

Before deciding to initiate a procedure, the Commission must formally consult the Member States, since they are represented in the TBR Advisory Committee.[194] In practice, such formal meetings will serve only for an exchange of views between national and Commission officials and to state any different opinions which may exist. But as the procedure foreseen for this decision is the advisory committee procedure,[195] the Commission does not, legally speaking,

[193] Article 5(4) of the TBR. This 45 day deadline may be suspended at the request of the complainant in order to allow the provision of complementary information. See *Brazilian Export Financing Programme*, O.J. 17.4.99 C108/33.

[194] Articles 8(1) and 7 of the TBR. The Commission will in fact also inform the 113 Committee. Article 7(2) TBR.

[195] Article 3 of Council Decision 99/468, laying down the procedures for the exercise of implementing powers conferred on the Commission, O.J. 17.7.99 L 184/23.

need the approval of the Committee in order to initiate a case. Although it would be hard to conceive of the Commission opening an investigation without being sure it has the support of most Member States, or at least that its decision is not opposed by the majority of them, no Member State or private party may challenge the Commission's decision to open an investigation. Only the complaining party may have its day in court and challenge the Commission's refusal to initiate an investigation. Thus, even if the Commission decided to refuse a TBR complaint which had previously been refused by the Article 113 Committee, the private party could still make itself heard by appealing to the Court of First Instance.

Despite the influence that Member States can exercise, the impossibility of challenging the Commission's decision to open an investigation is a fundamental enhancement of the Commission's powers and of its ability to run foreign trade policy unilaterally in comparison with the general Article 113 (now Article 133) procedure of the MAS. Whenever it is clear that there is a foreign violation of international trade law, the initiation of an investigation implies a serious threat of retaliation against this foreign country. This threat will provide the Commission with some flexibility to bargain with the foreign country and implement its trade policy without the strict control of the Member States.

The freedom of the Commission may further be seen by analysing the decisions which can be taken once an investigation has been initiated. It is the Commission which must conduct all investigations and negotiations. It must decide within five months from initiation, or seven months where complexity so demands, whether any actions should be taken.[196] During this investigation period, the Commission will try to determine whether there is a right of action for the Community and whether there are adverse effects or injury resulting from the foreign obstacle to trade. The Commission will send questionnaires to foreign governments, foreign and domestic companies, and will send missions to gather information. It would be naïve, of course, to think that it will not enter into some sort of negotiations. However the Commission will have no obligation to exhaust the five to seven month period mentioned in the Regulation. Article 12(1) of the TBR allows the Commission to make a decision on whether or not to take action without prior investigation if there is a clear-cut case. The Commission will thus have a certain degree of flexibility which allows it to speed up or slow down the procedure in accordance with its needs.

Once the Commission has concluded its investigation it may take the following decisions. It may decide to terminate the procedure,[197] it may decide to follow an international dispute settlement procedure,[198] to suspend the

[196] Article 8 of the TBR.

[197] *Mass Housing Levy in Turkey*, O.J. 17.12.96 L326/71; *Import Licensing for Steel Plates in Brazil*, O.J. 19.1.98 L32/38.

[198] *Rules of Origin for Textiles in the United States*, O.J. 4.3.97 L62/43; *United States Antidumping Act of 1916*, O.J. 28.4.98 L126/36; *Japanese Practices in Respect of Imports of Leather*, O.J. 3.6.98 L159/65; *Music Licensing Practices in the United States*, O.J. 22.12.98 L346/60; *Trade Obstacles to Leather in Argentina*, O.J. 4.11.98 L295/46.

procedure,[199] or that the Community should enter into an international agreement with the third state.[200] In all such cases, the Commission's decision will simply be subject to a safeguard committee procedure.[201] Thus, unlike the Article 113 (now Article 133) procedure, the Commission may go to the WTO or enter into bilateral consultations with a foreign country unless the Council, by a qualified majority, decides otherwise.

However, the TBR makes it clear that the Commission may not conclude any international agreement on its own.[202] All negotiations of international agreements following a TBR procedure must be carried out according to the general rules of Article 113 (now Article 133) of the Treaty.[203] The Regulation follows the European Court of Justice's decision which held that, subject to certain exceptions, the conclusion of international agreements is within the competence of the Council and not the Commission.[204] Member States, suspicious of the Commission's action and willing to preserve their influence in trade policy matters, have restrained all Commission's attempts to enhance further its negotiating powers in the international arena by means of TBR agreements.

After following an international dispute settlement procedure whenever the Community's commitments so require,[205] the Commission may propose the adoption of retaliation measures to the Council.[206] The latter may only be able to adopt retaliatory measures by a qualified majority vote. Any Member State, the complaining party or private parties affected by the measures may challenge the Council's decision before the ECJ. The free trade Member States limited the threat of retaliatory measures and, to a certain extent, the Commission's powers to manoeuvre, by establishing the need for a qualified majority within the Council.[207] However, whenever there is a clear-cut case of foreign violation of international trade law as contained in international agreements, the threat will be serious. It will be quite difficult for the Council to decide not to implement retaliatory measures allowed for by the dispute settlement body after the whole TBR procedure has been followed.[208]

The scope of the TBR and the powers of the Commission were seriously diminished by the power struggle between the Member States and the Community regarding trade policy. As a result of both the ECJ's Opinion on the

[199] *Piracy of Sound Recordings in Thailand*, O.J. 16.1.96 L 11/7.

[200] Article 11 of the TBR.

[201] Article 14 of the TBR; see also Article 6 of Council Decision 99/468, O.J. 17.7.99 L 184/23.

[202] Under the old Regulation, the Commission concluded international agreements on its own. See *Unauthorized Recordings in Indonesia*. O.J. 17.5.88 L 123/51.

[203] Article 11(3) of the TBR.

[204] Case C 327/91, *France* v. *Commission* [1994] ECR I-3641.

[205] Article 12 (2) of the TBR.

[206] Article 13(2) ibid.

[207] In this sense, anti-dumping and countervailing duties are imposed by simple majority within the Council. Article 15(1) of Council Regulation 2026/97, O.J. 21.10.97 L288/1; Article 9(4) of Council Regulation 384/96, O.J. 6.3.96 L56/1, as amended.

[208] Interview at the Commission, June 1997. Interview with an official of a Member State, Permanent Representation to the European Union, July 1997.

WTO and the Member States' continuing distrust of the Community institutions, some Member States in the Council were happy to introduce Article 2(8) of the Regulation. Furthermore, with the purpose of maintaining a sole legal basis and assuring the Uruguay Round implementation package, the Commission decided not to introduce any legal basis for the instrument other than Article 113. Thus, the Court's Opinion affected the TBR scope with regard to the protection of the Community interests concerning intellectual property rights (IPRs) and services.

As Article 113 (now Article 133) covers only the Community's customs measures affecting counterfeit goods, the scope of the TBR would, in principle, be seriously limited in the area of IPRs. However, with the consent of the Member States, the Commission has been able to adopt a broad interpretation which allows it to tackle, at least partially, foreign trade obstacles in this area.[209] Taking into account the fact that, from a strictly legal point of view, the TBR is simply a domestic procedural regulation, the Commission has, for the purpose of Article 113 (now Article 133), considered that what is important is not whether the protection of IPRs falls within its scope but rather whether the foreign practice affecting IPRs is an obstacle to the trade of goods and services which fall under its scope.[210] The Commission has rightly considered that the aim of the TBR is to use the threat of retaliatory measures in order to remove the foreign trade barrier. The foreign country's decision does not necessarily affect the division of powers between the Community and the Member States because this division is relevant only to the extent that it affects the Community's internal order. Rather, it is simply a foreign country's affair. The division of powers between the Member States and the Community, and the scope of Article 113 (now Article 133), would be of relevance only if after a whole investigation has been followed, and it is considered necessary to take retaliatory measures or to enter into an agreement. Only in such cases, would it be necessary to suspend the TBR procedure and take measures in accordance with other legal basis. At this point, two scenarios can be foreseen. First, the Community may have exclusive competence under a legal basis other than Article 113. Such a basis might require a different decision-making procedure than qualified majority voting. A different scenario would be that the Community does not have exclusive, or indeed any, competence to take the measure in question. Here, the Community and the Member States would have to act in the form of mixity.[211]

Thus, although from a legal point of view, the Commission's interpretation

[209] V Schuren and Luff, *supra* n. 114, at 217.

[210] *Trade Obstacles to Cognac in Brazil*, O.J. 2.4.97 C 103/3 (where the case referred to obstacles to trade of agricultural goods); *Music Licensing Practices in the United States*, O.J. 11.6.97 C 177/2 (where the case referred to obstacles to trade of cross-border services, fees in regard to music broadcasting); *Trade Practices Maintained by Canada in Relation to Imports of Prosciutto di Parma*, O.J. 22.6.99 C176/6 (where the case referred to obstacles to trade of agricultural products)

[211] P Kuipjer, "The New WTO Dispute Settlement System: The Impact on the European Community" (1995) 29(6) *J. World Trade* 49–71, 58–60.

seems to improve the possibilities of the TBR, the fact is that, from a strategic point of view, the TBR continues to be seriously ineffective with regard to the Community's protection of IPRs. Even with this interpretation, the threat of retaliation, and hence both the possibility of allowing the Commission to manoeuvre in world trade and the possibilities of the foreign country removing the obstacle to trade, has been diminished. The threat of retaliation is proportional to the chances of the Council either adopting retaliatory measures or taking any other form of action. But if the Community has to suspend the TBR and adopt measures under a more general legal basis, such as an article of the Treaty or in the form of mixity, the possibilities of the Council taking such measures are significantly reduced. Thus, even under the Commission's broad interpretation, the threat of retaliation does not seem to be credible, the best thing for a foreign country being to wait until the very last moment before Community action is decided. This will, of course, enhance the importance of the Council as the actor which takes the decisions and limit the credibility of the Commission in the external sphere. A second-best policy, with regard to the protection of IPRs, will be the price paid for stronger Member State influence.

The Commission's expansive interpretation seems to reflect the ambiguity of the entire Common Commercial Policy. While under Article 113 (now Article 133) of the Treaty the Community does not have powers to negotiate agreements in the area of IPRs other than customs measures affecting counterfeit in goods, the Commission, by simply following the safeguard committee procedure established in an instrument adopted on the basis of Article 113, may bring IPRs cases before the WTO.[212] Furthermore, this interpretation of the TBR highlights the mixity of the instrument and of the entire Common Commercial Policy. In the same proceeding, some measures may be taken by the Commission under the advisory committee procedure, others under the safeguard procedure, and finally others may even require unanimity under a different exclusive legal basis or on the basis of shared powers between the Community and the Member States. The Common Commercial Policy is thus on a continuum between supranationalism and intergovernmentalism. The power of the different actors to influence the outcome depends not only on the level of policy, as the comparison between the MAS and the TBR shows, but also on the step at which the decision must be taken as well as the international trade sector which is affected. Moreover, it highlights how the Common Commercial Policy is a balance between the need for efficiency and the need to take into account the diversity within the Community, and the sometimes resulting conflicting interests. The Member States' acceptance of this expansive interpretation shows how the issue of the division of powers in the trade policy area is, in fact, one of procedure, as it affects the input of the different trade policy actors. Member States will agree to common action but only as long as their interests are fully taken into consideration.

[212] *Music Licensing Practices in the United States*, O.J. 22.12.89 L346/60 (where the Commission, with the consent of the Member States in the Advisory Committee, decided to take a case to the WTO, on the US violation of IPRs with regard to music broadcasting).

The problems of the TBR are much more severe in regard to trade in services. As a result of Article 2(8), it will only be possible to open a TBR procedure with regard to those services which fall under the scope of Article 113 (now Article 133).[213] Thus, the Commission will be able to open investigations with regard to cross-border services only. Among such services, it will be possible to include banking services, but then only those which involve cross-border trade such as electronic transfers, counselling and financial analysis performed either through electronic communication or post, insurance services strictly limited to cross-border operations, telecommunications, audio-visual services which imply broadcasting via air or satellite but not cable, tourism services which are strictly limited to electronic or computer reservation services, etc.[214] The Community, however, will not be able to target foreign practices affecting important emerging areas of trade, such as services which involve the establishment of legal or physical persons or transport services.

The Commission, of course, hopes to change this situation. There may be two ways for the Community to broaden the scope of the instrument.[215] First, the Community could consider getting rid of Article 2(8), introducing other Treaty provisions as a legal basis for the TBR, under which the Community might have exclusive competence to conclude international trade agreements beyond that covered by Article 113 (now Article 133). This approach, however, could imply an alteration to the procedural elements of the TBR. The scope of the instrument would be broader but, very probably, both the threat of retaliation and the role of the Commission would be significantly limited. A second, more complicated, approach would be to extend the scope of the TBR to cover fields where the competence is shared between the Community and the Member States. The Community would establish a code of conduct whereby the Commission and the Member States would co-operate with the purpose of defending the Community's interests in international trade. But again this code of conduct would probably complicate the decision-making procedure and inevitably reduce the threat of retaliation and the role of the Commission.

It seems that the Commission has used the Advisory Committee in order to test the possibility of widening the scope of the instrument in the form of introducing a legal basis other than Article 113 of the Treaty. Thus, in one of the Advisory Committee meetings, the Commission tried to foresee the Member States' position in the event of a formal proposal by presenting a draft memorandum for an informal discussion. The response was rather discouraging but it illustrates how the question of the division of powers is one of conflicting trade interests between the Member States. While some Member States seemed to be ready to grant an expansion of the Community's powers under the TBR, key

[213] There have been several cases affecting foreign trade in services whose filing has been discouraged by the Commission because they did not fall under Article 113 of the Treaty.

[214] Interview at the Commission, March 1997.

[215] Interview at the Commission, June 1997.

Member States simply stated that there was no need for further changes. The idea was consequently dropped.[216]

Thus, the Commission waited until the end of the Amsterdam Intergovernmental Conference with the hope that an agreement between the Member States would extend the scope of Article 113 of the Treaty, and consequently that of the instrument. But again such expectations were never met. Nevertheless, the new Article 133 (5) could be read as allowing an extension of the application of Article 133 (ex 113) to services for the specific purposes of the TBR whenever the Council by unanimity decides to extend the application to an international agreement on services. Furthermore, if we were to adopt an expansive interpretation of Article 133(5) which would consider that services and the protection of intellectual property are within the scope of Article 133, no action of the Council would be needed to extend the action of the TBR to all services. While Article 113(5) of the Treaty refers only to the extension of the scope of Article 133 to conventional measures and not unilateral measures, Article 2(8) of the TBR defines services for which action is possible as those in respect of which international agreements can be concluded by the Community on the basis of Article 113 of the Treaty.[217] Another but less expansive interpretation of Article 133(5) would allow for an *ad hoc* extension of the application of Article 113 to services for the specific purposes of the TBR. The Member States would remain competent in all other aspects, but they would be able to use by unanimity the muscle of the Community in removing trade obstacles.

5.B.5. Conclusions

The TBR can be seen as an example of the Common Commercial Policy, in illustrating a shifting balance between an internal market diversity and the need to act efficiently in the external sphere.

First, the TBR's substantive and institutional features show how the persistence of different market economies within the Community, emphasised by the process of globalisation, led the Community to adopt a second-best instrument. The Member States' different approaches to international trade led them to distrust the Community institutions and to adopt a TBR limited both in its narrow scope and in its strict commitment to international trade law. As a result, the Community is bound to enforce an international liberal order which it can influence only to a very limited extent. By doing this, it oversees the existence of market diversity both at global and European level.

Second, the TBR shows how the Common Commercial Policy is a struggle for power between different actors. The trade instrument is an attempt to open a window for Commission action and European integration. It allows for more

[216] Interview at the Commission, Brussels, May 1997.

[217] See Chapter 4.

action on the part of the Commission in the external sphere; as well as the creation of links between the Commission and European business organisations. However, the Council has made sure that the Commission will not capture the instrument, by introducing elements such as the need to inform the Article 113 (now Article 133) Committee in addition to the Advisory Committee, the impossibility for the Commission to conclude agreements on its own, the need for qualified majority in the Council in order to take any retaliatory measures, and the formal limitation of the scope of the instrument.

However, the TBR also highlights the superficiality of analysing the role of the European Union in international trade either in supranational or intergovernmental terms. Thus, in the TBR, there is a blurring of the line between both forces. On the one hand, the degree of influence of each of the actors depends on the decision that must be taken. And as the threat of measures is the key element of the instrument, all such decisions have an impact on the external sphere. On the other hand, at each decision, all forces will be compelled to enter into a bargaining process. While the Commission has a strong control over most of the developments of the instrument, it must make sure that it has the support of the Member States. Similarly, although it is for the Member States to decide on the most serious decisions, the entire procedure ensures that the Commission will be able to influence the final outcome decisively.

6

Conclusions

THIS BOOK HAS been based on the idea that societies organise themselves differently and, consequently, states have different constitutional and market frameworks. They diverge in the way in which the distribution of power between different political units is constitutionally articulated and, thus, in the influence which they may have in the decision-making process. Furthermore, the book has rejected an ahistorical and structurally blind normative idea of free trade, arguing that political action prescribed by formal constitutions is part of a wider socio-economic context. The approach has focused on the strength or weakness of the government and the organisation or plurality of the market.

In the different parts of the study there has been an attempt to highlight the different socio-economic structures in which four market economies—the United States, France, Germany and Japan—are rooted, while arguing that these different structures result from diverse historical experiences. The foundation of America in a territory of unlimited resources and on the basis of a social *tabula rasa* led the United States to become a unique capitalist system which combines a fragmented government with a strong but disorganised business sector and an extremely weak labour. In sharp relief to this, the other three market systems were based on the existence of prior institutions which influenced their different capitalist developments. In France, the existence of a modern state with a centrally controlled bureaucracy prior to industrialisation led French capitalism to be characterised by a paternalistic relationship between a strong state and a plural and disorganised market. In contrast, in Germany, the development of capitalism on the basis of medieval institutions and the drama of the Second World War led to a market economy defined by the strategic relationship between an enabling state and a strong and organised market. Similarly, in Japan, the cultural tendency towards consensual ordering and a late industrialisation based on an alliance between an imperial bureaucracy and family conglomerates resulted in a capitalist system where networks between market actors are pervasive.

While globalisation entails important changes in the domestic sphere of each country, as change is path-dependent, the possibility of eliminating structural differences is limited. Although to a certain extent, international institutions may control different government policies, the structures that rule the organisation of the market and strongly condition the role of the state will undergo a very slow erosion process. On the one hand, international trade agreements and the creation of an international trade regime, are limited by the domestic structures of the major trading partners. As highlighted by the negotiation of the green light Research and Development subsidies provisions, as well as those concerning the definition of dumping, constitutional constraints and the wide divergences between the different economic systems require the adoption of a compromise which provides the appearance of a final legal solution yet leaves many issues unsolved. On the other hand, international trade law, while formally committing governments and limiting their policies to a certain extent, is incapable of dramatically changing the domestic structures of each partner. This much is evidenced by the United States' implementation of the Research and Development green light subsidies provisions and the European implementation of the Audio Tapes in Cassettes Panel Report.

Globalisation has thus been characterised both by homogeneity and diversity; as a process which does not create a completely homogenous world wide market place but instead enforces a thin Anglo-Saxon uniformity whilst making possible the interdependence of different market systems. Thin Anglo-Saxon uniformity prevails for two reasons. First, in building an international trade regime, negative integration (the reduction of trade barriers) is always easier than positive integration (the adoption of common market structures). The Anglo-Saxon model, characterised by government decentralisation and market pluralism, is the minimum common denominator of all market systems. Second, the United States has been the only trading partner with both the economic muscle and the ability to act efficiently in the international trading system so as to impose the rules of the game.

From an international point of view, the challenge of the World Trade Organisation is to put together different domestic systems and it is consequently bound to be characterised by trade conflicts and feuds. Thus, as the different GATT Panel Reports analysed throughout the study show, the international trade lawyer is compelled to put international trade law within an economic, political and sociological context.

This book, however, has taken a domestic perspective. It has considered globalisation as the result of the interaction, negotiations and policies among states. Globalisation does not imply the retreat of the state but a reshaping of its role, from domestic intervention towards an active trade policy. Taking into account the important role of states in the international trading system, the book has attempted to explain a state's trade policy as a result of its domestic factors. The question examined has been: if globalisation is characterised by diversity, how do such differences affect the trade policy of states in an era where nearly everything is subject to commerce?

For trading partners, the book has focused on the United States and the European Union. With regard to trade policy, it has analysed different institutional and substantive aspects of unfair trade instruments such as anti-dumping and countervailing measures and market access instruments. By domestic structures it has focused on both constitutional and socio-economic structures.

The study has analysed unfair trade instruments as an attempt to deal with the external world taking into account the conditions and constraints imposed by domestic constitutional and socio-economic structures. Thus, anti-dumping, countervailing measures and market access instruments have been examined as a reflection of the domestic systems of each trading partner from three perspectives, which the study has tried to merge. First, unfair trade instruments are *ad hoc* protectionism to compensate for the domestic constraints imposed by globalisation. Second, these instruments are intertwined with the trading partners' constitutional culture and trade policy-making process. Third, unfair trade instruments carry in their concept of fairness local views on the market behaviour of governments and market actors.

The study has considered unfair trade instruments as *ad hoc* protectionism to compensate for the inability of the domestic sphere to cope with the challenges of the external sphere. Both the substantive and procedural features of anti-dumping and countervailing duties are protectionist-biased. Such bias is consistent with the historical origins of these instruments. The rise of countervailing and anti-dumping law was part of a protectionist policy which took place as a result of an Anglo-Saxon system characterised by a domestic liberal tradition. *Ad hoc* protection was granted to safeguard a domestic system typified as having a government with a hands off tradition and a market marked by pluralism. Countervailing and anti-dumping laws were enacted not to protect against any market distortion but to guard the protectionism provided to a domestic industry, which was left to flourish on its own. Similarly, during the 1980s, the European institutions developed an anti-dumping asymmetry methodology to limit the flow of Asian, particularly Japanese, electronic goods which were seen as jeopardising the future of the European electronic industry. The limitation on government intervention, as a result of globalisation and at a regional level, European integration, led the European southern Member States, which had traditionally lacked forms of market co-operation and had relied instead on the active role of the state, to claim protection at the European level. The European institutions, eager to maintain their credibility, were thus, bound to develop an anti-dumping methodology which would guarantee a high level of dumping and, thus, of protection in the form of duties or procedural harassment.

Similarly, market access instruments, although based on the idea of opening markets and, thus, on a presumed free trade rationale, reflect a mercantilist approach to trade. Even justified under international trade rules they are means for governments to support domestic firms in exporting to foreign markets. Instead of protecting domestic industries at home they do so abroad. Thus, in the same way that the United States' use of Section 301 during the 1980s (and potentially in the years ahead) reflected the spectacular increase in the trade deficit and the inability of the American government to develop adequate policies to cope with this at home, the Trade Barriers Regulation reflects a third way between those Member States claiming protection in the form of defensive measures and those who prefer no protection at all.

The book has also considered unfair trade instruments as part of the paradox in which different trading partners are trapped. Unfair trade instruments are an attempt to deal efficiently with the global market diversity on the basis of the limitations posed by the domestic spheres. Thus, they reflect in their conceptions of fairness the different socio-economic frameworks in which markets are embedded. As the existence of different socio-economic structures within the globalisation process results in an interdependence between different market frameworks which has a great impact on the domestic life of each trading partner, globalisation is a struggle where states try to protect themselves by imposing on others, policies and rules that are in accordance with their own domestic structures.

States can influence the international trading system by two interrelated means. States can participate in international negotiations with other members. However, the positions held in international *fora* can be enhanced unilaterally by means of unfair trade instruments. While these instruments can be rationalised as interface mechanisms to smooth the exchange between different market systems, they can also be used to intervene in a foreign country's domestic structures in order to impose the same socio-economic framework that one has or to create an international precedent and, thus, influence the agenda for future trade negotiations. In this light, the United States' use of countervailing duty law against developing countries, in addition to its use of Section 301, served to bring the developing countries to the subsidies negotiation table and to influence the international rules on intellectual property rights, services and dispute settlement. Similarly, the United States' use of countervailing duties against European countries and the latter's massive anti-dumping duties against the People's Republic of China and Japan also amounted to interference in domestic sovereignty and an attempt to change the domestic structures of the targeted partners.

Whereas a common viewpoint has been that only market access instruments are offensive in the sense of interfering in foreign structures or defining the agenda of future negotiations, this book has considered that distinguishing between offensive and defensive instruments is somewhat limited. The dramatic case of the People's Republic of China, and to a lesser degree the change in attitude of the developing countries which were targeted by American countervailing duties, show the extent to which whether anti-dumping and countervailing duties are offensive or defensive depends on the magnitude of the asymmetrical relationship in market power as between the different trading partners.

However, globalisation itself creates the paradox. To influence the rules of the game to their benefit, states have to act rationally and as monoliths. States are required to act efficiently and with one voice as if there were no domestic differences. But as a result of the increasing effects of globalisation in the domestic spheres, since globalisation affects the life of everybody, all constitutional units of power will claim some degree of influence.

States are compelled to develop constitutional and political procedures which will provide them with the necessary domestic legitimacy to act efficiently in the global system. Globalisation requires the stretching of the domestic constitutional frameworks. But as political action prescribed by formal constitutions is part of a much wider socio-economic framework, the analysis of the trade policy of United States and European Union shows that while constitutional procedures can serve to reach, and crystallise, an agreement on common action, they are only possible when there is a minimum consensus on the common good. Thus, something seems to be wrong when the largest trading partners in the world do not have their own adequate and credible procedures to negotiate and conclude international trade agreements.

The lack of fast track would seem to put the United States on the verge of a U-turn. During the last few decades, America's trade policy has been a story of success due to its ability to allow the input of domestic constituencies whilst making sure that the country as a unified whole can speak strongly in the international trading system. Yet, just as the United States appears to be succeeding in modelling a world that is a reflection of its own system, it seems to retreat from the international trade *fora*.

Both the past success and the current impasse are a reflection of the American domestic structures. For fifty years, the success of United States' trade policy has not been due simply to its procedures for co-operation between the different constitutional actors, but rather to the fact that the policy was based on a broad national consensus. The United States has been committed to a long-standing and widely agreed policy which clearly reflected and fitted its domestic structures. Both fast track and unfair trade instruments were interwoven parts of a consensus based on increasing the pie for all by granting *ad hoc* protection at home, as an exception to the general rule of free trade, whilst globalising the American system abroad. Unfair trade instruments struck a balance between the protectionist worries of Congress and the export-enhancing policy of the Executive.

In matters of foreign trade, the United States Congress is sovereign. Through the mechanism of delegation the legislature has been able to enhance American effectiveness in world trade while reaffirming its control. As the implementation process of the Uruguay Round Agreement on the green light subsidies for Research and Development shows, trade policy has been characterised by the influence of Congress and especially that of the Senate Finance and the House Ways and Means Committees and the need for the Executive to broker between its own political agenda, its trading partners' positions and the legislature. Congress has been willing to delegate, but its price for opening the American market to foreign trade, either in the form authorising fast track procedures or implementing fast track trade agreements, has been the development of unfair trade instruments. Furthermore, Congress has reasserted its control over foreign trade and assured the effectiveness of its unfair trade laws by establishing an executive inter-agency mechanism and committing the latter to take into account the private sector. Thus, as the use of Section 301 in the banana feud highlights, to a larger extent than other governments, the American Administration is bound to act in the international trading system for the pursuit of what may be considered the narrow interests of private parties.

Unfair trade instruments fitted the American domestic system. The inability of the United States government to develop domestically coherent and co-ordinated economic redistributive policies, either in the form of industrial policy or social adjustment, together with the absence of any collective approaches to industrial crisis or globalisation coming from domestic market actors, tends to generate reactive responses in the form of calls for protection. Unfair trade instruments provide such protection on an exceptional basis while meeting the imperative requirement of safeguarding the autonomy of business against any attempt from government to intervene and plan the economy. If we are to consider globalisation as determined by the domestic constraints of the major trading partners, the dominance of the United States in the international trading system and its constant tendency to solve domestic problems through trade policy suggests that the system will never be characterised by stability.

Moreover, as the case on research and development subsidies shows, for Congress, developing unfair trade instruments is not only about granting *ad hoc* protectionism because there is no happier consumer than one with a job, but also about defending the American model both at home and abroad. The United States' provisions on research and development subsidies would signal to its trading partners how America expected the international rules to be implemented. As analysis of United States' methodology in general and the GATT Panel Report on European steel products, in particular, show the unfair trade instruments would mean preserving the American system at home and enhancing it abroad, since their standard of fairness conveyed the local view on the concept of market and the role which the government should play within it. Thus, the GATT Panel Report on European steel highlights how America, characterised by its domestic confrontation between the market and the state and the lack of cooperation between private market actors, was incapable of understanding that a concerted action between banks, government and industries was not unfair. The United States could not conceive that market actors could behave in a way which is different from its own. Likewise, the concept of unreasonableness in Section 301 of the 1947 Trade Act is a means by which the United States has been able to pursue an international trade system which reflects its own domestic structures. Through Section 301, America pursued a liberal regime for services and intellectual property rights, attempted to prevent collective action by private actors, as well as government intervention in foreign markets. The United States' radical liberalism leads to an activist, and at times aggressive, trade policy reflecting an intolerance towards other political and economic systems as a result of the fact that, domestically, it has never been seriously confronted. The irony is that unfair trade instruments globalise the features of government decentralisation and market plurality of an American system which is hindered from developing domestically collective responses to meet the challenge of globalisation. The result of this policy is, again, the world-wide increase of unfair trade instruments and trade conflict.

If the use of Section 301 during two decades highlights the success of America's trade policy by exemplifying how the United States Congress and Executive have been able to co-operate and influence the international trading system, its most recent practice is a signal of the collapse of the consensus which sustained that cooperation. As the United States Executive lacks fast track to credibly negotiate trade agreements, it is compelled to use Section 301 intensively within the WTO dispute settlement, to influence the development of new trade rules. But as the WTO Panel Report on the Kodak case shows, such an approach is limited. Furthermore, the need to obtain domestic support for the fast track project requires the Executive to demonstrate its willingness to defend strongly American interests, even at the cost of jeopardising the international trading system.

However, like all other American unfair trade instruments, Section 301 is of limited utility without fast track authority to negotiate trade agreements. Yet fast track, like unfair trade instruments, was based on a consensus. While fast track and unfair trade instruments, assured formally democratic control of Congress and the influence of the private sector, as the case on research and development subsidies highlighted, such control, in practice, came from the Senate Finance and the House Ways and Means Committees together with the private interests that supported them. Thus, fast track was only legitimate as long as there was a nation-wide consensus on trade policy. This consensus was based on free trade, *ad hoc* protectionism and globalising the American system. In short, the consensus assumed that what was good for American business was good for the American people.

Globalisation itself broke the American deal of increasing the pie for all through free trade. As globalisation increases the amount of wealth, but systematically and dramatically leaves some without a share, coping with it implies reaching a domestic agreement and establishing an adequate redistribution of the free trade benefits. But the decentralisation of the American government combined with the plurality of its market makes any credible domestic compromise impossible. America is thus left with trade policy. It can retrieve from the international trading system or reach a new compromise based on enforcing labour and environmental rights at an international level. As most of the Democrats have made clear, there will be no fast track unless the United States makes a strong commitment to enforce labour and environmental rights unilaterally and multilaterally. To the contrary, it has been argued that for each vote in favour of fast track which the President gets by promising to enforce worker rights, he will lose one Republican. Yet it is unbelievable that America's big business would give away its world hegemony by refusing to accept some changes in the trading system.

The analysis of United States trade policy can be useful for understanding the European Union's Common Commercial Policy. While both partners are trade superpowers, they diverge in their past ability to influence the developments of the international trading system. Unlike the United States, the experience of the

European Union is that of an economic power which cannot meet its expectations and be assertive in the international arena. The Community continues to act in the external sphere as a fragmented actor and therefore slowly to lose the struggle of globalisation.

Much of the literature has analysed the Common Commercial Policy as the result of inefficient intergovernmental procedures, which should be changed. Instead, this book has described the Community's trade policy institutional set up as a continuum between intergovernmental and supranational poles, arguing that, as with the United States trade policy, any changes of procedure require an agreement on the common good and, thus, the need to focus on the different market economies of which Member States are prisoners. The Common Commercial Policy is the result of a shifting balance between the need to cope together with the challenge of globalisation and the reality of a European internal market diversity.

As the implementation of the Audio Tapes in Cassettes Panel Report and the practice of the Trade Barriers Regulation show, considering trade policy as dominated by supranational or intergovernmental forces is somewhat limited. First, no Community institution can be considered as purely supranational or intergovernmentalist. The Commission is organised and works in such a way as to take into account at every step of its decision making process the very different national interests. Thus, in the implementation of the GATT Panel Report, whilst the Commission tried to champion what it considered as the overall interests of the Community, it took on board from the very first the different positions of the Member States. On the other hand, the way the Council and its different committees work makes it possible to achieve common positions that go beyond the single national interest. The implementation of the Trade Barriers Regulations shows that despite the strong differences within the Council at the conclusion of the Uruguay Round, it was capable of adopting a regulation which opened a window for Community action, although second best.

Second, the influence that each institution has within the Common Commercial Policy depends on the level of policy. The Trade Barriers Regulation shows how different actors will have varying degrees of influence depending on the decision to be taken. The Commission will have the last word when deciding to initiate, investigate, negotiate or go to the WTO dispute settlement body. On the other hand, it is the Council which must decide, after a proposal by the Commission and acting on a qualified majority, whether to take final retaliation. Furthermore, this distribution of powers is complicated even further by the problem of competence in relation to trade policy. Member States will want to act together while maximising their influence. However, even if all the important decisions should need the final decision of the Council, or the Member States acting collectively either by simple majority, qualified majority or under unanimity, this does not imply that other supranational forces will not be able to influence the trade output. The role of the European Parliament in cases where trade agreements do not fall under the limited scope of Article 113 (now Article 133) highlights how supranational forces can have a voice even when the Community has no exclusive competence.

Furthermore, the very fact of conflicting interests as between the Member States and the information advantage the Commission enjoys, may allow the latter to introduce and pass proposals which can benefit the Community as a whole. The implementation of the Audio Tapes in Cassettes Panel Report shows how, despite the broad differences between the Member States, the Commission was able to champion the Community interest; albeit in a second best manner. Similarly, the practice arising from the Trade Barriers Regulation illustrates that, whilst not being able to retaliate on its own, the Commission will, to a limited extent, have powers to pursue the Community's interests world-wide by informal negotiations and threatening an eventual retaliation or the possibility of a formal application to the WTO dispute settlement.

The Common Commercial Policy is an open, undefined arena where the different actors struggle for political power. As shown by the analysis of the creation of the market access strategy and the Trade Barriers Regulation, different political actors are in a constant process of opening windows for influence. The creation of the market access strategy was an idea masterminded to develop a common European trade action. The market access strategy would prove to European business that European institutions could be useful to them. Similarly, the Trade Barriers Regulation was an attempt to bypass the need for European industries to ask their national governments to take trade action. But as the final implementation of the Regulation shows, some Member States, but not all, would limit such initiatives. Member States would make sure that all TBR cases would be reported to, and reviewed in, the 113 (now Article 133) Committee. Furthermore, they would limit the scope of the instrument and require qualified majority for any retaliation. The trade policy influence of the fifteen Member States, the Commission, the Council and the Parliament varies, is often overlapping and, thus, ambiguous. In determining the governance of the Community's trade policy while we may identify the different elements, it will be impossible to adopt a precise formula between intergovernmentalism and supranationalism.

This trade policy process is not only ambiguous, scary and difficult to understand but from an efficiency point of view it also leads to second best outcomes. But a more efficient trade action in the form of qualified majority, democracy or technocratic decision-making is impossible when there is no consensus between the parties on the basic principles and interests of the Community trade policy. The Community's trade policy process is characterised by the all-encompassing persistence of different domestic structures within the European market which leads it to second best outcomes. Understanding the Community's Common Commercial Policy implies the need to focus on the different market economies to which the Member States are subject.

As this book has tried to highlight by focusing on the market economies of France and Germany, in spite of the Single Market Initiative, the European market is characterised by the survival of different national socio-economic structures. Rather than creating a uniform market, the initiative has resulted in the merger of 15 different market systems. As with globalisation, European liberalisation results in Member States maintaining certain differences while adopting a certain number of elements from the Anglo-Saxon market economies. This in turn raises the issue of how it could be possible to create a European identity while remaining open to the international system.

The analysis of the Trade Barriers Regulation and the Community's anti-dumping methodology shows the extent to which the survival of different market economies leads the Community to a second best trade policy. Member States are prisoners of their diverse market economies and consequently have contradictory trade interests. The challenge of the European Union is to act efficiently in the external sphere by creating legitimacy procedures on the basis of domestic heterogeneity.

First, the lack of a common good and the conflict between the Member States leads them to distrust the Community institutions and, therefore, the scope of the latter's powers. As the limits of the TBR with regard to trade in services and intellectual property rights demonstrates, the diverse trade interests of the Members States leads the Common Commercial Policy to be held back in establishing the rules of the game in new areas. Likewise, the use of undertakings in anti-dumping policy shows how the Community institutions will use second best instruments to by-pass the stringent procedures of trade agreements.

Secondly, the diverse trade interests among the Community Member States causes the Community to be a passive player in international trade. The conflict between these trade interests led the Community to adopt a TBR strictly committed to the rule of international trade law as contained in trade agreements. This commitment to international law results in the Community enforcing an international legal system whose development it cannot effectively influence.

Finally, the persistence of different domestic structures within the Community leads it to develop measures which can actually harm the Community itself. Since the Member States which traditionally relied on government intervention claimed some form of protection to compensate for the liberalisation resulting from globalisation and the internal market programme, the Community institutions, anxious to promote their prestige in Europe, were compelled to develop an anti-dumping methodology, and impose massive anti-dumping duties against Asian products while remaining more or less faithful to their international law commitment. But the irony is that those instruments were based on a liberal rationale and were never envisaged for European continental countries. Whilst the Community is enforcing the thin Anglo-Saxon homogenisation of both globalisation and European integration, it is jeopardising the long-standing economic traditions of European countries. By over-emphasising trade policy, and misusing unfair trade instruments, the Community has been playing the wrong game.

Bibliography

AMERICAN BAR ASSOCIATION, Section of International Law and Practice Report to the House of Delegates, "Fast Track Negotiating Authority" (1997) 31(3) *Int'l Lawyer* 955–959.

ABBOT, Kenneth W., "Modern International Relations Theory: A Prospectus for International Lawyers" (1989) 14 *Yale J. Int, L.* 335–411.

ACEVES, William J., "Lost Sovereignty? The Implications of the Uruguay Round Agreements" (1995) 19 *Fordham Int'l L. J.* 427–474.

ACKERMAN, Bruce and GOLOVE, David, "Is NAFTA Constitutional?" (1995) 108 *Harvard L. Rev.* 799–929.

ADAMS, William J., *Restructuring the French Economy: Government and the Rise of Market Competition since World War II* (Washington, The Brookings Institution, 1989).

ALBERT, Michel, *Capitalism versus Capitalism: How America's Obsession with Individual Achievement and Short Term Profit Had Led it to the Brink of Collapse* (New York, Four Wall Eight Windows, 1993).

AMERICAN SOCIETY OF INTERNATIONAL LAW, *The Future of the President's Authority to Negotiate International Trade Agreements after NAFTA and the Uruguay Round: What Should Congress Delegate?* (Proceedings of the 88th Annual Meeting of the American Society of International Law, Washington, April 6–9, 1994).

ANCHODOGUY, Marie, "Japanese-American Trade Conflict and Supercomputers" (1994) 109(1) *Political Science Quarterly* 35–80.

AOKI, Masahiko and HUGH, Patrick, *The Japanese Main Banking System: Its Relevance for Developing and Transforming Economies* (Oxford, Oxford University Press, 1994).

ARMSTRONG, Kenneth and BULMER, Simon, *The Governance of the Single European Market* (Manchester, Manchester University Press, 1998).

ARNOLD, M. and BRONCKERS, M., "The EEC New Trade Policy Instrument: Some Comments on its Application" (1988) 22(6) *J. World Trade* 19–38.

AXELROD, Robert, *The Evolution of Cooperation* (New York, Basic Books, 1984).

BADER, Gregory K., "The Keiretsu System of Japan: Its Steadfast Existence Despite Heightened Foreign and Domestic Pressure for Dissolution" (1994) 27 *Cornell Int'l L. J.* 365–386.

BAGLIONI, Guido and CROUCH, Colin (eds.), *European Industrial Relations: The Challenge of Flexibility* (London, Sage Publications, 1990).

BAILEY, GOLDSTEIN and WEINGAST, "The Institutional Roots of American Trade Policy" (1997) 49 *World Politics* 309–338.

BARCELO, John J., "Antidumping Laws as Barriers to Trade—The United States and the International Antidumping Code" (1972) 57 (4) *Cornell L. Rev.* 491.

—— "Subsidies and Countervailing Duties—Analysis and a Proposal" (1977) 9 *L.& Policy Int'l Business* 779–853.

—— "Subsidies, CVDs and Antidumping After the Tokyo Round" (1980) 13 (2) *Cornell Int'l L. J.* 25.

BARRINGER, William H. and DURLING, James P., "Out of Focus: The Use of Section 301 to Address Anticompetitive Practices in Foreign Markets" (1996) 1(1) *UCLA J. Int'l. & Foreign Affairs* 99–142.

BARSHEFSKY, MATTICE and MARTIN, "Government Equity Participation in State Owned Enterprises: An Analysis" (1983) 14 *L. & Pol'y Int'l Business* 1101–1158.

BASSOMPIERRE, Guy de, *Changing the Guard in Brussels: An Insider's View of the EC Presidency* (New York, Praeger, 1988)

BAYARD, Thomas O. and ELLIOT, Kimberly A., "Aggressive Unilateralism and Section 301: Market Opening or Market Closing?" (1992) 15 (6) *World Economy* 685–706.

BEEKMANN, Harry, "The 1994 Revised Commercial Policy Instrument of the European Union", 19 *World Competition* 53–75.

BEHBOODI, Rambod, *Industrial Subsidies in World Trade: Trade Policy or Trade Politics* (London, Routledge, 1994).

BELLO, Judith H. and HOLMER, Alan F., "The Heart of the 1988 Trade Act: A Legislative History of the Amendments to Section 301" (1988) 24 (1) *Stanford J. Int'l L.* 1.

—— "U.S. Trade Law and Policy Series No 23: Reflection on the NAFTA as a Turning Point in American Foreign Policy" (1994) 28(2) *Int'l Lawyer* 425–432.

—— "U.S. Trade Law and Policy Series No 24: Dispute Resolution in the New World Trade Organization, Concerns and Net Benefits" (1994) 28 (4) *Int'l Lawyer* 1095–1104.

—— "The Post Uruguay Round Future of Section 301" (1994) 25 *L. & Pol'y Int'l Bus.* 1297–1308.

—— "U.S. Trade Law and Policy Series No 21: GATT Dispute Settlement Agreement: Internationalization or Elimination of Section 301?" (1992) 26 *Int'l Lawyer* 795–802.

BENYON, Frank and BOURGEOIS Jacques H., "The EC-US Steel Arrangement" (1984) 21 *C.M.L. Rev.* 305–354.

BERGER, Suzanne and DORE, Ronald (eds.), *National Diversity and Global Capitalism* (Ithaca, Cornell University Press, 1996).

BERKEY, John, "International Trade: Countervailing Duties and the European Steel Imports" (1989) 23 (2) *Harvard Int'l L. J.* 443.

BESELER J. F. and WILLIAMS A. N., *Anti-Dumping and Anti-Subsidy Law: The European Communities* (London, Sweet & Maxwell, 1986).

BHAGWATI, Jagdish and HUDEC, Robert E. (eds.), *Fair Trade and Harmonization: Prerequisites for Free Trade?* (Cambridge, The MIT Press, 1996).

BHAGWATI, Jagdish, *Protectionism* (Cambridge, MIT Press, 1988).

—— *The World Trading System at Risk* (New York, Harvester Wheatsheaf, 1991).

BHAGWATI, Jagdish and PATRICK, Hugh T. (eds.), *Aggressive Unilateralism: America's 301 Trade Policy and the World Trading System* (New York, Harvester Wheatsheaf, 1991).

BIERSTEKER, Thomas J., "Reducing the Role of the State in the Economy: A Conceptual exploration of IMF and World Bank Prescriptions", 34 *Int'l Studies Quarterly* 477–492.

BLECKMANN, *Division of Powers Between the European Communities and their Member States in the Field of External Relations* (Deventer, Kluwer Law and Taxation, 1981).

BLISS, Julia C., "The Amendments to Section 301: An Overview and Suggested Strategies for Foreign Response" (1989) 20 *L. & Pol'y Int'l Bus.* 501–528.

BOGDANDY, Armin Von, "The Non-Violation Procedure of Article XXIII:2, GATT: Its Operational Rationale" (1992) 26 (4) *J. World Trade* 95–111.

BORCHARD, Edwin, "Treaties and Executive Agreements—A Reply" (1945) 54 *Yale L. J.* 611–664.

BOTTOMORE, Tom and BRIAN, Bryen, *The Capitalist Class: An International Study* (New York, Harvester Wheatsheaf, 1989).

BOLTUCK, Richard and LITAN, Robert E. (eds.), *Down in the Dumps: Administration of the Unfair Trade Laws* (Washington, The Brookings Institution, 1991).

BOURGEOIS, Jacques H., "The Tokyo Round on Technical Barriers and on Government Procurement in International and EEC Perspective" (1982) 19 *C.M.L. Rev.* 5–33.

—— "EC Rules Against 'Illicit Trade Practices'—Policy Cosmetics or International Law Enforcement?" (1988) *Annual Proceedings of the Fordham Corporate Law Institute: Europe/America Antitrust and Trade Law*, Chapter 6.

—— "The EC in the WTO and Advisory Opinion 1/94: An Echternach Procession" (1995) 32 *C.M.L. Rev.* 763–787.

BOURGEOIS, Jacques H. (ed.), *Subsidies and International Trade: A European Lawyers Perspective* (Deventer, Kluwer Law and Taxation, 1991).

BOURGEOIS, Jacques, "External Relations Powers of the European Community", 22 *Fordham Int'l L. J. 149–173.*

BOURGEOIS, J. H., BERROD and FOURNIER (eds.), *The Uruguay Round Results: A European Lawyer's Perspective* (Brussels, European Interuniversity Press, 1996).

BOURGEOIS, J. H., DEWOST, J. L. and GAIFEE (eds.), *La Communaute Europeenne et les Accords Mixtes: Quelles Perspectives?* (Brussels, Presses Interuniversitaires Europeennes, 1997).

BOURRINET, Jacques (ed.), *Les Relations Communaute Europeenne Etats Unis* (Paris, Economica, 1987).

BOYER, Robert and DRACHE, Daniel (eds.), *States Against Markets: The Limits of Globalization* (London, Routledge 1996).

BRONCKERS, Marco C. J., *Selective Safeguard Measures in Multilateral Trade Relations* (Deventer, Kluwer Law and Taxation, 1985).

—— "Private Participation in the Enforcement of WTO Law: The New EC Trade Barriers Regulation" (1996) 33 *C.M.L. Rev.* 299–318.

BROYER, Sylvain, *The Social Market Economy: Birth of an Economic Style* (Wissenschaftszentrum Berlin Fur Sozialforschung Working Paper 96–318, 1996).

BRYAN, Greyson, *Taxing Unfair International Trade Practices* (Lexington, Lexington Books, 1980).

BULMER, Simon and PATERSON, William, *The Federal Republic of Germany and the European Community* (London, Allen & Unwin, 1987).

BULMER, Simon, "Domestic Politics and European Community Policy Making" (1983) 21 *J.C.M.S.* 339–363.

BURROWS, Noreen, "No General External Relations Competence for the Commission" (1995) 20 *European L. Rev.* 210.

BURTLESS, LAWRENCE, LITAN and SHAPIRO, *Globaphobia: Confronting Fears About Open Trade* (Washington, The Brookings Institution, The Progressive Policy Institute & The Twentieth Century Found, 1998).

CAFRUNY, A. and PETERS, P. (eds.), *The Union and the World: The Political Economy of a Common Foreign Policy* (The Hague, Kluwer Law, 1997).

CAMPBELL, Colton C. and DAVIDSON, Roger H., "U.S. Congressional Committees: Changing Legislative Workshops," (1998) 4(1) *Legislative Studies* 124–142 (1998).

CARTLAND, Michael, "Antidumping and Competition Policy" (1996) 28(1) *L. & Pol'y Int'l Bus.* 289–296.

CASSESE, Antonio (ed.), *Control of Foreign Policy in Western Democracies: A Comparative Study of Parliamentary Foreign Affairs Committees* (New York, Oceana Publications, 1982).

CASTILLO DE LA TORRE, Fernando, "The EEC New Instrument of Trade Policy: Some Comments in the Light of the Latest Developments" (1993) 30 *C.M.L. Rev.* 687–719.

CATER, Ralph G. and EDEN, Lorraine, "Who Makes US Trade Policy?" (1999) 13(1) *Int'l Trade J.* 53–100.

CHATAIN, Carmel Ni, "The European Community and the Member States in the Dispute Settlement Understanding of the WTO: United or Divided?" (1999) 5(4) *European L. J.* 461.

CONGRESSIONAL BUDGET OFFICE, *A Review of U.S. Antidumping and Countervailing Duty Law and Policy* (Washington, CBO, 1994).

CERNY, Philip G., "Globalization and Other Stories: The Search for a New Paradigm for International Relations" (1996) *Int'l. J.* 617–635.

CHAPMAN, Kimberly, "Separation of Powers and Unilateral Executive Action: The Constitutionality of President Clinton's Mexican Loan Initiative" (1996) 26 *G.A. J. Int'l Comp. L.* 163–185.

CHARNOVITZ, Steve, The Future of Fast Track in U.S. Trade Policy, 14(15) *BNA Int'l Trade Rep.* 655 (April 9, 1997).

CHICK, Martin, *Governments, Industries and Markets: Aspects of Government-Industry Relations in the U.K., Japan, West Germany and the U.S.A. Since 1945* (Aldershot, Edward Elgar 1990).

CHO, Sung-Joon, "GATT Non-Violation Issues in the WTO Framework: Are they the Achilles' Heel of the Dispute Settlement Process" (1998) 39(2) *Harvard Int'l L. J.* 311–355.

CHRYSSONCHOU, Dimitris N., "New Challenges to the Study of European Integration: Implications for Theory Building" (1997) 35(4) *J.C.M.S.* 521–542.

CHUA, Adrian T. L., "Reasonable Expectation and Non-Violation Complaints in GATT/WTO Jurisprudence" (1998) 32(2) *J. World Trade* 27–50.

CHUBB, John E. and PETERSON, Paul, E., *Can the Government Govern?* (Washington, The Brookings Institution, 1989).

CLINE, William, *Trade Policy in the 1980* (Washington, Institute for International Economics, 1983).

CINI, Michelle, *The European Commission: Leadership, Organisation and Culture in the E.U. Administration* (Manchester, Manchester University Press, 1996).

CODEVILLA, "Discouraging the Practice of What we Preach: Saarstahl I, Inland Steel and the Implementation of the Uruguay Round of GATT 1994" (1995) 3 *Geo. Mason Independent L. Rev.* 435–472.

COFFIELD, Shirley A., "Using Section 301 of the Trade Act as a Response to Foreign Government Trade Actions: When, Why and How" (1981) 6 *N. C. J. Int'l L. & Comm. Reg.* 381–405.

—— "Section 301 of the Trade Act of 1974: New Life in the Old Dog" (1986) 33 (6) *Fed. Bar News. J.* 248–251.

COHEN, Benjamin J., "The Political Economy of International Trade" (1990) 44 *Int'l Org*. 261–28.

COHEN, Stephen D., *The Making of United States International Economic Policy* (New York, Praeger Publishers, 1977).

COLLINS-WILLIAMS, Terry and SALEMBIER, Gerry, "International Disciplines on Subsidies" (1996) 30(1) *J. World Trade* 5–17.

COLLINSON, Sarah, "Issues Systems, Multi-Level Games and the Analysis of the EU's External Commercial and Associated Policies: A Research Agenda" (1999) *J. European Public Policy* 206–224.

COMMISSION OF THE EUROPEAN COMMUNITIES, Directorate General for Economic and Financial Affairs, *European Economy 48: Fair Competition in the Internal Market: Community State Aid and Policy* (Luxembourg, Office of the Official Publications of the EC, 1991).

—— *Third Survey on State aids in the European Community in the Manufacturing and Certain other Sectors* (Luxembourg, Office for the Official Publications, 1992).

COMMITTEE ON WAYS AND MEANS, U.S. House of Representatives, *Overview and Compilation of U.S. Trade Statutes, 1997 Edition, 105th Congress 1st Session* (Washington, U.S. Government Printing Office, 1997).

COOMBES, David, *Politics and Bureaucracy in the European Community: A Potrait of the Commission of the EEC* (London, Allen & Unwin, 1970).

COTTIER, Thomas, "Dispute Settlement in the World Trade Organization: Characteristics and Structural Implications for the European Union" (1998) 35 *C.M.L. Rev*. 325–378.

COUNCIL OF COMPETITIVENESS, *Road Map for Results: Trade Policy, Technology and American Competitiveness* (Washington, Council of Competitiveness 1993).

COWHEY, Peter F., "Domestic Institutions and the Credibility of International Commitments: Japan and the United States" (1993) 47 *Int'l Org*. 299–327.

COX, Andrew (ed.), *Politics, Policy and the European Recession* (London, The Macmillan Press, 1982).

—— *The State, Finance and Industry* (Brighton, Wheatsheaf, 1986).

CRAIG, Paul and DE BURCA, Grainne (eds.), *The Evolution of E.U. Law* (Oxford, Oxford University Press, 1999).

CRAIG Paul and HARLOW, Carol, *Lawmaking in the European Union* (The Hague, Kluwer Law, 1998).

CRAM, Laura, "The European Commission as a Multi-Organisation: Social Policy and IT Policy in the European Union" (1994) 1 *J. European Public Pol'y* 195–217.

CROCCIONI, Pietro, "The GATT Rules on Industrial Subsidies" (1994) 47 *Austrian J. Pub. Int'l L*. 49–80.

CROUCH, Colin and STREECK, Wolfgang (eds.), *Political Economy of Modern Capitalism: Mapping Convergence and Diversity* (London, Sage Publications, 1997).

CROUCH, Colin, *Industrial Relations and European State Tradition* (Oxford, Clarendon Press, 1993).

CUNNINGHAM, Richard O., *Countervailing Capital Subsidies: Commerce's Methodologies Approach: A Fundamental Breakdown* (The Georgetown University Law Center's Annual International Trade Update, Washington D.C., June 24, 1994).

DALEY, Anthony (ed.), *The Miterrand Era: Policy Alternatives and Political Mobilization in France* (New York, New York University Press 1996).

DASHWOOD, Alan, "The Limits of European Community Powers" (1996) 21 *European L. Rev.* 113–128.

—— "External Relations Provisions of the Amsterdam Treaty" (1998) 35 *C.M.L. Rev.* 1019–1045.

DAVIS, F., "The Regulation and Control of Foreign Trade" (1966) 66 *Columbia L. Rev.* 1428.

DEEG, Richard, *Finance Capitalism Unveiled: Banks and the German Political Economy* (Ann Arbor, The University of Michigan Press, 1999).

—— *German Banks and Industrial Finance in the 1990s* (Wissenschaftszentrum Berlin Fur Sozialforschung WP 96–323, 1996).

DEERING, Christopher J. and SMITH, Steven S., *Committees in Congress* (Washington, Congressional Quarterly Press, 3rd 1997).

DEMARET, P. (ed.), *Relations Exteriueres de la Communaute Europeenne et Marche Interieur: Aspects Juridiques et Fonctionnels* (Gent, Storia Scientia, 1986).

DENENBERG, R.V., *Understanding American Politics* (London, Fontana Press, 1996).

DESTLER, I. M., *American Trade Politics* (Washington, Institute for International Economics, 1992)

—— *Renewing Fast Track Legislation* (Washington, Institute for International Economics, 1997).

DEVUYST, Youri, "The E.C.'s Common Commercial Policy and the Treaty of the European Union: An Overview of the Negotiations" (1992) 16 *World Trade Competition* 67–80.

—— "The European Community and the Conclusion of the Uruguay Round", in Carolyn Rhodes and Sonia Mazey (eds.), *The State of the European Union: Building a European Polity?* (Boulder, Lynne Rienner, 1995), 449–467.

DIAMOND Richard, "Economic Foundations of Countervailing Duty Law" (1989) 29 *Virginia J. Int'l L..* 767.

—— "A Search for Economic and Financial Principles in the Administration of U.S. Countervailing Duty Law" (1990) 21 *L. & Pol'y Int'l Bus.* 514.

—— "Changes in the Game: Understanding the Relationship Between Section 301 and U.S. Trade Strategies" (1990) 8 (2) *B. U. Int'l L. J.* 351–361.

DIDIER, Pierre, "EEC Antidumping: The Level of Trade Issue After the Definitive CD Player Regulation; Japanese Proposal to GATT on the Level of Trade Issue" (1990) 24(2) *J. World Trade* 103–109.

DOANE, Michael L., "Green Light Subsidies: Technology Policy in International Trade" (1995) 21 *Syracuse J. Int'l L. & Com.* 155–179 (1995).

DOBSON, John, *Two Centuries of Tariffs: The Background and Emergence of the U.S. International Trade Commission* (Washington, US ITC,1976).

DOREMUS, Paul, KELLER, William, PAULY, Louis and REICH, Simon, *The Myth of the Global Corporation* (Princeton, Princeton UP, 1998).

DYE, Thomas R., *American Federalism: Competition Among Governments* (Lexington, Lexington Books, 1990).

DYSON, Kenneth, *The State Tradition in Western Europe* (Oxford, Martin Robertson, 1980).

—— "Cultural Issues and the European Single Market: Barriers to Trade and Shifting Attitudes" (1993) 64 *Political Quarterly* 84–98.

DYSON, Kenneth and WILKS Stephen (eds.), *Industrial Crisis: A Comparative Study of State and Industry* (Oxford, Martin Robertson, 1983).

ECKES, Alfred E., *Opening America's Market* (Chapel Hill, The University of North California Press, 1995).

EDWARDS, Geoffrey and SPENCE, David (eds.), *The European Commission* (Harlow, Longman, 1994).

EDWARDS, Jeremy and FISHER, Klaus, *Banks, Finance and Investment in Germany* (Cambridge, Cambridge University Press, 1994).

EHR, T., "Allocation of Coutervailable Benefits over Time", in *The Commerce Department Speaks, 1990* (New York, Practising Law Institute, 1990).

EICHMANN, Erwin P. and HORLICK, Gary N., "Political Questions in International Trade: Judicial Review of Section 301" (1988) 10 *Michigan J. Int'l L.* 735.

ELHERMANN, Claus D., "Mixed Agreements: A List of Problems", in O'Keeffe and Schermers (eds.), *Mixed Agreements* (Deventer, Kluwer Law and Taxation, 1983).

—— "The Scope of Article 113 of the EEC Treaty", in *Etudes de Droit Communautes Europeennes: Melanges Offerts a Pierre Henry Teitgen* (Paris, Pedone, 1984).

EMILIOU, Nicholas and O'KEEFFE, David, *The European Union and World Trade Law after the Uruguay Round* (Chichester, John Wiley & Sons, 1996).

ENGERING, DE BRABANDER and VERMULST, "EC Antidumping Policy in a Globalized World: A Dutch Perspective" (1998) 32(6) *J. World Trade* 115–126.

EUROPEAN PARLIAMENT SESSION DOCUMENT, *Second Report of the Committee on External Economic Relations* (18 January 1994).

THE EUROPEAN PARLIAMENT, Directorate General for Research, *Working Paper: The World Trade Organisation and the European Community* (Luxembourg, The European Parliament, 1995).

THE EUROPEAN POLICY CENTRE, *Challenge Europe: Making Sense of the Amsterdam Treaty* (Brussels, The European Policy Centre, 1998).

EVERLING, Ulrich, "Possibilities and Limits of European Integration" (1980) 18 *J.C.M.S.* 217–228.

EVANS, Peter B., JACOBSON, Harold K. and PUTMAN Robert D. (eds.), *Double Edge Diplomacy: International Bargaining and Domestic Politics* (Berkeley, University of California Press, 1993).

EVANS, Andrew and MARTIN, Stephen, "Socially Acceptable Distortion of Competition: Community Policy on State Aids" (1991) 16 *European L. Rev.* 79–111.

FALLOWS, James, *More Like Us: Making America Great Again* (Boston, Houghton Mifflin Company, 1989).

—— *Looking at the Sun: The Rise of the New East Asian Economic and Political System* (New York, Pantheon Books, 1994).

FARBER, Henry and KRUEGER, Alan B, *Union Membership in the United States: The Decline Continues* (Washington, National Bureau of Economic Research, Working Paper No 4216, 1992).

FARBER, Henry, "The Decline of Unionization in the United States: What Can Be Learned from Recent Experience?" (1990) 8(1) *J. Labour Economics* S75–S105.

FELLER, Peter Buck and WILSON, Ann Carlise, "United States Tariff and Trade Law: Constitutional Sources and Constraints" (1976) *L.& Pol'y Int'l Bus.* 105–123.

FINGER, J. Michael and NOGUES, Julio, "International Control of Subsidies and Countervailing Duties" (1987) 1 *World Bank Economic Rev.* 707–725.

FINGER, J. Michael, *The Uruguay Round: A Handbook for Multilateral Trade Negotiations* (Washington, World Bank, 1988).

FINGER, J. Michael, "The Meaning of Unfair in United States Import Policy" (1992) 1 *Minn. J. Global Trade* 35–56.

FINLAYSON, John A. and ZACHER, Mark W., "The GATT and the Regulation of Trade Barriers: Regime Dynamics and Functions" (1981) 35 *Int'l Org*. 561.

FISHER, Bart S. and STEINHARDT, Ralph G., "Section 301 of the Trade Act of 1974: Protection for U.S. Exports of Goods, Services and Capital" (1982) 14 *L. & Pol'y Int'l Bus*. 569–690.

FLIGSTEIN, Neil and MARA-DRITA, Iona, "How to Make a Market: Reflections on the Attempt to Create a Single Market in the European Union" (1996) 102 (1) *Am. J. Sociology* 1–33.

FLIGSTEIN, Neil and FREELAND, Robert, "Theoretical and Comparative Perspectives on Corporate Organization" (1995) 21 *Annual Rev. Sociology* 21–43.

FLORY, Thiebaut and MARTIN, Frederic-Paul, "Remarques A Propos des Avis 1/94 et 2/92 de la Cour de Justice des Communautes Europeennes au Regard de L'Evolution de la Notion de Politique Commerciale Commune" (1996) 32 (3–4) *C. D. E*. 379–400.

FRANCOIS, Joseph F., "Countervailing the Effects of Subsidies: An Economic Analysis" (1992) 16 *J. World Trade*. 5–13.

FRANKS Julian and MAYER, Colin, "Capital Markets and Corporate Control: A Study of France, Germany and the UK" (1990) 10 *Economic Pol'y* 189–223.

FREYMAN, Jeffrey B., "Industrial Policy: Patterns of Convergence and Divergence", in Jerold L. Waltman and Donley T. Studlar (eds.), *Political Economy: Public Policies in the United States and Britain* (Jackson, University Press of Mississippi, 1987), 44–68.

GAGNE, Gilbert, "The Canadian-US Softwood Lumber Dispute: An Assessment after 15 Years" (1999) 33(1) *J. World Trade* 67–86.

GENERAL ACCOUNTING OFFICE, *Report to the Secretary of Commerce and the United States Trade Representative, Benefits of International Agreement on Trade-Distorting Subsidies not Yet Realized* (Washington, GAO/NSIAD-83–10, August 15, 1983).

GARDNER, Richard, *Sterling-Dollar Diplomacy in Current Perspective* (New York, Columbia University Press, 1980).

GARTEN, Jeffrey E., "American Trade Law in a Changing World Economy" (1995) 29(1) *Int'l Lawyer* 15–41.

GESAU, Frans A. M. Alting Von, "The External Representation of Plural Interests" (1967) 5 *J.C.M.S*. 426–453.

GILDSFORD, Peter, "Portee et Delimitations des Competences Communautaires en Materie de Politique Commerciale" (1989) 328 *Revue du Marche Comun* 196.

GILL, Stephen R., "Neo-Liberalism and the Shift Towards a US Centered Transnational Hegemony", in Henk Overbeek (ed.), *Restructuring Hegemony in the Global Political Economy: The Rise of Transnational Neo-Liberalism in the 1980s* (London, Routledge, 1993).

GLENON, Michael J., *Constitutional Diplomacy* (Princeton, Princeton University Press, 1990).

GOETZ, Charles, GRANET, Lloyd and SCHAWRTZ, Warren, *The Meaning of Subsidy and Injury in the Countervailing Duty Law* (1986) *Int'l Rev. L. & Economics*. 17–32.

GOLDMAN, Patti, "The Democratisation of the Development of United States Trade Policy" (1994) 27 *Cornell Int'l L. J*. 631–697.

GOLDSTEIN, Judith and KEOHANE, Robert O. (eds.), *Ideas and Foreign Policy: Beliefs, Institutions and Political Change* (Ithaca, Cornell University Press, 1993).

GOLDSTEIN, Judith, "Ideas, Institutions and America's Trade Policy" (1988) 42 *Int'l Org.* 179–198.

—— *Ideas, Interests and American Trade Policy* (Ithaca, Cornell University Press, 1993).

GORLIN, Jacques J., "Foreign Trade and the Constitution", in Robert A. Goldwin and Robert A. Licht (eds.), *Foreign Policy and the Constitution* (Washington, The AEI Press, 1990), 54–71.

GRAHL, John and TEAGUE, Paul, "The Cost of Neo-Liberal Europe" (1989) 174 *New Left Rev.* 33–50.

GRASSTEK, Craig Van, "Is the Fast Track Really Necessary?" (1997) 31(2) *J. World Trade* 97–119.

GREENWALD, John, "Protectionism and U.S. Economic Policy" (1987) 23 *Stanford J. Int'l L.* 233–261.

GRIER, Jean H., "The Use of Section 301 to Open Japanese Markets to Foreign Firms" (1992) 17 *N.C. J. Int'l Commerce &Reg.* 1–44.

THE GROUP OF LISBON, *Limits to Competition* (Cambridge, MIT Press 1995).

GRUNWALD, Joseph and FLAMM Kenneth, *The Global Factory: Foreign Assembly in International Trade* (Washington, The Brookings Institution, 1985).

HAGELSTAM, Jarl, "Mercantilism Still Influences Practical Trade Policy at the End of the Twentieth Century" (1991) 25 (1) *J. World Trade* 95–105.

HALEY, John O., "Luck, Law, Culture and Trade: The Intractability of United States-Japan Trade Conflict" (1989) 22 *Cornell Int'l L. J.* 403–423.

HALL, Peter A., *Governing the Economy: The Politics of State Intervention in Britain and France* (London, Polity Press, 1986).

HALL, HAYWARD and MACHIN (eds.), *Developments in French Politics* (London, MacMillan 1990).

HALL, J. (ed.), States in History (Oxford, Basil Blackwell 1986).

HAMILTON, Alexander, "Report on manufactures: Communicated to the House of Representatives on December 5, 1791", in Henry Cabot Lodge (ed.), *The Works of Alexander Hamilton. Volume IV* (New York, Haskell House Publishers Ltd 1971).

HANCHER, Leigh and MORAN, Michael (ed.), *Capitalism,Culture and Economic Regulation* (Oxford, Clarendon, 1989).

HANCKE, Bob, *Modernisation Without Flexible Specialisation: How Large Firms Restructuring and Government Regional Policies Became the Step Parents of Autartic Regional Production Systems in France* (Wissenschaftszentrum Berlin Fur Sozialforschung Working Paper 97–304, 1997).

HANSEN, Wendy L. and PARK, Kee Ok, "Nation-State and Pluralistic Decision Making in Trade Policy: The Case of the International Trade Administration" (1995) 39 *Int'l Studies Quarterly* 181–211.

HANSEN, Patricia I, "Defining Unreasonableness in International Trade: Section 301 of the Trade Act of 1974" (1987) 96 *Yale L. J.* 1122–1146.

HANSEN, Susan B., "Industrial Policy and Corporativism in the American States" (1989) 2(2) *Governance* 172–197.

HANSON, Brian T., "What Happened to Fortress Europe? External Trade Policy Liberalization in the European Union" (1998) 52 (1) *Int'l Org.* 55–85.

HART, Jeffrey A., *Rival Capitalists: International Competitiveness in the United States, Japan and Western Europe* (Ithaca, Cornell University Press, 1992).

HART, John, *The Presidential Branch: From Washington to Clinton* (Chatham, Chatham House Publishers, 2nd 1995).

HARTZ, Louis, *The Liberal Tradition in America* (New York, Harcourt, Brace & World, 1955).
HAYES, J. P., *Making Trade Policy in the European Community* (New York, St. Martin Press, 1993).
HAYES-RENSHAW, LEQUESNE and MAYOR LOPEZ, "The Permanent Representation of the Member States of the European Communities," (1989) 28 *J.C.M.S.* 119–137.
HAYWARD, Jack, *The State and the Market Economy: Industrial Patriotism and Economic Intervention in France* (Brighton, Wheatsheaf Books, 1986).
HENKIN, Louis, *Foreign Affairs and the Constitution* (New York, Norton, 1975).
—— "The Constitution and United States Sovereignty: A Century of Chinese Exclusion and its Progeny" (1987) 100 *Harvard L. Rev.* 853–886.
—— "Foreign Affairs and the Constitution" (1987/88) 66(2) *Foreign Affairs* 284–309.
—— *Constitutionalism, Democracy and Foreign Affairs* (New York, Columbia University Press, 1990).
HENRY, John B, "The Legislative Veto: In Search of Constitutional Limits" (1979) 16(3) *Harvard J. Legislation* 735–762.
HILF, Meinhard and PETERSMANN Ernst-Ulrich (eds.), *National Constitutions and International Economic Law* (Deventer, Kluwer Law and Taxation, 1983).
HILF, Meinhard, "The E.C.J.'s Opinon on the WTO—No Surprise but Wise?" (1995) 6 *European J. Int'l L.* 245–259.
—— "Unwritten EC Authority in Foreign Trade Law" (1997) *E.F.A. Rev.* 437–454.
HINDLEY, Brian, "Dumping and the Far East Trade of the European Community" (1988) 11 *World Economy* 445–464.
HIRSHMAN, Albert O., *Rival Views of Market Society and Other Recent Essays* (New York, Viking, 1986).
HIRST, Paul, "The Global Economy—Myths and Realities" (1997) 73(3) *Int'l Affairs* 409–425.
HIX, Simon, "The Study of the European Community: The Challenge of Comparative Politics" (1994) 17 *West European Politics* 1–30.
HODGES, Michael and WOOLCOCK, Stephen, "Atlantic Capitalism versus Rhine Capitalism in the European Community" (1993) 16 *West European Politics* 329–344.
HODGSON, Geoffrey, "The Evolution of Socioeconomic Order in the Move to a Market Economy" (1994) 1(3) *Rev. Int'l Pol'y & Economy* 387–404.
HOEKAM, Bernard M. and MAVROIDIS, Petros C., "Dumping, Anti-Dumping and Antitrust" (1996) 30(1) *J. World Trade* 27–52.
HOFHANSEL, Claus, "The Harmonisation of Export Control Policies" (1999) 32 (2) *Comparative Political Studies* 229–256.
HOLLINGSWORTH, J. Rogers and BOYER, Robert (eds.), *Contemporary Capitalism: The Embeddedness of Institutions* (Cambridge, Cambridge University Press, 1997).
HOLLINGSWORTH, SCHMITTER and STREECK (eds.), *Governing Capitalist Economies: Performance & Control of Economic Sectors* (Oxford, Oxford University Press 1994).
HOLMER, Alan F. and BELLO, Judith H., "U.S. Trade and Policy Series No 20: The Fast Track Debate: A Prescription for Pragmatism" (1992) 26 *Int'l Lawyer* 183–194.
HOLMER, HAGGERTY and HUNTER (eds.), "Identifying and Measuring Subsidies", in *The Commerce Department Speaks on Import and Export Administration 1984* (New York, Practising Law Institute, 1984).

HOLMES, Peter and KEPTON, Jeremy, "EU Anti-Dumping Policy: A Regulatory Perspective" (1996) 3(4) *J. European Pub. Pol'y* 647–664.

HOWELL, BARLET and GADBOW (eds.), *Conflict Among Nation: Trade Policies in the 1990s* (Boulder, Westview Press, 1992).

HORLICK, Gary N., "Subsidies and Suspension Agreements in Countervailing Duty Cases", in *Commerce Department Speaks on Dumping and Countervailing Duties* (New York, Practising Law Institute, 1982), 33–53.

—— WTO Dispute Settlement and the Dole Commission, 29(6) (1995) *J. WORLD TRADE* 45–48.

HORLICK, QUICK and VERMULST, "Government Actions Against Domestic Subsidies, an Analysis of the International Rules and an Introduction to U.S. Practice" (1986) (1) *L.I.E.I.* 1–56.

US HOUSE OF REPRESENTATIVES, *Hearings before the Subcommittee on Technology, Environment and Aviation of the Committee on Space and Technology of the United States House of Representatives, The GATT Subsidies Code and its Impact on R&D* 103rd Cong. 2nd Session (1994).

HOUSMAN, Robert F., "Democratizing International Trade Decision-Making" (1994) 27 *Cornell Int'l L. J.* 699.

HOWELL, Thomas R., "Trade Protection: Rethinking the American Perspective" (1992) 25 *N.Y. U. J. Int'l L. & Pol'y* 251–262.

HOWSE, Robert and TREBILOCK, Michael, "The Fair Trade-Free Trade Debate: Trade, Labor and the Environment," (1996) 16 *Int'l Rev. L. & Economics* 61–79.

HUDEC, Robert E., "Circumventing Democracy: The Political Morality of Trade Negotiations" (1992) 25 *N.Y. J. Int'l L. & Pol'y* 311–322.

—— "International Economic Law: The Political Theatre Dimension" (1996) 17(1) *U. PA: J. Int'l Economic L.* 9–15.

HUFBAUER, Gary Clyde, and ERB, Shelton, *Subsidies in International Trade* (Cambridge, MIT Press, 1984).

HUNTER William and KUHBACH Susan H., "Subsidies and CVD: Highlights Since 1984", in *The Commerce Department Speaks 1987* (New York, Practising Law Institute, 1987).

HYMER, Stephen, "The Internationalisation of Capital" (1972) 6 *J. Economic Issues* 91–11.

JACKSON, John H., "The General Agreement on Tariffs and Trade in United States Law" (1967) 66 *Michigan L. Rev.* 250.

—— *World Trade and the Law of the GATT* (Indianapolis, Bobbs Merrill, 1969).

—— "The Jurisprudence of International Trade: The DISC Case in GATT" (1978) 72 *Am. J. Int'l L.* 747–78.

—— "The Crumbling Institutions of the Liberal Trading System" (1978) 12 (2) *J. World Trade* 93.

—— "United States-EEC Trade Relations: Constitutional Problems of Economic Interdependence" (1979) 16 *C.M.L. Rev.* 453.

—— "Perspectives on the Jurisprudence of International Trade: Costs and Benefits of Legal Procedures in the United States" (1984) 82 *Michigan L. Rev.* 1570–1587.

—— *The World Trading System: Law and Policy of International Economic Relations* (Cambridge, The MIT Press 1989).

—— *Restructuring the GATT System* (Chatham, Chatham House Papers, 1990).

JACKSON, John H., "Status of Treaties in Domestic Legal Systems: A Policy Analysis" (1992) 86 *Am. J. Int'l L.* 310–340.
—— "Perspectives on Countervailing Duties" (1989) 21 *L. & Pol'y Int'l Bus.* 739–761.
—— "The General Agreement on Tariffs and Trade in United States Law" (1967) 66 *Michigan L. Rev.* 250.
—— "The Uruguay Round Results and National Sovereignty", in Jagdish Bhagwati and Mathias Hirsch (eds.), *The Uruguay Round and Beyond: Essays in Honour of Arthur Dunkel* (Berlin, Springer, 1998).
JACKSON, John H. and VERMULST Edwin (eds.), *Antidumping Law and Practice: A Comparative Study* (New York, Harvester Wheatsheaf, 1990).
JACKSON, John H., LOUIS, J. V. and MATSUSHITA, Matsuo, *Implementing the Tokyo Round: National Constitutions and International Economic Rules* (Ann Arbor, The University of Michigan Press, 1984).
JACKSON, J. H. and SYKES, Alan O. (eds.), *Implementing the Uruguay Round* (Oxford, Clarendon Press, 1997).
JAMERSON, Paul, "The Administration Of U.S. Countervailing Duty Laws with Regard to Domestic Subsidies: Where it's Been, Where it Stands and Where it May Go" (1985) 12 *Syracuse J. Int'l L. Comm.* 549–124 .
JONES, Charles O., *The Presidency in a Separated System* (Washington, The Brookings Institution, 1994).
JONES, Carol A. G., "Capitalism, Globalization and Rule of Law: An Alternative Trajectory of Legal Change in China" (1994) 3 *Social & Legal Studies* 195–221.
JOERGES, Christian and NEYER, Jurgen, "From Intergovernmental Bargaining to Deliberative Political Process: The Constitutionalisation of Commitology" (1997) 3(3) *European L. J.* 273–299.
KARNS, Margaret P. and MINGST, Karen A. (eds.), *The United States and Multilateral Institutions* (Boston, Unwin Hyman, 1990).
KATZENSTEIN, Peter J. (ed.), *Between Power and Plenty: Foreign Economic Policies of Advanced Industrial States* (Madison, The University of Wisconsin Press, 1978).
KATZENSTEIN, Peter J., *Small States in World Markets: Industrial Policy in Europe* (Ithaca, Cornell University Press, 1985).
KATZENSTEIN, Peter (ed.), *Industrial Politics in West Germany: Towards the Third Regime* (Ithaca, Cornell University Press, 1989).
KEOHANE, Robert O. and NYE, Joseph S., *Power and Interdependence* 4th ed. (Boston, Little Brown, 1977).
—— "The World Political Economy and the Crisis of Embedded Liberalism", in John H. Goldthorpe (ed.), *Order and Conflict in Contemporary Capitalism: Studies in the Political Economy of Western European Nations* (Oxford, Clarendon Press 1984).
—— "Reciprocity in International Relations" (1986) 40(1) *Int'l Org.* 1–27.
KEOHANE, Robert O. and MILNER Helen (eds.), *Internationalization and Domestic Politics* (Cambridge, Cambridge University Press 1996).
KITCHELT, LANGE, MARKS and STEPHENS (eds.), *Continuity and Change in Contemporary Capitalism* (Cambridge, Cambridge University Press, 1999).
KLEINFELD, George and KAYE, David, "Red Light, Green Light?: The 1994 Agreement on Subsidies and Countervailing Measures, Research and Development Assistance, and U.S. Policy" (1994) 28 (6) *J. World Trade* 43–63.
KOH, Harold Hongju, "Congressional Controls on Presidential Trade Policymaking after I.N.S. v. Chadha" (1986) 18 *N.Y. U. J. Int'l L. & Pol'y* 1191–1233.

—— "The Legal Markets of International Trade: A Perspective on the Proposed United States-Canada Free Trade Agreement" (1987) 12(2) *Yale J. Int'l L.* 193–249.

—— "Why the President (Almost) Always Wins in Foreign Affairs: Lessons of the Iran-Contra Affair" (1988) 97(7) *Yale L. J.* 1255–1342.

—— "The Fast Track and United States Trade Policy" (1992) 18 (1) *Brooklyn J. Int'l L.* 143–180.

KOMURO, Norio, "EC Antidumping Measures Vis-A-Vis Japan", in *The European Union in a Changing World* (Brussels, Third ECSA-WORLD Conference, 19–20 September 1996).

—— "Kodak-Fuiji Film Dispute and the WTO Panel Ruling" (1998) 32(5) *J. World Trade* 161–217.

KONSTADINIDIS, Stratos V. (ed.), *The Legal Regulation of the European Community's External Relations After the Completion of the Internal Market* (Aldershot, Dartmouth 1996).

KOSKENNIEMI, M. (ed.), *International Law Aspects of the European Union* (Deventer, Kluwer Law and Taxation, 1998).

KRAUS, Ellis S. and REICH Simon, "Ideology, Interests and the American Executive: Towards a Theory of Foreign Competition and Manufacturing Trade Policy" (1994) 46(4) *Int'l Org.* 857–897.

KRUEGER, Anne O. (ed.), *The Political Economy of Trade Protection* (Chicago, The University of Chicago Press, 1996).

KUILWIJK, Kees Jan, *The European Court of Justice and the GATT Dilemma: Public Interest versus Individual Rights?* (Beuningen, Nexed Editions, 1996).

KUYPJER, Pieter Jan, "The EC's Common Commercial Policy: Which Way the Swing of the Pendulum?", in *The Future of the President's Authority to Negotiate International Trade Agreements after NAFTA and the Uruguay Round: What Should Congress Delegate?, Proceedings of the 88th Annual Meeting of the American Society of International Law*, Washington, April 6–9, 1994.

KUYPJER, Pieter J., "The Conclusion of the Uruguay Round Results by the European Community" (1995) 6 *European J. Int'l L.* 222–244.

KUYPJER, Pieter Jan, "The New WTO Dispute Settlement System: The Impact on the European Community" (1995) 29 (6) *J. World Trade* 49–71.

LABBE, Dominique, "Trade Unionism in France Since the Second World War" (1994) 17 *West European Politics* 146–168.

LANKOVSKI, Carl F. (ed.), *Germany and the European Community: Beyond Hegemony and Containment?* (New York, St. Martin Press 1993).

LAY, William, "Redefining Actionable Subsidies under U.S. Countervailing Duty Law" (1991) 91(6) *Columbia L. Rev.* 1495–1518.

LEHRER, Mark, *The German Model of Industrial Strategy in Turbulence: Corporate Governance and Managerial Strategies in Lufthansa* (Wissenschaftszentrum Berlin Fur Sozialforschung Working Paper 96–307, 1996).

LEIVO, Kirsi, *The Need for an Exclusive External Competence of the European Community with Regard to International Trade in Services* (College of Europe Working Papers No 17, European Interuniversity Press, 1997).

LEW, Ginger, *The Commerce Department Speaks on International Trade and Investment 1994* (New York, Practising Law Institute, 1994).

LINEARLY, John, "International Trade Relations and the Separation of Powers Under the United States Constitution" (1995) *Dick. J. Int'l L.* 203–239.

LIPSET, Seymour Martin, *American Exceptionalism: A Double-Edge Sword* (New York, Norton, 1996).

LOHMANN, Susanne and O'HALLORAN Sharyn, "Divided Government and U.S. Trade Policy: Theory and Evidence" (1994) 58(4) *Int'l Org.* 595–632.

LOOMIS, Burdett, *The Contemporary Congress* (New York, St. Martin Press, 1996).

LOW, Patrick, *Trading Free: The GATT and the U.S. Trade Policy* (Washington, Twentieth Century Fund, 1993).

LOWENFILED, Andreas, "Remedies Along Rights: Institutional Reform in the New GATT" (1994) 88 *Am. J. Int'l L.* 477–488.

LUTZ, Susanne, "The Revival of the Nation State? Stock Exchange Regulation in an Era of Globalised Financial Markets" (1999) 5(1) *J. European Public Policy* 153–168.

MACLEAN, Robert M. and ECCLES, Richard J., "A Change of Style Not of Substance: The Community's New Approach Towards the Community Interest Test in Anti-Dumping and Anti-Subsidy Law" (1999) 36 *C.M.L. Rev. 123–148.*

MACPHERSON, Cranford Brough, *The Political Theory of Possessive Individualism: Hobbes to Locke* (Oxford, Oxford University Press, 1964).

MAHLER, Vincent A., "Domestic and International Sources of Trade Policy: The Case of Agriculture in the European Community and the United States" (1991) 24 *Polity* 27–47.

MALMROSE, M., "Interest Rate Benchmarks in Countervailing Proceedings", in *Commerce Department Speaks 1990* (New York, Practising Law Institute, 1990).

MARESCEAU, M. (ed.), *The European Community's Commercial Policy After 1992: The Legal Dimension* (Dordrecht, Martinus Nijhoff Publishers 1993).

MARKS, HOOGHE and BLANK, "European Integration from the 1980s: State-Centric v. Multi-Level Governance" (1996) 34(3) *J.C.M.S* .341–378.

MASON, Mark, "Elements of a Consensus: Europe's Response to the Japanese Automotive Challenge" (1994) 32 (4) *J.C.M.S.* 433–453.

MATSUMOTO, Ken and FILAYSON, Grant, "Dumping and Antidumping: Growing Problems in World Trade" (1990) 24 (4) *J. World Trade* 5–19.

MAUNU, Antti, "The Implied External Competence of the European Community after the ECJ Opinion 1/94—Towards Coherence or Diversity?" (1995/2) *L.I.E.I.* 115–127.

MCCLAFFERTY, Eric R., "Identifying Level of Trade in U.S. Antidumping Law" (1996) 36(4) *Virginia J. Int'l L.* 1021–1078.

MCDONOUGH, Patrick J., "Subsidies and Countervailing Measures" in Terence P. Stewart (ed.), *The GATT Uruguay Round: A Negotiating History (1986–1992)* (Deventer, Kluwer Law and Taxation, 1993).

MCDOUGAL, Myers S. and LANS, Asher, "Treaties and Congressional-Executive or Presidential Agreements: Interchangeable Instruments of National Policy I" (1945) 54(2) *Yale L. J.* 181–351.

MCKINLAY, Robert D. and LITTLE, Richard, *Global Problems and World Order* (London, Pinter, 1986).

MEGRET, WAELBROECK, LOUIS, *et al.*, *Le Droit Communaute Economique Europeenne Volume XII: External Relations* (Brussels, Editions de l'Universite de Bruxelles, 1981).

MESSERLIN, Patrick A., *The Uruguay Negotiations on Subsidies and Countervailing Measures: Past and Future Constraints, in Subsidies and Countervailing Measures: Critical Issues for the Uruguay Round* (Washington, World Bank Discussion Papers No 77, 1989).

MEUNIER, Sophie and NICOLAIDES, Kalypso, "Who Speaks for Europe? The Delegation of Trade Authority in the EU" (1999) 37(3) *J.C.M.S.* 477–501.

MILNER, Helen V., *Resisting Protectionism: Global Industries and the Politics of International Trade* (Princeton, Princeton University Press, 1988).

MINKLER, Majorie A., "The Omnibus Trade Act of 1988, Section 301: A Permissible Enforcement Mechanism or a Violation of the United States' Obligations Under International Law?" (1992) 11 *J. L. & Comm.* 283.

MIRANDA, TORRES and RUIZ, "The International Use of Antidumping—1987–1997" (1998) 32(5) *J. World Trade* 5–71.

MIYASHITA, Kenichi and RUSSELL, David, *Keiretsu: Inside the Hidden Japanese Conglomerates* (New York, McGraw-Hill, 1994).

MOBERG, David, "Union Busting, Past and Present: Charting an Old American Tradition" (1992) 39 *Dissent* 73–80.

MONAR, Joerg, *Western Europe's Dual System of Foreign Affairs: The EC and the EPC System and their Coherence After the Single European Act* (Florence, E.U.I. PhD Thesis, 1991).

MORAVSICK, Andrew, "Preferences and Power in the European Community: A Liberal Intergovernmentalist Approach", in Simon Bulmer and Andrew Scott (eds.), *Economic and Political Integration in Europe: Internal Dynamics and Global Context* (Oxford, Blackwell Publishers 1994), 29–80.

MOUGIN, Catherine Flaeasch, "Le Traite de Maastricht et les Competences Externes de la Communaute Europeenne: A la Recherche d'une Politique Externe de l'Union" (1993) *C.D.E.* 351–398.

MOYER, Homer E., "How Will the Uruguay Round Change the Practice of Trade Law in the United States? U.S. Institutions, Not the WTO, May Hold the Answer" (1996) 30(3) *J. World Trade* 63–85.

MULLER, KHAN and NEUMANN, *EC Anti-Dumping Law—A Commentary on Regulation 384/96* (New York, John Wiley & Sons, 1998).

MURPHY, Anna, *The European Community and the International Trading System: The European Community and the Uruguay Round* (Brussels, CEPS, 1990).

MYERSON, Toby, "Barriers to Trade in Japan: The Keiretsu System-Problems and Prospects" (1992) 24 *Int'l L. & Politics* 1107–1113.

MYRDAL, Gunnar, *The Political Element in the Development of Economic Theory* (London, Routledge & Kegan Paul, 2nd 1955).

NATIONAL ECONOMIC COUNCIL, *Future Visions for US Trade Policy* (Washington, The National Economic Council of Foreign Relations, 1998).

NAU, Henry R. (ed.), *Domestic Trade Politics and the Uruguay Round* (New York, Columbia University Press, 1988).

NEFRAMI, Eleftheria, "Quelques Reflexions Sur la Reforme de la Politique Commerciale par le Traite D'Amsterdam: Le Maintien du Statu Quo et l'Unite de la Representation Internationale de la Communaute" (1998) 34 (1–2) *C.D.E.* 137–159.

NEUWAHL, Nanette A., "Shared Powers or Combined Incompetence? More on Mixity" (1996) 33(4) *C.M.L. Rev.* 667.

NICOLAIDES, Phendon, "How Fair is Fair Trade?" (1987) 21 *J. World Trade.* 147–162.

NIVOLA, Pietro S., "Trade Policy: Referring the Playing Field", in Thomas E. Mann, *A Question of Balance: The President, the Congress and Foreign Policy* (Washington, The Brookings Institution 1990).

NOEL, Emile and ETIENNE, Henry, "The Permanent Representatives Committee and the Deepening of the Communities" (1971) 6 *Government & Opposition* 422–447.
NOEL, Emile, "Reflexions Sur le Processus de Decision dans le Counseil des Communautes Europeennes", in *Etudes de Droit des Communautes Europeennes: Melanges Offerts a Pierre Henry Teitgen* (Paris, Pedone, 1984).
NOLAND, Marcus, "Chasing Phantoms: The Political Economy of USTR" (1997) 51(3) *Int'l Org.* 365–387 (1997).
NORRAL, Christopher, "New Trends in Anti-Dumping Practice in Brussels" (1987) *World Economy* 97.
—— "Some Thoughts on the New Community Trade Barriers Regulation" (1995) 3 *Int'l Trade L. R.* 67.
O'HALLORAN, Sharyn, *Politics, Process and American Trade Policy* (Ann Arbor, The University of Michigan Press, 4th 1997).
O'NEAL TAYLOR, C., "Fast Track, Trade Policy and Free Trade Agreements: Why the NAFTA Turned into a Battle" (1994) 28 *Geo. Washington J. Int'l L. & Economy* 1–132.
O'REILLY, James T., "Stop the World, We Want Our Own Labels, Treaties, State Voter Initiative Laws and Federal Pre-Emption" (1997) 18(2) *U. PA. J. Int'l Economy L.* 617–653.
OSTRY, Sylvia, "Europe and the Evolution of the Multilateral Trading System" (1990) 22 *Case W. Re. J. Int'l L.* 311–329.
OYE, Kenneth, "Explaining Cooperation Under Anarchy" (1985) 38 *World Pol'y* 1–24.
PAEMEN, Hugo and BENSCH, Alexandra, *From the GATT to the WTO: The European Community in the Uruguay Round* (Leuven, Leuven University Press, 1995)
PALMETER, David, "Torquemada and the Tariff Act: The Inquisitor Rides Again" (1985) 20 (2) *Int'l Lawyer* 641–657.
—— "The Capture of Antidumping Law" (1989) 14 *Yale J. Int'l L.*182–198.
PANGRATIS, Angelos and VERMULST, Edwin, "Injury in Anti-Dumping Proceedings—The Need to Look Beyond the Uruguay Round Results" (1994) 28(5) *J. World Trade* 61–96.
PASTOR, Robert A., *Congress and the Politics of U.S. Foreign Economic Policy 1929–1976* (Berkeley, University of California Press, 1980)
PASTOR, Robert, "The Cry and Sigh Syndrome: Congress and Trade Policy", in Allen Schick (ed.), *Making Economic Policy in Congress* (Washington, AEI Studies, 1983)
PAULY, Louis W. and REICH, Simon, "National Structures and Multinational Corporate Behaviour: Enduring Differences in the Age of Globalization" (1997) 51(1) *Int'l Org.* 1–30.
PEARCE, Joan and SUTTON, John, *Protection and Industrial Policy in Europe* (London, Routledge, 1985).
PESCATORE, Pierre, "External Relations in the Case Law of the Court of Justice of the European Communities" (1979) 16 *C.M.L. Rev.* 615–645.
—— "Contribution to the Discussion", in C. Timmermans and Volker (eds.), *Division of Powers Between the European Communities and their Member States in the Field of External Relations* (Deventer, Kluwer, 1981).
—— "Drafting and Analyzing Decisions on Dispute Settlement", in P. PESCATORE, W. DAVEY and A. LOWENFELD, *Handbook of WTO/GATT Dispute Settlement* (New York, Oceana, 5th 1995).
—— "Opinion 1/94 on Conclusion of the WTO Agreement: Is there an Escape from a Programmed Disaster" (1999) 36 *C.M.L. Rev.* 387–405.

PETERSMANN, Ernst-Ulrich, Application of GATT by the Court of Justice of the European Communities, 20 *C.M.L. Rev.* 397–437 (1983).

—— "Violation-Complaints and Non-Violation Complaints in Public International Trade Law" (1991) 34 *G.Y.B. Int'l L.*175 (1991).

—— "International Competition Rules for Governments and for Private Business: The Case of Linking Future WTO Negotiations on Investment, Competition and Enviromental Rules to Reforms of Anti-Dumping Laws," (1996) 30(3) *J. World Trade* 5–35.

—— "The Transformation of the World Trading System through the 1994 Agreement Establishing the World Trade Organization" (1995) 6 *European J. Int'l L.* 161–221.

—— "The Moral Foundations of the European Union's Foreign Constitution: Defining 'European Identity' and 'Community Interests' for the Benefit of EU Citizens" (1996) 51 *Aussen Wirtschaft* 151–176.

PETERSMANN, Ernst-Ulrich and MEINHARD, Hilf (eds.), *The New GATT Round of Multilateral Trade Negotiations, Legal and Economic Problems* (Deventer, Kluwer Law and Taxation, 1991).

PETERSON, John, "Decision-making in the European Union: Towards a Framework of Analysis" (1995) 2 *J. European Public Pol'y* 69–93.

PHILLIPS, Steven R., "The New Section 301 of the Omnibus Trade and Competitiveness Act of 1988: Trade Wars or Open Markets?", (1989) 22 *Vanderbilt J. Transnat'l L.* 491–579.

PERRAU DE PINNICK, Fernando, "Les Competences Communautaires dans le Negociations sur Le Commerce des Services" (1991) 27 *C.D.E.* 390.

PITOFSKY, Robert, "Competition Policy in the Global Economy –Today and Tomorrow" (1994) *J. Int'l Economic L. 403–411.*

POLANYI, Karl, *The Great Transformation: The Political and Economic Origins of Our Time* (Boston, Beacon Press, 1957).

POSTER, Roger B., "The President, Congress and Trade Policy" (1988) 15(2) *Congress & the Presidency* 165–184.

POTLER, T., "Preferentiality under the Proposed Regulations" in *Commerce Department Speaks 1990* (New York, Practising Law Institute, 1990).

PRESTON, Lee E. and WINDSOR, Duane, *The Rules of the Game in the Global Economy: Policy Regimes for International Business* (Amsterdam, Kluwer, 1992).

PRICE, Victoria Curzon, "The Threat of 'Fortress Europe' from the Development of Social and Industrial Policies at the European Level" (1991) 46 *Aussenwirtschaft* 119–138.

PROSSER, Tony, "The State, Constitutions and Implementing Economic Policy: Privatization and the U.K., France and the U.S.A" (1995) 4 *Social & Legal Studies* 507–516.

PUCKETT, A. Lynne and REYNOLDS, William L., "Rules, Sanctions and Enforcement under Section 301: At Odds with the WTO?" (1996) 90 *Am. J. Int'l L.* 675–689.

REGINI, Marino, *The Future of Labour Movements* (London, Sage, 1992).

REINICKE, Wolfgang H., *Banking, Politics and Global Finance: American Commercial Banks and Regulatory Change 1980–1990* (Aldershot, Elgar, 1995).

RENSHAW, Fiona Hayes and WALLACE, Helen, *The Council of Ministers* (London, MacMillan Press, 1997).

RESTANI, Jane A., "Judicial Review in International Trade: Its Role in the Balance Between Delegation by Congress and Limitation of Executive Discretion" (1988) 37 *Am. U. L. Rev.* 1075–1086.

RHODES, Martin and APELDOORN, Bastian van, *Capital Unbound? The Transformation of European Corporate Governance* (1998) 5(3) *J. European Public Pol'y* 406–427.

RICARDO, David, *The Principles of Political Economy and Taxation* (London, Dent & Sons, 1973).

RISSE-KAPPEN, Thomas, "Exploring the Nature of the Beast: International Relations Theory and Comparative Policy Analysis Meet the European Union" (1996) 34(1) *J.C.M.S.* 53–80.

RITCHIE, Mark, "Democratizing the Trade Policy-Making Process: The Lessons of NAFTA and Their Implications for the GATT" (1994) 27 *Cornell Int'l L. J.* 749–754.

RIVERS, Richard and GREENWALD, John, "The Negotiation of a Code on Subsidies and Countervailing Measures: Bridging Fundamental Policy Differences" (1979) 11 *L. & Pol'y Int'l Bus.* 1447–1495.

ROBE, Jean Philippe, *Countervailing Duties, State Protectionism and the Challenge of the Uruguay Round* (European University Institute Working Paper No 372, 1989).

RODRIK, Dani, *Has Globalization Gone Too Far?* (Washington, Institute for International Economics, 1997).

ROESSLER, Frieder, "Should Principles of Competition Policy Be Incorporated into WTO Law Through Non-Violation Complaints?" (1994) *J. Int'l Economic L.* 413–421.

ROHRLICH, Paul Egon, "Economic Culture and Foreign Policy: The Cognitive Analysis of Economic Policy Making" (1987) 41 *Int'l Org.* 61–92.

ROSENCRANCE, Richard and STEIN, Arthur (eds.), *The Domestic Bases of Grand Strategy* (Ithaca, Cornell University Press 1993).

ROWAT, Malcom D., "Protectionist Tilts in Antidumping Legislation of Developed Countries and the LDC Response: Is the Race to the Bottom Inevitable?" (1990) 24 (6) *J. World Trade* 5–27.

RUGGIE, John G., "International Regimes, Transactions, and Change: Embedded Liberalism in the Postwar Economic Order" (1982) 36(2) *Int'l Org.* 379–415.

—— "Trade, Protectionism and the Future of Welfare Capitalism" (1994) 48 *J. Int'l Affairs* 1–11.

—— *Winning the Peace: American and World Order in the New Era* (New York, Columbia University Press, 1996).

SACK, John, "The European Community's Membership of International Organisations" (1995) 32 *C.M.L. Rev.* 1227–1256.

SALVATORE, Dominick (ed.), *National Trade Policies* (Amsterdam, North-Holland, 1992).

SANTOS, Leonardo E., "Trade Politics of the American Congress" (1995) 29 (6) *J. World Trade* 74–78.

SBRAGIA, A. M., "The European Community: A Balancing Act" (1993) 23 *Publius* 23–38.

SCHARPTZ, Fritz, "The Joint Decision Trap: Lessons from German Federalism and European Integration" (1988) 66 *Public Administration* 239–278.

SCHARPTZ, Fritz W., "Economic Integration, Democracy and the Welfare State" (1997) 4(1) *J. European Pub. Pol'y* 18–36.

SCHAWB, Susan C., "Politics, Economics and U.S. Trade Policy" (1987) 23 *Standford J. Int'l L.* 155–176.

SCHMIDT, Robert J., "International Negotiations Paralyzed by Domestic Politics: Two-Level Game Theory and the Problem of the Pacific Salmon Commission" (1996) 26 *Environmental L.* 95–139.

SCHMIDT, Vivien A., *From State to Market: The Transformation of French Business and Government* (Cambridge, Cambridge University Press 1996).

—— "Loosening the Ties that Bind: The Impact of European Integration on French Government and its Relationship to Business" (1996) 34(2) *J.C.M.S. 223–254.*

SCHOTT, Jeffrey J. (ed.), *Completing the Uruguay Round* (Washington, Institute for International Economics, 1990).

—— *Restarting Fast Track* (Washington, Institute for International Economics, 1998).

SCHWARTZ, Warren F. and HARPER, Eugene W., "The Regulation of Subsidies Affecting International Trade" (1972) 70 *Michigan L. Rev.* 831.

SCHAEFER, Matthew, "Section 301 and the World Trade Organization: A Largely Peaceful Coexistence to Date" (1998) 1 *J. Int'l Economic L.* 156–160.

—— "Twenty First Century Trade Negotiations, the US Constitution and the Elimination of US State Level Protectionism" (1999) *J. Int'l Economic L.* 71–111.

SCHONOVELD, Frank, "The European Community Reaction to the Illicit Commercial Trade Practices of Other Countries" (1992) 26 (2) *J. World Trade* 17–34.

SHONFIELD, Andrew, *Modern Capitalism: The Changing Balance of Public and Private Power* (Oxford, Oxford University Press, 2nd 1970).

SCHOLTE, Jan Aart, "Global Capitalism and the State" (1997) 73(3) *Int'l Affairs* 427–452.

SHULL, Steven A. and COHEN, Jeffrey E. (eds.), *Economics and Politics of Industrial Policy: The United States, and Western Europe* (Boulder, West View Press 1986).

SIM, Edmun W., "Derailing the Fast Track for International Trade Agreements" (1990) *5 Florida Int'l L. J.* 471–534.

SKLAMBERG, Howard R., "The Meaning of Advice and Consent: The Senate's Constitutional Role in Treatymaking" (1997) 18 *Michigan J. Int'l L.* 445–474.

SMITH, Michael, "The European Union, Foreign Economic Policy and the Changing World Arena" (1994) 1(2) *J. European Public Policy* 283–302.

SMITH, Steven S., *The American Congress* (Boston, Houghton Mifflin Company, 1995).

SNYDER, Francis, *New Directions in Community Law* (London, Weidenfeld & Nicolson, 1990).

—— *International Trade and Customs Law of the European Union* (London, Butterworths, 1998).

DE SOUSA SANTOS, Boaventura, "Globalization, Nation-States and the Legal Field: From Legal Diaspora to Legal Ecumenism?", in *Toward a New Common Sense: Law, Science and Politics in the Paradigmatic Transition* (New York, Routledge, 1995).

STATEMENT OF ADMINISTRATIVE ACTION, in *Message from the President of the United States Transmitting the Uruguay Round Trade Agreements, Texts of Agreements Implementing Bill, Statement of Administrative Action and Required Supporting Statements* 103rd Congress, 2nd Session, House Document 103–316, Volume 1 (September 27, 1994).

STEENBERGEN, Jacques, "The New Commercial Policy Instrument" (1985) 22 *C.M.L. Rev.* 421.

STEIN, Eric, "External Relations of the European Community: Structure and Process", in *Collected Courses of the Academy of European Law, Vol I, Book 1* (Dordrecht, Martinus Nijhoff,1990).

STERN, Paula, "Reaping the Wind and Sowing the Whirlwind: Section 301 as a Metaphor for Congressional Assertiveness in U.S. Trade Policy" (1990) 8(1) *B.U. Int'l L. J.* 1–19.

STERN, Robert, *The Multilateral Trading System—Analysis and Options for Change* (New York, Harvester Wheatsheaf, 1993).

STEWART, Eugen L., "Existing Remedies and the Trade Deficit: The Promise of Reform Through Judicial Review" (1986) 18 *N.Y. U. J. Int'l L. & Pol'y*1165–1189.

STEWART, Alistair, "Market Access: A European Community Instrument to Break Down Barriers to Trade" (1996) 4 *Int'l Trade L. Rep.* 121.

STRANGE, Susan, *Casino Capitalism* (Oxford, Basic Blackwell, 1986).

—— *States and Markets* (London, Pinter Publishers, 1988).

STREECK, Wolfgang and SCHMITTER, Philippe, *Community, Market, State- and Associations: The Prospective Contribution of Interest Governance to Social Order* (European University Institute Working Paper No 94, 1984).

STREIT, Mansfred E. and MUSSLER, Werner, "The Economic Constitution of the European Community: From Rome to Maastricht" (1995) 1 (1) *European L. J.* 5.

SUMNER, C., *Reading Ideologies: An Investigation into the Marxist Theory of Ideology and Law* (London, Academic Press, 1979).

SYKES, Alan O., "Constructive Unilateral Threats in International Commercial Relations: The Limited Case for Section 301" (1992) 23 (2) *L. & Pol'y Int'l Bus.* 263–330.

TARULLO, Daniel K., "Law and Politics in Twentieth Century Tariff History" (1986) 34 *UCLA L. Rev.* 285–370.

—— "Beyond Normalcy in the Regulation of International Trade" (1987) 100 *Harvard L. Rev.* 547–628.

—— "U.S.-E.C. Trade Relationship and the Uruguay Round", 24 *C.M.L. Rev.* (1987) 411–426.

TARULLO, Daniel, "Competition Policy for Global Markets" (1994) *J. Int'l Economic L.* 445–455.

TAYLOR, C. O'Neal, "The Limits of Economic Power: Section 301 and the World Trade Organization Dispute Settlement System" (1997) 30 *Vanderbilt J. Transnat'l L.* 209–315.

TERRY, J., "Sovereignty, Subsidies and Countervailing Duties in the Context of the Canada-U.S. Trading Relationship", 46 *U. Toronto Faculty Rev.* 48.

THARAKAN, P. K. M. (ed.), *Policy Implications of Antidumping Measures* (Amsterdam, North Holland, 1991).

THARAKAN, P. K. M., "The Political Economy of Anti-Dumping Undertakings in the European Communities" (1991) 35 *European Economic Rev.* 132–1359.

TONDSON, Alan, "Beating Back Predatory Trade" (1994) 73 (4) *Foreign Affairs* 123.

TOUGAS, F., "Softwood Lumber from Canada: Natural Resources and the Search for a Definition of a Domestic Countervailable Subsidy" (1989) 24 *Gonzaga L. Rev.* 135.

TREBILOCK, Michael, "Is the Game Worth the Candle? Comments on a Search for Economic and Financial Principles in the Administration of Countervailing Duty Law" (1990) 21 *L. & Pol'y Int'l Bus.* 723–733.

TRIBE, Laurence H., "Taking Text and Structure Seriously: Reflection on Free-Form Method in Constitutional Interpretation" (1995) 108 *Harvard L. Rev.* 1221–1303.

TRIDIMAS, Takis and EECKHOUT, Piet, "The External Competence of the Community and the Case Law of the Court of Justice: Principle versus Pragmatism" *Y.B.E.L.* 143–177.

TRIMBLE, Phillips, "International Trade and the Rule of Law" (1985) 83 *Michigan L. Rev.* 1016–1032.

UNITED STATES INTERNATIONAL TRADE COMMISSION, *Report to the Committee on Finance, U.S. Senate, on Investigation No 332–212 Under Section 332(g) of the Tariff Act of 1930: Review of the Effectiveness of Trade Dispute Settlement under the GATT and the Tokyo Round Agreements* (Washington, USITC 1985).

—— *Annual Report Fiscal Year 1992* (Washington, International Trade Commission 1993).

UNITED STATES SENATE, *GATT Implementating Legislation: Hearings on S. 2467 Before the Committee on Commerce, Science and Transportation* 103rd Cong., 2nd Sess (1994).

UNDERHILL, Geoffrey R., "Markets Beyond Politics? The State and the Internationalisation of Financial Markets", 19 *European J. Political Research* 197–225 (1991).

UPHAM, Frank K., "Privatized Regulation: Japanese Regulatory Style in Comparative and International Perspective" (1996) 20(2) *Fordham Int'l L. J.* 396–511.

US SENATE, *Hearings before the Committee of Finance of the United States Senate, Results of the Uruguay Round Trade Negotiation*, 103rd Cong. 2nd Session (1994).

US SENATE, *GATT Implementing Legislation: Hearings on S. 2467 Before the Committee on Commerce, Science and Transportation*, 103rd Cong. 2nd Sess. 290–312 (1994).

VAKERICS, WILSON and WIEGEL, *Antidumping, Countervailing Duty and Other Trade Actions* (New York, Practising Law Institute 1987).

VAN BAEL, Ivo and BELLIS, Jean-Francois, *Anti-Dumping and other Trade Protection Laws of the EC*, 3rd ed. (Bicester, CCH, 1996).

VANDER SHUEREN, Paulette and LUFF, David, "The Trade Barriers Regulation and the Community's Market Access Policy", *European Foreign Affairs Rev.* 211–230.

VANDER SHUEREN, Paulette, "New Anti-Dumping Rules and Practice: Wide Discretion Held on a Tight Leash?" (1996) 33 *C.M.L. Rev.* 271–297.

VERRECKEN, Marc, "La Competenza della Comunita a Concludere Accordi Internationali in Materia di Servizi" (1996) 35 (1) *Diritto Comunitario e degli Scambi Internationali* 87–106.

VERMULST, Edwin and DRIESSEN, Bart, "An Overview of the WTO Dispute Settlement System and its Relationship with the Uruguay Round Agreements: Nice on Paper but Too Much Stress for the System?", 29 *J. World Trade* 132–163 (1995).

—— "New Battle Lines in the Anti-Dumping War: Recent Developments on the European Front", (1997) 31(3) *J. World Trade* 135–157.

VERMULST, Edwin and DRIESSEN, Bart, "Commercial Defense Actions and Other International Trade Developments in the European Communities IX: 1 July 1994–31 December 1994" (1995) 6 *European J. Int'l L.* 287–316.

VERMULST, Edwin A. and GRAAFMA, Folkert, "A Decade of European Community Anti-Dumping Law and Practice Applicable to Imports from China" (1992) 26 *J. World Trade* 5–59.

VERMULST, Edwin and KOMURO, Norio, "Anti-Dumping Disputes in the GATT/WTO: Navigating Dire Straits", 1997) 31 (1) *J. World Trade* 5–43.

VERMULST, Edwin and WAER, Paul, "The Post Uruguay Round EC Anti-Dumping Regulation—After a Pit Stop, Back in the Race" (1995) 29 (2) *J. World Trade* 53–76.

—— *AC Anti-Dumping Law and Practice* (London, Sweet & Maxwell, 1996).

VERMULST, Edwin, *Antidumping Law and Practice in the United States and the European Communities: A Comparative Analysis* (North-Holland, 1987).
VICTOR, Paul A., "Antidumping and Antitrust: Can the Inconsistencies Be Resolved?" (1983) 15 *N.Y. U. Int'l L. & Pol'y* 339–350.
VINER, Jacob, *Dumping: A Problem in International Trade* (New York, Augustus M. Kelly Publishers, 1966).
VITOLIS, Sigurt, *German Industrial Policy: An Overview* (Wissenschaftszentrum Berlin Fur Sozialforschung Working Paper 96–321, 1996).
VOGUEL David, "Why Businessmen Distrust their State: The Political Consciousness of American Corporate Executives" (1978) 8 *British J. Political Science* 45–78.
—— *Fluctuating Fortunes: The Political Power of Business in America* (New York, Basic Books, 1989).
VOLKER, E. L. M. and STEENBERGEN, J., *Leading Cases and Materials on the External Trade Relations Law of the E.C.* (Deventer, Kluwer Law and Taxation, 1985).
VOLKER, E. L. M. (ed.), *Protectionism and the European Community* (Deventer, Kluwer Law and Taxation, 1987).
VOS, Ellen, "The Rise of Committees" (1997) 3(3) *European L. J.* 210–229.
WALLACE, LOFTUS and KRIKORIAN, *Interface Three: Legal Treatment of Domestic Subsidies* (Washington, International Law Institute 1984).
WAER, Paul and VERMULST, Edwin, "EC Anti-Dumping Law and Practice after the Uruguay Round-A New Lease of Life?" (1994) 28 *J. World Trade* 5–21.
—— "The GATT Panel Report on the EC Anti-Dumping Proceedings Concerning Audio Tapes in Cassettes: Back to Basics in the Concept of Dumping?" (1995) 29 (6) *J. World Trade* 31–44.
WAER, Paul, "Constructed Normal Values in EC Dumping Margin Calculations—Fiction or Realistic Approach?" (1993) 7(4) *I. World Trade* 5–22.
WEAVER, R. Kent and ROCKMAN, Bert A. (eds.), *Do Institutions Matter: Government Capabilities in the United States and Abroad* (Washington, The Brokings Institution, 1993).
WEBBER, Douglas, "High Midnight in Brussels: An Analysis of the September 1993 Council Meeting on the GATT Uruguay Round" (1998) 5(4) *J. European Public Pol'y* 578–594.
WEILER, Joseph H., "The External Relations of Non-Unitary Actors: Mixity and the Federal Principle", in O'Keeffee and Schermers (ed.), *Mixed Agreements* (Deventer Kluwer Law and Taxation, 1983), 35–83.
WENT, Robert, "Globalization: Myths, Reality and Ideology: The EU in a Globalized World" (1997) 26(3) *Int'l J. Political Economy* 35–59.
WILKS, Stephan, and WRIGHT, Maurice (eds.), *Comparative Government-Industry Relations: West Europe, the United States and Japan* (Oxford, Clarendon Press, 1987).
WILKS, Stephen, *Regulatory Compliance and Capitalist Diversity in Europe*, 3(4) *J. European Public Policy* 536–559 (1996).
WILLKIE, Wendell L. (ed.), *The Commerce Department Speaks 1992: Developments in Import Administration: Export and Investment Abroad* (New York, Practicing Law Institute 1992).
WINHAM, Gilbert R., "Robert Strauss, the MTN, and the Control of Faction" (1980) 14 *J. World Trade L.* 377–397.
—— *International Trade and the Tokyo Round Negotiations* (Princeton, Princeton University Press, 1986).

WINTERS, L. A., "The EC and Protection: The Political Economy" (1994) 38 *European Economic Rev.* 596–603..

WOLF, Martin, "Cooperation or Conflict? The European Union in a Liberal Global Economy" (1995) 71 *Int'l Affairs* 325–337.

YAMANE, Hiroko, "EU Efforts to Open the Japanese Market: Government, Market Structures and Private Practices" (1998) 3 *E.F.A. Rev.* 481–504.

YANNOPOULOS, George N., "The European Community's Common External Commercial Policy: Internal Condradictions and Institutional Weakneses" (1985) 19 *J. World Trade L.* 451–465.

YOUNG, James P., *Reconsidering American Liberalism: The Troubled Odyssey of the Liberal Idea* (Boulder, Westview Press, 1996).

ZETTERHOLM, Staffan, *National Cultures and European Integration: Exploratory Essays on Cultural Diversity and Common Policies* (Oxford, Berg, 1994).

ZILJMANS, J. M., "The Exclusive External Competence of the European Community" (1995) 2 *M. J.* 405–429.

ZOLLER, Elisabeth, "Remedies for Unfair Trade: European and U.S. Views" (1985) 18 *Cornell Int'l L. J.* 227–245.

ZYSMAN, John, *Political Strategies of Industrial Order: State, Market and Industry in France* (Berkeley, University of California Press, 1977).

—— *Government, Markets and Growth: Financial Systems and the Politics of Industrial Change* (Ithaca, Cornell University Press, 1983).

ZYSMAN, John and TYSON, Laura (eds.), *American Industry in International Competition: Government Policies and Corporate Strategies* (Ithaca, Cornell University Press, 1983).

ZYSMAN, John, "How Institutions Create Historically Rooted Trajectories of Growth" (1994) 3(1) *Industrial & Corporate Change* 243–283.

ZYSMAN, John, "The Myth of a Global Economy: Enduring National Foundations and Emerging Regional Realities" (1996) 1(2) *New Political Economy* 157–184.

Index

www.ingramcontent.com/pod-product-compliance
Ingram Content Group UK Ltd.
Pitfield, Milton Keynes, MK11 3LW, UK
UKHW020239290926
15470UKWH00002B/629

9 781841 131320